CW01263176

CRITICAL INSIGHTS

The Catcher in the Rye

by J. D. Salinger

CRITICAL INSIGHTS

The Catcher in the Rye

by J. D. Salinger

Editor
Joseph Dewey
University of Pittsburgh

Salem Press
Pasadena, California   Hackensack, New Jersey

Cover photo: ©Terry Alexander/Dreamstime.com

Copyright © 2012 by Salem Press,
a Division of EBSCO Publishing, Inc.

Editor's text © 2012 by Joseph Dewey
"The *Paris Review* Perspective" © 2012 by David Matthews for *The Paris Review*

All rights in this book are reserved. No part of this work may be used or reproduced in any manner whatsoever or transmitted in any form or by any means, electronic or mechanical, including photocopy, recording, or any information storage and retrieval system, without written permission from the copyright owner except in the case of brief quotations embodied in critical articles and reviews or in the copying of images deemed to be freely licensed or in the public domain. For information address the publisher, Salem Press, at csr@salempress.com.

∞ The paper used in these volumes conforms to the American National Standard for Permanence of Paper for Printed Library Materials, Z39.48-1992 (R1997).

Library of Congress Cataloging-in-Publication Data
The catcher in the rye, by J.D. Salinger / editor, Joseph Dewey.
 p. cm. — (Critical insights)
Includes bibliographical references and index.
 ISBN 978-1-58765-837-2 (alk. paper) — ISBN 978-1-58765-821-1 (set for Critical insights : alk. paper)
 1. Salinger, J. D. (Jerome David), 1919-2010. Catcher in the rye. 2. Caulfield, Holden (Fictitious character) 3. Runaway teenagers in literature. 4. Teenage boys in literature. I. Dewey, Joseph, 1957-
 PS3537.A426C3224 2012
 813'.54—dc23
2011019114

PRINTED IN CANADA

Contents

About This Volume, Joseph Dewey vii

The Book and Author

On *The Catcher in the Rye*: An American Koan, Joseph Dewey . . . 3
Salinger and Holden, Disappearing in Plain Sight: Biography of
   J. D. Salinger, David Klingenberger 18
The *Paris Review* Perspective, David Matthews for *The Paris Review* . . . 27

Critical Contexts

Catching Holden Through a Cultural Studies Lens, Robert Miltner . . . 33
Holden at Sixty: Reading *Catcher* After the Age of Irony,
   Jeff Pruchnic 49
The Catcher in the Rye: "Paul's Case" in Anticipation of
   Holden Caulfield, Matthew Evertson 64
Critical Mass: Holden Among the Critics, Jill Rollins 81

Critical Readings

Memories of Holden Caulfield—and of Miss Greenwood,
   Carl Freedman 97
J. D. Salinger, Novelist of Modern Anomie, Dead at 91,
   Tom Teicholz 118
J. D. Salinger, Adam Gopnik 122
"Holden Caulfield in Doc Martens": *The Catcher in the Rye*
   and *My So-Called Life*, Barbara Bell 126
Holden Caulfield's Legacy, David Castronovo 141
The Catcher in the Rye and All: Is the Age of Formative Books
   Over?, Sanford Pinsker 152
Cherished and Cursed: Toward a Social History of *The Catcher*
   in the Rye, Stephen J. Whitfield 170
Reviewers, Critics, and *The Catcher in the Rye*, Carol and
   Richard Ohmann 205
Catcher In and Out of History, James E. Miller, Jr. 235

On First Looking into Chapman's Holden: Speculations on
   a Murder, Daniel M. Stashower   241
The Language of *The Catcher in the Rye*, Donald P. Costello   251
The Saint as a Young Man: A Reappraisal of *The Catcher
   in the Rye*, Jonathan Baumbach   265
In Memoriam: Allie Caulfield in *The Catcher in the Rye*,
   Edwin Haviland Miller   279
Symbolic Resolution in *The Catcher in the Rye:* The Cap,
   the Carrousel, and the American West, Kermit Vanderbilt   297
The Burning Carousel and the Carnivalesque: Subversion and
   Transcendence at the Close of *The Catcher in the Rye*,
   Yasuhiro Takeuchi   306

Resources

Chronology of J. D. Salinger's Life   331
Works by J. D. Salinger   333
Bibliography   334

About the Editor   339
About *The Paris Review*   339
Contributors   341
Acknowledgments   345
Index   349

About This Volume
                                                    Joseph Dewey

> STAN: Did you get to the dirty parts yet?
> KYLE: No. It's still just some whiny annoying teenager just talking about how lame he is.
> STAN: I don't get it. What's so controversial? All he's done is say "shit" and "fuck" a couple of times.
> KYLE: I'm almost at the end and there's nothing.
> —*South Park*, episode 197

In March 2010, barely a month after the death of J. D. Salinger, *South Park*, the irreverent cutting-edge animated series on cable's Comedy Central, broadcast an episode in which the fourth graders at South Park Elementary School are assigned to read *The Catcher in the Rye*, just removed from the district's list of banned books. Initially objecting—the kids would prefer not to read anything—the teacher entices them by casting about the book the nearly irresistible lure of the forbidden, telling them school systems across the country have routinely banned the book for its risqué content, its vulgarity, its adult themes, and its tendency to twist the minds of its most impressionable readers. The kids naturally cannot wait to read it. That night, their disappointment is palpable; their disdain for the book and for being tricked into reading causes them, in turn, to set about writing a really vulgar book just to get it banned; the book—titled *The Tale of Scrotie McBoogerballs*—is so disgusting that readers vomit after only a few sentences. It becomes a national sensation.

With signature impudence, the show's cocreator, Trey Parker, who wrote the episode, skewers the half-century reputation *The Catcher in the Rye* has maintained as the bogeyman of post-World War II American literature and in so doing raises fundamental questions about what readers now are to do with the book. For more than fifty years, *Catcher*, easily the most banned book of the twentieth-century American canon, the favorite target of conservative school systems, earnest parents' groups, and strident church organizations, has thrived on its reputation as an underground text, passed with cultlike fanaticism among ardent readers, hard-core fans who have found in the lonely misfit Holden Caulfield a companion, a friend for life. Given the intimate accessibility of Holden's colloquial first-person narration, high school and university teachers have long recognized that amid a formidable reading list of nonoptional novels, often ponderous and hefty tomes whose sculpted, overwrought prose can seem inaccessible and, worse, irrelevant to kids, *The Catcher in the Rye* would be a welcome change, its dangerous edginess making it a book their students would actually want to read. In turn, *Catcher* became a cause célèbre for brash, recklessly quixotic teachers eager for a crusade, spoiling for a fight over First Amendment freedom and the oppressive hand of censorship. And, given Holden's own emphatic argument that the very best books make you want to shake hands with the author, that same generation of readers came under the considerable enchantment of the monkish Salinger himself, the hermit crab of New England, the subject of increasingly bizarre urban legends, eventually promulgated on the free range of the Internet, an eccentric figure whose very absence made him a formidable presence, whose deep disdain for celebrity was irresistibly fascinating for a postmodern culture that accepted as a given that everyone wants to be famous.

But that was then. What *South Park* asks in its own iconoclastic way is, What exactly are we to do now with a shocking book that no longer shocks, an incendiary text that no longer incites? What happens when the bogeyman no longer terrifies? Parents' groups and conservative think tanks long ago moved on to quash other more contemporary (and far hipper) texts. The first generation of impressionable postwar readers who fell so completely under the spell of Holden's voice have now moved off, and what is emerging is a new generation of young readers unfazed by the cultural tsunami that was Holden Caulfield. Indeed, by any contemporary measure of cool, Holden can come across as a shrill, obnoxious, judgmental, whiny, arrogant kid whose entire psychic stability has been unhinged by a single death (his younger brother's), a reaction that can seem self-indulgent melodrama to a generation of post-postmodern kids raised with ultraviolent video games, in-your-face action movies, and slash-and-gash horror flicks in which dead bodies stack up like cordwood. By contemporary standards, Holden's swearing lacks fire and, far worse, originality (just listen for a minute to the kids at South Park Elementary); Holden's antiauthoritarianism seems cliché; his rants against phony adults, pedestrian; his apprehensions over sex, trivial; his terror over growing up, childish. And far more telling, in our culture's hard-won environment of diversity, Holden can appear to have little to say to, well, just about everyone, to minorities, to women, to the religiously devout, to gays; indeed, he speaks for a distinctly narrow demographic—spoiled, horny, white, private school-educated agnostic American male children of privilege.

What, then, are we to do with *The Catcher in the Rye*? This volume in the Critical Insights series argues that, with the death of Salinger, we are at a threshold moment in our long obsession with Holden and his eccentric author, a chance to reapproach *The Catcher in the Rye* not as fans, misfits searching for a comrade-in-angst, or as agitators looking for a First Amendment cause, or as wannabe paparazzi intrigued into reading the novel with Talmudic intensity to explicate finally the mystique of the absent/present Salinger. Rather, we can approach the book now as readers. As it turns out, there is more to Holden Caulfield than, well, Holden. And there is more to *The Catcher in the Rye* than Sonny Salinger. Liberated from the need to identify with (or the zeal to condemn) Holden Caulfield, liberated from the dark charisma of its troubled hermit-author, we can at last confront a novel whose argument, as it turns out, we have only begun to measure. *The Catcher in the Rye* stands like some enticing, barely trammeled wilderness. *Catcher* is at that fortuitous moment when a book that has had such a galvanizing effect on its culture—and in American literature, such novels can be counted on the fingers of a single hand—ceases to be an event or a cause or even a companion and becomes as it began, a book, puzzling, engaging, layered, at least as much an intellectual challenge as an emotional experience.

This volume gathers essays—now-classic investigations into the novel as well as new perspectives—that collectively offer the opportunity to begin such a reintroduction. Included here are, of course, essays that detail the emotional impact of first hearing Holden's voice. In these poignant essays, readers set aside the pedagogical imperative and attempt to understand the human ties they felt with Holden. These essayists—Carl Freedman, Tom Teicholz, and Adam Gopnik (the last two writing in the wake of Salinger's death)—remind readers today that once upon a time novels, and the characters in them, had the deeply personal impact that is now routinely associated with films, music, and television. However, beyond such intimacy, the private identification with a book and a charismatic main character, *Catcher* speaks to a much broader community. Scholars have positioned the novel within the wider currents of American literature. After all, *Catcher*'s genre—the coming-of-age novel—is intrinsic to American narrative. The American imagination has produced a stunningly original array of such narratives largely because it has itself struggled for its comparatively brief two hundred years as a kind of unruly adolescent. *Catcher* indeed offers a wide range of tantalizing influences to track, both backward and forward. Several essays in this volume position *Catcher* historically, tracing its genealogy, the literary ancestors of Holden Caulfield's troubling and troubled adolescent psyche; others remind us how profoundly Holden has shaped the perception of adolescence in novels, films, music, and television since the novel's publication. In the essays of Barbara Bell, David Matthews, Jeff Pruchnic, Matthew Evertson, Joseph Dewey, and David Castronovo we are given compelling discussions on the sheer reach of Salinger's influence. Such measures of the breadth of the novel's lineage are critical to understanding the complex relationship between the novel and its cultural community—as Sanford Pinsker's essay discusses, we are most likely past the time when a novel can have such an impress.

That impact, in turn, is the subject of other essays offered here. Stephen J. Whitfield, for instance, reviews the novel's tumultuous history, the fierce condemnation and profound admiration that *Catcher*, alone among novels of postwar America, generated. Carol and Richard Ohmann articulate how *Catcher* was part of the 1950s and that decade's complex assessment of the rewards (and dangers) of capitalism when, in the economic postwar boom, writers critiqued the mercenary assumptions of prosperity and ambition and the whole range of suburban gray-flannel aspirations. James E. Miller, Jr., in turn, reminds us that Salinger's novel is ultimately both bound to its era and timeless, an expression of the collective imagination that makes such a tender, defiant book resonate across generations. What drives Holden to his ferocious discontent, Miller concludes, is what troubles all American adolescents—the settling into a stultifying routine, the disenchantment that comes with growing up. Robert Miltner opens *Catcher* to a new and vibrant range of perspectives by challenging newcomers to the book to approach the novel through the argument of contemporary critical schools, including gender studies, social psychology, and media studies. And, finally, it is the sobering reminder of Daniel M. Stashower's essay that the novel's impact has at times been problematic: Salinger's novel has been implicated in horrific incidents in which troubled, emotionally stunted misfits have found in Holden's voice encouragement to act on their latent violent impulses.

Ultimately, however, a casebook such as this, positioned as it is at a pivotal moment in *Catcher*'s evolution (the book, after all is barely sixty years old, young by the standards of other classics), takes us back into the novel, reminding us that the privilege of reading comes ultimately from analysis, noticing patterns of events, matrices of symbols, levels of conflicts, and a complication of contradictory and provocative themes—in short, the excavation into a book that has long been the essence of the act, indeed the art, of reading. The present collection offers a range of such stimulating close readings: Donald P. Costello reconstructs Holden as a carefully designed vocal event, Salinger's deft shaping of a teenage voice consistent with the 1950s, a tour de force of authorial creation (given that Salinger was at the time in his thirties); Jonathan Baumbach elaborates a close reading of Holden's fiercely contradictory character by suggesting the rich dimension of Christian compassion to Holden's doomed, quixotic struggle to preserve innocence; and Edwin Haviland Miller explicates the symbolic implications of the death of Holden's younger brother, the emotional crisis that, despite Holden's reluctance to share much about it, shapes his brooding temperament and inevitably raises significant cautions about Holden's reliability as a narrator. And the tantalizing, teasing close of the novel, the (re)solution Holden achieves in the rain of Central Park, provides the opportunity for Yasuhiro Takeuchi and Kermit Vanderbilt to explore from different angles the implications of Holden's epiphany, his decision to forsake his naive (and sweetly romantic) dream of protecting the innocent. In sum, these essays do not offer definitive textual analyses; rather, collectively they implicitly encourage further work, *Catcher* doing what any great novel does—inciting responsible speculation, the endlessly rewarding round of a community of engaged readers assembling and defending provocative readings of a provocative text.

If the kids at South Park Elementary felt duped, tricked into reading a forbidden novel that did not titillate, their frustration signals the opportunity the rest of us have now to approach a book we have for too long treated with too much deference or too much hostility. *The Catcher in the Rye* is a book that, like the landmark works of our national literature, suggests who and what we are at our imaginative depth—Holden speaks in a voice that is, finally, distinctly, defiantly American. It is the argument of this collection that if at last we stop listening to Holden, we will finally start to hear him.

THE BOOK AND AUTHOR

On *The Catcher in the Rye*:
An American Koan

Joseph Dewey

America, it appears, is in the uneasy twilight of the Age of the Novel. Even the most ardent readers—and the most dedicated English teachers—acknowledge that. Given the sheer reach that visual technologies have achieved in just fifty years—film, advertising, television, video games, and, supremely, the Internet—the act (and art) of reading the printed word has been gracelessly shuffled off to the margins. Americans are now pixel-fed and image-fat. Novels themselves seem bulky, impractical, clumsy, ink pressed on paper fast becoming like Morse code and cathedral radios, rotary phones and print newspapers, quaint relics of ways we use to communicate. And serious literature—those novels that challenge willing, alert readers to interact with characters and symbols to formulate compelling themes—has been all but relegated to the protective hothouse of the classroom. Airport terminals, beaches, living rooms, bedrooms, park benches—there readers indulge the serious trivia of low-octane mass-market entertainments: complicated whodunits, edgy political thrillers, breezy romances, futuristic sci-fi sagas, multivolume fantasy epics about wizards and dragons, gothic vampire tales. Save those infrequent titles deemed Oprah-worthy, serious fiction never receives the lavish hype routinely accorded the most inconsequential new films or reality television shows. Landmark novels momentarily stir heady excitement among a narrow coterie of professional readers and then promptly, utterly sink into the heavy tomb dust of library shelves. In America, in the twenty-first century, serious fiction has lost its clout, its cultural privilege.

When cultural historians come to chronicle these end days of the American novel, they will most assuredly mark July 16, 1951, as the novel's last hurrah. On that day, Little, Brown, with little fanfare, released J. D. Salinger's *The Catcher in the Rye*, a slender, unprepossessing novel, barely two hundred pages, centered on a confused and depressed sixteen-year-old kid named Holden Caulfield, who, after flunking out of prep school (for the third time), delays returning home to his family's swanky Central Park townhouse to wander the streets of New York City for three days. In the process, he struggles to come to terms not only with his academic failure but with the death, three years earlier, of his younger brother, Allie, from leukemia. It is not an easy adjustment. Indeed, by novel's end, we learn Holden has been institutionalized at a psychiatric facility near Hollywood, where his older brother works as a screenwriter.

On its surface, the novel was yet another coming-of-age narrative in which a sensitive and traumatized adolescent must negotiate the difficult threshold into adulthood. If the genre was conventional, however, the book was anything but. Holden told his own story. And that voice—at once smart-alecky and vulnerable, worldly-wise and engagingly naive—touched a generation of readers, mostly under twenty-five, in a tectonic way that novels today simply don't. Holden spoke in the syllable-crisp pitch-perfect immediacy of colloquialisms, the click and rhythm of clichés laced with swear words. Holden sounded real. And American teens, born too late to share in the euphoria of World War II and compelled rather to adjust to the anxieties of the Cold War and imminent atomic apocalypse, found in Holden Caulfield a friend who shared their discontent with authority, their anger over the middle-class status quo, their frustration with conventional measures of success, their angst over their own futures. Unlike the polite and restrained child-heroes of the serious fiction of an earlier time, Holden reflected a hipper sensibility—he chain-smoked, he drank Scotch and soda, he talked back to his teachers, he rejected the expectations of career ambition, he declined to commit effort to school, he swore with remarkable agility, he mocked Christians, he obsessed over sex. Within the free energy field of the early 1950s—an edgy kinetics that included the leather jacket-tight jeans movies of James Dean and Marlon Brando, Allen Ginsberg's tormented "Howl," Jack Kerouac's epical peregrinations, Jackson Pollock's splatter canvasses, John Coltrane's shattered melodies, Lenny Bruce's incendiary performance pieces, and, supremely, rock and roll's raucous rhythms—Holden Caulfield gave a voice to a generation in rebellion. *The Catcher in the Rye* quickly became the book every twenty-something *had* to read. Despite mixed reviews from the establishment press (who simply didn't "get" Holden), the novel dominated best-seller lists and stayed there for more than a year. Indeed, in this twilight of the Age of the Novel, the book has *never* been out of print.

Thus—it appears, for the last time—a work of serious fiction simultaneously realigned the dynamics of American fiction and the dynamics of American culture. Holden helped incite the younger generation amid the narcoleptic calm of Eisenhower's America to upend conventions, defy authority, and, in the process, attend to the suddenly serious business of reconsidering the very premise of their own lives and the nature of their own identities. Not surprisingly, perhaps inevitably, *The Catcher in the Rye* was quickly perceived to be a dangerous work, a work from which kids needed to be protected, second only to Mark Twain's *Adventures of Huckleberry Finn* (a work to which it is often compared) as the most frequently banned book in the American literary canon. Since 1951, Holden has been blamed for virtually every expression of adolescent rebellion. Swearing, the use of recreational pharmaceuticals, dropping out of school, premarital sex, underage drinking—they are all cool because of Holden. Holden has been read into the DNA for every angry white male rock music icon from Jerry Lee Lewis to Eminem, Bob Dylan to Kurt Cobain. Holden's strident antiauthoritarianism and his uncompromising sense of honesty have been seen at the heart of the civil disobedience of the social and political upheavals in the 1960s. But far more problematically, parents and teachers, child psychologists, and guidance counselors have long blamed Holden, given his obsession with death (his own and others), for the gothic sensibility among teenagers and the dark appeal of suicide. The novel routinely comes up in any roundtable convened to consider the implications of some heinous act of violence perpetrated by a young maladjusted misfit. Fans of the novel have included Mark David Chapman, who shot John Lennon four times in the back; John Hinckley, Jr., who shot President Ronald Reagan outside a Washington hotel to impress a film actress; and Dylan Klebold and Eric Harris, who wreaked the havoc at Columbine High School.

Quite simply, no other work of American serious fiction in the last half century has achieved such reach. And given that Salinger's novel has never been translated into film (Salinger had been angered by a film adaptation of one of his early short stories and resisted numerous lucrative offers to bring *Catcher* to the big screen), Holden has existed entirely as words, as ink pressed on paper. We get little physical description of him, save his unusual height and his patch of prematurely gray hair. He is conjured entirely by language. Imagine that. The most notable and engaging adolescent characters of the last generation (many of them intriguing avatars of Holden)—Dawson Leery, Kevin Arnold, Richie Cunningham, Hannah Montana, Bart Simpson, Luke Skywalker, Benjamin Braddock, and, of course, a cluster of Disney animations, most notably Simba and Ariel—have achieved their considerable cultural impress entirely through visual presentation, through film and television. And even those few landmark adolescent characters first introduced in books have had their presentations inalterably defined (and simplified) by movies. We *see* Daniel Radcliffe's Harry Potter or Elijah Wood's Frodo Baggins or Robert Pattinson's Edward Cullen. But we read Holden, happily seduced by the verbal suction of that mesmerizing voice.

It is an understatement to say that Holden has intrigued readers, eager and determined to do what readers of serious fiction have been doing for nearly five centuries: gather textual evidence to construct a consistent reading of an engaging character. Readers have asked, Who is Holden Caulfield? The results have been curious. Holden is the prototype hippie, an antieverything nonconformist, a perspicacious outsider who irreverently skewers the hypocrisies and shallowness of postwar America. Holden is a spoiled whiner, an arrogant slacker, a smart-alecky (and not terribly bright) child of privilege who, given all the advantages of wealth, cannot find his way to maturity or responsibility. Holden is a complex con man, a moral chameleon, a shallow, superficial phony, a compulsive liar and an inveterate fraud who assumes identities with casual ease to mock teachers, friends, strangers—and us, the readers. Holden is a victim, traumatized by the hammer stroke of mortality, haunted by the death of his younger brother and by the suicide of a kid in prep school who jumped out a window in a turtleneck he had just borrowed from Holden. Holden is a tragic romantic, gentle and naive, who wants what every dreamer since Quixote has wanted, the impossible, to protect the tenderhearted from the painful realities of this sad and imperfect world. Holden is a raging latter-day prophet, indicting his era's mercenary capitalism, its soulless consumerism, its competitive acquisitiveness, and, supremely, its moral shallowness. Holden is a lost heart yearning for love. Estranged from his parents, shuffled off to a succession of boarding schools, he reaches out again and again—to strangers on trains and in bars, to old classmates and former teachers. Holden, a virgin, is deeply conflicted (like most sixteen-year-olds) by the idea of physical intimacy, confused about his own sexual identity; the socially awkward Holden needs the reassuring stability of love in a cold and hostile world. Holden is a textbook sociopath, at sixteen already committed to an institution, a simmering misanthrope, a lunatic fringer, hostile, mocking, menacing, mean-spirited, given to explosive fits of violence, and who, tormented by private demons, refers to the odd deer-hunting hat he sports as his "people shooting" hat.

You get the idea. This is a singularly contentious record of readings, one in irresolvable conflict with itself. This is not to dismiss the considerable body of articulate and careful explications engendered by *The Catcher in the Rye*—after a half century an accumulation of more than three hundred separate readings—but rather to suggest that such abundant effort has left Holden Caulfield undefined, voiding the very contract upon which reading fiction has always rested. Take Charles

Dickens's *David Copperfield* or *Oliver Twist*, both classic coming-of-age novels that Holden invokes (and mocks). As traditional realistic novels, both are sustained by the emotional energy generated between and among the characters (we are engaged by the unfolding action) and between the reader and the main character (we are engaged by a character we recognize, a character that we feel we "know"). In turn, our responsibility has been to define that main character, to fix our sympathies. Main characters are designed to yield only two readings—you either like them or you don't, they are perceived either sympathetically or ironically. Indeed, virtually any primary character in any serious novel in the realist tradition is intended to be clarified by the reader into an agreeable consistency. The reader gathers evidence from the narrative—significant moments, telling symbols, revealing quotes, critical decisions—and makes the case, one way or the other: hero or villain.

But Holden presents a dilemma. He is at once a good guy *and* a bad guy, a saint *and* a provocateur, a prophet *and* a sociopath, a romantic *and* a cynic. If he frets over the fate of the ducks in Central Park during the winter, he as well fantasizes about riding an atomic bomb down into the crowded sidewalks of Manhattan. He is and he is not—he is/is not. It is not that Holden is ironic or ambiguous or that he is some sort of Rorschach inkblot that readers are free to define as they "see." Rather, Holden resists analysis, defies definition. Any single reading of Holden—and all of those listed above have been articulated in published readings of *Catcher*—is valid only if a generous body of evidence from the text is ignored. Holden violates the assumptions upon which, for centuries, we have erected our understanding of the act of reading itself.

Unless, of course, consistency was never the point. Either Salinger is a remarkably inept writer—unable to construct a consistent character—or he is up to something vastly different. What if *The Catcher in the Rye* was conceived as something other than a traditional novel and Holden Caulfield as something other than a traditional character?

What has been lost amid the passionate disputations centered on defining Holden—identifying with him, loathing him, sympathizing with him, excusing him, blaming him, analyzing him, counseling him, diagnosing him, fixing him, judging him—is the obvious: Holden Caulfield is not real, he is not a friend nor is he a fiend, he is not a "he" at all. "He" is an it, a textual event, a construction, a word chord, a ventriloquist act conducted by a writer-authority. The question we should ask is not Who is Holden Caulfield? but rather, What is Holden Caulfield?

What he is, is the creation of a traumatized thirty-something World War II veteran, a disquieted soul at once profoundly lonely and deeply spiritual, named Jerome David Salinger. Of course, as anyone familiar with the odd biography of Salinger knows, therein is a problem. Although he lived more than ninety years, Salinger never shared much insight into his life, much less into his writing processes. His decision shortly after *Catcher*'s publication to reject the coaxing lure of celebrity rendered him for a half century an intriguing absence. Salinger never granted a professional interview, never worked the lucrative lecture circuit, never appeared on television, never wrote an autobiography, never taught fiction at a university. But an understanding of Salinger would be central to any approach to *Catcher* that does not indulge Holden-mania. Holden Caulfield was not created by some foul-mouthed slacker kid addled by hormones, indifferent to school, and terrified by the prospects of growing up. Rather, he was deftly, subtly fashioned by a grown man who, by his early thirties, had been appalled by what the world had shown him: the economic catastrophe of the Great Depression, the dark brutalities of field combat in World War II, the horrific inhumanity of the Nazi concentration camps, the paranoid hysteria of the early Cold War, and the wonderland logic of mutual assured destruction.

Salinger was of the troubled generation that had witnessed firsthand the failure, the hypocrisies, the corruption, the venality of Western civilization and its most dominant expressions: Judeo-Christianity, Enlightenment science, and consumer capitalism. For them, Christianity was far too driven by its certainty that right and wrong are definable, that good and evil are quantifiable, and too obsessed with the competitive pilgrimage to the afterlife. Christianity divided society, separated nations and cultures, made bloodshed logical, even inevitable. For them, science, determined to reject the spiritual as a valid plane of experience, committed to explanation and definition, dwelled too contentedly in the empirical realm of material fact, smugly certain that the universe would inevitably be domesticated, its vastness mapped into clarity. And capitalism? For them, it relentlessly pushed the privilege of possessions, too certain that the accumulation of stuff and the ambitious (and fiercely competitive) pursuit of wealth justified itself, despite creating a troubling chasm between a handful of the wealthy and all the rest.

For Salinger (as well as other East Coast college-educated liberals in his generation), Christianity, science, and capitalism simply did not work. Each, in turn, is tested in *Catcher*. Holden's precocious younger sister, Phoebe, for instance, embodies the best—and the worst—of Judeo-Christianity. Produced by the same disturbing family circumstances that have unsettled Holden—distant parents, an upscale lifestyle of cold materialism, and the death of a brother from cancer—Phoebe is strong and clearheaded. In the novel's close, Phoebe, in her offer to accompany Holden in his foolish plans to head out West, calls his bluff as a way to compel him to acknowledge that he must rejoin the responsibilities of living in a difficult, hazardous now. Phoebe is determined to fix her brother, to put his pieces back together (when Holden accidentally breaks a 45 record he has bought for Phoebe, she insists that he give her the bag with the pieces). Phoebe's loving concern is familiar love-thy-neighbor Judeo-Christian rhetoric.

But here Phoebe does not sustain admiration—like some caricature of Jesus the healer, she comes across as a bossy control freak (she claims she can control her own body temperature), an egomaniac (her school notebooks are decorated with columns of her own signature), an intrusive, steamrolling busybody (she sports elephants on her pajamas) who cannot endure mystery (in her spare time she writes detective fiction) and who lives too easily in a world of cause and effect, good and evil. And, in the end, Holden cannot be healed anyway, cannot be fixed. At one point, Holden says that of all the characters in the Bible he most sympathizes with the man afflicted by demons recounted in Mark 5. The man has long lived on the outskirts of a village in Gergesa, left to roam amid the broken tombs in the cemetery, shrieking in his madness, cutting himself with jagged stones. Jesus, ever the busybody, takes a moment to cast out the demons. But when the man tries to follow Jesus, Jesus tells him no. The man is left behind, healed, yes, but now an outcast. Jesus has moved on and the villagers still look upon the man with understandable wariness. Christian caring, then, is tender cruelty. Perhaps the most genuine gesture to help Holden comes from his former English teacher, Mr. Antolini, who gives Holden a place to sleep his last night in Manhattan. Mr. Antolini cautions Holden that he is heading for a painful fall and counsels him to find his place in this most imperfect world and to turn that spiritual anguish into great art—perhaps the best advice Holden receives. But when Holden wakes up the following morning to discover Mr. Antolini stroking his hair, Holden overreacts, assumes the teacher is making a homosexual pass, and summarily bolts. Again and again gestures of love, gestures of compassion, fail. For all of Jesus' rhetoric, then, the Christian world resists cleansing. In the novel's harrowing closing pages, Holden struggles to erase the obscenities scrawled on the walls of his sister's elementary school, but even as he erases one "Fuck you" he finds another.

If Christian compassion fails, science does little better. Holden's brother invests his faith in therapy, real doctors in real hospitals. It is the stuff of the Hollywood screenplays D. B. churns out—a (melo)dramatic recovery, a feel-good last-reel recovery through the rigorous application of medical attention. D. B. has placed his troubled little brother in an institution on the outskirts of Hollywood where medical science will "help" Holden through administering therapeutic rest and rehabilitation centered largely on Holden's talking his way through his considerable anxieties. But the more Holden "confides," the more we see he evades. He dodges any sort of honest confrontation with his troubled past, refuses to be straightforward, and never actually opens up about the most critical emotional crises of his life. He obfuscates, digresses, teases, and taunts his listener—indeed, given the numerous times he lies, we are never really sure how much of what he confesses actually happened. And capitalism? It fares little better than science or Christianity. Money and privilege—Holden's father is an influential attorney—have given little to Holden. And as he walks amid the garish holiday displays and the throngs of weary shoppers at Christmastime, we are reminded how the crass materialism of capitalism is a measure of the spiritual bankruptcy of Judeo-Christianity.

If Western civilization, then, is deemed soulless, mercenary, corrupt, spiritually rotten, where do you turn? Living amid the heady artistic environs of New York City and attending Columbia University in the late 1940s (the time that *Catcher* was being written), Salinger, like other Greenwich Village intellectuals, found in the powerful persuasion of Eastern thought, particularly Zen Buddhism, a profound consolation, a way out of the wasteland despair over Western civilization's evident failures. In a world intent on coming apart at every nail, Buddhism, with its emphasis on individual spiritual development, offered a compelling rationale for letting go, for achieving an inner balance and maintaining the integrity of a private sense of wholeness and spiritual wellness. Like the phalanx of free-spirited Manhattan writers and avant-garde poets, hip jazz musicians, coffeehouse philosophers, and experimental painters known collectively as the Beats, Salinger studied with care the argument of Zen Buddhism and responded to its striking simplicity, its emphasis on interior exploration as the way to spiritual peace amid great suffering, and its advocacy of intuitive meditation and the rich expression of silence as central in the search for enlightenment. Against the suffocating materialism and economic anxieties of consumer capitalism, against the barbaric irony of civilized war, against the apocalyptic implications of science's atomic age, Buddhism offered a signal consolation, a spiritual awakening that accords the seeker a resilient interior equanimity amid the distracting universe of chaos and noise.

The experience of reading *Catcher*, specifically frustrations over defining Holden, shifts dramatically if we factor in Salinger's burgeoning interest in Buddhism. The problem, of course, is that contemporary Americans have little interest in spiritual complexities. Evangelical Protestantism, Christian Catholicism, Judaism, Islamism, even atheism—all are simplified into T-shirt slogans and bumper stickers. Zen Buddhism is no exception. Enjoy the Ride; Less Is More; Don't Sweat the Small Stuff . . . It's All Small Stuff; It's All Fun and Games and Then Someone Loses an I; Meditation—It's Not What You Think!; Be Mindful; See the (*insert any noun*); be the (*insert the same noun*). Indeed, the mention of Zen Buddhism to a contemporary audience is likely to be associated with feng shui templates for interior redecorating using elaborate gardening layouts and tumbling water; or paramilitary martial arts academies in strip malls where suburban kids are drilled with concepts of mental toughness; or low-key exercise regimens in which, to soothing instrumental music with gauzy sound effects such as rain or ocean waves and glass wind chimes, practitioners assume pretzel-like positions on floor mats; or the power motivation bromides of knockoff Zen masters from NBA coach Phil Jackson to cable news spiritual healer Deepak Chopra. The profound wisdom literature of centuries of Buddhism has been simplified, popularized as the wit and wisdom of a succession of pop-culture icons, the Tao of Pooh or Mr. Spock, Eric Cartman or Dwight Schrute. Buddhism's rich sense of paradox, its celebration of insight, the Zen moment, has long been a punch line for comedians who, in exaggerated broken "Oriental" syntax, offer nonsensical phrases that inevitably begin "Confucius say." Or Buddhism has been appropriated as the fuzzy feel-good wisdom delivered with appropriate inscrutability and unshakable calm by a series of faux-sensei characters in scores of television series and films, from a succession of character actors in the role of detective Charlie Chan to tight-lipped martial arts actors from Chuck Norris to David Carradine, from gnomic wisdom-spouting characters from the Jedi master Yoda to Mr. Miyagi in *The Karate Kid* to the giant anthropomorphic sewer rat Master Splinter in *Teenage Mutant Ninja Turtles*. But the impact of Buddhism in energizing the avant-garde underground of New York City of the late 1940s was profound, and Salinger, we know, was particularly engaged by its argument. Not only are there abundant references to the vocabulary and rich imagery of Buddhism in *Catcher* but also the handful of cryptic stories Salinger would publish in the decade after *Catcher* confirmed his serious interest. *Catcher* itself is the work of a man, at once deeply spiritual (his father was Jewish, his mother Catholic) and deeply dissatisfied with his materialist culture, who had found in Zen Buddhism the consolation of spiritual discipline.

For Salinger and his troubled generation, Zen Buddhism freed the mind. Indeed, Zen Buddhism has no designated deity to pray to, no scriptures to study, no rituals to attend, no formal teachings to learn. Rather, it seeks to stretch the mind to the point where it grasps its own limits. These occasions for meditation center on a kind of story called a koan, the meaning of which, unlike traditional narrative parables, cannot be apprehended by thought or analysis; indeed, the argument of a koan cannot be reconstructed through discussion or lecture. Koans are entirely private experiences. Novitiates to the Buddhist tradition are given these perplexing stories to focus their meditations. From a Western perspective, koans can seem silly—of the nearly two thousand koans compiled in Buddhist tradition, most Westerners know only the one that ponders the sound of one hand clapping. But the intention of koans is to confound logic and in turn to ignite illumination, what Buddhists term a satori. Koans are not themselves the source of enlightenment; rather, they are the call to insight, like a knock at the door or the ring of a telephone. That intuitive moment of illumination is a profoundly private moment that comes, by all accounts, only from the rigorous application of the intellect until its very processes give way, a moment that cannot be forced, cannot even be earned, cannot be shared, indeed cannot even be articulated. Thus the satori runs counter to the expectations of Christian tradition, which sees the moment of spiritual awakening as a public moment, a saving moment when the absurd universe suddenly coheres, suddenly makes sense.

Which brings us back to Holden. Shifting the focus away from Holden and positioning the reader at the center of the narrative experience defines a far different, and far more ambitious, novel. If the novel takes place not among the characters or between Holden and the reader but rather between Salinger and the reader, then Salinger becomes the sensei, the teacher, who has subtly created the conditions in which and through which we readers may teach ourselves. We are reluctant, of course, students often are. As good Western readers, at once smugly clever and joylessly analytical, we seek a good story, a sympathetic character, a handy symbol or two, a tidy lesson. But Salinger wants nothing less than to enlarge the vision of the readers, to change not so much the conditions of our lives—that would be grossly inappropriate from a Buddhist perspective—but rather our perceptions of those conditions. Whatever epiphany Holden apparently achieves is left decidedly (deliberately) problematic—he has numerous opportunities in the closing pages, in the museum, in his conversation with Phoebe, at the park watching the carousel in the rain, later in the California hospital bed. Is he redeemed? Is he doomed? Is he sick? Is he on the mend? It's not that we do not know, it's that we cannot know.

But now shift to the reader. As with all wisdom literature, the reader, not the character, is invited to learn. Holden is a complex riddle, a puzzling contradiction, a paradoxical multireality that refuses to conform to the expectations of logic and rationality. We dutifully consider the evidence that Salinger so carefully orchestrates in his narrative. We realize that frustration until (and here is where the illumination comes in) we glimpse the far more profound truth that Salinger seeks to teach, that fact cannot lead to clarity, that reality itself does not abide by the cloying imperatives of logic, that the mind needs to be roused to the reality of its own limits. Unlike Christianity or science or capitalism, Buddhism celebrates that moment of frustration when we grasp how ungraspable, how wonderfully elusive the material cosmos is. It is a moment of bracing, breathlessly expansive awareness. In executing a koan, Salinger uses *The Catcher in the Rye* as a spiritual exercise that rewards patience, concentration, discipline, and focus. We are not to define Holden—we are to ponder him.

Thus like Melville's elusive white whale, Hawthorne's ornate scarlet letter, Fitzgerald's shadowy gangster Jimmy Gatz, all literary progenitors of Holden Caulfield, Holden is less a textual event and more a daring, defiant refutation of the dreary Western imperative to put faith in the intellect. Holden is dangerously/wonderfully undefinable, a hieroglyph, a conundrum that opens the reader to the terrifying/exhilarating energy of possibility. What is Holden? A pattern emerges. He is a confrontational pacifist, an uncommunicative confidant, a lonely egomaniac, a humble braggart, a loving sociopath, a sophisticated innocent, a caring homophobe, an authentic phony, an honest liar, a friendly loner, a spiritual atheist, a rebellious conformist, a pragmatic idealist, a compassionate misanthrope, a loving misogynist, a likable cad, a wandering paralytic, a Marxist capitalist, a hopeful manic-depressive, a moribund joker, a metaphysical existentialist, a selfless narcissist, an impotent savior, an erotic virgin, an egomaniac with an inferiority complex, a noble soul uncomplicated by a conscience. Pause to consider each yin-yang construction, how each construction defies reason, how each makes irony ironic—clear sight and insight are suddenly not the same thing. The more you think, the more confused you are, the wiser you become. The less you understand, the more you see.

If contemplating Holden seems suspiciously eggheaded and irredeemably impractical compared to the far more efficient process of extracting symbols and coining themes, that is exactly why Salinger wants so earnestly for us to engage this character. For Salinger, it is the faith in analysis that has spiraled Western civilization into its catastrophic dead end. It is thus not so much ironic as appropriate that this last grand expression of the serious novel in American culture, the last American novel to find a wide and deep place in American culture, would so audaciously and so confidently reject its own genre. But Salinger is returning the novel to its beginnings—to what invented stories did long before they so pleasantly distracted readers with plot and character, symbol and theme. In its beginnings, narrative offered the complex rejuvenation of wisdom. As a latter-day exemplum of such a narrative, *Catcher* is indeed a dangerous book. But not because Holden smokes or swears or disrespects teachers or because he hires a prostitute or mocks Jesus' disciples or even because he fantasizes about killing people. It is dangerous because what Salinger counsels runs so completely counter to the relentless materialism, the superficial certainties, and the aggressive pursuit of the trivial that define Western culture. Salinger offers the difficult gift of an Eastern perception. If we can achieve that satori, if the didactic construction that is Holden can lead us to the intuitive embrace of paradox, an insight beyond language, beyond logic, then we are presented with a viable avenue to what so completely eludes the tormented and haunted Holden—spiritual contentment amid the obscenities of an inscrutable universe.

Salinger and Holden, Disappearing in Plain Sight:
Biography of J. D. Salinger _____

David Klingenberger

    It would appear at best ironic, at worst irrelevant to preface any approach to the work of J. D. Salinger with his biography. After all, what use is the biography of an eccentric and monkish figure who so deliberately thinned himself into shadow, who resisted so early and so completely the fetching lure of celebrity, who spent more than half a century in self-imposed exile in a remote, if rustic, corner of rural New Hampshire, and who actually sought legal protection against those few hardy souls who, over that half century, thought to piece together a biography of a man who was by any measure among the most influential literary voices of his generation. Despite a man who so fashioned his life that it stands now as a cautionary tale against importing a writer's biography into that writer's fiction, that argues read the work and forget the author, the reality is that Holden Caulfield, by many estimates the defining creation of the American imagination of the second half of the twentieth century, did not materialize out of thin air; he was the creation of a particular person in a particular time and place—and the biography of that person, Jerome David Salinger, if spare by contemporary standards when we know so much about so many, is salient, even necessary, to any approach to *The Catcher in the Rye*.

    What do we know? Salinger was born in New York City on New Year's Day, 1919; a writer who would live to 2010 was born a scant six weeks after the end of World War I. Salinger grew up in upper-middle-class comfort—his father was a highly successful importer of European cheeses and meats. Salinger was raised Jewish, although his mother was Catholic. Young Sonny, as he was called, found school uninspiring and struggled with grades. He attended a number of private prep schools before his exasperated father sent him to Valley Forge Military Academy just outside Philadelphia. There, Salinger, who had been drawn to the theater and had considered training to be an actor, began to write short stories, mostly satiric pieces about life at the academy. In 1936, he matriculated at New York University with loose plans to pursue teaching. He stayed one full semester. His father, determined to help his misfit son, sent him to Vienna, Austria, to learn firsthand the meat and cheese import business. The rapid rise of Adolf Hitler and the advent of the Anschluss sent Salinger back to the United States in 1938.

He tried college again—this time at Ursinus College, a small prestigious liberal arts school just outside Philadelphia. Again, he stayed a single semester. In 1939 he returned to New York determined to become a writer. He enrolled in a night class in creative writing at Columbia, where his professor, Whit Burnett, a fiction editor at *Story* magazine, encouraged him to publish one of his stories in the magazine. Salinger did—his first story appeared in March 1940. It was clear to Salinger that he would write—he set his sights on publishing in the prestigious (and lucrative) *New Yorker*, then as now the bellwether for promising fiction writers. After several rejections, the magazine accepted "Slight Rebellion off Madison," a story set in New York about a troubled teenager named Holden Caulfield who struggles with the evident absurdity of his prep school education. When Japan attacked Pearl Harbor and war was declared, however, the magazine decided a story about a troubled teen without clear goals would be counterproductive to the war effort—it would not appear until 1946. Salinger himself, after initially being rejected for service because of a heart condition, was eventually drafted into the Army infantry, where he would participate in some of the bloodiest action in the war, including D-Day and later the Battle of the Bulge. He was also part of the counterespionage intelligence corps and was responsible for intense interrogation sessions with suspected spies. He was part of the brigades that first liberated the Nazi concentration camps—the Jewish Salinger witnessing the grim evidence of Hitler's barbarism. In the weeks following Germany's surrender in 1945, Salinger was hospitalized for exhaustion and what today might be called post-traumatic stress syndrome.

Throughout his harrowing war experience, however, Salinger never stopped writing—indeed, among his fondest war memories was the chance to meet novelist Ernest Hemingway in Paris.

When Salinger returned to the United States in April 1946, he came home married, to a French doctor. The marriage did not last—within six months his wife had returned home. The two would never speak again. Over the next eight years, Salinger perfected the short-story form, publishing widely in a host of prominent marketplace magazines, including *Collier's*, the *Saturday Evening Post*, *Esquire*, and *Cosmopolitan*, but most prominently in *The New Yorker*. It was the publication of what would be his first and only novel, *The Catcher in the Rye*, in 1951 that would catapult a reluctant Salinger into iconic status. The novel's tectonic impact on Eisenhower's America made Salinger a much sought-after figure—fans of the novel swarmed his 57th Street Manhattan apartment just to meet him, even catch a glimpse of him. For Salinger, who was himself turning to the contemplative principles of Zen Buddhism, such distracting noise proved overwhelming—he moved to the rural wilds outside Cornish, New Hampshire, and began what would become more than fifty years of simply, absolutely tuning the world out.

He published three more books, collections of stories that each shot to the top of best-seller lists. But Salinger maintained his distance—although a fixture of Cornish's community life, he steadfastly refused to pursue any opportunity for celebrity, save a single interview in 1974 with the *New York Times*. After 1965, he stopped publishing entirely, although rumors would swirl for decades of stacks of finished manuscripts he was hoarding away in his compound at Cornish. He was writing, it was said, just not deigning to publish. The last forty years of Salinger's life, until his death on January 27, 2010, were remarkably unremarkable—he married twice and had two children, he studied and pursued a variety of exotic religions, and he practiced an assortment of extreme dietary regimens. A memoir published in 2000 by Salinger's daughter provided a kind of voyeuristic glimpse into elements of the recluse's life: his meticulous hygiene, his obsession with old movies, his fascination with alternative medicine. And with the advent of the Internet, admirers and fanatics had a forum for propounding often bizarre stories of Salinger's private life, little of it ever substantiated. Attempts by well-intentioned academics and journalists to meet Salinger were all frustrated—most famously in 1988 when British writer Ian Hamilton was contracted to write a biography on Salinger and ended up writing a kind of story about writing the biography, *In Search of J. D. Salinger*, and even that Salinger contested in court (unsuccessfully) when Hamilton planned to publish excerpts from letters Salinger had written. For the next twenty years, Salinger maintained his strict isolation, never breaking his silence, never coaxed to an interview or a public appearance. In 1992, when his farmhouse caught fire, reporters swarmed onto his property hoping to get even a single photograph of the hermit-writer—they were unsuccessful. Salinger died of natural causes in 2010 at the age of ninety-one.

Undoubtedly, in an age when everyone wants to be famous, when everyone seeks the hot white light of celebrity even for fifteen minutes, the central mystery of J. D. Salinger is his nearly fifty-year absence. Are there indications in the character of Holden Caulfield, Salinger's most developed character, that might explain or at least clarify such a consummate dedication to isolation? Why did Salinger simply, so completely walk away? Athletes never retire at the top of their game; singers don't simply quit recording after a string of hit songs. After publishing more than a dozen highly acclaimed short stories in major magazines and then the landmark *Catcher in the Rye*, in 1951, Salinger was easily the most influential writer of his time. Salinger and his work were regularly dissected in college classrooms and routinely discussed around dinner tables. He became a celebrity in the United States and around the world: the Great American Writer. And then he disappeared. After 1965 he never again published, not a word. He never again spoke publicly. Gone.

Of course, Salinger disappeared in plain sight. Everyone was looking at him and everyone knew where he went, that 90-acre farm outside Cornish. In retrospect, we can find evidence of how important privacy was for him. For instance, the original cover of *Catcher* had his picture on the back. Salinger was so upset at what he perceived as an intrusion into his life that he not only had the photo removed from subsequent printings of the novel, he also went on to have his remaining three books published with absolutely plain covers, bearing simply the title and the author's name. Even with that, why Salinger decided to vanish so publicly was never answered. With Salinger's death, it is unlikely that there will ever be answers. Of course, Holden also wants to disappear. One of the first revelations he shares with the reader about himself is that his favorite story, which his brother wrote, is "The Secret Goldfish." This ability—or desire—on the part of the goldfish to vanish behind glass seems remarkably like Salinger's later trick of evanescing in plain sight. Later, when watching Ernie, the piano player at one of the bars he visits, Holden decides that if he were a piano player he would go and just play in a closet so that no one could watch him. Throughout the book, Holden has a number of elaborate fantasies of disappearing, ranging from going West and living on a ranch to pretending to be a deaf-mute gas station owner who will never have to talk to anyone. It is as if Holden's fantasies simply became Salinger's reality.

Is Holden autobiographical? In *Catcher* the word "autobiography" appears on the first page. Holden references *David Copperfield*, perhaps the most autobiographical of Charles Dickens's novels, and tells us that we will probably want to know about his birth and childhood. Connections between a writer and a character should not surprise a reader, but they become especially charged when the life of the artist has become such a public mystery. Basic biographical parallels between Salinger and Holden are also numerous. The book begins at Pencey Prep; Salinger attended Valley Forge Military Academy. Holden tells us that his father is wealthy; Salinger's father's food import business brought in enough money that the family was well-off.

Holden attended a series of schools with varying degrees of success, and that describes Salinger's academic career. Holden's parents are of different religions; Salinger's father was Jewish, his mother Catholic. The Salingers lived on 91st Street in Manhattan; the Caulfields on 71st. Although all of these may simply reflect the adage that authors write about what they know, the last fact—that both Holden and Salinger are products of New York City—is particularly telling.

Although *Catcher* bustles with events, the action of the book actually covers only three days, and almost all of that occurs in New York City. Although some of the first day ("where I want to start telling") happens at Pencey Prep, the reader discovers that the morning had been spent in New York City—where Holden left the fencing equipment on the subway—and the day ends with his travel back into that city. Along the way, *Catcher* becomes a veritable Baedeker of sites associated with New York City—Central Park, Broadway, Radio City Music Hall, Fifth Avenue, Grand Central Station—but the novel is also privy to places known only to locals. Yes, Holden is familiar with the Museum of Natural History, but he also knows about the two French singers, Tina and Janine, who used to perform at the Wicker Bar in the Seton Hotel. Unlike so much of American literature that takes place in the wilderness or in the suburbs, *Catcher* is set in the city and that the quintessential American city. It is the story of a high school student, but instead of cheerleaders and prom it concerns taxicabs and jazz clubs, cocktails and prostitutes. It is an urban tale of a kid attempting to pick up women in bars and take voyeuristic peeks through windows into the sexual lives of others.

One of the most powerful elements of living in—or even visiting—a city is the ability not only to disappear but also to disappear, as Salinger did, in plain sight. Surrounded by literally millions, the individual walks down the street invisible and unconnected. The ability to be alone among millions is one of the great paradoxes of the city. And it happens to Holden. Certainly the most terrifying passage in the novel occurs in the midst of the city at its busiest. It is the middle of the day and Holden is on Fifth Avenue, one of the major thoroughfares of the city. All of the stores are open; it's Christmastime. The streets are packed, especially with children.

> Then all of the sudden, something very spooky started happening. Every time I came to the end of a block and stepped off the goddam curb, I had this feeling that I'd never get to the other side of the street. I thought I'd just go down, down, down, and nobody'd ever see me again. Boy, did it scare me. You can't imagine. I started sweating like a bastard—my whole shirt and underwear and everything. Then I started doing something else. Every time I'd get to the end of a block I'd make believe I was talking to my brother Allie. I'd say to him, "Allie, don't let me disappear. Allie, don't let me disappear. Allie, don't let me disappear." (197-98)

Holden has a near-complete psychological break with external reality while in the middle of a New York City street. The book ends shortly after this, and that ending reinforces the reader's knowledge that Holden's mental instability has resulted in his travel out to California, that he is recounting the events of the three days of the action of the novel as therapy. But what could cause an intelligent, humorous, and economically stable kid to end up so destroyed? And, more important, does Holden's fear of disappearing become Salinger's reality?

The novel is designed not to give the reader a simple cause and effect for Holden's disassociation from reality—or insight into Salinger's future action—but one telling aspect often overlooked is the intensity of violence that runs throughout the novel. The murder/suicide of James Castle sits emotionally at the center of the book, and there are also the pummeling Holden receives from Maurice and the beating from Stradlater. But throughout the novel the level of violence in Holden's head is quite graphic. One of Holden's recurring fantasies involves shooting someone or being shot himself. He repeatedly imagines giving or getting a bullet in the gut. He tells us that he would rather push a guy out a window or chop his head off with an ax than sock him in the jaw. Holden's favorite biblical character is a raving maniac haunted by legions of devils who lives amid the tombs in a village cemetery and cuts himself with shards of rock (Mark 5:11). When he sees the word "fuck" scratched into a surface, Holden not only wants to kill the vandal but also pictures himself smashing the culprit's head on the stone steps "till he was good and goddam dead and bloody" (201). Cruelty of this intensity does not sound like the Holden the reader remembers upon finishing the novel. And then there is the most memorable physical item that defines Holden: that red hat. A red hat is an odd clothing choice, and certainly its color and repeated appearance in the story call attention to it. But this hat is not just any hat, it is a hunting hat. Although Ackley tells him that it is a deer-hunting hat, to Holden the hat is more ominous. "Like hell it is. . . . This is a people shooting hat . . . I shoot people in this hat" (22). The hat transforms from an object bought on a whim that morning during a field trip to New York into a helmet that protects and inspires violence.

Perhaps with more knowledge of Salinger's life, a book about the travels and troubles of an adolescent boy in Manhattan at Christmastime may become a painfully autobiographical story of a young writer who somehow survived the incredible violence of World War II. After all, Salinger witnessed some of the ugliest conflicts in the European theater. He must have seen suffering and destruction on a level few people can imagine. As with so many wounds, the physical mark heals but the mental scar causes the most pain and remains the longest. Salinger was famously quiet about his military service, but the results of his psychic battle scars perhaps surface, obliquely, in *Catcher* and also in his ultimate desire for silence on a New England farm.

War wounds, childhood memories, or adult desires, the biographical piece that ties them all and acts as the most powerfully personal element of *The Catcher in the Rye* must be Salinger's profession as a writer. Returning from the horrors of the war, Salinger turned immediately to writing. Not surprisingly, the book is replete with examples of

Holden's love of writers and of writing; he does his best work in English class, he ghostwrites essays for struggling students, he reads voraciously—he even wants to shake the writer's hand after finishing a particularly great book. Both Holden and J. D. Salinger believe in the power of the written word to communicate the ineffable pain and bliss and peculiarity of being human. Seeing Holden at the depths of his suffering, Mr. Antolini counsels the troubled kid:

> "Among other things, you'll find that you're not the first person who was ever confused and frightened and even sickened by human behavior. You're by no means alone on that score, you'll be excited and *stimulated* to know. Many, many men have been just as troubled morally and spiritually as you are right now. Happily, some of them kept records of their troubles. You'll learn from them—if you want to. Just as someday, if you have something to offer, someone will learn something from you. It's a beautiful reciprocal arrangement." (189)

Salinger writes these words for Mr. Antolini to give to Holden, who in turn gives them to us. It is indeed a beautiful reciprocal arrangement.

Work Cited

Salinger, J. D. *The Catcher in the Rye*. 1951. Boston: Little, Brown, 1971.

the PARIS REVIEW

The *Paris Review* Perspective
David Matthews for *The Paris Review*

Some works of art transcend valuations of *good* or *bad* and are merely *important*. Crucial even. *The Catcher in the Rye* happens to be not only good—impossibly so, in fact—but also indispensible.

I'll go one step further: there would be nothing we recognize today as American youth/popular/postmodern culture without *The Catcher in the Rye*. No Warhol, Dylan, James Dean, Brando, Woodstock, Woody Allen, Updike, Bellow, Eggers, Vonnegut, Mailer, Franzen, Selby, Roth, or Kerouac. No rock and roll, no hipsters, beatniks or iconoclasts, no—by now clichéd, but at the time of the novel's publication, in 1951, like a bucket of cold coffee in the face—trope of the snarky, damaged young man with a heart too big for this world, which has inspired countless geeks to pick up pens, guitars, cameras. Salinger's sixteen-year-old narrator, Holden Caulfield, so acutely presented the schizoid face of maleness at the dawn of the atomic age that some of those geeks lost themselves in his consciousness and picked up *guns*, too. Rock stars and presidents took bullets, induced, in some twisted way, by Holden's primal yawp of pain. *The Catcher in the Rye* is a book that burrowed into the brain and saved lives and created culture and killed.

Until Mark Twain came along, with *Adventures of Huckleberry Finn*, in 1884, American fiction was stuck in a rut of romanticism—guys in the woods moping about their place in the world, or Puritans getting it on or witch burning, or whaling stories in need of a good edit. There weren't many heroes, though.

It wouldn't be too far from the mark to suggest that Huck was the first American literary hero, Odysseus in dungarees and a straw hat. Twain was the first American novelist to use vernacular successfully, closing the wide chasm between narrator and reader. For the first time, the central voice of the story—in this case, Twain's thirteen-year-old first-person narrator—reflected the sensibilities and rhythms of, if not people we knew, then people we would like to have known. Novels before then were a monologue. *Huck Finn* felt like a dialogue. The first word in the text is "you," as in you, the reader.

Huck's character flaws could mostly be rubbed off with some discipline, education, and a hot washcloth. Holden Caulfield is Huck's bastard son. His troubles run deeper and his worldview skews darker. Salinger appropriates the structure of the man-child's heroic journey (a conceit going back as far as the Homeric tradition) and retrofits it for post-World War II America. Holden is *Catcher*'s hero, but he's no hero. He is a liar, a hypocrite, a misogynist, a homophobe, a regressive, delusional, first-rate whack-job, either an insufferable boor or a prig, depending on his circumstance, and kind of a jerk. He is also perhaps the most varied and confounding fictional character extant, until that point. Like Twain, Salinger decides to do away with the fourth wall in order to allow a marrow-deep access into Holden's psyche. Not coincidentally, the *second* word in Salinger's text is "you." We're involved from the start.

The premise of *Catcher* is simple: Holden Caulfield, sixteen, privileged, has been kicked out of yet another private school just before Christmas and has to make his way from Connecticut into Manhattan to inform his parents of yet another failure.

Salinger commits to the character completely. The book is purposefully discursive and hyperbolic, the documentations of a self-absorbed, hormone-addled man-child. He is grandiose; his speech is filled with unnecessary adverbs—everything is "really" this or "very" that—and waterlogged with qualifiers—"if you ask me," or "if you really want to know the truth." Adolescent journals to this day are filled with that kind of crap. If readers find Holden a solipsistic pain in the ass—a common complaint—that is part of Salinger's authorial intent. Holden is annoying in precisely the way teenagers everywhere are annoying, in their insistence that their small, insulated dramas are the stuff of life or death. Which is not to minimize the seriousness of Holden's descent into near-madness. It's heavy stuff, heavier than Jay Gatsby by tons.

In keeping with the heroic tradition, Holden's transition to adulthood is not an easy one. For every advance he makes toward some insight into what it means to be a man, he retreats back into the safety of childhood. Once he is in Manhattan—an ostensible adult on his own—he solicits a hooker to relieve him of his virginity. Then he chickens out, the final (physical) frontier of sexual maturity too frightening to broach. Eventually, Holden takes shelter in the Museum of Natural History, a place devoid of sexuality, a monument to grade school-era adventures and a simpler time.

Coming only a few years after the second global world war, and in the wake of the first atomic bombs dropped on mass populations, the path to adulthood seemed less sure than ever when *Catcher* was published in 1951. Why grow up, if there may not be a world to grow into?

It is the vaguely nihilistic, informed cynicism that Salinger infuses his narrator with that sets the tone for the modern antihero, and for youth culture as we now know it. Most of the cinematic and literary descendants of Holden share a particular trait (in addition to being almost exclusively male): they all lack, in the beginning of their narratives, the ability to communicate with, or meet the expectations of, adult (read: productive, conventional) society. Think about the tortured, misunderstood character James Dean plays in the seminal film *Rebel Without a Cause*. Or faux-suicidal Harold in *Harold and Maude*, or practically any character from a John Hughes movie. All of Woody Allen's nebbishy characters are based on a rough outline of Holden. They are always smart (smarter than the phonies they are surrounded by), doomed to a life outside the mainstream (which they are also smarter than—it's their curse), and on a futile quest for the girl/woman who is smart enough to appreciate their genius—but not so smart as to outshine them. Holden created the paradigm for the comic leading man, post-World War II. (It's not all gravy—Holden also helped ratify the idea that self-absorbed slackers are actually misunderstood geniuses. Sorry, ladies.) How about the unnamed narrator of Jay McInerney's novel *Bright Lights, Big City* (a 1980s update of *Catcher*), or everything Bret Easton Ellis has ever written? Jack Kerouac's Beat lyricism is an avant-garde update of Holden's stylized, urbane riffing. Even nonfiction bears the mark of Salinger's creation: Dave Eggers and David Sedaris and even Norman Mailer, with his journalistic legitimation of the hipster/outsider as a cultural force, cop freely from Holden's eccentricities.

Youth popular culture, especially rock and roll and its derivatives—also have their basis in the sneering iconoclasm of Salinger's narrator. Hippies rallied around music and a lifestyle that eschewed mainstream acceptance and "adult" hypocrisy. Nearly thirty years after *Catcher* was published, when punker Johnny Rotten famously sneered at his audience, "Ever get the feeling you've been cheated?" he was channeling Holden's contempt for the status quo. Pop music's insistence on rebellion and "authenticity" is Holden, set to three chords.

If it sounds like I'm overstating the importance of *The Catcher in the Rye*, I'm not. It's not possible. The changes in the cultural landscape the book has affected are too numerous. Every angry young man, every outsider looking in on a world he despises, but ultimately must conform to, is—first and best—manifested in Salinger's novel.

It's okay if you hate Holden. You're kind of supposed to. It's okay if you don't like the novel, even. And it's okay if you don't think the world of art and culture has been shaped, to a large degree, by *Catcher*. I mean, you're *wrong*, but it's okay.

Copyright © 2012 by David Matthews.

CRITICAL CONTEXTS

Catching Holden Through a Cultural Studies Lens

Robert Miltner

One helpful way to approach *The Catcher in the Rye* is to consider the title that J. D. Salinger selected. Midway through the novel, Holden Caulfield, having dropped off his suitcases at Grand Central Station before he is to meet Sally Hayes at the theater, observes a family coming from church. Holden's focus falls on their six-year-old child:

> The kid ... was walking in the street, instead of on the sidewalk, but right next to the curb. He was making out like he was walking a very straight line, the way kids do, and the whole time he kept singing and humming. I got up closer so I could hear what he was singing. He was singing that song, "If a body catch a body coming through the rye. . . ." The cars zoomed by, brakes screeched all over the place, his parents paid no attention to him, and he kept on walking next to the curb singing "If a body catch a body coming through the rye." It made me feel better. It made me feel not so depressed any more. (115)

The cinematic elements of this scene are worth noting. Holden's narrative distance closes in like a camera moving in for a close shot. A sound track of sorts is introduced, the title song that is in fact appropriate to the story because in this small cinematic moment, Holden is established as the book title's catcher in the rye. The child is off the curb and in a dangerous street, but he is singing and doing fine—so much so that Holden feels "not so depressed any more." Holden's identification with the child is emblematic of his own arrested development and his own need to overcome the unresolved death of his younger brother, Allie, from leukemia and the concurrent loss of his own innocence. If the idea of a camera lens can be borrowed from this scene and the concept of a lens or focus for critical inquiry be substituted, *Catcher* can be as vibrant and fresh to readers of all ages today as it was when first published. The best lens for the camera of critical inquiry is perhaps cultural studies, one large enough, given its panoramic sweep, to see the broad swath of the narrative yet able to include, for close-up study, the ways in which gender studies and media studies help readers understand the dilemmas Holden Caulfield faces.

Raymond Williams, who helped establish the field of cultural studies, believed that, as a means of critical inquiry, cultural studies would examine the "structure of the family, the structure of institutions which express or govern social relationships, [and] the characteristic forms through which members of the society communicate" (qtd. in Sardar and Van Loon 5). Cultural studies is not one unified lens; instead, it borrows from and uses the social sciences, the arts, and the humanities: psychology, sociology, anthropology, political science, philosophy, art theory, literary criticism, gender studies, pop culture, media, musicology. Imagine cultural studies as a whirlwind that encircles *Catcher*; by using cultural studies, one can undertake critical inquiry by moving across disciplines, selecting and adopting whatever suits a particular passage, section, chapter, or the book as a whole. Because cultural studies is a collective comprising numerous fields of study, a change or advance in any one of them can affect the others, ever allowing for new and exciting critical insights. However, because this field of study often must reconcile discrete or conflicting forms of knowledge, it "assumes a common identity and common interest between the knower and the known" (Sardar and Van Loon 9). Although this split can potentially lead to inconsistency, hierarchy, and conflict, British theorist Stuart Hall sees cultural studies as an intellectual practice that "must always remain at the cutting edge of knowledge and theory" and through which "one may attempt to reconcile conflicting forces by channeling them in creative directions." "Society is driven by conflicts based on sex, race, religion, and region, as well as class," notes Hall, and "culture shapes people's sense of identity just as much as economics" (qtd. in Sardar and Van Loon 36-37). If *The Catcher in the Rye* is ultimately about Holden's sense of identity, or rather his interrupted identity development, the broad umbrella of cultural studies serves as a useful methodology to reinvigorate readings of a story set on the cusp between modernism and postmodernism.

Why are Holden Caulfield and this book so suited for a cultural studies critical lens? Perhaps it is because, as J. P. Steed observes, Holden is a

> precocious, romantically cynical, cynically romantic teenager who—in all his Americanness—often embodies that which he criticizes, while nobly grasping (and perpetually failing) to protect that which he idealizes. In the 1950's post-World War II, pre-Civil Rights Movement America, Holden Caulfield—do we dare say single-handedly?—(re)defined the identity of the American teenager and subsequently reconstructed the identity of Americans. (2-3)

But how much perpetual appeal is there to teenagers for Holden Caulfield, a literary figure? Given that in the United States alone, *The Catcher in the Rye* sells about 250,000 copies a year, with more than 65 million copies sold worldwide since its publication, the book seems to speak to teenagers and adults decade after decade. As different generations of readers encounter Holden Caulfield, a critical inquiry relative to each generation emerges, offering a lens that opens up the text in new and relevant ways for those readers. Contemporary readers—either new to the book or returning to it—can benefit from applying an appropriately fine-tuned cultural studies critical lens. In this case, the aspects of cultural studies most applicable to *The Catcher in the Rye* are gender studies, social psychology, and media studies.

Gender studies is concerned with the social construction of gender rather than its biological determinism. Although gender studies encompasses feminist theory, queer theory, and men's studies, it is the last of these that is most useful for a close reading of *Catcher*. "Culture is a place where the social arrangements of gender can be contested," writes Ziauddin Sardar. "This is particularly so . . . in the dominant modes of cultural *representation*, such as literature and the visual arts, where the constructed notions of gender have a strong presence" (Sardar and Van Loon 139). *Catcher*, then, can be read as a cautionary tale of an American teenage boy in mid-twentieth century, a period of great social readjustment after World War II. As linguist Bill Bryson observes:

> So little had [adolescents] been noticed in the past that *teenager* had entered the language only as recently as 1941. . . . In the heady boom of the postwar years, however, America's teenagers made up for lost time. Between 1946 and 1960, when the population of the United States grew by around 40 percent, the number of teenagers grew by 110 percent. (335)

Holden was at the forefront of the teenage population explosion collectively referred to as the Baby Boom. This discrepancy in population growth that produced more teenagers than adults led to some unanticipated social consequences. During the early years of the twentieth century, adults in the community served as role models for young men. Adults are traditionally seen as necessary for modeling, a socialization process that allows young people to imitate elders until the young people's acquired responses become habitual. Parents are often the "most significant adults in the lives of adolescents," followed by siblings and nonrelated significant adults, such as teachers (Rice 96). Holden suffers from having no effective adult figures on which to model himself. Suspended between the world of prep schools and an upper-middle-class New York lifestyle, between childhood and adulthood, Holden is cast adrift amid peers every bit as adrift as he is. By accepting peer guidance from what amounts to a society composed of siblings, young men come of age without the guidance of strong male role models; poet Robert Bly, in *The Sibling Society*, argues that this leads to ineffective "socialization of young males in the absence of fathers and mentors" (180). A brief review of the adult male role models available, or not available, to Holden Caulfield illustrates how he struggles because of a chronic lack of effective mentors.

The most important missing person, of course, is Holden's father, a corporate lawyer. Physically absent from the story, this "shadowy figure" (Rowe 89) is presented in offstage snippets: driving the family car to a party in Norwalk, Connecticut (162-63), flying to California for business (162), and even sympathetically described as lunching with Mr. Antolini, Holden's teacher, to discuss how "terribly concerned" he is about Holden (186). Moreover, because Mr. Caulfield is a typical 1950s male who goes to work early and works hard and with discipline to maintain his family, when he cannot convince Holden to be psychoanalyzed after Allie dies, he threatens to send Holden to military school (166), that is, to a rigorously disciplined version of the prep schools to which Holden has already been unable to adjust. Given that his father never actually interacts with Holden, we recognize him now as an absentee parent, typical of "fathers [who] abandon the family emotionally by working fourteen hours a day" (Bly 36); by doing so, Mr. Caulfield presages the social construct of the contemporary father who has vanished physically, emotionally, and conceptually. Holden, rather than being angry with or resentful of his father, is merely ambivalent about his father, who embodies the traits of adults in general.

As an alternative role model, Holden turns to his older brother. In the sibling order, Holden is the middle child. After Allie's death, he would naturally look up to his older brother, who has written and published a book of short stories, *The Secret Goldfish*, which Holden admires. By attending Allie's funeral when Holden was still in the hospital after hurting his hand by breaking the garage windows the night Allie died, D. B. acted as Holden's surrogate. But D. B. has deserted him and has abandoned what Holden views as his artistry as a writer of short stories to go to Hollywood, making himself "as emotionally remote from [Holden] as is his father" (Rowe 89). D. B. now writes for the movies, an act that leads Holden to label his brother a "prostitute" (2); D. B.'s relocation connects him with his father, who flies from New York to California for business. Because older siblings function as "surrogate parents, acting as caretakers, teachers, playmates and confidants," they are "vitally important" as role models for younger siblings in the development of an adolescent's personality traits and behavior (Rice 441).

With both his father and older brother unavailable as meaningful role models during the events related by Holden in the narrative, he must turn elsewhere for guidance. One older male to whom Holden turns is his former student adviser at Whooton School, Carl Luce, who was known for "giving sex talks" to the younger students (143), serving a role usually reserved for older brothers or fathers, though Holden still admits, "Sex is something I just don't understand" (63). Acting as a surrogate older brother, Luce, three years older than Holden, has graduated from Whooton and now attends Columbia and is dating an older woman. In a sense, Luce represents a version of Holden's future in which he finishes prep school and attends college. In this meeting, despite his apparent disinterest in Holden's current problem, Luce reminds Holden that the last time he saw him, he recommended Holden should see a psychoanalyst, someone like his own father, who could help Holden "recognize the patterns of [his] mind" (148). Although all he does is offer Holden the same advice he had given previously, at the least Luce has consistently tried to point Holden in the direction of recommended help.

A second older male is Holden's English teacher from Elkton Hills, Mr. Antolini, a "pretty young guy," not much older than D. B. (174), who had read D. B.'s stories and had "phoned [D. B.] up and told him not to go [to Hollywood]" (181). So with D. B. away, Mr. Antolini is the logical surrogate older brother, someone his brother's age Holden can talk to. He also functions as a "substitute father," observes Jonathan Baumbach, "after all the other fathers of his world have failed him, including his real father" (463). This is suggested by Mr. Antolini's calling him "Holden, m'boy!" (181) and by his having changed since Holden's Elkton Hills days by marrying an older woman (181) and taking a teaching position at New York University

(173). Additionally, Mr. Antolini offers Holden the best advice of anyone in the book, cautioning him regarding the consequences of repeating his pattern of failure at prep schools:

> This fall I think you're riding for—it's a special kind of fall, a horrible kind. The man falling isn't permitted to feel or hear himself hit bottom. He just keeps falling and falling. The whole arrangement's designed for men who, at some time or other in their lives, were looking for something their own environment couldn't supply them with. (187)

Here, even as he voices what Holden has already intuited, that the prep school environment is not helping him, Mr. Antolini ties together two important, previously unconnected details. The first is the death of James Castle, a student Holden knew at Elkton Hills. Castle was harassed by students for not retracting a statement he believed to be true about another boy at the school; as a result, he jumped from his dorm room window to his death. Holden recalls looking at Castle on the ground, how "his teeth and blood were all over the place" (170). Castle is emblematic of integrity and truth, and his actions exemplify the price paid for adhering to such principles. Castle is linked to Holden in a significant way: at the time of his death, Castle was wearing a turtleneck he had borrowed from Holden, linking them by the turtleneck as object-signifier. It can be inferred further that Holden has the potential to follow Castle because he mentions jumping out a window once when thinking about Stradlater with Jane Gallagher in Ed Banky's car (48) and again after Maurice punches him (104); even more pointedly, Holden says that "all I knew about [James Castle] was that his name was always right ahead of me at roll call. Cabel, R., Cabel, W., Castle, Caulfield—I can still remember it" (171). Finally, when Holden reveals that it was Mr. Antolini who found Castle after he had jumped from the window and "took off his coat and put it over James Castle and carried him all the way over to the infirmary" (174), readers can see a connection as Mr. Antolini, taking in Holden for the night at his apartment, provides sheets and blankets with which he indirectly covers Holden, only, in this case, before a jump from a window or a fall from a cliff.

The second connecting detail occurs after Holden tells his sister, Phoebe, when he sneaks back home after being kicked out of Pencey Prep, about the Robert Burns poem that the boy was singing when he walked in the street next to the curb—"If a body catch a body comin' through the rye." He shares with Phoebe a vision that he has:

> I keep picturing all these little kids playing some game in this big field of rye and all. Thousands of little kids, and nobody's around—nobody big, I mean—except me. And I'm standing on the edge of some crazy cliff. . . . I mean if they're running and they don't look where they're going I have to come out from somewhere and *catch* them. That's all I'd do all day. I'd just be the catcher in the rye and all. (173)

This anecdote can be unpacked in several ways. On one hand, Holden wants to save all innocent, unprepared children—like his sister Phoebe—from falling off the "crazy cliff," a metaphor for falling too quickly into the adult world. Second, as a "catcher," he would like to have used Allie's ball glove to save Allie from an early death. Third, he could be wishing he could have caught and saved James Castle when he jumped from the window. But last, and most important, Holden is projecting his desire to have someone save him from having to fall off the cliff into adulthood, the "horrible fall" Mr. Antolini warns him about. Granted, Holden is sixteen, but he often mentions that he is immature for his age, saying he acts more like he is thirteen. What is important to note is that Holden was thirteen when Allie died of leukemia, leaving Holden frozen in time in a state of arrested development. Perhaps subconsciously, Holden believes he is able to stay close to Allie this way—after all, he still talks with Allie (198), and Phoebe is just a year younger than Allie was when he died. Therefore, whereas Holden wants to save the "little kids," Mr. Antolini recognizes that it is

Holden who is headed for a "horrible kind" of fall, which he fears could be, like James Castle's fall, his demise.

Mr. Antolini tries to differentiate between Holden himself and James Castle by quoting the psychoanalyst Wilhelm Stekel: "The mark of the immature man is that he wants to die nobly for a cause, while the mark of the mature man is that he wants to live humbly for one" (188). Antolini, who presumably knows more about the events surrounding James Castle's death than Holden does, suggests to Holden that he need not experience a horrible fall like Castle, dying for a noble cause (truth). As he tells Holden, "I can very clearly see you dying nobly, one way or another, for some highly unworthy cause" (188). Instead, he implies that Holden could live humbly, become "educated and scholarly" (189), for an "academic education ... [will] begin to give you an idea what size mind you have. What it'll fit and, maybe, what it won't. After a while, you'll have an idea of what kind of thoughts your particular size mind should be wearing" (191). The model Mr. Antolini suggests for Holden is the one that Carl Luce and he have both taken: Luce has graduated from prep school and is now in college, learning what fits his mind, and Antolini has left teaching boys at a prep school to teach young men at the university what fits their "particular size minds." Each recommends that Holden undertake psychoanalysis, either with Luce's father or through applying the doctrine of the psychoanalyst Wilhelm Stekel.

Should Holden choose not to follow the advice of Luce or Mr. Antolini, and in the absence of his father and brother, his only recourse is to turn to his peer group, the other boys who attend his prep schools—Elkton Hills, Whooton School, and Pencey. These educational institutions are similar in social structure to what Bly calls a sibling society, places where "the socialization of young males [takes place] in the absence of fathers and mentors" (180), so that Holden's socialization is with the likes of Stradlater, Ackley, Castle, Luce, Marsalla, and Ernest Morrow. Christopher Brookeman, discussing the operant cultural codes of Pencey, views the institution as representative of single-sex private boarding schools, places where "young future professionals of the middle and upper classes experienced an extended period of training and socialization" (59), and, because students live at the schools rather than commuting from home, prep schools function as an "idealized family standing in loco parentis" (61), with students acting like siblings within the peer group. Sociologists identify family and peer groups as the most influential agents in the socialization process, and Brookeman sees Salinger locating Holden as "socializing with . . . members of his peer group" (63). As a result,

> what Salinger shows us is a world . . . of teenagers, the peer group and its culture, [which have] become a way of life. . . . there is something tragic about the sadly contracted state of Holden's world from which other [previous] generations have withdrawn, leaving his own generation in its one-dimensional fate. (64)

In the absence of fathers, brothers, and older peer mentors, Holden is adrift in a world of peers, most of whom, because he considers them phonies, will not be effective peer-siblings. Pencey Prep first appears in the second paragraph of the novel, showing its media-created image—promoting class, status, leisure, and character—which is in contrast with the real place: "[Pencey Prep] advertise[s] in about a thousand magazines, always showing some hot-shot guy on a horse jumping over a fence. Like as if all you ever did at Pencey was play polo all the time. I never saw a horse anywhere *near* the place" (2). Deconstructing the concept of character building at Pencey Prep and schools like it, Holden adds:

> And underneath the guy on the horse's picture, it always says: "Since 1888 we have been molding boys into splendid, clear-thinking young men." Strictly for the birds. They don't do any damn more *mold*ing at Pencey than they do at any other school. And I didn't know anybody there that was splendid and clear-thinking and all. Maybe two guys. If that many. And they probably *came* to Pencey that way. (2)

The underlying assumption here is that, during a child's formative years at home, character, morals, and ethics are developed and that in the sibling society of the prep school environment, each adolescent manifests the character traits when he encounters them. What Holden encounters instead are students who are mean, crooked, or phony, boys who, as the antithesis of "splendid and clear-thinking," gather into "these dirty little goddam cliques. The guys that are on the basketball team stick together, the Catholics stick together, the goddam intellectuals stick together, the guys that play bridge stick together. Even the guys that belong to the goddam Book-of-the-*Month* Club stick together" (131). For Holden, as he tries to tell Sally Hayes, the only alternative to the peer group sibling society of the prep school is escape: rural Massachusetts, Vermont, or Colorado—places unlike the prep schools where Holden feels miserable.

Unable to run off and escape to an isolated rural setting, however unrealistic as it may seem, Holden makes his escape by fantasizing a life that parallels the movies or by looking for reinforcing images in magazines. Media studies, another aspect of cultural studies, uses its critical lens like a camera, focusing on the visual aspects of characters within the literary narrative as well as the representations that are shaped by media codes. The media industry is shaped by four basic components that package its messages: product, audience, technology, and final look; the variable components that are "interacting simultaneously in a surrounding social and cultural world . . . lead to different patterns of representation" (Sardar and Van Loon 155). In films, the composite representation creates a sequence that is the basic element of the moving picture (Sardar and Van Loon 156). Holden is critical of the movie industry, especially regarding how it has affected him. His brother, D. B., whom he admires as a writer, has moved to Hollywood to write for the movies, an act that has left Holden disillusioned: "If there's one thing I hate, it's the movies," Holden states (2). Yet, in times of stress, Holden acts out scenes as if he is a character in a film.

Early in the novel, before he leaves Pencey Prep, Holden parodies the media. With Ackley, for example, Holden horses around, behaving like an over-the-top actor playing a scene in a hoarse voice: "I started groping around in front of me, like a blind guy, but without getting up or anything. I kept saying, 'Mother darling, why won't you give me your *hand*?'" (22). In a more detailed scene, while Stradlater is shaving, Holden tap-dances in a parody of Hollywood musicals, "It's the opening night of the *Ziegfeld Follies*," he says:

> I backed up a few feet and started doing this tap dance. . . . I started imitating one of those guys in the movies. In one of those *musicals*. I hate the movies like poison, but I get a bang imitating them. Old Stradlater watched me in the mirror while he was shaving. All I need's an audience. I'm an exhibitionist. "I'm the goddam Governor's son," I said. I was knocking myself out. Tap-dancing all over the place. "He doesn't want me to be a tap dancer. He wants me to go to Oxford. But it's in my goddam blood, tap-dancing." (29)

The cinematic effects of Holden's need to perform are noticeable in this passage: Holden's backing up sets up a long shot as he locates himself away from Stradlater and in the larger visual frame necessary to show him (in the reader's mind) in the open space required for the dance scene. Holden's telling the reader that he was "knocking himself out . . . dancing all over the place" is the equivalent of speeding up the visual action, for Stradlater's stationary position at the sink heightens the movement of Holden's tap dancing, creating the appearance of speed that leaves him "out of breath" (29). Moreover, he incorporates mock-dialogue of the rags-to-riches dancer who must overthrow the oppressive father who wants his son to attend a prestigious university such as Oxford. Because "dialogue can also encode literary meanings" and "visual metaphors often allude to real world objects and symbols and connote social and cultural meanings" (Sardar and Van Loon 157), media studies makes it possible to interpret this scene as a parody of Holden's own life: he feels he is just tap-dancing, not applying himself at Pencey to prepare him for college when he graduates, as his father (represented here by the authority figure, the governor) did, because he has something else in his blood, suggesting Holden's fixation on Allie's death from the blood cancer leukemia.

Other references to movies also appear in the novel. Holden, accompanied by two students from Pencey, takes a bus to nearby Agerstown to see a Cary Grant comedy, but because the others have seen it, they eat hamburgers and play pinball instead. He also recounts when he and his brother D. B. took Phoebe to a French film, *The Baker's Wife*. Holden tells of taking her to see *The 39 Steps* "about ten times" (67), telling the reader that Phoebe actually participates in the film, saying "right out loud in the movie—right when the Scotch guy in the picture says it—'Can you eat the herring?'" (67) and holding up her finger to Holden when the spy on the screen does so to the star of the film, Robert Donat (68). When Holden checks into the Edmont Hotel upon his arrival in New York City, he looks out his window and into the windows on the other side of the hotel and describes a variety of curious scenes, as if each window is a small movie. His comment that what he sees is "sort of fascinating to watch, even if you don't want it to be" (62) suggests a connection between movie watching and voyeurism, the uninvited viewing of other people's intimate spaces or actions. Alfred Hitchcock's 1954 *Rear Window* is a suspense thriller based on a similar premise of a man with a broken leg who voyeuristically watches the "stories" in the windows of his neighbors' apartments.

Additionally, there are two scenes in which Holden, much like when he imitates the tap dancer in a musical, imitates a wounded movie gangster. The first of these occurs when he is punched by Maurice at the Edmont. As he is walking to the bathroom, he begins to fantasize himself in a film sequence. He pretends to be shot in the gut:

> Old Maurice had plugged me. Now I was on my way to the bathroom to get a good shot of bourbon or something to steady my nerves. . . . I pictured myself coming out of the goddam bathroom, dressed and all, with my auto-

matic in my pocket. . . . Then I'd walk downstairs . . . hold[ing] onto the banister and all, with this blood trickling out of the side of my mouth a little at a time. What I'd do, I'd walk down a few floors—holding onto my guts, blood leaking all over the place. (103-4)

The scene in Holden's mind concludes with the imagined arrival of Jane Gallagher, who would "come over and bandage up my guts. I pictured her holding a cigarette for me to smoke as I was bleeding and all" (104).

Holden's fantasy borrows from the cinema tradition of the film noir, movies produced largely in the 1940s in which tough, hard-boiled detectives, often loners, use their wit and grit to survive enough gunshots to save the heroines. Film noir story lines use "witty, razor-sharp and acerbic dialogue, and/or reflective and confessional, first-person voice-over narration" (Dirks), techniques Salinger borrows so that Holden can imitate the conventions of the genre. The scene recurs as a flashback when a drunken Holden has been left in the Wicker Bar by Carl Luce:

I started that stupid business with the bullet in my guts again. I was the only guy at the bar with a bullet in my guts. I kept putting my hand under my jacket, on my stomach and all, to keep the blood from dripping all over the place. I didn't want anyone to know I was even wounded. (150)

The wound suggests Holden's pain over Allie's death, whereas the blood suggests his haunting obsession with James Castle. Moreover, by transferring his emotions to an objectified projection of himself as a tough detective, Holden is able to push away his subjective duress. In this sense, the characters from movies unintentionally become role models for him, at least in his fantasies.

Holden is also drawn to print media. He recognizes that they present unrealistic portraits of adult males, or rather role models that he would reject. When leaving Pencey Prep, Holden dismisses the idea of buying a magazine to read on the train because it would have "a lot of phony, lean-jawed guys named David in it, and a lot of phony girls named Linda or Marcia that are always lighting all the goddam Davids' pipes for them" (53). Later, Holden reads a magazine he has found at Grand Central Station. After reading an article about how an adolescent with healthy hormones should look and a second article about how to tell if one has cancer, he concludes that he "looked exactly like the guy in the article with lousy hormones" and that he "was getting cancer" (195-96). His cheeky comment that the magazine was a "little cheerer upper" shows his grudging acceptance of the influence of print media.

Holden no more matches the image of a healthy adolescent that he sees in the magazine than he matches Stekel's definition of a mature man. Despite how Holden's "sense of alienation is almost complete—from parents, from friends, from society in general as represented by the prep school" (Jones 24), his unexpected rescue comes from Phoebe. As he watches her reach for the gold ring while riding the carousel in Central Park, he concludes, "If [kids] fall off, they fall off" (211), and in doing so, he accepts that he need not be the catcher in the rye.

Works Cited

Baumbach, Jonathan. "The Saint as Young Man: A Reappraisal of *The Catcher in the Rye*." *Modern Language Quarterly* 25.4 (1964): 461-472.

Bly, Robert. *The Sibling Society*. Reading, MA: Addison-Wesley, 1990.

Brookeman, Christopher. "Pencey Preppy: Cultural Codes in *The Catcher in the Rye*." *New Essays on "The Catcher in the Rye."* Ed. Jack Salzman. New York: Cambridge UP, 1991. 57-76.

Bryson, Bill. *Made in America: An Informal History of the English Language in the United States*. New York: Morrow, 1994.

Dirks, Tim. "Film Noir." AMC Filmsite. Web. Http://www.filmsite.org/filmnoir.html.

Jones, Ernest. "Case History of All of Us." *Critical Essays on Salinger's "The Catcher in the Rye."* Ed. Joel Salzberg. Boston: G. K. Hall, 1990. 24-25.

Rice, F. Philip. *The Adolescent: Development, Relationships, and Culture*. 6th ed. Boston: Allyn & Bacon, 1990.

Rowe, Joyce. "Holden Caulfield and American Protest." *New Essays on "The Catcher in the Rye."* Ed. Jack Salzman. New York: Cambridge UP, 1991. 77-95.
Salinger, J. D. *The Catcher in the Rye*. 1951. New York: Little, Brown, 1991.
Sardar, Ziauddin, and Borin Van Loon. *Introducing Cultural Studies*. New York: Totem Books, 1998.
Steed, J. P. "Introduction: *The Catcher in the Rye* at Fifty, 1951-2001." *"The Catcher in the Rye": New Essays*. Ed. J. P. Steed. New York: Peter Lang, 2002. 1-5.

Holden at Sixty:
Reading *Catcher* After the Age of Irony
Jeff Pruchnic

It is not at all unusual for the death of a celebrated writer to occasion retrospective appraisals of the writer's career, the end of the author's life a natural opportunity for reflecting on the impact of his or her work on the lives of others and on literary or popular culture as a whole. Nor, of course, is it uncommon for this attention to focus on the author's major work and its more specific legacy. However, what was unique about the wide variety of appreciations, evaluations, and tributes that immediately followed J. D. Salinger's passing in early 2010 was their consistent turn toward a much more particular question: Does *The Catcher in the Rye* still speak meaningfully to audiences today?[1] Does *Catcher*, long a touchstone of mid-twentieth-century American literature and, perhaps even more important, a novel whose reading has long been regarded as a rite of passage for American adolescents, still function as a shared cultural commonplace? Or, to put it in the even more specific format followed by many of these reflections: Does *Catcher* still capture the experience of contemporary adolescents the way that it did for their parents or grandparents?

What we might call the question of *Catcher*'s "universality"—the presumption that its story is somehow timeless or narrates an experience that crosses differences of generation, gender, and cultural experience—is, of course, far from new. Indeed, the majority of reviews and critical responses published in the year following *Catcher*'s publication were already attributing an ecumenical appeal to the novel and referring to the "eternal" nature of its story. In an early, influential write-up in *The Nation*, Ernest Jones suggested that Holden's story amounts to a "case history for all of us," the sources of Holden's frustrations and anger being just obscure enough for all readers to relate to his experiences and to conjure up similar feelings from their own pasts. Critics largely ignored consideration of the novel's particular setting

(1950s New York, particularly Manhattan) and the background of the protagonist (a white upper-middle-class prep school student) and instead tended to interpret it along the lines of mythic and archetypal themes that harked back to the earliest days of Western literature (emphasizing, for instance, how the book fit the format of a literary tragedy, or how Holden functioned as an Everyman character, or how his travels mirrored those of other quest narratives in which the heroes undergo harrowing journeys while maturing or changing internally in the process).[2] Similarly, comparisons of *Catcher* with other literary works were far less likely to mention other twentieth-century American novels and far more likely to point readers toward texts composed in the nineteenth century (Herman Melville's *Moby Dick* and a variety of works by Fyodor Dostoevski in addition to the most frequent comparison: Mark Twain's *Adventures of Huckleberry Finn*), if not earlier (Holden was frequently compared to William Shakespeare's Hamlet).[3]

The early perception of the novel as something of an "instant classic" is undoubtedly at least one reason that so many commentators seemed interested in considering the contemporary vitality of the novel shortly after Salinger's death. However, I want to suggest that there is at least one more important factor that prompted the interest in whether *Catcher*'s influence had spread to yet another generation and the hope that contemporary adolescents are finding Holden to be an empathetic, rather than just plain pathetic, figure. More specifically, I am interested in how, whether or not we take the novel to be truly timeless, at least some of the major concerns of the novel might speak all the more powerfully today, specifically in light of the last ten years or so of American culture. More precisely, it seems to me that the concerns behind the question of *Catcher*'s contemporary relevance are, on one hand, very much written into the book itself: Holden is also concerned about whether and how great works of literature may continue to affect people's lives and behavior or whether they are being crowded out by other, newer forms of media. Additionally, it seems to me that there is something particularly timely about turning back to

Catcher and to a character that is likely unsurpassed in prizing the personal, the sincere, and the idiosyncratic against the conventional, the phony (to use one of Holden's favorite words), and the quotidian during a moment in which American culture has itself become obsessed with self-disclosure and the public sharing of private experience. Although early critical responses to *Catcher* may have already been predicting its longevity into the next century, there is something poignant about considering the value of Salinger's words today, after the end of the so-called Age of Irony (a period often suggested to have terminated with the events of September 11, 2001) and its attendant effects of cynicism and emotional distance. In other words, although it may be impossible to consider whether the words of Holden Caulfield still speak to readers today without also tracking changes in American culture and the role of literature within it, shifting perceptions of private and public life, and whether what made the work so vital in the early 1950s still applies in the early twenty-first century, *Catcher* is a particularly salutary text for working through these questions—these concerns are, indeed, quite literally written into its pages.

All of which is to say that asking after the relevance and vitality of *The Catcher in the Rye* today requires posing different questions from those posed by scholars just checking in, every decade or so, to take the temperature of how well the book and its central character have been aging (as critic Louis Menand did in his 2001 essay "Holden at Fifty") or by those querying whether the book holds an eternal message, its teenage protagonist frozen in midcentury but destined to be discovered by those of a similar age in every generation to come (as the novelist Bruce Brooks argued in 2004 in his essay "Holden at Sixteen"). It compels us to think at least as much about today's cultural landscape as about the midcentury Manhattan where a prep school exile takes readers on a very circuitous journey toward something like maturity or self-awareness.

Holden's Time(s); or, The Partial Goddam Autobiography

Indeed, with the benefit of hindsight, concerns about the role of literature in culture and in individuals' private experiences as well as about the (lack of) sincerity or self-disclosure evidenced in people's everyday behavior are in many ways the central subjects of *Catcher*, a novel that has often been faulted, despite the immense critical acclaim it received at the time of its publication, for lacking a formal plot or theme. In fact, both of these issues emerge as early as the very first line of the novel:

> If you really want to hear about it, the first thing you'll probably want to know is where I was born, and what my lousy childhood was like, and how my parents were occupied and all before they had me, and all that David Copperfield kind of crap, but I don't feel like going into it, if you want to know the truth. (3)

In this single sentence, we are presented with the points that Holden will continue to return to throughout *Catcher*. First, Holden is acutely aware of the emotional connections that form between a reader (or listener in the dramatic context of his story as a spoken monologue) and the story or its writer that can emerge in the telling. He is also, however, equally wary of the ways that connection can become something artificial or manipulative, the ways that a narrator's self-description (or the author's of a character) can be played for sympathy or can be used to excuse bad behavior. Thus Holden goes out of his way to include everything about himself and his thoughts, both good and bad, while at the same time attempting to preempt or stymie any sympathy the reader might feel. For instance, Holden's disclosure of his brother Allie's untimely death and Holden's explosive reaction to it is immediately followed by Holden's forestalling of any concern for the emotional as well as physical damage that he may have suffered in his grieving from breaking all the windows in the family garage. Overall, Holden is not going to tell us, as he says, his "whole goddam autobiography or anything" (3), particularly those elements that might explain away his often less-than-admirable actions, but his "partial" autobiography—covering a few days but with frequent, often aleatory, digressions into his past experiences—is going to come across as sincere and unsparing.

Despite his dismissal of "all that David Copperfield kind of crap" (referencing a novel that, perhaps not coincidentally, is widely surmised to be based on the childhood experiences of its author, Charles Dickens), Holden, who is "flunking everything else except English" (17), spends considerable time praising the importance and intimacy of literary works as opposed to more modern forms of entertainment—theater shows and musicals, movies, television—all of which Holden disdains. Shortly after expressing strong admiration for his brother D. B.'s first story collection, *The Secret Goldfish*, and bemoaning his brother's subsequent prostitution as a writer for the movies, Holden identifies the surprising familiarity or affection a reader can feel for an author: "What really knocks me out is a book that, when you're all done reading it, you wish the author that wrote it was a terrific friend of yours and you could call him up on the phone whenever you felt like it"(25), an experience Holden mentions he would like to have with Isak Dinesen, Ring Lardner, and Thomas Hardy, but not Somerset Maugham. Holden's deep appreciation for, and positive descriptions of, literary works that move him—from the above examples to F. Scott Fitzgerald's *The Great Gatsby*, from D. B.'s short-story collection to the Robert Burns lyric that provides *Catcher* its title—is mirrored by his fascination with the idiosyncratic behavior and attachments of other characters in the book for which Holden feels admiration or closeness. In both situations, these examples (and they are numerous in *Catcher*, from pretty much everything Holden mentions about Phoebe and about Jane Gallagher to his former teacher Spencer, who can "get a big bang out of buying a blanket"[10]) are joined by Holden's perception of them as exhibiting something true or authentic about either themselves or the human condition in general.

The contrast to these experiences is, of course, the vast number of people, things, and behaviors that Holden finds phony (a word that, as numerous critics have pointed out, appears in some variation every few pages). Holden's blanket judgment of the multitude of phony phenomena with which he is currently confronted has been the source of much criticism of the novel; critics have noted particularly how the obverse of phoniness—authenticity or sincerity—seems like an abstract ideal (and one primarily negatively defined) in the work, and this puts forward an all-too-easy portrayal of Holden as its only authentic character, or at least the only one who is allowed to divide the world into the real and the phony. It is true that Holden's judgments tend toward the ideal or the abstract, notably in Holden's vision, late in the novel, of his moving to a rural cabin in which he'd "have this rule that nobody could do anything phony when they visited" (266). Similarly, Holden often uses the accusation of insincerity to dismiss behavior that annoys or frustrates him, such as when he describes the intermission of the performance he attends with Sally by telling the reader that he had never seen "so many phonies in [his] life, everybody smoking their ears off and talking about the play so that everybody could hear and know how sharp they were" (164).

However, a careful reading of Holden's more complex references to artifice and insincerity reveals that his central critique of various phonies or phony behavior is not so much an abstract critique of conformity or of the ways that profit and respectability drive people's actions as it is a more complicated meditation on the difficulty of telling the difference between the authentic and mere imitations of the same—in particular, the challenge of parsing out someone's motivations for public self-expression and self-disclosure. Thus, for instance, Holden's disaffection for the performance of the much-heralded Lunts in the show he attends with Sally results from his perception of the actors as seemingly too real, or their expression seemingly too much like what one might imagine in the situation being dramatized as to call into question the authenticity or spontaneity of the performance itself.

Holden states that the Lunts "didn't act like people and they didn't act like actors" but acted more like they "knew they were celebrities and all" (164). But their "acting like celebrities" rather than "acting like actors" is, strangely, revealed by the realism of their stage performance: "It was supposed to be like people really talking and interrupting each other and all. The trouble was, it was *too* much like people talking and interrupting each other" (164).

Similarly, Holden finds he is unable to really enjoy the tuxedoed, joke-telling roller skater who is part of the Rockettes show; although he admires the performer's athletic ability and timing, Holden cannot help but imagine the motivation and practice behind such a stylized performance: "He was a very good skater and all, but . . . I kept picturing him *prac*ticing to be a guy that roller-skates on the stage. It seemed so stupid" (178). The nature of the roller skater's routine as developed and designed explicitly for public performance, for the satisfaction of others and in pursuit of acclaim, ruins its value for Holden; as he tells us earlier in the novel, "If I were a piano player, I'd play it in the goddam closet" (110). Perhaps most significantly, however, when pressed by Phoebe to tell her what he would really like to do with his life, Holden expresses his own confusion about what might motivate people's actions in public and private and whether it is possible for us even to be aware of our own motivations. After mentioning that it might not be bad to be a lawyer if you focused on protecting the innocent and standing up for the persecuted, Holden backpedals to show how even in this case it would not be possible to figure out if these actions were done in a selfless or a selfish way or whether the motivation could be known at all:

> "Even if you *did* go around saving guys' lives and all, how would you know if you did it because you really *wanted* to save guys' lives, or because you did it because what you *real*ly wanted to do was be a terrific lawyer, with everybody slapping you on the back and congratulating you in court. . . . How would you know you weren't being a phony? The trouble is, you wouldn't." (223-24)

It would be too easy, I take it, to associate Holden's overarching concern with the authentic and the phony as a mere anticipation of questions of middle-class and consumer conformity of 1950s America, the stereotypical cookie-cutter houses and cookie-cutter mind-sets that still in many ways shape our contemporary imagination of that moment in American cultural life. Nor does Holden's rebellion hold up well as an avatar of the "youthful" rebellion of the 1960s (either as the pop-cultural phenomenon of the teenage rebel or the very real actions of protest and resistance against the Vietnam War and American foreign policy and in support of civil rights and women's rights), as some have suggested. Finally, as tempting as it may be, taking *Catcher*'s protagonist as a prescient proxy of sorts for its author, Salinger, composing never-to-be-published manuscripts while secluded in Cornish, New Hampshire—the literary equivalent of Holden playing the piano in a goddam closet—will not gain us much. Instead, it seems that Holden's concerns are, on one hand, and as many critics in the 1950s surmised, eternal ones about the general nature of authentic and simulated feelings and the difficulty of determining whether the attachments we feel for others emerge from some real knowledge of their inner selves or just from a stylized self-presentation to the world. Yet, on the other hand, they are also ones that might, however strangely, be all the more timely now than they were in Holden's day, might be all the more pressing for those of us living after the Age of Irony, when these questions that might have seemed inconsequential to American culture of the past few decades have reemerged with a vengeance as a result of a new seriousness following the experience of one national trauma (9/11) and two long-standing wars and in the wake of a new sincerity or new concern with the personal and authentic on display in venues from reality television, our enmeshment in ever-greater communicative connectivity via media technology, and the generally intertwined status of personal lives and public personas demanded of politicians, athletes, and assorted celebrities.

Particular Universals and the Universally Particular; or, Reading *Catcher* after the Age of Irony

The notion of American culture from the late 1970s onward constituting an Age of Irony—a moment in which irony and its corollary categories of emotional distance, self-referentiality, and strategic self-presentation became the master tropes of not just the arts but in many ways of mass media and even interpersonal exchange—became a common reference during the 1980s. However, this way of thinking about these years in American culture became prominent and widespread only as a result of the moment of cultural reflection that took place after 9/11, largely because of an influential *Time* magazine article by journalist and playwright Roger Rosenblatt that was written less than one week after the fall of the World Trade Center's Twin Towers. For Rosenblatt, if there was any positive effect to be seen coming from the tragedy of 9/11, it was to be found in the way in which the event might wake up Americans from a three-decade-long slumber in which we were urged to keep an ironic distance in both our private and our public lives, a time when, with a "giggle and a smirk, our chattering classes—our columnists and pop culture makers—declared that detachment and personal whimsy were the necessary tools for an oh-so-cool life" and during which the "good folks in charge of America's intellectual life have insisted that nothing was to be believed in or taken seriously. Nothing was real." In a particularly poignant reference, Rosenblatt reminded readers of the endless mocking and parodying of a statement made by Bill Clinton during the 1992 presidential campaign. Confronted by ACT UP activist Bob Rafsky's claim that HIV sufferers were dying not only because of the disease itself but also because of a decade of governmental neglect in focusing on and treating HIV, Clinton famously responded, "I feel your pain." This response became something of a cultural catchphrase in the 1990s, used as shorthand for the ironic dismissal of another's complaint or suffering, or to suggest the impossibility of a political figure's actually relating to the pain of another, or to indict the possibility of empathy between strangers altogether. During and immediately after the terrorist attacks of 9/11, however, Rosenblatt asserted, people were in fact compelled to feel the pain of others, unable to not respond or not empathize with the victims of the attacks and their families as they watched nonstop coverage of the events on television. Rosenblatt stated his hope that such a dramatic shift in cultural feeling might signal the end of the Age of Irony and the beginning of a new seriousness and sincerity in American cultural life.

It is, of course, debatable whether such a moment was the end or merely a pause in the cultural conditions Rosenblatt associates with the Age of Irony.[4] However, among the numerous other aftereffects one might attribute to 9/11—the divergent resurgence of American patriotism and renewed debates over civil liberties, religious freedom, and international relations—there does seem to have been a cultural shift toward if not the immediately empathetic then at least the interpersonal and the prizing of the authentic private lives and experiences of individuals. In the realm of literature, one need look no further than the dramatic rise of the memoir, a genre whose value depends quite literally on how much the reader believes the experiences detailed to be wholly those of the author (as seen, for instance, in the massive controversies that have arisen when best-selling memoirs have been shown to be partially fictionalized).

Similarly, electronic media, from (the surprisingly still prevalent) online message boards and online personal journals to blogs and Facebook pages, have shown an increasing trend toward formats that encourage the listing of personal data and preferences and the sharing of interpersonal experiences. The most familiar examples, however, are as close as the nearest television. Even reality shows that ostensibly focus on competition—*American Idol*, *Survivor*, *The Amazing Race*, *America's Got Talent*—have become equally, if not more, about the personal histories and challenging experiences of their contestants (to say nothing of the spread of other shows—from *The Bachelor* and *The Bachelorette* to *Intervention* and *Hoarders*—that specifically make public often private behavior and experiences). In televised athletics, beyond the Olympic Games (which traditionally have had an interest in at least the differing cultural experiences of competitors), even extreme sports athletes, once expected to embody ironic detachment almost physically, are now just as often called upon to relate their personal histories and private journeys toward success during coverage of their games. Finally, we might also point to the return of a focus on interiority in popular music; today everyone from indie rockers to hip-hop artists share a concentration on self-narration not seen since the 1960s singer-songwriter movement (Eminem, in particular, has marked the transformation of rapping about oneself in relation to success and skill to rapping about one's pain and feelings of inadequacy or lack of control).

Critic Jeffrey T. Nealon has referred to this new trend toward the authentic and the interior within culture as a moment of "cultural privatization" (one he also extends to phenomena such as student-centered pedagogies in university instruction, the focus on personal rather than cultural narratives in documentary films, and the replication of residential environments within sport-utility vehicles [75]). If, as is often suggested, a key moment in the economic and cultural life of the 1980s and the early 1990s was the "privatization" of formerly public services (the transfer of functions formerly done by the government or held in common to the private sector and private ownership), according to Nealon, since then we have seen a concomitant privatization of culture in which what we increasingly share are, however paradoxical it might at first seem, our personal experiences. In other words, the way we are asked to relate to people through mass media (and increasingly in daily life) is more and more through the self-disclosure of our own authentic identities and experiences rather than through our generic social roles. Such a shift, however, bring its own challenges, particularly in determining what motivates such disclosures and to what degree authenticity has itself become a commodity or an act of conformity, the same way irony was in previous decades. And it is in such an environment, as I see it, that Holden Caulfield's concerns about the true and the phony might take on a new relevance, if not an entirely new meaning, and the question of *Catcher*'s universal appeal might be rethought, particularly the value of Holden's simultaneous dismissal of ironic distance and wariness of the seemingly authentic or personal.

A little more than a decade after *Catcher*'s publication, critic Joseph L. Blotner reaffirmed, with a few qualifications, earlier suggestions that *Catcher* was likely to remain relevant to readers for the foreseeable future:

> One suspects that as long as preparatory schools remain much as they are today, *The Catcher in the Rye* will continue [to be] popular. And, more fundamentally, as long as aspects of the process of growing-up—call it initiation or maturation as you will—particularly among the sensitive young, remain the same, the novel will continue to speak to younger readers. Not only this, but its exposure of shame and the humor which is often the vehicle of exposure would seem to guarantee an audience all across the age spectrum. (100-101)

It is important to note that these caveats are not entirely insignificant; although Blotner ended up affirming the universal reading of *Catcher*, his reference to attending private preparatory school (not at all common for teenagers of Holden's time, let alone today) cannot but be read as dated or at least restricted to the experiences of a certain economic class. Indeed, a little more than a decade later, class issues and historical context in *Catcher* were the sources of a debate carried on in the venerable literary theory journal *Critical Inquiry*. Carol and Richard Ohmann, in their article "Reviewers, Critics, and *The Catcher in the Rye*" (reprinted in this volume), took earlier studies of the novel to task for ignoring what they took to be a central feature of the narrative: the ways that Holden's anxiety and dissatisfaction can be read as a specific indictment of life under capitalist culture during a time in which alternative (socialist and communist) systems were on display in other countries. For the Ohmanns, universal readings of *Catcher* ignore the specific historical particularities to which Salinger was responding. One of the critics targeted by the Ohmanns, James E. Miller, Jr., responded (in an essay titled "*Catcher* In and Out of History," also reprinted in this volume) by suggesting that the Ohmanns were themselves beholden to a certain historical moment (that of the present), their focus on the "historical particulars" of *Catcher* itself a symptom of the currency of Marxist literary criticism in contemporary academics.

With the benefit of hindsight, perhaps the universal and particular readings of *Catcher* are available to be historicized while also available to be taken as universals in their own right. During the 1950s, when questions of authenticity as well as critical interest in the transhistorical mythemes of Western literature were at a high point, *Catcher* offered readers much by way of thinking the universal as a category. In the mid-1970s, when what the Ohmanns call the "historically particular" was a central concern, *Catcher* also seemed to be relevant for working through the questions of our relations to historical contexts and cultural change. Today, it seems to me that in a time after the Age of Irony but not quite in an Age of Authenticity, when, as Nealon suggests, the new common or universal is the private or particular, *Catcher* might be relevant once again, but in a new way: as a text that mediates what we might call the "universally particular" nature of contemporary American cultural life.

Here also we might find a working out of this particular logic or problem in the very pages of *Catcher*. In an often-referenced scene in the novel, Holden considers how the displays in the Museum of Natural History stay the same but the viewers are different each time they encounter them, marking changes from the quotidian (what you're wearing, which teacher accompanies you) to the potentially dramatic ("you'd heard your mother and father having a terrific fight in the bathroom") to the poetic ("you'd just passed by one of those puddles in the street with gasoline rainbows in them"). Although the import of this scene is often keyed to Holden's subsequent longing that more things could stay in stasis—"Certain things they should stay the way they are. You ought to be able to stick them in one of those big glass cases and just leave them alone" (158)—perhaps it is the earlier consideration of the way the permanent and the protean, the universal and the particular, the public display and the private self interact that has the most relevance for us today. And it is in this sense that *Catcher* still speaks to us today, the way in which the words of an unusually privileged and unusually damaged fictional teenager of the mid-twentieth century has something to offer the real teenagers and adults of the early twenty-first. Holden may still not be the Everyman identified by critics in the 1950s, but at least for every man and woman forced to rethink the nature of the personal and the performative, the authentic and the phony, after the end of the Age of Irony, Holden still has important things to say.

Notes

1. See, for example, Harpaz and Levithan, as well as the *New York Times* feature "Reaching Holden Caulfield's Grandchildren" (Parini et al.) and *Slate*'s "Audio Book Club" segment on Salinger (Metcalf et al.), in which a total of eight different authors, educators, and critics weigh in on this question. Perhaps the real testament to the popularity of this query, however, is its recent appearance as an available topic on Web sites selling academic term papers.

2. In the third chapter of her book *In Cold Fear* (44-66), Steinle provides a helpful overview of early critical responses to *Catcher*. Ohmann and Ohmann's mid-1970s reevaluation of the novel's reception (mentioned below) stresses in particular critics' reluctance to draw any connections between *Catcher* and the coverage of current world events that were quite literally surrounding their reviews in newspaper and magazine publications (particularly the Korean War and the beginnings of the Cold War).

3. For early reviews and analyses of this type, see, for instance, Heiserman and Miller, Kaplan, and Longstreth. A notable exception to this trend are comparisons made with James Joyce's *A Portrait of the Artist as a Young Man* and *Ulysses*, though these novels themselves feature characters and plots explicitly fashioned on the patterns of early Western mythological narratives (see, for instance, Heiserman and Miller as well as Smith). A noteworthy exception to the trend of ignoring the historical and geographic contexts of *Catcher*, though one that still disregards the connection be-

tween these contexts and the story itself, is Donald P. Costello's often-cited study (reprinted in this volume) of how well Holden's speech patterns match the vernacular of a boy of his age and upbringing.

4. See, for instance, Williams for one popular rejection of Rosenblatt's prediction.

Works Cited

Blotner, Joseph L. "Salinger Now: An Appraisal." *Wisconsin Studies in Contemporary Literature* 4.1 (Winter 1963): 100-108.

Brooks, Bruce. "Holden at Sixteen." *Horn Book Magazine* May/June 2004. Web.

Costello, Donald P. "The Language of *The Catcher in the Rye*." *American Speech* 34.3 (Oct. 1959): 172-81.

Harpaz, Beth J. "Is *Catcher in the Rye* Still Relevant to Teens?" *Associated Press* 9 Feb. 2010. Web.

Heiserman, Arthur, and James E. Miller, Jr. "J. D. Salinger: Some Crazy Cliff." *Western Humanities Review* 10.2 (Spring 1956): 129-37.

Jones, Ernest. "Case History of All of Us." *The Nation* 1 Sept. 1951: 176.

Kaplan, Charles. "Holden and Huck: The Odysseys of Youth." *College English* 18.2 (Nov. 1956): 76-80.

Levithan, David. "How J. D. Salinger's *The Catcher in the Rye* Helped Create Young Adult Literature." *Wall Street Journal* 18 Jan. 2010. Web.

Longstreth, T. Morris. "New Novels in the News." *Christian Science Monitor* 19 July 1951: 11.

Menand, Louis. "Holden at Fifty." *The New Yorker* 1 Oct. 2001. Web.

Metcalf, Stephen, et al. "The Audio Book Club on J. D. Salinger." *Slate* 18 Jan. 2010. Web.

Miller, James E., Jr. "*Catcher* In and Out of History." *Critical Inquiry* 3.3 (Spring 1977): 599-603.

Nealon, Jeffrey T. "Periodizing the 80s: The Cultural Logic of Economic Privatization in the United States." *A Leftist Ontology: Beyond Relativism and Identity Politics*. Ed. Carsten Strathausen. Minneapolis: U of Minnesota P, 2009. 54-79.

Ohmann, Carol, and Richard Ohmann. "Reviewers, Critics, and *The Catcher in the Rye*." *Critical Inquiry* 3.1 (Autumn 1976): 15-37.

Parini, Jay, et al. "Reaching Holden Caulfield's Grandchildren." Room for Debate Blog. *New York Times*. 29 Jan. 2010. Web.

Rosenblatt, Roger. "The Age of Irony Comes to an End." *Time* 16 Sept. 2001. Web.

Salinger, J. D. *The Catcher in the Rye*. 1951. Boston: Little, Brown, 1979.

Smith, Harrison. "Manhattan Ulysses, Junior." *Saturday Review* 14 July 1951: 12-13.

Steinle, Pamela Hunt. *In Cold Fear: The "Catcher in the Rye" Censorship Controversies and Postwar American Character*. Columbus: Ohio State UP, 2000.

Williams, Zoe. "The Final Irony." *The Guardian* 28 June 2003. Web.

The Catcher in the Rye: "Paul's Case" in Anticipation of Holden Caulfield
Matthew Evertson

The death of J. D. Salinger in January of 2010 prompted a nationwide discussion of the very subject of loss that *The Catcher in the Rye* had explored so powerfully nearly sixty years earlier. As parents have handed the book off to their children and teachers have passed it on to their students, *Catcher* has become a common subject of literary comparison as young readers seek out new voices to speak similarly for *that* generation's alienated youth.[1] Although further comparative studies could be made with many contemporary novels that seem to reflect Salinger's influence, I would like to explore, instead, how these same themes and issues can be found in works that predate Salinger and that maybe even influenced his own take on coming-of-age. Mark Twain's *Adventures of Huckleberry Finn* is perhaps the most common antecedent cited, but I would like to focus on an author rarely thought of in conjunction with Salinger: Willa Cather.

At first glance, this turn-of-the-century Nebraska writer—a woman who grew up in a small prairie town, became a devoted Episcopalian, and wrote that "the world broke in two for her around 1922 or thereabouts" when she felt like modernity had left her behind—would hardly seem to have much in common with a World War II combat veteran who was raised in an upper-middle-class Manhattan Jewish family and who has been celebrated as one of the key figures in the emerging modernism of American fiction.[2] I believe, however, that a productive exploration can be made between Salinger and Cather because Cather in many ways anticipates the themes explored in *Catcher* and because her books are often taught in high school and college classrooms. Analyzing her works side by side with *Catcher*, young readers will be able to contrast the narrative techniques and approaches that these two authors use in exploring the initiation of youth into adulthood.[3]

Youthful protagonists are at the heart of many of Cather's most famous works, and they often confront the same issues that operate so poignantly in Salinger. *O Pioneers!* (1913), for example, follows the fates of a young brother and sister, Alexandra and Emil Bergson, who are forced to grow up quickly, taking over their father's isolated Nebraska homestead after his untimely death. Emil's story, in particular, touches on themes similar to those in Holden's story: the pains of being forced to grow up too soon without the guidance of trusted adults, college and career conflicts, and a desperate and mostly platonic love affair that ends in violence. Cather's novels *One of Ours* (1922), *A Lost Lady* (1923), and *The Professor's House* (1925), especially the section titled "Tom Outland's Story," all contain substantial plot elements that revolve around the experiences of young men or women coming of age in the turmoil of trying to find a meaningful place in society. Several of Cather's short stories similarly focus on young protagonists who feel out of place in their communities and struggle to find satisfying directions in their lives, focusing particular attention on that threshold between high school and college or career choices and the adult voices that guide, inhibit, or sometimes corrupt those decisions.

Despite being set primarily in the sparse settlements of isolated rural Nebraska at the turn of the twentieth century, *My Ántonia* (1918), Cather's most famous and most critically acclaimed novel, touches on many of the themes that Holden confronts fifty years later on the streets of Manhattan. The story is told in a first-person, confessional style by the protagonist, Jim Burden, who, Cather claims in the introduction to the novel, has written it all out in a manuscript she is sharing "substantially as he brought it to me" (xiii). Both *My Ántonia* and *The Catcher in theRye* feature young protagonists who are exposed early in their lives to images of death and suicide, and both show those teenagers feeling trapped in their respective communities. As Holden imagines fleeing "someplace way the hell off" (170), maybe a ranch in Colorado, Jim Burden dreams of escaping the constraints and conflicts of small-town Nebraska—first to the state university, then to Harvard

Law, eventually becoming legal counsel to a large railroad and working out of offices in New York City. Jim's desire as a young man to head East for greater opportunity casts him as a "reverse Holden" who dreams of heading in the opposite direction, but Cather's preface to the novel lets us know immediately that Jim, like Holden, has become disenchanted by the big city and high-society promises that seem quite phony indeed: he suffers an unhappy, childless marriage to a wealthy New York socialite and makes frequent trips back West, going "off into the wilds hunting for lost parks or exploring new canyons" and is "still able to lose himself in those big Western dreams" (xi). In the Bohemian "hired girl" that he came to know as a child and revisits at the end of the novel, Jim finds an authentic answer for a meaningful existence, as Ántonia has remained on the prairie all her life, has worked hard, and has cultivated a farm and family so fertile that Holden would have a major challenge catching all of her rambunctious children running through the rye.

Although a close attachment to nature and to the innocence of childhood pervades both novels, *My Ántonia* often surprises readers with its rather frank depiction of youthful passions, the sexual awakenings of major characters as well as their initiations into the perversities that occur in adult society (Mr. Antolini's supposed "flitty pass" at Holden seems tame compared to the young Jim Burden's own violent encounter with the lecherous Wick Cutter, for example). The most compelling trait that these two novels share, however, is an exploration of time, focusing on how adolescents ache to join the world of adults only to realize later how much is lost as they cast their childlike innocence away and lose their primary connection to what William Wordsworth famously calls in his "Ode: Intimations of Immortality from Recollections of Early Childhood" the "visionary gleam" of youth. The title page of *My Ántonia* includes an epigraph taken from book 3 of Vergil's *Georgics*, a work that also extols rural living: "Optima dies . . . prima fugit," which translates, "The best days are the first to flee from wretched mortals." Similarly, *The Catcher in the Rye* is filled with

Holden's obsessions with preserving time and innocence, such as his aching nostalgia toward the Museum of Natural History, where the displays never change—the Eskimo and the Indian, the bird and the deer—always frozen in the same comforting poses. When he would go to visit "nobody'd be different," Holden recalls. "The only thing that would be different would be you" (158).

The most obvious Cather work to offer up for comparison to *Catcher*, however, is "Paul's Case," which was published in her first collection of short stories, *The Troll Garden*, in 1905, first appearing that May in *McClure's Magazine*, a prominent and prestigious venue for short-story writers.[4] Readers familiar with both Cather and Salinger have noted for years fascinating similarities between the two works (although no scholar, to my knowledge, has ever demonstrated that Salinger had read or was influenced by Cather's story as he composed *Catcher*). In a 2007 issue of *Notes on Contemporary Literature*, Hal Blythe and Charlie Sweet published a short exploration that outlines the key plot parallels: both stories focus on disaffected high school male protagonists who get kicked out of their schools in Pennsylvania, are fond of exaggerating and lying, construct elaborate fantasies about how they would like to live their lives, flee their parents and escape to New York City over the winter holiday in pursuit of their own wild adventures, and, finding such experiences far short of their romanticized ideals, descend into mental breakdowns: Holden eventually winds up in a hospital in California; Paul commits suicide.

Although these two works—written nearly fifty years apart—share similar plots, the stories offer contrasting analyses and explorations of the teenage psyche. Unlike *Catcher*, "Paul's Case" is not told in the first person, so the narrative voice is not nearly as confessional as Holden's. However, it mirrors the psychological realism much in vogue in the late nineteenth and early twentieth centuries among writers such as Henry James and Edith Wharton. "Paul's Case" was originally published with the subheading "A Study in Temperament," which is precisely how Cather wants us to explore the narrative. What is wrong with Paul? What might explain his behavior? What is his *case*? Unlike Holden, Paul does not tell us about his troubles directly, forcing the reader to stand outside of the protagonist's confidence, trying to solve the puzzle; whereas we live in Holden's mind and share his experiences, "Paul's Case" compels readers to study the protagonist's actions from a clinical distance.

A good example of this objective viewpoint occurs at the beginning of the story, where we learn that Paul has been called into a meeting with his school's principal and several of his teachers who cannot quite pinpoint their frustrations with his behavior: "Each of his instructors felt that it was scarcely possible to put into words the real cause of the trouble, which lay in a sort of hysterically defiant manner of the boy's; in the contempt which they all knew he felt for them, and which he seemingly made not the least effort to conceal" (60). As they attempt to correct Paul's behavior, they become enraged by his shrugging attitude and even his dandified way of dressing, punctuated by a "flippantly red carnation flower" that he wears in his lapel; they fall "upon him without mercy, his English teacher leading the pack," as Paul simply sits there smiling. When Paul is given an example of an "impertinent remark" he had made to one of his teachers, the principal demands to know if Paul felt it proper to say such things. Paul replies, "I don't know.... I didn't mean to be polite or impolite, either. I guess it's sort of a way I have of saying things regardless" (61).

This passage calls to mind Holden Caulfield's own struggles to articulate his motives at the beginning of his narrative and his reticence to share such language at the end. When his psychologist asks whether Holden will "apply himself" when he gets back to school, Holden thinks it is a "stupid" question. "I mean how do you know what you're going to do till you *do* it?... The answer is, you don't." When his older brother, D. B., asks him at the end of the novel what he "thought about all this stuff I just finished telling you about," Holden responds, "I didn't know what the hell to say. If you want to know the truth, I don't *know* what I think about it" (276-77). Both Holden and Paul reveal in such scenes the eternal anxiety of youth, the desire, on one hand, for choice and control over their circumstances and the inability, on the other, to explain their actions and desires.

Like Paul, Holden faces many awkward confrontations with people in authority. Early in the novel, when he visits his convalescing history teacher, Mr. Spencer, we witness a similar examination of motive. "What's the matter with you, boy?" he asks, as Holden can "feel a terrific lecture coming on" (14). He demands to know why Holden never applies himself as a student, pulling out Holden's most recent exam for evidence, handling the paper "like it was a turd or something" (15). In what Holden calls a "very dirty trick," Mr. Spencer forces him to sit there as he reads aloud his nonsense answers, including a personal note from Holden at the end of the essay telling his teacher that "it is all right with me if you flunk me though as I am flunking everything else except English anyway" (17). The ailing Spencer presses Holden: "How do you feel about all this, boy? I'd be very interested to know. Very interested." Holden cannot really explain *why* he didn't try harder to pass history or his other subjects or why he keeps flunking out. "I didn't feel like going into the whole thing with him. . . . He wouldn't have understood it anyway" (18). The biggest problem, Holden reveals, is that wherever he has gone he has been "surrounded by phonies" (19). Then he proceeds to give examples of ways in which, he believes, adults around him have behaved hypocritically.

Though we are not privy in the same way to Paul's thoughts, it appears that the "case" that Paul shares with Holden is an inability to articulate what he wants out of life in the face of demanding grown-ups who claim to have his best interests at heart but whom he deeply distrusts. Both characters have little interest in conforming to the conventional roles their peers so eagerly adopt as part of their ambitions toward becoming adults. Instead, Paul prefers the world of his imagination and, especially, the world of the theater. If he slacks off at school, Paul makes up for it in his job as an usher at Carnegie Hall in downtown Pittsburgh. He is good at this work—enthusiastic about showing patrons to their seats and managing his section of the auditorium, maintaining the romantic escape that he so loves.[5] The reprieve is short for Paul. After spending time among the dazzling lights of the theater, he dreads the return to what he perceives to be the dull conformity of his home, where he lives with his stern widower father:

> It was a highly respectable street, where all the houses were exactly alike, and where business men of moderate means begot and reared large families of children, all of whom went to Sabbath-school and learned the shorter catechism, and were interested in arithmetic; all of whom were as exactly alike as their homes, and of a piece with the monotony in which they lived. Paul never went up Cordelia Street without a shudder of loathing. (66)

As when Holden sneaks into his upper East Side apartment to see his little sister, Paul feels completely estranged from his own household. To avoid a confrontation with his father one night after coming home from the theater, Paul breaks into his basement and spends the night sleeping near the furnace—and, like Holden, imagines his father mistaking him for a burglar and shooting him. Moreover, Cather's narrative anticipates Holden's own sense that everyone around him is buying into a conforming, unsatisfying pathway into the corrupted values of adult society. The description of a Sunday-afternoon gathering of all the "burghers of Cordelia Street" drips with the same antipathy toward all the "big shots" gathered around as does Holden's expression of his distaste for prep school snobs and their parents and the hypocritical administrators and smarmy teachers he has encountered over the years. Surrounded by the businessmen of his father's social set, Paul paints a vapid, materialistic portrait and mocks their conventional obsessions with profits and business, marriage, family, and church. As they tell stories of their expanding industries and their chief executives opening up new markets in faraway lands, Paul has "an awful apprehension that they might spoil it all before he got there" (69).

Eventually, Paul is kicked out of school, and his father sets him to work as an office boy at the company he manages, completely cutting him off from Carnegie Hall. This has a devastating effect on Paul, for, we are told, "it was at the theatre and Carnegie Hall that Paul really lived; the rest was but a sleep and a forgetting" (71).[6] If the allusion to Wordsworth does not make clear to the reader how much Paul lives in his mind and emotions, the narrator tells us that "it would be difficult to put it strongly enough how convincingly the stage entrance of that theatre was for Paul the actual portal of Romance," offering Paul a "secret temple, his wishing carpet, his bit of blue-and-white Mediterranean shore bathed in perpetual sunshine" (71-72). When this last bastion of control over his life is taken away, Paul snaps, stealing a small fortune in bank deposits from his father's firm and, just as Holden will do fifty years later, fleeing Pennsylvania by train to New York City. All his life Paul has been "tormented by fear, a sort of apprehensive dread that, of late years, as the meshes of lies he had told closed about him, had been pulling his muscles tighter and tighter" (76). But now, in the city—much like Holden in his escape from Pencey Prep—Paul feels relief and reprieve in finally taking some control over his life. For the first time in a long while, he is able to sleep peacefully.

> When he awoke, it was three o'clock in the afternoon. He bounded up with a start; half of one of his precious days gone already! He spent more than an hour in dressing, watching every stage of his toilet carefully in the mirror. Everything was quite perfect. He was exactly the kind of boy he always wanted to be. (77)

Paul's adventures in the city are remarkably similar to Holden's. He passes as an independent young man of means, not as an impertinent kid drawing unwelcome attention to himself. He dines in the finest restaurants, drinks wine as if he had been doing it all his life, attends the best concerts, and luxuriates in his expensive room at the Waldorf. "He felt now that his surroundings explained him. . . . He had only to glance down at his attire to reassure himself that here it would be impossible for any one to humiliate him" (79). But, as with Holden, we know that Paul's charade cannot last; on his eighth day in the city, Paul discovers that the Pittsburgh newspapers are filled with stories of his disappearance. He will soon have to return to the world he so despises:

> It was to be worse than jail, even; the tepid waters of Cordelia Street were to close over him finally and forever. The grey monotony stretched before him in hopeless, unrelieved years; Sabbath-school, Young People's Meeting, the yellow-papered room, the damp dish-towels; it all rushed back upon him with a sickening vividness. (81)

This brings us to the final and most compelling theme shared in the two novels: an emphasis on falling. Such imagery occurs throughout *Catcher* but finds its most potent exploration in the last part of the novel as Holden's mental health deteriorates. Grappling for direction, Holden visits a favorite former teacher, Mr. Antolini, who warns Holden that he is "riding for some kind of terrible, terrible fall" (242) and that "it's a special kind of fall, a horrible kind. The man falling isn't permitted to feel or hear himself hit bottom. He just keeps falling and falling" (244). For the first time in the narrative, Holden seems to take heart, but when he later wakes up in Mr. Antolini's apartment and finds his former teacher touching his head, what he later describes as a "flitty pass," he flees and feels even more distraught.[7] He tries to get a bite to eat but cannot keep the food down. He sees all the Christmas displays up and down Fifth Avenue and grows more and more depressed. His fall accelerates. "Every time I came to the end of a block and stepped off the goddam curb, I had this feeling that I'd never get to the other side of the street. I thought I'd just go down, down, down, and nobody'd ever see me again" (256). He becomes physically ill and begins calling out to his dead brother: "Allie, don't let me disappear. Allie, don't let me disappear. Allie, don't let me disappear. Please, Allie" (257). Only his little sister Phoebe, in the end, is able to stop his descent. Having confided in her his desire to be a catcher in the rye, to prevent kids from falling off that cliff into adulthood, she in essence catches *him*. Arriving at their planned goodbye, she has a suitcase packed and insists on heading West with Holden. Instead, he relents and takes her to the carousel in Central Park. He is at first fearful that she might fall off the horse but then recognizes that she has to be allowed to reach for the gold ring. He promises to go home with her and then get help, which he does.

Holden's final acceptance of the fact that he cannot stop time or preserve innocence and that he needs the help of others to get well contrasts with Paul's concluding that he simply cannot return to his former life and that he is completely alone in the universe. Rather than getting on the train back to Pittsburgh, he follows the tracks out into the countryside and finds a ravine where the train will pass beneath him. There he pulls out a bunch of red carnations—the flower associated with his flippancy at the beginning of the story—and looks at them "drooping with the cold, he noticed, their red glory all over" (83-84). He buries them in the snow. From the moment that Paul enters New York City with such hope and anticipation, both flowers and snow surround him as a ripe symbol of his own repressed growth. When he first checks into the Waldorf, he has flowers brought up to his room. With snow falling steadily outside, he luxuriates in their beauty and their soft fragrance. If the metaphor is lost on the reader—here is a young man who in his own mind has not been allowed to flower in his cloudy and oppressive dome of a world—Cather makes the connection overt as Paul hits the streets of the city. "Here and there on the corners were stands, with whole flower gardens blooming under glass cases, against the sides of which the snow flakes stuck and melted; violets, roses, carnations, lilies of the valley—somehow vastly more lovely and alluring that they blossomed thus unnaturally in the snow" (77). Now, as he awaits his final train "home," Paul sees nothing but drifted snow in the open fields, with only here and there "dead grass or dried weed stalks" that project, "singularly black, above it" (83). Burying the flowers where he is about to jump before the train, he thinks that all the flowers he had seen in the glass cases that first night must have gone the same way, long before this. It was only one splendid breath they had, in spite of their brave mockery at the winter outside the glass; and it was a losing game in the end, it seemed, this revolt against the homilies by which the world is run. (84)

What Cather does here at the end of the story, then, is quite similar to what Salinger has Holden confront. The adolescent troubles the two protagonists face center on feeling out of place in their respective worlds, unable to blossom in environments that they find inhibiting. They are also at heart romantics trying to shield the young, the natural, against the encroaching concerns, corruptions, and materialism of the adult world. "Certain things they should stay the way they are," Holden argues. "You ought to be able to stick them in one of those big glass cases and just leave them alone" (158). He shares with Paul, then, a desire to preserve a kind of timeless innocence. As I have argued elsewhere, the very title of the novel references this idea of Holden the protector of youth, the "only big kid around" trying to keep the children from falling off the cliff, willing to sacrifice himself to protect others from the experiences and growing pains that he has suffered—and reaffirming the underlying source of his angst, that he knows that he *can't* be the catcher in the rye because those days of careless youth are numbered and that the reality of inevitable initiation, growth, and the loss of childhood is a universal condition.

Unlike Paul, however, who compares himself to the winter flowers that "mock" the cold environment outside the glass case and "revolt against the homilies of the world," Holden, shaken by the death of his little brother, ultimately realizes the futility of such rebellion and recognizes that none of us can live as if preserved in some museum diorama. Whereas Paul seems to be preparing his own sacrifice, burying the flowers in the snow as a kind of romantic ritual, Holden recognizes that flowers and the beauty of nature are for the living. "I hope to hell when I do die somebody has sense enough to just dump me in the river or something," he declares. "Anything except sticking me in the goddam cemetery. People coming and putting a bunch of flowers on your stomach on Sunday, and all that crap. Who wants flowers when you're dead? Nobody" (201). This lesson comes to Paul much too late, literally as he is falling in front of the train and for a split second realizes he has made a terrible mistake:

> As he fell, the folly of his haste occurred to him with merciless clearness, the vastness of what he had left undone. There flashed through his brain, clearer than ever before, the blue of Adriatic water, the yellow of Algerian sands. (84)

The train smashes into Paul and, "because the picture making mechanism was crushed, the disturbing visions flashed into black, and Paul dropped back into the immense design of things" (84). Paul, like those children Holden imagines falling off the cliff, realizes in a flash that he has held an unrealistic view of the world, sold to him by grown-ups, that his only options are to conform or to be destroyed. As long as his own mind is intact, however, he can at least fight to keep alive his flowering vision of the world. This final point is surely the lesson that Mr. Antolini tries to impart to Holden as he faces his fall. "The whole arrangement's designed for men who, at some time or other in their lives, were looking for something their own environment couldn't supply them with," Mr. Antolini argues. "Or they thought their own environment couldn't supply them with. So they gave up looking. They gave it up before they ever really even got started" (244-45). Paul's tragic mistake, in the end, is giving up because he cannot stand his surroundings instead of thinking of ways—beyond theft, materialism, and unrealistic daydreams—that he might effectively change his environment. Instead of trying to bloom unnaturally in a winter world, like the flowers he has buried in the snow, he should seek his own proper season to grow.[8]

At the end of his narrative Paul exits into oblivion; Holden, at the end of his, tells us, "Don't ever tell anybody anything. If you do, you start missing everybody" (277). Both Cather and Salinger conclude their stories with erasure. Perhaps that is the "case" that we all face and that Holden has to learn to confront and deal with as an adult and that Paul is unable to survive. Cather, like Salinger, crafts young characters who need to produce authentic responses to the realization that life is, ultimately, about loss. When Holden describes visiting his brother's grave, with the cold rain percolating through the soil to Allie's lonely body, he sets in stark terms what ultimately awaits us all. "It was awful. It rained on his lousy tombstone, and it rained on the grass on his stomach." Death indeed cures Holden of all sentiment, uncomforted by the hope that "it is only his body and all that's in the cemetery, and his soul's in Heaven and all that crap" (202). All the theology in the world cannot overcome Holden's justified fear of disappearing. Nor does it temper his sense that the world we live in is a corrupt place, that in the end we cannot even control the final words that conclude our existence. "I think, even, if I ever die, and they stick me in a cemetery, and I have a tombstone and all, it'll say 'Holden Caulfield' on it and then what year I was born and what year I died, and then right under that it'll say 'Fuck You.' I'm positive in fact" (204).

Perhaps Cather, and the way out West that Holden dreams of, can offer an antidote for such pessimism. At heart, Holden—and *The Catcher in the Rye*—shares a sense of romanticism with Cather. Although Paul's overactive and unrealistic imagination dooms him, in her later works Cather offers characters who return to their youthful places and find deeper meaning in life, closer to the earth—away from the cliff face of lost innocence or oblivion—places where their younger selves can teach them what matters most. Perhaps she was not so far away from Salinger after all. Cather may have begun her life on the prairie, and few of her works after "Paul's Case" would be set in cities, but she spent the vast majority of her professional career in close proximity to the world that Salinger himself inhabited. A private funeral was held for Cather in New York City when she died in

1947, but she was then buried in the rural and rolling hills of Jaffrey, New Hampshire, roughly 75 miles north of where Salinger himself passed away. The words on her gravestone are taken from a passage in *My Ántonia*, from a scene early in the novel where Jim Burden, as a boy slowly learning to appreciate his new prairie home, is lying against the ground amid the bounty of his grandmother's garden. "The Earth was warm under me, and warm as I crumbled it through my fingers," he explains:

> I kept as still as I could. Nothing happened. I did not expect anything to happen. I was something that lay under the sun and felt it, like the pumpkins, and I did not want to be anything more. I was entirely happy. Perhaps we feel like that when we die and become part of something entire, whether it is sun and air, or goodness and knowledge. (18)

This seems to be the cure that Holden seeks, that Paul never seeks, and that Cather's young protagonists struggle to discover themselves. The last lines from the passage mark her epitaph: "That is happiness; to be dissolved into something complete and great." What a comforting contrast to Holden's dread of disappearing and what he fears might be the final conclusion marked on his own gravestone.

Notes

1. Writing after Salinger's death in *The New Yorker*, where Salinger had published the majority of his short stories, Adam Gopnik called *Catcher* the "handbook of the adolescent heart," asserting that Salinger's writing continues to resonate due to its "essential gift of joy" in a "message" that "was always the same: that, amid the malice and falseness of social life, redemption rises from clear speech and childlike enchantment, from all the forms of unselfconscious innocence that still surrounds us" (20). This sense that Salinger captured in his writing something essential about the perspective of our younger selves and the loss associated with our passage into the adult world has resulted in a curious transaction between adults and young readers ever since, in the very passing of the book itself from generation to generation.

2. Cather's famous remark appears in the preface to her 1936 essay collection *Not Under Forty*, where she argues that her book will "have little interest for people un-

der forty years of age. The world broke in two in 1922 or thereabouts, and the persons and prejudices recalled in these sketches slid back into yesterday's seven thousand years. . . . It is for the backward, and by one of their number, that these sketches were written" (v). Part of my argument in this exploration is that Cather's take on adolescence and coming-of-age—regardless of her seeming old-fashionedness—touches on the same key issues that find success in the best works in this genre. Cather was exploring teenage angst before Salinger was even born.

3. In my comparative reading of *Catcher* and Cormac McCarthy's *All the Pretty Horses*, for example, I identify three major areas that I feel the two works share and that operate at the heart of most successful coming-of-age narratives. First is a focus on the choice and control that young adults yearn for in their lives, the opportunities to make their own unique paths into an adult world they feel is corrupt or has failed them. Second are compelling explorations of innocence and youth and the ability or inability to control the processes of time and maturation. Finally, the controlling themes of love and death elevate these works into the American canon (103-4).

4. A slightly revised version of "Paul's Case" appeared in Cather's 1920 collection of short stories, *Youth and the Bright Medusa*. For my exploration, I am using the original text of the story as it appeared in 1905.

5. This is one area where Holden differs greatly with Paul: Holden hates the theater. When he secures tickets for a Broadway show to impress his girlfriend, he confesses: "I didn't much want to see it, but I knew old Sally, the queen of the phonies, would start drooling all over the place when I told her I had tickets for that, because the Lunts were in it and all. She liked shows that are supposed to be very sophisticated and dry and all, with the Lunts and all. I don't. I don't like any shows very much, if you want to know the truth" (152).

6. See verse 5, lines 58-66, of William Wordsworth's "Ode: Intimations of Immortality from Recollections of Early Childhood." The specific lines are worth reviewing for this study: "Our birth is but a sleep and a forgetting:/ The Soul that rises with us, our life's star,/ Hath had elsewhere its setting,/ And cometh from afar:/ Not in entire forgetfulness,/ And not in utter nakedness,/ But trailing clouds of glory do we come/ From God, who is our home:/ Heaven lies about us in our infancy!" It makes sense that Cather would have Wordsworth in mind here, both for exposing Paul's romantic obsessions and for keying the reader into the theme of lost youth and the potential corruption of adulthood. This same theme is at the heart of *Catcher* as Holden laments the loss of innocence and the childlike view of the world as we grow up.

7. Beyond the scope of this study but pertinent to the question of coming-of-age is the fact that many of Cather's narratives contain underlying elements of interest to contemporary literary critics involved in lesbian, gay, bisexual, and transgendered studies (also known as queer theory). In this way, Cather's allusions to homosexuality and shifting gender roles in her narratives address an element of youthful angst that Salinger mostly avoids in *Catcher*. Cather herself lived for most of her life with female companions and never married or had children. Critics over the years have noted that many of Cather's characters are shown to be "strange" or "artistic" and struggle with being out of synch with their surrounding society. In "The Sculptor's Funeral," for example, an effeminate, overly sensitive artist is ostracized by his small rural community

for not fulfilling the role of a conventional male. The narrative structure of *My Ántonia* offers tantalizing room for speculation—Cather chose to inhabit the voice of a male protagonist, Jim Burden, who in many areas of the narrative reflects strong desires toward the female characters, particularly the hypersexualized "Hired Girls" section. *The Professor's House* contains many elements that literary scholars have interpreted as homoerotic, particularly the relationship between the protagonist, Godfry St. Peter, and his young student, Tom Outland (as well as a strikingly intimate relationship that Tom shares with his best friend, Roddy). Many critics have asserted that "Paul's Case" is one of the first American short stories to deal with a possibly gay central character. These critics frequently cite this passage as validation:

> [Paul] fell in with a wild San Francisco boy, a freshman at Yale, who said he had run down for a "little flyer" over Sunday. The young man offered to show Paul the night side of the town, and the two boys went out together after dinner, not returning to the hotel until seven o'clock the next morning. They had started out in the confiding warmth of a champagne friendship, but their parting on the elevator was singularly cool. (80)

Such examples as this are suggestive rather than overt, but Paul's love of the theater and his close relationship with a young actor, Charley Edwards, in whose dressing room Paul spends much time until Edwards "remorsefully promised the boy's father not to see him again" (73), lend further evidence that Cather was likely exploring issues of sexual orientation nearly a century before that term became common and well before the issue was openly explored in American literature.

8. Holden shares with Paul similar suicidal tendencies. After he is assaulted by the pimp, Maurice, at his hotel, Holden confesses that he "felt like jumping out the window. I probably would've done it, too, if I'd been sure somebody'd cover me up as soon as I landed. I didn't want a bunch of stupid rubbernecks looking at me when I was all gory" (136). This brings to mind the story of James Castle, a former classmate of Holden's, "a skinny weak-looking guy, with wrists about as big as pencils," who fell victim to bullies and jumped out a window at their school. The reality of suicide as Holden has witnessed it and the fantasy he carries of wanting to "catch" youngsters from such falls contrast darkly with Paul's final descent into the "immense design of things." Such broken bodies reinforce the notion that youth is fragile, impermanent, and violent to anyone who becomes marked as strange or unconventional.

Works Cited

Blythe, Hal, and Charlie Sweet. "Willa Cather's 'Paul's Case' and Salinger's *The Catcher in the Rye*." *Notes on Contemporary Literature* 37.1 (2007): 10-11.

Cather, Willa. *My Ántonia*. Scholarly edition. Ed. Charles Mignon and Kari A. Ronning. Lincoln: U of Nebraska P, 1994.

———. *Not Under Forty*. Lincoln: U of Nebraska P, 1988.

_____. "Paul's Case." 1905. *Great Short Works of Willa Cather*. Ed. Robert K. Miller. New York: HarperPerennial, 1993. 59-84.

Evertson, Matt. "Love, Loss, and Growing up in J. D. Salinger and Cormac McCarthy." *"The Catcher in the Rye": New Essays*. Ed. J. P. Steed. New York: Peter Lang, 2002. 101-41.

Gopnik, Adam. "Postscript: J. D. Salinger." *The New Yorker* 8 Feb. 2010: 20-21.

Salinger J. D. *The Catcher in the Rye*. Boston: Little, Brown, 1951.

Critical Mass:
Holden Among the Critics

Jill Rollins

In 1951, many of *The Catcher in the Rye*'s reviewers were already familiar with the eleven years of Salinger's writing that preceded it. They had met prototypes of *Catcher*'s larger-than-life protagonist, Holden Caulfield, in the best of Salinger's short stories published in magazines before 1951. Holden had materialized in six stories, but most fully as the Holden we know in "I'm Crazy" (*Collier's*, 22 December 1945) and in "Slight Rebellion off Madison." The latter story marked Salinger's publishing debut in the prestigious *New Yorker* (21 December 1946), where he continued to publish all his stories until the end of his publishing career in 1965. When *The Catcher in the Rye* was launched in July 1951, it immediately provoked a critical conversation that has waxed and waned but has persisted. Though not a blockbuster at its debut, it was a work of immediate, contentious, and, it turns out, lasting interest. *Catcher* appeared on the *New York Times* best-seller list at number fourteen (out of sixteen) two weeks after its publication; it remained on the list for seven months, rising as high as number four and staying there for ten weeks.

American critics have been trying to figure out why ever since. Critic and editor Robert Gutwillig, in a *New York Times Book Review* retrospective written five years after *Catcher*'s publication, spoke for many when he noted the "shock and thrill of recognition" (39) that Holden Caulfield evoked in readers, particularly youthful ones. Initial reviews of *Catcher* were plentiful, even if mixed in their verdicts, and set the pattern for criticism to come. James Stern's review, published in the weighty *New York Times Book Review* to accompany the novel's release, relegated *Catcher* to the category of "minor achievement." Stern (like Salinger, a short-fiction writer for the elite *New Yorker*) wrote his self-congratulatory review, "Aw, the World's a Crumby Place," in the style of Holden's adolescent speech and idiom. Despite

Stern's declared admiration for Salinger's skills as a short-fiction writer, it seems plain that he read only the beginning and end of Salinger's debut novel with any attention because "it's too long. Gets kind of monotonous."

Stern typifies many early reviewers who had no inkling of how quickly and permanently *Catcher* would become lodged in the American cultural consciousness. Reviewer Harvey Breit, in *The Atlantic* (August 1951), even categorized *Catcher* as a "summer novel." But Breit also recognized something about the novel that led him to wonder why it was a "near miss." Indeed, that something in *Catcher* must have explained the more than two hundred additional reviews of Salinger's first novel that quickly followed its publication. These appeared over the next several months in a variety of American periodicals, such as the *Saturday Evening Post, Harper's, The Nation*, the *New York Times Book Review*, the *Washington Post*, and the *Christian Science Monitor*, to name a very few. *Catcher*'s immediate success was also boosted by the support of respected *New Yorker* book editor Clifton Fadiman, the then-guru of popular literature, who endorsed the Book-of-the-Month Club's decision to make *Catcher* its summer selection. Other influential reviewers were equally smitten. Salinger's *New Yorker* associate S. N. Behrman declared of *Catcher* in a long review published in the magazine, "I loved this one" (76). Stamps of more measured approval came from many other critics, such as respected *Saturday Review* writer Harrison Smith and *Harper's* reviewer Charles Poore.

Detractors tended to doubt or even deride the teenage Holden's credibility. Many dismissed Holden's sufferings as the whining of one of the very privileged preppies Holden himself rejected. But the most vociferous critics attacked, condemned, and generally threw up their hands in horror at Holden's frankness and profanity (missing the novel's humor, of course). The novel's explicit language and its negative view of contemporary America put religious, social, and educational institutions on alert. Reviews such as T. Morris Longstreth's in the *Christian Science Monitor* declared *Catcher* a danger to young people: "One finds it hard to believe that a true lover of children could father this tale." Similar warnings in publications such as *Catholic World* immediately sent school administrators, parents, librarians, and other would-be censors scurrying to keep the novel out of the hands of America's youth. Yet in the *New York Herald Tribune*, reviewer Virgilia Peterson, though also reviling young Holden's vulgar language, was astute enough to recognize his most ardent audience—the one, she felt, that could truly measure the novel's success (or, she implied, its failure): "It would be interesting and enlightening to know what Holden Caulfield's contemporaries, male and female, think of him. Their opinion would constitute the real test of Mr. Salinger's validity." Although the huffing of censors no doubt simply added to the novel's initial wicked appeal for rebellious teenagers, Peterson's observation acknowledged the ability of these same teenagers not only to relate wholeheartedly to Holden's alienation, rebelliousness, and foul language but also to discern the genuine from the phony in both Holden and his creator's art.

Catcher would be Salinger's only novel, though nobody knew that at the time. After 1951, he resumed writing short stories and novella-length fiction that dealt exclusively with the brittle, brilliant Glass family. He continued to publish exclusively in *The New Yorker*. *Catcher* came along at a time when a methodology called New Criticism dominated the complex world of literary criticism. In 1963, in their introduction to their still-indispensable *Studies in J. D. Salinger: Reviews, Essays, and Critiques of "The Catcher in the Rye" and Other Fiction*, editors Marvin Laser and Norman Fruman rejected New Criticism as a valid methodology for analyzing *Catcher*: "It is a technique more easily practised [*sic*] on a poem or short story than on even so brief a novel as *The Catcher in the Rye*" (vii). Yet the novel's shortness does seem to have stimulated critics in the late 1950s and early 1960s to the depth and breadth of critical commentary that New Criticism demanded. Critical essays and articles of the time contained intense discussion and interpretation of Holden, his speech and idiom, his spiritual journey, his innocence, his search for pure love, and his place in the American literary tradition. The liveliest pieces considered whether or not Salinger was a literary artist of lasting importance.

In 1956, *Catcher* was five years old. It still enjoyed strong sales, which may have puzzled the critics but certainly not college students, the novel's most enthusiastic readers. Their intense identification with Holden and his anguished sojourn in a worrying post-World War II world was continuing to grow. The pressure that university students applied to their professors to include *Catcher* for study in literature curricula ensured both the novel's steady sales and its place in the critical spotlight. In a gracious 1959 *Saturday Review* article, columnist, author, and professor Granville Hicks acknowledged his New York University students' discernment: "For the college generation of the Fifties, Salinger has the kind of importance that Scott Fitzgerald and Ernest Hemingway had for the young people of the Twenties. . . . in the first place, he speaks their language. . . . In the second place, he expresses their rebellion . . . they rejoice in his gestures of defiance" (30). Furthermore, Salinger's mystique was increasing with every year since he had, in 1953, withdrawn from public life to Cornish, New Hampshire. And when it was perceived that *Catcher* was not going to go away and enough time had passed for the phenomenon that is Holden to settle comfortably into the American imagination, many literary critics and academics (often one and the same) began to explore the novel more seriously.

In the spring of 1956, Arthur Heiserman and James E. Miller, Jr., both professors at the University of Chicago and authors of other literary critical studies, published "J. D. Salinger: Some Crazy Cliff" in the highly respected academic journal *Western Humanities Review*. Here was the critical endorsement the novel had not, until then, achieved. *Catcher*, the authors declared admiringly, clearly is a novel that belongs to the classic quest tradition. As a contemporary protagonist in that tradition, they continued, Holden is unique because he both explores and repudiates the sick contemporary world in which he lives. That Holden can suffer and at the same time be funny, profane, and innocent further endorsed Salinger's achievement in the critics' eyes. Reaction to Heiserman and Miller's assessment was mixed but opened the door wider to critical discussion of *Catcher* in academia. Critic Charles H. Kegel responded in his own 1957 article in *Western Humanities Review* that "[Heiserman and Miller's] article serves as a very convincing notice to students of recent American fiction that *The Catcher in the Rye* deserves careful, critical attention" (188). Kegel also placed himself in the ranks of the novel's admirers.

Edgar Branch's thorough, respectful 1957 examination of the parallels between Holden and Huck Finn (noted but not so completely explored by others) seemed to fix *Catcher* even more firmly in the realm of serious literature. In "Mark Twain and J. D. Salinger: A Study in Literary Continuity," Branch discussed the parallels in character, experience, and language between the two young protagonists, declaring, "*The Catcher in the Rye* is a haunting reminder of *Huckleberry Finn*" (150). In *Radical Innocence: Studies in the Contemporary American Novel* (1961), English professor and critic Ihab Hassan's assessment ranked Salinger's fiction among the most exemplary of his era. Responding to some critical rejection of the novel and its adolescent protagonist as somehow superficial, phony, and not worthy of serious attention, Hassan rejected "the small talk of criticism" (260) and concluded robustly that "we can see how *The Catcher in the Rye* is *both* a funny and terrifying work" (275). That same year, in *Wisconsin Studies in Contemporary Literature*, Carl F. Strauch lent even more gravitas to Salinger's achievement. Summarizing the widely varied critical opinion on *Catcher* to date, Strauch chastised his fellow critics for their shortsightedness in not recognizing the novel as a modern American masterpiece.

Throughout *Catcher*'s first decade, however, the novel's detractors gathered steam as well. As the work aged, the more caustic and personal their criticism seemed to become, particularly regarding

Salinger's long, fruitful membership in what was dismissively referred to as the *New Yorker* school of fiction. Although some of the snarkier critical commentary could be attributed to professional jealousy, many respected writers and critics did scorn in *Catcher* the sentimentality, elitism, superficiality, and almost puritanical mores (*Catcher*'s profanity notwithstanding) that *The New Yorker* seemed to them to endorse in its fiction. Among the first to dismiss *Catcher* on these grounds was Professor John W. Aldridge, a worried observer of the American postwar generation. In his 1956 book *In Search of Heresy: American Literature in an Age of Conformity*, Aldridge included a chapter each on Salinger and his promising contemporaries Saul Bellow and William Styron. Refuting parallels between Huckleberry Finn and Holden, Aldridge scathingly concluded: "The innocence of Mr. Salinger's Holden Caulfield, on the other hand, is a compound of urban intelligence, juvenile contempt and *New Yorker* sentimentalism. . . . And for ourselves, there is identification but no insight, a sense of pathos but not of tragedy" (130-31).

Influential critic and literary scholar Maxwell Geismar offered a chapter on Salinger in his book *American Moderns: From Rebellion to Conformity* (1958) that was even more scathing, damning the novel with very faint praise. Geismar's own tastes were for the more muscular, socially engaged authors such as Theodore Dreiser, Thomas Wolfe, and Sinclair Lewis, about whom he wrote extensively. Geismar found Holden a precocious poseur. Snidely, he dubbed Salinger the "spokesman of the Ivy League Rebellion during the early Fifties," the voice of "undergraduate circles, and particularly in the women's colleges," and a "leading light in the *New Yorker* school of writing" (195), which champions "that lost world of childhood" to which "Salinger, like the rest of the *New Yorker* school, always returns" (209). Geismar did acknowledge that *Catcher* was so far "Salinger's best work, if a highly artificial one" (199), but concluded it was of little consequence to any but over-earnest adolescents searching for Meaning. Freelance writer Dan Wakefield, though, observed in 1958 that Salinger's writing was reaching a wider audience. Its appeal was in its confessional nature; its interest, Holden's anguished spiritual search for love. When Beat generation writers denounced Salinger's writing as slick, Wakefield wryly challenged the Beats' own credibility, observing that their search for love and relevance "ended . . . not with love but with heroin" (72).

As the turbulent 1960s unfolded, much *Catcher* criticism took an even more personal turn, deriding Salinger for his increasing obsession with Eastern religion, his continued seclusion, and his failure to produce a more substantial body of work. George Steiner sourly attributed Salinger's steady popularity partly to his appeal as fresh meat for publish-or-perish young professors in search of subject matter. And in a savage, funny article, "J. D. Salinger: 'Everybody's Favorite,'" Alfred Kazin chastised Salinger for the "self-conscious charm and prankishness of his own writing" (30) and dismissed Holden and his suffering as cute. So much critical interest in *Catcher* and Salinger spurred the publication of several thick volumes of Salinger criticism still seminal today: Frederick L. Gwynn and Joseph L. Blotner's study (1958), Henry Anatole Grunwald's anthology of critical essays with his editorial commentary (1962), and Laser and Fruman's astutely chosen collection (1963), among others. Warren French took a career-long interest in Salinger's work, publishing three engaging books on his writing between 1963 and 1988.

Salinger's last published story, "Hapworth 16, 1924," appeared in *The New Yorker* in the summer of 1965. Typically, critical reaction ranged from fervently admiring to strongly negative, the balance tipping to the latter view, which tended to blame *The New Yorker* for its continuing indulgence of Salinger. After that, additional critical studies appeared that treated *Catcher* with the rest of Salinger's fiction; these included James E. Miller, Jr.'s *J. D. Salinger* in the respected University of Minnesota Pamphlet series (1965) and a special Salinger issue of *Modern Fiction Studies* in 1966. Then critical near-silence fell until the mid-1970s, though the censors' vigorous attempts to have the novel removed from school reading lists and libraries continued unabated (and carries on today). Maybe the reason for the decline in critical interest is best expressed in Gwynn and Blotner's gentle but telling assessment of Salinger's talent made in 1958 at the height of Salinger's popularity in the introduction to their study *The Fiction of J. D. Salinger*:

> The present study . . . comes to the early conclusion that Salinger's achievement . . . occurs in what may currently be called the middle of his career, and that the progress of his creativity has run up from second-rate magazine items to the half-dozen masterworks [*Catcher* included], and thence downward, most recently, to ambitious failures. (3)

Just such an ambitious failure was "Hapworth 16, 1924." After that, Salinger published no more fiction—ever.

Perhaps as well the growing threat of nuclear holocaust, the assassination of President John F. Kennedy, the civil rights movement, and the Vietnam War focused even literary critical attention elsewhere. Instead, as Raychel Haugrud Reiff points out in her 2008 Salinger study, "[*Catcher*] became the mouthpiece for the counterculture of the activist anti-Vietnam War generation of the 1960s. In the following decades this counterculture became the culture of the universities and the media" (80). It became as well the culture of a new generation of critics, fewer of whom seemed interested in returning to the novel. But also critics had long wrestled with *Catcher*'s perceived failure to engage with the troubled American society of the 1950s that Holden reviles but, paradoxically, ends up edging back into. This was a line of critical argument that would receive closer attention as the politically and economically unstable 1970s unfolded.

Gerald Rosen's long, intelligent 1977 article "A Retrospective Look at *The Catcher in the Rye*" and James Lundquist's *J. D. Salinger* (1979) were among the best of the 1970s criticism, but two substantial articles, both published in 1976 issues of the academic journal *Critical Inquiry*, can be considered the most significant in the critical history of

Catcher during the decade. The first (reprinted in this volume) is Carol and Richard Ohmann's long, self-important article "Reviewers, Critics, and *The Catcher in the Rye*," delivered from a declared Marxist critical stance and aiming grandiosely to provide a "case study of capitalist criticism" (16). In the Ohmanns' view, Salinger fell short with the novel by only faithfully reflecting its materialistic American society without analyzing or castigating that society. And reviewers, the Ohmanns alleged, were content with describing "*Catcher* as a literary work and plac[ing] it vis-à-vis other works similar in genre and style" (19), focusing on its universality rather than on its lack of political or socioeconomic specificity. Toward the many critics who had so far assessed Salinger's writing (particularly *Catcher*), the Ohmanns were condescending; however, they warned that reviewers and critics practicing New Criticism and other critical methodologies might soon be in decline for economic as much as intellectual reasons: "As thousands of people in our field join the unemployed or ill-employed, it will be surprising if most teachers of English maintain a separation of culture from society, and keep on writing the kind of criticism that mediated *Catcher*'s acceptance as a classic" (37).

Literary scholar Geoffrey Hartman's even gloomier assessment of literary criticism's future in American academia followed, in "Literary Criticism and Its Discontents." In observations that seem particularly pertinent to the critical fate of *Catcher*, Hartman mourned the decline of New Criticism and its replacement with what he called "post-New Critical critics" (207). The latter, he asserted, were not up to the task of practicing authoritative criticism in an academia that was itself undergoing a sea change. "We teach and write in a mass culture" (206), Hartman observed; "Then how do we deal with this multiplying burden of books, sources, texts, interpretations?" (211). Hartman accused post-New Critics in the universities of being more interested in self-promotion than in addressing the literary text itself. Though "post-New Critical critics remain intense readers, devoted to the study of writing in all its modes . . . [they are] presently reduced to quarreling about what particular interpretation (evaluation) is or is not correct" (219). In the uproar of competing critical voices, he maintains, the literary work is lost. Hartman's assessment indeed seems to foreshadow the self-promoting nature of some of the ever-more-meager Salinger criticism that followed.

From the 1980s on, less attention was paid to *Catcher*, then more than a generation old. Instead, publicity and criticism during the 1980s played up Salinger's roles as a cult figure and a recluse. Events and publications sustained those perceptions. In 1980 and beyond, much was made of John Lennon assassin Mark David Chapman's misguided inspiration by *Catcher*. In 1988, much was also made of Ian Hamilton's failure in court to gain Salinger's authorization for Hamilton's biography, *In Search of J. D. Salinger*. The book was certainly more about Hamilton's search than a revelation of Salinger or his art, critics agreed. By 1990, *Catcher* remained on academic reading lists, and some critical interest persisted. In his thoughtful introduction to *New Essays on "The Catcher in the Rye"* (1991), editor Jack Salzman remained optimistic: "But surely the public that continues to read *The Catcher in the Rye*, even that part of the public which demands that the book not be read, is more concerned with the fiction written than with the man in New Hampshire who may or may not be writing more stories" (2). The five commissioned essays in the collection, said Salzman, "also reveal the diversity of critical approaches to the novel" (16). Indeed they do, but the five essays scarcely provide the diversity of the much larger numbers of critical essays published in the collections of the late 1950s and early 1960s.

Where newer critical insights into Salinger and his work might have been expected, potential sources failed. In 1998, writer Joyce Maynard titillated Americans with the details of her youthful 1972 affair with Salinger in *At Home in the World: A Memoir*. However, to a public increasingly jaded by seamy details of the lives of celebrities, the affair was a seven-day wonder and offered few insights into Salinger's creative output. In 2000 Margaret A. Salinger published *Dream Catcher:*

A Memoir, which shed light on her eccentric father but had little to say about his writing, *Catcher* in particular. Increasingly, now that it was a fixture in American culture, *Catcher* seemed to become more alluded-to than read: Mel Gibson's seriously damaged character in the film *Conspiracy Theory* (1997) owns multiple copies of *Catcher*; Will Smith's character, Paul, delivers a lengthy monologue on *Catcher* (interestingly, on the death of imagination in American culture) in the film version of John Guare's play *Six Degrees of Separation* (1993). With the advent of the Internet and the speedy displacement of print with visual media, Geoffrey Hartman's gloomy 1976 predictions for mass culture might seem to be coming true. However, surfing the Internet quickly reveals that *Catcher* is still a topic of discussion among readers and critics. On academic reading lists, *Catcher* remains largely in high schools rather than in universities (an easy read, sniff some critics) for teachers and students born long after the 1950s.

Today, the hoped-for counterculture that Warren French evoked in 1988 in *J. D. Salinger, Revisited* is best observed on YouTube, where student "movies" of the novel, online readings by Holden aspirants, and thousands of commentary "bites" keep Holden alive, but without the immediacy of his character and voice as they leap from *Catcher*'s pages. Today, in the blogosphere, everyone's a critic. Conversation on the novel continues, with opinion as varied and contentious (though sometimes less well-informed or literate) as it was in the first two decades following *Catcher*'s publication. In a clever, nasty 2004 revisiting of *Catcher* by Jonathan Yardley, book reviewer for the *Washington Post*, the title says it all—almost. In "J. D. Salinger's Holden Caulfield, Aging Gracelessly," Yardley opines that today's youth find Holden (and his profanity) archaic; he is struck by "how sentimental—how outright squishy—[the novel] is. . . . [Salinger] said everything he had to say in it, which may well be why he has said nothing else."

Catcher can still provoke public interest, however. A brief flurry occurred around the 2009 publication in Britain of a *Catcher* "sequel." *Sixty Years Later: Coming Through the Rye*, by John David California (pseudonym for Swedish writer and publisher Fredrik Colting), depicts Holden as incontinent old crank. Unimpressed by the flattery offered by imitation, Salinger successfully blocked the novel's American publication on grounds of plagiarism, once again proving his career-long adroitness at bringing lawsuits in defense of his work and privacy, although the decision was overturned in April 2010. Salinger's death on January 27, 2010, provoked a round of retrospectives on his life and work, mostly respectful. Daniel Geddes's thoughtful essay "J. D. Salinger: *In Memoriam*" deems Holden a great comedic character, praises the body of Salinger's fiction, and declares that "*Catcher* is clearly the cornerstone of Salinger's reputation." And the rumors of a cache of unpublished Salinger fiction? Don't hold your breath, says Geddes.

What's left? Well, *The Catcher in the Rye: The Movie*. Hollywood producers have unsuccessfully pursued rights to the novel for decades. Salinger steadfastly rebuffed them. After Salinger's death, legal representatives closely guarded details of Salinger's will and wishes so that "Hollywood might have to wait the best part of a century until the book is out of copyright" (Allen). Even in death, Salinger seems to be calling the shots. More than 65 million copies sold and a huge body of critical study confirms the lasting impact of *The Catcher in the Rye*. Whether negative or positive, almost all criticism has recognized that *Catcher* occupies a permanent place in great twentieth-century American fiction.

Works Cited

Aldridge, John W. *In Search of Heresy: American Literature in an Age of Conformity*. New York: McGraw-Hill, 1956.

Allen, Nick. "*Catcher in the Rye* Still Baffles." *The Gazette*. Arts. 23 June 2010: C6.

Behrman, S. N. "The Vision of the Innocent." *The New Yorker* 11 Aug. 1951: 71-76.

Branch, Edgar. "Mark Twain and J. D. Salinger: A Study in Literary Continuity." *American Quarterly* 9.2 (Summer 1957): 144-58.

Breit, Harvey. "Reader's Choice." *The Atlantic* Aug. 1951: 82.
California, John David [Fredrik Colting]. *Sixty Years Later: Coming Through the Rye*. London: Windupbird, 2009.
French, Warren. *J. D. Salinger*. Boston: Twayne, 1963.
_____. *J. D. Salinger*. Rev. ed. Boston: Twayne, 1976.
_____. *J. D. Salinger, Revisited*. Boston: Twayne, 1988.
Geddes, Daniel. "J. D. Salinger: *In Memoriam*." *The Satirist*. Apr. 2010. Web.
Geismar, Maxwell. *American Moderns: From Rebellion to Conformity*. New York: Hill & Wang, 1958.
Grunwald, Henry Anatole, ed. *Salinger: A Critical and Personal Portrait*. New York: Harper, 1962.
Gutwillig, Robert. "Everybody's Caught *The Catcher in the Rye*." *New York Times Book Review* 15 Jan. 1961: sec. 7, 38-39.
Gwynn, Frederick L., and Joseph L. Blotner. *The Fiction of J. D. Salinger*. Pittsburgh: U of Pittsburgh P, 1958.
Hamilton, Ian. *In Search of J. D. Salinger*. New York: Random House, 1988.
Hartman, Geoffrey. "Literary Criticism and Its Discontents." *Critical Inquiry* 3.2 (Winter 1976): 203-20.
Hassan, Ihab. *Radical Innocence: Studies in the Contemporary American Novel*. Princeton, NJ: Princeton UP, 1961.
Heiserman, Arthur, and James E. Miller, Jr. "J. D. Salinger: Some Crazy Cliff." *Western Humanities Review* 10.2 (Spring 1956): 129-37.
Hicks, Granville. "J. D. Salinger: Search for Wisdom." *Saturday Review* 25 Jul. 1959: 13, 30.
Kazin, Alfred. "J. D. Salinger: 'Everybody's Favorite.'" *The Atlantic Monthly* Aug. 1961: 27-31.
Kegel, Charles H. "Incommunicability in Salinger's *The Catcher in the Rye*." *Western Humanities Review* 11 (Spring 1957): 188-90.
Laser, Marvin, and Norman Fruman, eds. *Studies in J. D. Salinger: Reviews, Essays, and Critiques of "The Catcher in the Rye" and Other Fiction*. New York: Odyssey Press, 1963.
Longstreth, T. Morris. "New Novels in the News." *Christian Science Monitor* 19 July 1951: 11.
Maynard, Joyce. *At Home in the World: A Memoir*. New York: Picador, 1998.
Miller, James E., Jr. *J. D. Salinger*. University of Minnesota Pamphlets on American Writers. Minneapolis: U of Minnesota P, 1965.
Modern Fiction Studies. Special issue on Salinger. 12.3 (1966).
Ohmann, Carol, and Richard Ohmann. "Reviewers, Critics, and *The Catcher in the Rye*." *Critical Inquiry* 3.1 (Autumn 1976): 15-37.
Peterson, Virgilia. "Three Days in the Bewildering World of an Adolescent." *New York Herald Tribune Book Review* 15 July 1951: 3.
Reiff, Raychel Haugrud. *J. D. Salinger: "The Catcher in the Rye" and Other Works*. Tarrytown, NY: Benchmark Books, 2008.
Rosen, Gerald. "A Retrospective Look at *The Catcher in the Rye*." *American Quarterly* 29.5 (Winter 1977): 547-62.

Salinger, Margaret A. *Dream Catcher: A Memoir*. New York: Washington Square Press, 2000.

Salzman, Jack, ed. *New Essays on "The Catcher in the Rye."* New York: Cambridge UP, 1991.

Steiner, George. "The Salinger Industry." *Nation* 14 Nov. 1957: 360-63.

Stern, James. "Aw, the World's a Crumby Place." *New York Times Book Review* 15 July 1951: 5.

Strauch, Carl F. "Kings in the Back Row: Meaning through Structure—A Reading of Salinger's *The Catcher in the Rye*." *Wisconsin Studies in Contemporary Literature* 2.1 (1961): 5-30.

Wakefield, Dan. "Salinger and the Search for Love." *New World Writing*. Vol. 14. New York: New American Library, 1958. 68-85.

Yardley, Jonathan. "J. D. Salinger's Holden Caulfield, Aging Gracelessly." *Washington Post* 19 Oct. 2004: C1.

CRITICAL READINGS

Memories of Holden Caulfield— and of Miss Greenwood
Carl Freedman

Two years ago, the fiftieth anniversary of J. D. Salinger's *The Catcher in the Rye* took place. The book is almost exactly the same age I am. To be precise, it's about three months younger: I appeared in April 1951, the novel—after a much longer gestation period—in July. Inevitably, a good many essays about it have recently been published, and, though they indicate little consensus about the exact meaning or value of the novel, they do generally agree that it is still, in some sense, an extraordinary text. At the height of Salinger's reputation—the 1950s and 1960s—his was in many ways the dominant voice in contemporary American fiction, despite his slender output, and it was not unusual for him to be discussed in tones that suggested a genius almost on the order of Shakespeare's or Tolstoy's to be at stake. His stature has long since assumed much more modest proportions. Few, I suppose, would maintain now that *The Catcher in the Rye* belongs in the absolute first rank of the modern novel: on a level, that is, with Conrad's *Nostromo* (1904) or Lawrence's *Women in Love* (1920) or Joyce's *Ulysses* (1922) or Faulkner's *Absalom, Absalom!* (1936) or Pynchon's *Gravity's Rainbow* (1973). Yet if it is, in this strict sense, a work of the second rank, it is also a novel that possesses a remarkable hold on its readers, or at least on a good many of them. There are more than a few of us for whom *The Catcher in the Rye* still feels less like a canonical book than like a personal experience, and one of the most powerful of our lives. Though I earn a living chiefly by producing materialist criticism of literary texts (on the page and in the classroom), I think of this text mainly as a part—a phase, really—of my personal history, and of its protagonist as someone I know, or once knew: attitudes that do not necessarily exclude a properly critical approach but that by no means inevitably make for one either. Accordingly, though what follows will certainly have its critical moments, it is at least as much a memoir as a critical essay, a memoir of the Holden Caulfield I knew and of an earlier self, both of whom are now long in the past but also still with me.

But this must also be a memoir of Miss Greenwood. No, I do not mean Sylvia Plath's Esther Greenwood, protagonist of *The Bell Jar* (1963) and the most memorable, perhaps, of all the many fictional characters conceived under the direct influence of Holden Caulfield. The real Miss Greenwood was my eighth-grade English teacher and my first teacher who was also, in some important way, a friend. Not that I had gotten along badly with my earlier teachers—quite the contrary. But before Miss Greenwood a teacher was no more to be counted as a friend than was a parent, a doctor, or a rabbi. Teachers were all just adults, authority figures, and one took it for granted that they inhabited a world different from one's own. Miss Greenwood, somehow, was different. Doubtless this was at least partly because she was quite young herself, no more than a year or so out of college. It is a somewhat staggering thought that, during the time I am remembering, she was thus only slightly older than the seniors I teach today, and younger than nearly all of my graduate students. It is even more staggering to think that, if she and I were to meet today, we would be, for most practical purposes, about the same age. In the eighth grade, of course, the gulf was much wider—and yet bridgeable in a way that the age gulf between an adult and me had never quite been before.

I still have before me a fairly clear mental image of Miss Greenwood. She was thin, of about average height, with brown hair cut relatively short and a pleasant, freckled face. Her looks were not those of a bombshell or head-turner, but I expect that a fair number of men would have found her—I expect that a fair number of men *did* find her—attractive, and increasingly attractive as they got to know her better. But you would probably have had to be in love with her to call her beautiful. I was in love with her, though it is a love that I recognized as such only many years later. I am pretty sure that, at the time, I never consciously thought of Miss Greenwood in a romantic or even a sexual way, and in retrospect that seems a curious omission. After all, I was a horny, virginal fourteen-year-old boy, and I was preoccupied with sex in that intense, yearning way typical of my age and gender; but, as far as I can recall, the guest stars in my lustful fantasies tended to be either female classmates my own age or else generically "good-looking" women whose images were based on models and movie stars. Why not Miss Greenwood? She was pretty enough for the role. Perhaps I just respected her too much. Perhaps it was just that, in those more innocent days, the idea of "doing anything" with Miss Greenwood was literally beyond (conscious) comprehension.

In retrospect, however, it seems clear that nothing short of sexual love could have driven me to do what I frequently did during the eighth grade: namely, to *stay* in the school building after the final bell had rung, to use some of those precious hours of freedom between the end of school and dinner at home to talk with a teacher whose class I had been required to attend earlier in the day. Miss Greenwood was often in her classroom for a while after classes had ended, doing various chores—cleaning blackboards, arranging papers, and the like—and I got in the habit of dropping by. I would help her to the extent I could, and we would chat about various things. Some of these talks were brief—no more than ten or fifteen minutes—but others went on for an hour or even more. My house was within walking distance of the school, but sometimes, especially after one of our longer chats, Miss Greenwood would give me a lift home in the used, battered Volkswagen bug that she had recently purchased and about whose mechanical soundness she was, as I remember, a bit nervous. She took some consolation in the relatively low number on the odometer, and was mildly alarmed when I told her that odometer readings could be faked. Our relations were by no means completely informal. It was always clear that we were teacher and pupil, and certainly I never called her anything except "Miss Greenwood" (with the result that today I am not sure of her first name, though I once knew it well—Mary, perhaps?). But we were definitely friends.

Our conversations were mainly about two of our strongest common interests, politics and literature, which, as it happens, are the two main fields about which I write professionally today. We probably talked more about politics than about literature. The school year was 1964-65, and we shared happiness and relief that, in the presidential election, Lyndon Johnson defeated Barry Goldwater so resoundingly, though Miss Greenwood, I believe, was somewhat discreet about her political preferences (doubtless a prudent habit for any schoolteacher, but especially wise since the school principal was widely thought to be a rather unbalanced right-winger). I think the first political bet that I ever made—and won—in my life was with Miss Greenwood. In January 1965, Hubert Humphrey was inaugurated as vice-president and so had to give up his seat in the Senate, where he had been the Democratic whip. Several senators competed to succeed him, with the frontrunners generally agreed to be John Pastore of Rhode Island and Russell Long of Louisiana. Miss Greenwood liked Pastore's chances—a choice she shared with most journalistic pundits and by no means a stupid one, for Pastore's political profile resembled Humphrey's own, and his northeastern liberalism seemed in tune with the (very brief) moment of triumph that American liberalism was then enjoying. But I already knew a fair bit about how the Senate worked, and I reckoned that the southerners—still the dominant force in that body, despite the huge defeat they had recently suffered when the Civil Rights Act of 1964 was passed—would prove strong enough to win the post for one of their own. As indeed they did.

Long's victory brought him a position for which he never displayed much aptitude and which he lost to Edward Kennedy four years later. But it brought me the copy that I still possess of Salinger's fourth (and, as things now seem to have turned out, last) book, the one that collected the long stories, "Raise High the Roof Beam, Carpenters" and "Seymour—An Introduction." The volume was already out in hardcover, and Miss Greenwood and I agreed that the loser of the bet would buy the winner a copy of the paperback as soon as it appeared. It was a logical choice, for there was nothing we shared more intensely than our common admiration for Salinger. I think that I vaguely knew who

Salinger was even before meeting Miss Greenwood—I browsed through the current paperbacks frequently, and those Salinger paperbacks, with their covers nearly blank save for title and author, were hard to miss—but I had never read his work until Miss Greenwood recommended *The Catcher in the Rye* to me. I didn't realize at the time how typical an enthusiasm for Salinger was among intelligent college students of her generation, nor did it occur to me that, in urging me to read *The Catcher in the Rye*, Miss Greenwood was running something of a risk. Salinger's novel was one of three strictly banned throughout our public school system (Aldous Huxley's *Brave New World* [1932] and George Orwell's *Nineteen Eighty-four* [1949] were the others); and, though recommending it to a single student in an after-school chat was not, presumably, a transgression on the order of assigning it to a whole class, I'm sure she could have gotten into some trouble if, for instance, my parents had been the sort to make a fuss. Looking back, I suspect that, out of college and living on her own in a new city, Miss Greenwood was missing companions with whom she could discuss her favorite writer, and so she took a chance on me.

Her recommendation was about as successful as a recommendation can be. The book just knocked me out, as Holden himself would say. Today it seems clear to me that, technically, the main source of the novel's overwhelming power is its almost unparalleled mastery of voice. Except for *Huckleberry Finn* (1884)—often enough proposed as the chief precursor text of *The Catcher in the Rye*—there is not a novel in American literature, perhaps not a novel in the world, that more convincingly invents and sustains a young colloquial voice, page after page after page, with virtually not a single false note, and while managing to avoid both sentimentality and condescension on the part of the unseen author. If it is difficult to believe that Holden Caulfield is "just" a literary fabrication, it's because the reader seems to hear an entirely real human being talking to him or her for more than two hundred pages without interruption. But at the age of fourteen, of course, I was less struck by Salinger's technique than by the reality that his technique appeared to convey. Simply put, Holden seemed absolutely right to me—in some ways the rightest human being I had ever encountered. His world was basically similar to my own—never mind the differences between an upper-class northeasterner in the late 1940s and a middle-class southerner in the mid-1960s—and, at two or three years older than me, he was just young enough to be a peer and just enough older to seem automatically savvier and more worldly wise. Again and again Holden hit off exactly what a morass of mendacity the world had prepared for children in the process of leaving childhood behind; again and again he articulated, with painful but exuberant and wonderful accuracy, the essential inauthenticity of bourgeois American society that I myself was just beginning to be able to name.

Take Holden's roommate Stradlater, for instance: crude, obtuse, brash, outgoing, handsome, athletic, and, Holden believes, one of the few boys at Pencey Prep who actually succeeds in "giving the time" to the girls that he dates. I knew the type, and I resented the all-but-universal envy and admiration that the type attracted from his fellows. Who but Holden would have had the clear-sightedness and courage to dismiss him simply as "a stupid bastard"? And who, really knowing the type, could deny that Holden was exactly right? Or take Mr. Spencer, the history teacher who pompously and uselessly lectures Holden about his future: "Life *is* a game, boy. Life *is* a game that one plays according to the rules." I heard this sort of thing all the time, and Holden knew exactly what it was worth: "Game, my ass. Some game. If you get on the side where all the hot-shots are, then it's a game, all right—I'll admit that. But if you get on the *other* side, where there aren't any hot-shots, then what's a game about it? Nothing. No game."

Or take "this guy Ossenburger," the wealthy mortician and Pencey alumnus after whom Holden's dorm is named:

> The first football game of the year, he came up to school in this big goddam Cadillac, and we all had to stand up in the grandstand and give him a locomotive—that's a cheer. Then, the next morning, in chapel, he made a

speech that lasted about ten hours. He started off with about fifty corny jokes, just to show us what a regular guy he was. Very big deal. Then he started telling us how he was never ashamed, when he was in some kind of trouble or something, to get right down on his knees and pray to God. He told us we should always pray to God—talk to Him and all—wherever we were. He told us we ought to think of Jesus as our buddy and all. He said *he* talked to Jesus all the time. Even when he was driving his car. That killed me. I can just see the big phony bastard shifting into first gear and asking Jesus to send him a few more stiffs.

Though at the age of fourteen I had never even set eyes on a school precisely similar to Pencey, this passage seemed to sum up practically every school assembly I had ever been forced to attend; and future assemblies were made a little more bearable for knowing that at least one other person saw them for exactly what they were.

Sometimes it seemed to me that there was almost no variety of phony that Holden had not managed to spot and expose, from the insufferably pretentious pseudo-intellectual Carl Luce, an old schoolmate with whom he has an extended conversation in a bar, to the young naval officer ("His name was Commander Blop or something") he meets briefly in Ernie's nightclub: "He was one of those guys that think they're being a pansy if they don't break around forty of your fingers when they shake hands with you. God, I hate that stuff." Though most of Holden's insights are delivered in this ad hoc manner, there are a few more synoptic passages. Perhaps the best is the summary of Pencey he offers to Sally Hayes, herself an excruciating phony—the sort who appears much more intelligent than she is because she knows "quite a lot about the theater and plays and literature and all that stuff" and whom Holden finds harder to shake than most phonies because she is physically very attractive and usually willing to make out with him.

"You ought to go to a boys' school sometime. Try it sometime," I said.
"It's full of phonies, and all you do is study so that you can learn enough to

be smart enough to be able to buy a goddam Cadillac some day, and you have to keep making believe you give a damn if the football team loses, and all you do is talk about girls and liquor and sex all day, and everybody sticks together in these dirty little goddam cliques. The guys that are on the basketball team stick together, the Catholics stick together, the goddam intellectuals stick together, the guys that play bridge stick together. Even the guys that belong to the goddam Book-of-the-*Month* Club stick together. If you try to have a little intelligent—"

Sally is technically correct, as Holden himself agrees, when she interrupts him to object, "Lots of boys get more out of school than *that*." But no matter—Holden has Pencey, and the world, dead to rights.

Holden's wisdom seemed all the more impressive to me because there is no trace of superiority about it. He is never the detached, self-sufficient bystander, coolly and ironically observing life from its foyer; instead, he is passionate and disappointed, always newly indignant at every fresh instance of phoniness that life offers. It is also true that he is therefore extremely unhappy—an aspect of the book that I rather glossed over in my first few readings. I was able to see that Holden almost never seems to be having a good time, but I was not particularly unhappy myself—allowing for the fact that hardly any fourteen-year-old can be unambiguously called happy—and I hesitated to attribute to such a powerfully kindred spirit the extreme degree of psychic misery that now seems to me one of the principal features of Holden's character. Or to put it another way: The almost unerring acuteness of Holden's insights, and the superb colloquial vigor with which he could express them, seemed to make for a kind of intellectual high spirits that I could not, at the age of fourteen, easily reconcile with underlying pain. To see phonies so clearly could not exactly be a recipe for happiness in a world where phonies were so numerous, but surely, I felt, truth itself had its own consolations.

Not everyone has felt such a deep affinity with Holden as I did. Some readers—most prominently Mary McCarthy—believe that

Holden is too harsh in his judgments of others, that he is too much the pitiless phony-spotter. "I was surrounded by jerks," says Holden of his fellow patrons at Ernie's, and for some this sentence sums up almost the entirety of Holden's world view. Miss Greenwood to some extent held this opinion. Indeed, one of the things that slightly divided us in our shared passion for Salinger was that for me, then as now, Salinger was first and foremost the author of *The Catcher in the Rye*, whereas Miss Greenwood preferred his stories about the Glass family. Looking back, I suspect that this difference of opinion was largely a gendered one. Holden's outlook is intensely masculine (though never macho), and I suppose that from the other side of the gender divide it might well often seem suffocatingly masculine. But this point never occurred to me at the time, and I doubt it did to Miss Greenwood either. The problem with Holden, she once said to me, is just that you get the idea he probably wouldn't like you very much—whereas Buddy Glass, Holden's successor as Salinger's principal narrator and alter ego, was Miss Greenwood's idea of a very nice guy indeed.

I now think that Holden's supposed pitilessness in judging others has been greatly exaggerated. It has become conventional to say that he likes nobody except his three siblings; and, since one of them, his younger brother Allie, is dead, and since another, his older brother D. B., seems, as an evidently successful Hollywood screenwriter, to be in danger of becoming a bit of a phony himself, only his kid sister Phoebe ("himself in miniature or in glory," as McCarthy insisted) would be left as an unambiguously Good Person, a certified nonphony, in the land of the living. But in fact Holden likes quite a lot of people: people of both sexes and of various ages, and chance acquaintances as well as old friends. He immensely likes Jane Gallagher, sort of his girlfriend but not exactly, who always kept her kings in the back row whenever they played checkers. He equally likes his old English teacher Mr. Antolini, even though he is understandably disconcerted when Mr. Antolini makes what appears to be a homosexual pass at him. He likes the nuns he meets in a sandwich bar, and he likes Mrs.

Morrow, the mother of a classmate, whom he meets on a train. He even likes Selma Thurmer, the daughter of the headmaster at Pencey, despite her big nose and her falsies and her fingernails bitten bloody. He likes children in general, and so tries to rub out dirty words scrawled where children might see them; and, of course, he fantasizes about being the catcher in the rye, spending every day keeping children safely in the field of rye and away from the cliff's edge. He likes the ducks in the Central Park lagoon, and worries about what happens to them when the pond freezes solid in winter. Furthermore, Holden (unlike the Hemingway heroes with whom McCarthy so unjustly compares him) usually manages a good deal of concrete human sympathy even for those whom he cannot bring himself to like: his obnoxious, pimple-squeezing schoolmate Ackley, for instance, and Sunny, the prostitute who cheats him out of five dollars. His encounter with the latter makes for one of the book's most memorable scenes. At the end of a very long, very lonely, and frequently horny evening, Holden accepts a pimp's offer to send a whore to his hotel room. But when Sunny (who is "[n]o old bag," just as the pimp Maurice promises) actually arrives, Holden is so overcome with sadness at the thought of her life that his enthusiasm for losing his virginity evaporates into thin air and he offers to pay Sunny full price for just a few minutes of conversation.

In the eighth grade it did not occur to me to point out this deeply sensitive and compassionate side of Holden's character in reply to Miss Greenwood's criticism of him as too astringently judgmental. Nonetheless, her (perhaps not wholly intentional but clear enough) implication—that Holden might not like *me*—bothered me very little. It was not so much that I disagreed with her suggestion as that it somehow seemed beside the point. Maybe Holden wouldn't necessarily like me, but so what? Holden was me. And indeed, Holden by no means expresses invariable liking for himself throughout the long monologue that constitutes the novel. Though most readers have, I think, failed to notice the fact, he frequently confesses to acts of phoniness on his own part. Precept, as Samuel Johnson said, may be very sincere even when practice is very imperfect, and the fact that Holden—as sturdy a moralist, in his own way, as Dr. Johnson—is capable of self-criticism, that he can recognize his own involvement in the whole system of phoniness from which he recoils so bitterly, only made (and makes) him all the more admirable and all the more right in my eyes.

Whatever Holden might have thought of me, though, Miss Greenwood had an explanation for why I liked Holden and *The Catcher in the Rye* so much more than her own favorite, Buddy Glass, and the stories centered on his family. She once commented that people closer to her own age—people in their late teens, I believe she meant—often liked *The Catcher in the Rye* because people that age often felt rebellious toward society (this conversation took place, remember, just as the 1960s was coming into focus as a political and cultural era). She suggested that I myself was feeling that kind of rebelliousness, at an earlier age than was typical. At the time, I recall, I felt slightly uncertain as to exactly what Miss Greenwood's attitude toward my supposed rebelliousness was, though I took her remark as basically flattering, if only for the precocity it implied. Today, especially in view of the fact that I did not, at that point overtly fit the usual profile of the school rebel—I had never, by the eighth grade, detonated firecrackers in the school bathroom, or brought a subversive petition to class, or smoked marijuana, or even grown my hair long—hers must surely be counted as a pretty shrewd, prescient judgment of a fourteen-year-old boy who grew up to become a Marxist literary critic.

But it must also be pointed out that Holden himself is not really a rebel. True enough, his acute penetration into the life of his society could in principle supply the basis for rebellion, but Holden is never able to take the step from diagnosis to action, or even to serious planning. The only action he ever even contemplates is a strategy not of rebellion but of withdrawal: He imagines leaving civilization (like Huck Finn at the end of Mark Twain's novel, though in Holden's America the frontier has been long closed) and living somewhere out west in a cabin on the edge of the woods, pretending to be a deaf mute in order to avoid conversations with phonies. Even this is pure fantasizing, as Holden at heart always knows. Not only is Holden not a rebel, but (like Hamlet, who is in many ways almost as much Holden's predecessor as Huck is) he even has great difficulty acting meaningfully in *any* way. Etymologically, the opposite of an actor is a patient—someone who is acted upon—and it is no accident that a patient is precisely what Holden is during the time present of the novel. It is also significant that, though everyone knows that Holden tells his story from some sort of medical institution ("this crumby place," as he calls it), there has been considerable disagreement among readers as to exactly what sort of hospital it is and why Holden is there. Is it because he is threatened by tuberculosis and needs a long rest in a sanatorium? Or because he has suffered some sort of mental collapse and requires psychiatric help? The source of the confusion is that Salinger definitely allows both explanations. Holden is a mess, physically and psychologically.

Holden, then, might be seen as basically pathetic, someone who, despite all his advantages (intelligence, eloquence, evident good looks, family money), is essentially incapable of coping with life—hence his removal not to an isolated Thoreauvian cabin where he can practice Emersonian self-reliance, but to an expensive private hospital where a professionally trained staff is on call twenty-four hours a day to tend to his physical and emotional weaknesses. This was not, needless to say, an interpretation that occurred to me during my first reading of the novel, or my second, or even my third. But by about the fourth reading—undertaken when I was eighteen or nineteen, and so about as much older than Holden as I had been younger when in Miss Greenwood's class—I did begin to see Holden less as a hero or a kindred spirit than as a pathetic weakling. I remember some feeling of loss when I began to view him in this way, but on the whole I welcomed my changed perception: It seemed to me a more adult perception, and I considered the fact that I could now look down on Holden to be a sign of my own increasing maturity. One of the advantages of middle age, however, is that it often allows us to see how much more wisdom there usually is in even the most callow idealism of adolescence than in the superior "knowingness" of young adulthood. Yes, Holden is defeated by life, at least temporarily, and we don't know what path he will take "after" the end of the novel. He might begin to act on the insight that Mr. Antolini (quoting the psychoanalyst Wilhelm Stekel) tries to convey to him—"The mark of the immature man is that he wants to die nobly for a cause, while the mark of the mature man is that he wants to live humbly for one"—though it is also conceivable that he will gradually abandon his revulsion from phoniness and learn to "adjust" better to the latter. The incontestable point is that Holden's defeat is an honorable one, and honorable defeats are in the scheme of things more valuable than most victories. I think that I was right, at the age of fourteen, to gloss over the pain and weakness in Holden's character, for at that stage of life I probably couldn't have taken the full pressure of those things and still properly appreciated just how right Holden is.

Proust suggests somewhere that the "first edition" of a book ought to mean the edition in which one first happened to read it, and it may seem that I am now advocating a somewhat similar privileging of the first reading, at least insofar as my own first reading of *The Catcher in the Rye* is concerned. Though I do indeed maintain the essential validity of my original pro-Holden and indeed "Holdencentric" interpretation (it is noteworthy that Holden dominates his text as relatively few great characters other than Hamlet and Huck Finn have done), I am not actually proposing an emulation of Peter Pan. Growing up can have its virtues. When I first read the book, I gave little thought to the historical contexts of Holden's character, because for me Holden's "context" was simply life itself, life as I knew it. But as a professional critic and teacher, I now insist that a more specific and rigorous analysis of context can enhance rather than diminish one's appreciation of Holden.

One such context, for example, is the Second World War. As part of the revival of interest in America's last "good war" that has in recent years played such a prominent role in American popular culture, the notion that *The Catcher in the Rye* is in some sense about that war—that it is, as Louis Menand suggested in a fiftieth-anniversary essay published in the *New Yorker*, more a book of the 1940s than the 1950s—has gained a certain currency. It has some biographical plausibility. Like several of his characters—D. B. Caulfield, Seymour Glass, the unnamed American soldier who narrates "For Esmé—with Love and Squalor"—Salinger did serve in the war. He landed on Utah Beach during the fifth hour of the Normandy invasion and in the following months took part in some of the fiercest combat of the twentieth century; his daughter Margaret (author of a fascinating and remarkably even-tempered memoir called *Dream Catcher* [2000]) has said that he was among the first American soldiers to enter a liberated Nazi concentration camp. As a result of his combat experience he suffered something like a nervous breakdown—but only after the German army had surrendered—and, again according to his daughter, has remained forever after possessed by memories of the war and by a sense of his own identity as a soldier. It is often said that the truest and most sincere pacifists are combat veterans, and there may well be a direct connection between Salinger's experience of war at its most ferocious and Holden's description of himself as "a pacifist, if you want to know the truth."

But there are no combat scenes in *The Catcher in the Rye*. A brief mention of D. B.'s military service is the most explicit indication the novel gives that World War II even took place. But perhaps it is the professional writer D. B. who himself supplies the best clue to reading the book as a war novel. Holden well remembers the occasion on which Allie suggests to D. B. that at least one advantage of D. B.'s time in the army must be that it gave him a good deal of material about which to write; D. B. replies by asking Allie to compare Rupert Brooke with Emily Dickinson and then to say who ranks as the greater war poet. The correct answer, as Allie sees at once, is of course Emily Dickinson. If Dickinson is indeed the great poet of the American Civil War—and if, for that matter, Virginia Woolf's *Mrs. Dalloway* (1925), with its unforgettable portrait of Septimus Smith, is one of the great World War I novels—then in much the same way *The Catcher in the*

Rye can be read as a record of the war against Hitler. One way to express the gap between Holden's shrewd perceptions and his pathetic inability to act effectively is to say that he (again like Hamlet) just takes everything a little too hard. Wealthy and privileged as his background may be, Holden's world is every bit as bad as he says it is; but nothing plainly in it, not even Allie's death from leukemia, *quite* accounts for the extreme degree of pain and loneliness and psychic dislocation that often seems to lie just beyond Holden's awesome powers of self-expression. Life appears to have a kind of wrongness for Holden that neither he nor Salinger can ever completely verbalize, and it may be that this wrongness is finally to be identified with the inexpressible barbarism of the Second World War.

Doubtless what is at issue here is not only the war in general but the Holocaust in particular, and at this point a war-centered reading of the novel may shade into an ethnic one. Again biography seems pertinent. Salinger's own ethnic make-up—of Jewish background on his father's side and Irish Catholic background on his mother's, just like the seven Glass children—was pretty unusual in his generation, and he is said to have felt severely dislocated by his mixed heritage, especially as regards his being, yet not being, Jewish. One can easily understand that, under these circumstances—and especially given the fact that during the 1920s, the 1930s, and well into the 1940s, anti-Semitism existed in the United States at levels that are practically unimaginable today—the annihilation of European Jewry was bound to be a deeply complex and traumatic event for him, especially after seeing some of the machinery of extermination with his own eyes: "You never really get the smell of burning flesh out of your nose entirely, no matter how long you live," he told Margaret. A further complexity was that he evidently had a tense, distant relationship with his father (who vainly wished that young Jerry would join the family business, a prosperous firm that imported kosher meats and cheeses), but a warm, loving one with his mother, to whom *The Catcher in the Rye* is dedicated: a situation perhaps reflected in Salinger's giving Holden an Irish surname and a home address not on the (stereotypically Jewish) Upper West Side of Manhattan, where he himself was raised, but on the (stereotypically Gentile) East Side—while also, however, supplying a note of Jewishness in the name of the Caulfields' next-door neighbors, the Dicksteins.

The context of war and ethnicity—the two categories intimately and complexly linked by the mediating term of the Holocaust—thus enters the novel as a determinate absence. We do not get overt scenes of combat or extermination, but instead something like the negative imprint of the unspeakable physical violence visited upon the world during the decade or so prior to 1951, the period during which Salinger worked, on and off, toward the completion of his novel. This context may well illuminate Holden's sadness and mental instability, though it hardly says much about his intelligence and sensitivity. Another context, however, and one that illuminates both these sides of his character, is presented far more explicitly: the context of class relations under capitalism, which constitute a different kind of violence.

Though Holden is constantly talking about the injuries of class, this dimension of the book has been astonishingly—or maybe not so astonishingly—ignored by journalistic and academic Salinger critics, as Richard and Carol Ohmann show in "A Case Study in Canon Formation: Reviewers, Critics, and *The Catcher in the Rye*" (perhaps the single most perceptive critical treatment of the novel to date, at least insofar as my own—fairly extensive though far from exhaustive—reading of the secondary literature goes). Class, of course, has been the great taboo subject in American discourse for more than half a century, a taboo so strong that it extends, to some degree, even into the overtly "progressive" circles of institutionalized cultural studies, where elaborate attention to race and gender is taken for granted. Still, it seems extraordinary that Salinger criticism has been able so thoroughly to erase a subject with which Salinger himself deals so overtly and so often.

Consider, for instance, Mr. Haas, the headmaster at Holden's old prep school Elkton Hills, who bears the remarkable distinction of being, in Holden's opinion, "the phoniest bastard I ever met in my life." Mr. Haas's general practice is to ingratiate himself as much as possible with the parents of his pupils, and he normally turns on as much charm as he can. But he does make exceptions:

> I mean if a boy's mother was sort of fat or corny-looking or something, and if somebody's father was one of those guys that wear those suits with very big shoulders and corny black-and-white shoes, then old Haas would just shake hands with them and give them a phony smile and then he'd go talk, for maybe a half an *hour*, with somebody else's parents. I can't stand that stuff. It drives me crazy. It makes me so depressed I go crazy.

Holden understands that, in the American upper bourgeoisie at the middle of the twentieth century, a fashionable suit and pair of shoes are *de rigueur* for a man, as a trim, elegant body is for a woman. He understands, too, that Haas cares nothing for his pupils or their parents as individuals: He is interested only in toadying up to those who unambiguously appear to be members in good standing of the class with which he identifies and toward which, probably, he aspires. Or consider—again—the successful businessman Ossenburger, who has amassed a fortune through a chain of cut-rate mortuaries ("these undertaking parlors all over the country that you could get members of your family buried for about five bucks apiece"). Holden has not, perhaps, read his Max Weber as carefully as he might have, and so fails to remark that Ossenburger's speech suggests the links between capitalist acquisitiveness and Protestant spirituality as clearly as any Weberian sociologist could wish. But he does plainly see that Ossenburger is considered important enough at Pencey to rate a cheer at the football game and a speech in the chapel simply and solely because of his ability to throw large sums of money around: "[H]e gave Pencey a pile of dough, and they named our wing after him." Holden also possesses a shrewd sense of the routine fraudulence that so typically underlies capitalist success in modern America: "You should see old Ossenburger.

He probably just shoves them [i.e., the remains of his customers] in a sack and dumps them in the river."

Haas and Ossenburger, then, are especially odious because of the relative purity, so to speak, with which they incarnate the market-based relations of the capitalist class structure. Conversely, the nuns that Holden meets at the sandwich bar are admirable not so much for their religious vocation (Holden admits to being "sort of an atheist"), but because they have chosen to live outside the class system to the maximum extent feasible. It is not merely that they spend their lives teaching school and collecting money for charity. Holden, after all, has known plenty of phony teachers, and charity can be practiced by those of his own high-bourgeois background—his mother, for instance, and his aunt (who is "pretty charitable—she does a lot of Red Cross work and all"), and Sally Hayes's mother—but when such women perform good works it is with no renunciation, or even qualification, of their privileged place in the socioeconomic hierarchy. Holden's aunt may help out the Red Cross, but "when she does anything charitable she's always very well-dressed and has lipstick on and all that crap. I couldn't picture her doing anything for charity if she had to wear black clothes and no lipstick while she was doing it"—that is, if she had to abandon, even temporarily, the uniform of her class position. As for Sally's mother, she (like her daughter) craves attention as a spoiled child does, and "[t]he only way *she* could go around with a basket collecting dough would be if everybody kissed her ass for her when they made a contribution." Otherwise, "[s]he'd get bored. She would hand in her basket and then go someplace swanky for lunch." But the nuns are genuinely different: "That's what I liked about those nuns. You could tell, for one thing, that they never went anywhere swanky for lunch." Holden immediately adds that he is saddened by the nuns' inability to enjoy the swankiness that is routine for his own people—he does not sentimentalize the poverty they have chosen—but at the same time their integrity remains an inspiration in a world so heavily populated by those obsessed with scrambling up, or staying on top of, the class ladder.

Even before striking up a conversation with the nuns (who turn out to be moving from a convent in Chicago to one in New York), Holden notices that they have with them a pair of cheap suitcases, "the ones that aren't genuine leather or anything," and this observation provokes what is perhaps the most remarkable meditation on class in the novel. Holden thinks back to his roommate at Elkton Hills, Dick Slagle, who, like the nuns, had cheap suitcases, whereas Holden's own "came from Mark Cross, and they were genuine cowhide and all that crap, and I guess they cost quite a pretty penny." Holden finds Dick to be smart and funny, and the two are capable of having a good time together. But their relationship is soon poisoned by class. Dick is resentful and envious of the superior class position that the Mark Cross suitcases symbolize: He ridicules Holden suitcases as "bourgeois" (an adjective he then extends to Holden's fountain pen and other possessions) while also pretending to other people that the Mark Cross suitcases really belong to him. Holden is baffled as to what to do. He tries stuffing his suitcases out of sight under his bed, and is perfectly willing to throw them away or even to trade suitcases with Dick, if doing so will save the friendship. But nothing avails, and within two months both boys ask to be moved. Holden sadly sums up the lesson:

> The thing is, it's really hard to be roommates with people if your suitcases are much better than theirs—if yours are really *good* ones and theirs aren't. You think if they're intelligent and all, the other person, and have a good sense of humor, that they don't give a damn whose suitcases are better, but they do. They really do. It's one of the reasons why I roomed with a stupid bastard like Stradlater. At least his suitcases were as good as mine.

On personal grounds, Holden likes and admires Dick, and despises Stradlater, but such purely personal factors are finally less powerful than the social realities of class.

So the reality Holden confronts—the reality whose phoniness he so acutely diagnoses—is not "the human condition" or "the pains of adolescence" or any of the other ahistorical clichés that have dominated Salinger criticism; it is, rather, the specific historical conjuncture of a particular time and place. What I find especially remarkable—and this is a point that even the Ohmanns, to whose excellent analysis I am much indebted, do not, I think, sufficiently emphasize—is the extent to which Holden, while perched near the top of capitalist America's class hierarchy, is nonetheless capable of understanding how much misery class relations cause. *The Catcher in the Rye* is about as far from being a proletarian novel as a novel can be, and it would sound odd to describe Salinger as a political writer. But the novel demonstrates that the standpoint of the proletariat is not the only one from which the injustices of capitalism can be glimpsed, and Holden's situation irresistibly suggests an impeccably Marxist point: namely, that any comprehensive system of oppression corrupts the quality of life for *everyone*, even for those who materially gain the most from it. In the eighth grade, of course, I was hardly capable of constructing a class analysis of a work of literature—though I strongly suspect (especially in view of Miss Greenwood's evident prescience as regards my political tendencies) that the sheer *rootedness* of Holden's outlook, the historical concreteness of his insights, did subliminally contribute to my spontaneous sense that Holden saw things as they really were. In any case, today this concreteness helps to confirm my sense that I was always justified in seeing Holden as simply right, and, though in chronological age he is only a few years older than my own daughter is now, there are important ways in which he remains for me a kindred spirit and even a hero. Miss Greenwood was clearly a far-seeing teacher—but could she have guessed anything like the actual impact on me of being introduced to J. D. Salinger?

And what, you may ask, became of Miss Greenwood herself? I have almost no idea. Not long after she taught me, she got married—becoming, after the all-but-universal fashion of the time, Mrs. Walker—and soon after that she left the school, probably because she and her new husband moved out of town. She is most likely a grandmother today—yet another staggering thought. I am tempted to try to get in touch with her, though it is not clear to me that this is feasible. How much, after all, do I have to go on? One possible—and very common—first name, two common Anglo-Saxon surnames, and the certain knowledge that, for a brief time in the mid-1960s, she taught English at Leroy Martin Junior High School in Raleigh, North Carolina. The evidence is scant, and the trail very cold. Still, I suppose a professional detective could do the job, and, given the resources of the telephone and the Internet, even an amateur might have a reasonable shot. But, beyond the question of whether the thing could be done, there is also the question of whether it would be a good idea. Such reunions sometimes produce much pleasure and even joy—such, indeed, has been my own personal experience—but one hears that sometimes they yield little but disappointment and embarrassment. It is possible that, in the aging grandmother I now imagine Miss Greenwood to be, I would plainly see traces of the skinny kid just out of college who once so enchanted my much younger self. But it is also possible that her whole manner and personality would seem utterly different and unfamiliar to me, whether because of actual changes in her, or because of flaws in my adolescent perceptions of more than three and a half decades ago, or because of the tricks that memory can play. Perhaps she would not even remember me except after detailed prompting, or—most humiliating possibility of all—not even *with* such prompting. So I remain undecided about trying to see Miss Greenwood again. One of the most startling and disconcerting things about living in a world with other human beings is the thousand and one ways they have of turning out to be different from what one had thought or assumed or expected or remembered them to be. The Miss Greenwood of this memoir may or may not (still) exist. But—and this is, of course, one of the most magical things about art—I am quite certain that for me Holden Caulfield will always, *always*, be there.

From *The Southern Review* 39.2 (2003): 401-417. Copyright © 2003 by Carl Freedman. Reprinted with permission of Carl Freedman.

J. D. Salinger, Novelist of
Modern Anomie, Dead at 91
Tom Teicholz

J. D. Salinger, the novelist whose *Catcher in the Rye* was the gateway drug for a generation of teenagers, readers and writers resisting the social conformity, and who became almost as famous for being reclusive as he was for his novel and his collections of short stories, died at his home in New Hampshire, at 91. He last published in 1965; Salinger claimed that he continued to write and would no longer be published during his lifetime.

With Salinger's death, the literary world awaits to find out, after more than 50 years of waiting, whether in fact Salinger left completed work—stories, novels, even poems—and whether it is coherent and intelligible, interesting or out-of-date—whether any of it is good, or even perhaps, great.

In *Catcher in the Rye* he created a teenage character who spoke the feelings of teenagers of all ages, in decrying the behavior of "phonies." In his subsequent short story collections, *Franny and Zooey* and *Raise High the Roof Beam, Carpenters*, Salinger described characters at odds with themselves—and though many readers found them plain odd, they found them compelling. *The Catcher in the Rye* remains one of the perennial best-selling novels, read in schools across the country and the globe, holding a special place on the bookshelves of many. But Salinger's last published stories, increasingly influenced by Salinger's own experiments in Eastern thinking, give one pause about what direction his unpublished writing may have taken. Hopefully we will know soon.

After Mark David Chapman murdered John Lennon, he was found with a copy of *Catcher in the Rye*, and various writers and filmmakers have expounded on the connections between the two. Readers formed great attachment to *Catcher in the Rye*, and perhaps this as much as anything was reason for Salinger to remove himself from society and live as a recluse in New Hampshire.

Born Jerome David Salinger in New York City in 1919, his father Sol worked in the food industry. One of the accounts I read online claims that Salinger's mother was born Marie but called herself Miriam, and it was only after his Bar Mitzvah that Salinger discovered that she was not in fact Jewish.

Salinger attended several schools in New York, including McBurney, before attending Valley Forge Military Academy, and several colleges, including New York University and Columbia University's evening program, where he attended a writing class taught by Whit Burnett of *Story* magazine, who would publish some of his early work.

In 1941 *The New Yorker* magazine accepted "Slight Rebellion off Madison," a short story featuring a character named Holden Caulfield.

At that time, Salinger also courted Oona O'Neil, playwright Eugene O'Neil's daughter, who was a teenager at the time—she would eventually marry Charlie Chaplin. The courtship is mentioned in Aram Saroyan's "Trio," his account of the young lives of Oona O'Neil, Gloria Vanderbilt, and Carol Matthau (Saroyan's mother).

It is also reported that around that time Salinger worked on a cruise ship, and perhaps performed on board.

Salinger served in World War Two, landing in France on D-Day and fighting in the Battle of the Bulge. While in France, he met Ernest Hemingway, who impressed Salinger and who was in turn impressed by Salinger's writing—they began a correspondence. Salinger also served in a Counter-Intelligence Unit that interrogated prisoners of war, and he was among the first soldiers to enter a recently liberated concentration camp. Shortly thereafter, Salinger reportedly had a nervous breakdown and was hospitalized for combat-related stress in an Army hospital.

Upon his return to the States, Salinger continued to write short stories. "A Perfect Day for Bananafish" was published in *The New Yorker* and established Salinger as an important contemporary writer. At the same time, Salinger became interested in Buddhism and various variants of Eastern religions and religious practices, which he would continue to explore the rest of his life.

With the publication of *Catcher in the Rye*, Salinger, who was living in Westport, Connecticut, moved with his then wife Claire to Cornish, New Hampshire, which continued to be his residence until his death. Salinger had two children, Margaret and Matt, who survive him.

Salinger continued to publish stories in *The New Yorker*, many of them about the Glass family, until 1965, with "Hapworth 16, 1924," his last published story. After that Salinger claimed that he continued to write but would no longer publish during his lifetime.

At first, Salinger gave interviews to the local paper and high school but he stopped that after a certain time. For a while, journalists would take it upon themselves to travel to Cornish and wait in town for Salinger to pick up his mail and then try and strike up a conversation. Salinger gave his last interview in 1980.

Over the last many decades several persons have written memoirs of knowing Salinger. These include his daughter Margaret and the writer Joyce Maynard, who dated Salinger as a teenager.

Salinger was protective of his life and his work and over the years sued to block publications, biographies, and unauthorized collections of his short stories, or works too closely inspired by his own.

My own Salinger experiences begin with *Catcher in the Rye*, one of four books a bookstore clerk insisted I needed to read, as a teenager, to educate myself (the other three were Aldous Huxley's *Brave New World*, George Orwell's *1984*, and Richard Farina's *Been Down So Long*)—and yes, I became attached to the book. Whenever I had a swimming meet against the McBurney School I thought of Salinger and his description of his fencing team adventure in *Catcher*. And when we thought of where to meet near Grand Central, we thought of the clock in the Vanderbilt Hotel.

When the *New York Times Magazine* placed Joyce Maynard on its cover, I was not alone in developing a crush and felt validated in my attraction when it was reported that she had begun an affair with J. D.

Salinger. The fact that Salinger was so much older didn't matter—the creator of Holden was, no doubt, in touch with his inner teenager.

A few years later, I learned that a friend of mine's high school girlfriend had also had a relationship with Salinger which had developed by correspondence. According to the gossip, third hand, Salinger loved to come to New York, much like any tourist, and have tea at the Plaza, see a show and visit friends at the *New Yorker* and in the city—by being a recluse, he had created anonymity for himself in New York—no one knew what he looked like, and no one recognized him.

One summer in the mid-1970s I found myself in the Catalyst bookstore in Santa Cruz. There on the counter by the cash register were two paperbacks, *The Uncollected Stories of J. D. Salinger*, volumes 1 and 2. Someone had taken all the stories that Salinger had published over the years in magazines that remained uncollected and published them. I remember holding them in my hands and poring over them, looking at stories I had never heard of. Shortly thereafter, Salinger sued to halt what the publishers called a "samizdat publication"—and those copies were not seen again.

Matt, Salinger's son, is an actor and producer who has lived for many years in LA—I don't know if he still does—I met him once (possibly twice)—he seemed nice and very unaffected. Given that his father wanted at some point to be an actor and/or entertainer, perhaps his father found some pleasure in his son being a working actor who would turn up on TV programs with some regularity. In any event, please accept our condolences on your loss.

Although Salinger had one of his early stories optioned for film, the way in which his work was mangled for the screen convinced him to never again option anything. Joyce Maynard once commented that the only one who could ever have played Holden was Salinger himself.

Holden is dead. Long Live Holden.

From *Jewish Journal* 28 January 2010. Copyright © 2010 by Tom Teicholz. Reprinted with permission of Tom Teicholz.

J. D. Salinger
Adam Gopnik

J. D. Salinger's long silence, and his withdrawal from the world, attracted more than the usual degree of gossip and resentment—as though we readers were somehow owed more than his words, were somehow owed his personal, talk-show presence, too—and fed the myth of the author as homespun religious mystic. Yet though he may seem to have chosen a hermit's life, Salinger was no hermit on the page. And so his death throws us back from the myth to the magical world of his writing as it really is, with its matchless comedy, its ear for American speech, its contagious ardor and incomparable charm. Salinger's voice—which illuminated and enlivened these pages for two decades—remade American writing in the fifties and sixties in a way that no one had since Hemingway. (The juvenilia of most American writers since bear the mark of one or the other.) But if it had been Hemingway's role to make American writing hardboiled, it was Salinger's to let it be soft, even runny, again.

"For Esmé—with Love and Squalor," which appeared here in the issue of April 8, 1950, is an account of the horror and battle shock of the Second World War—which the young Salinger fought during some of its worst days and battles—only to end, amazingly, with the offer of an antidote: the simple, direct, and uncorrupted speech that young Esmé's letter holds out to the no longer entirely broken narrator. It was the comedy, the overt soulfulness, the high-hearted (to use an adjective he liked) romantic openness of the early Salinger stories that came as such a revelation to readers. The shine of Fitzgerald and the sound of Ring Lardner haunted these pages, but it was Salinger's readiness to be touched, and to be touching, his hypersensitivity to the smallest sounds and graces of life, which still startles. Suicides and strange deaths happen in his stories—one shattering story is devoted to the back and forth on the telephone between a betrayed husband and the man in bed with his wife at that very moment—but their tone is alive with an appetite for experience as it is, and the certainty that religious epiphanies will arise from such ordinary experience. A typical Salinger hero is the little boy who confuses "kike" with "kite," in "Down at the Dinghy"—who thinks that his father has been maliciously compared to "one of those things that go up in the air. . . . With string you hold."

Salinger was an expansive romantic, an observer of the details of the world, and of New York in particular; no book has ever captured a city better than "The Catcher in the Rye" captured New York in the forties. Has any writer ever had a better ear for American talk? (One thinks of the man occupying the seat behind Holden Caulfield at Radio City Music Hall, who, watching the Rockettes, keeps saying to his wife, "You know what that is? That's precision.") A self-enclosed writer doesn't listen, and Salinger was a peerless listener: page after page of pure talk flowed out of him, moving and true and, above all, funny. He was a humorist with a heart before he was a mystic with a vision, or, rather, the vision flowed from the humor. That was the final almost-moral of "Zooey," the almost-final Salinger story to appear in these pages: Seymour's Fat Lady, who gives art its audience, is all of us.

As for Holden Caulfield, he is so much a part of the lives of his readers that he is more a person to phone up than a character to analyze. A "Catcher" lover in his forties handed Holden's Christmas journey to his own twelve-year-old son a few years ago, filled with trepidation that time and manners would have changed too much for it to still matter. Not a bit—the boy grasped it to his heart as his father had, as the Rough Guide to his experience, and used its last lines as his yearbook motto. In American writing, there are three perfect books, which seem to speak to every reader and condition: "Huckleberry Finn," "The Great Gatsby," and "The Catcher in the Rye." Of the three, only "Catcher" defines an entire region of human experience: it is—in French and Dutch as much as in English—the handbook of the adolescent heart. But the Glass family saga that followed is the larger accomplishment. Salinger's retreat into that family had its unreality—no family of Jewish intellectual children actually spoke quite like this, or revered one of the members quite so uncritically—but its central concern is universal. The golden thread that runs through it is the question of Seymour's suicide, so shockingly rendered in "A Perfect Day for Bananafish." How, amid so much joyful experience, could life become so intolerable to the one figure who seems to be its master?

Critics fretted about the growing self-enclosure of Salinger's work, about a faith in his characters' importance that sometimes seemed to make a religion of them. But the isolation of his later decades should not be allowed to obscure his essential gift for joy. The message of his writing was always the same: that, amid the malice and falseness of social life, redemption rises from clear speech and childlike enchantment, from all the forms of unself-conscious innocence that still surround us (with the hovering unease that one might mistake emptiness for innocence, as Seymour seems to have done with his Muriel). It resides in the particular things that he delighted to record. In memory, his writing is a catalogue of those moments: Esmé's letter and her broken watch; and the little girl with the dachshund that leaps up on Park Avenue, in "Zooey"; and the record of "Little Shirley Beans" that Holden buys for Phoebe (and then sees break on the pavement); and Phoebe's coat spinning on the carrousel at twilight in the December light of Central Park; and the Easter chick left in the wastebasket at the end of "Just Before the War with the Eskimos"; and Buddy, at the magic twilight hour in New York, after learning from Seymour how to play Zen marbles ("Could you try not aiming so much?"), running to get Louis Sherry ice cream, only to be overtaken by his brother; and the small girl on the plane who turns her doll's head around to look at Seymour. That these things were not in themselves quite enough to hold Seymour on this planet—or enough, it seems, at times, to hold his creator entirely here, either—does not diminish the beauty of their realization. In "Seymour: An Introduction," Seymour, thinking of van Gogh, tells Buddy that the only question worth asking about a writer is "Were most of your stars out?" Writing, real writing, is done not from some seat of fussy moral judgment but with the eye and ear and heart; no American writer will ever have a more alert ear, a more attentive eye, or a more ardent heart than his.

Originally published in *The New Yorker*, 8 February 2010, pp. 20-21. Copyright © 2010 by Condé Nast Publications. Reprinted with permission of Condé Nast Publications.

"Holden Caulfield in Doc Martens":
The Catcher in the Rye and *My So-Called Life*
Barbara Bell

> If you really want to hear about it, the first thing you'll probably want to know is where I was born, and what my lousy childhood was like, and how my parents were occupied and all before they had me, and all that David Copperfield kind of crap, but I don't really feel like going into it, if you want to know the truth.
>
> (Salinger 1)

These lines opening J.D. Salinger's *The Catcher in the Rye* are expressed by his 16-year-old protagonist and narrator, Holden Caulfield, who indeed **does** go into it. First published in 1951, Salinger's novel communicates the confusion and chaos of adolescence in the late 1940's. "In *Catcher*," claims Joel Salzberg, ". . . Salinger . . . capture[s] the image, the imagination, and the emotions of an urban American adolescent in his time and place, as no one else before or since . . ." (17). However, Salzberg made this comment in 1990, four years before Angela Chase was introduced to American television audiences:

> So I started hanging out with Rayanne Graff. Just for fun. Just 'cause it seemed like if I didn't, I would die or something. Things were getting to me. Just how people are. How they always expect you to be a certain way, even your best friend . . . School is a battlefield for your heart. So when Rayanne Graff told me my hair was holding me beck, I had to listen. 'Cause she wasn't just talking about my hair. She was talking about any life. (*My So-Called Life*)

And so begins the pilot episode of *My So-Called Life*, a dramatic series produced by *thirtysomething* creators Marshall Herskovitz and Edward Zwick that explores the aforementioned life of 15-year-old Angela Chase. When the show made its debut in the fall of 1994, several reviewers alluded to its Salingeresque nature. Matt Zoller Seitz claimed that "[t]he spirit of Holden Caulfield lives on" (34) through the series, while Harry F. Waters referred to Angela as "a kind of Holden Caulfield in Doc Martens" (68). These writers made their observations after reviewing only the first few episodes of the series. Nineteen episodes later, however, these first impressions prove to be accurate in a variety of ways. Both the novel and the series make use of realistic language, a first person and often unreliable narrator, and similar thematic concerns.

When *Catcher* was first published, many reviews referred to Salinger's accurate rendering of teenage colloquial speech. For example, Harrison Smith writes "[t]he magic of this novel does not depend on this boy's horrifying experience but on the authenticity of the language he uses and the emotions and memories which overwhelm him" (29). In Donald Costello's comprehensive linguistic study (published in 1959), he draws attention to *Catcher* as "an example of teenage vernacular in the 1950's" (44). It is this kind of verisimilitude writer Winnie Holzman was seeking in her *MSCL* scripts. She even took a teaching position in a suburban Los Angeles high school so that she could "research" the language and subject matter (Waters 68). The other *MSCL* writers took her cue, prompting one reviewer's observation that "[t]he dialogue and mannerisms are probably as close as one can get to bringing the sensibility of that age (Generation Y?) to a network show" (Martin 24).

One reason the characters on *MSCL* sound so authentic is because the writers have a keen ear for spoken teenage dialogue. Thus the scripts are full of awkwardly constructed sentences, sentence fragments, run-ons and false starts—dialogue that would be impossible to diagram, but that sounds realistic when spoken:

> There's this thing at this coffee house Vertigo, and, like, I promised Rayanne I would ask you if I could go, but I don't even really want to go, and I feel so guilty. See, she's singing with this band—all right, fine, it's

Jordan Catalano's band, but this had nothing to do with Jordan, or the fact that we broke up, or anything, that's what's so weird. It's this thing between Rayanne and me I can't even describe that's there, and it's been there for, like, a while. Since that night when you had to drive her to the hospital? It's this thing we never talk about. (Angela to her parents)

This type of structure, of course, is to be expected from scripted dialogue that's meant to be spoken; it's much harder to pull off in written speech. But several critics have commented on how Holden Caulfield's written narrative "offers us the 'sound' and flavor of Holden talking" (Cowan 37). Costello argues that "[t]he structure of Holden's sentences indicates that Salinger thinks of the book more in terms of spoken speech than written speech" (51). For instance, Holden explains his decision to go to New York this way: "So what I decided to do, I decided I'd take a room in a hotel in New York—some very inexpensive hotel and all—and just take it easy till Wednesday" (Salinger 51). Thus Salinger's style seems to place us in the same room with Holden where we can almost hear him telling us about that "madman stuff" that happened last Christmas (1).

Within the overall speech-like structure of *Catcher* are elements of Holden's vocabulary and grammar that reflect the typical teenage speech habits of his contemporaries. For example, throughout the novel Holden uses the phrases "and all," "or something," "or anything" to provide "a sense of looseness of expression . . . and thought" (Costello 45). These phrases suggest that Holden could expand on the subject, but isn't going to bother:

> I wasn't supposed to come back after Christmas vacation, on account of I was flunking four subjects and not applying myself *and all*. (Salinger 4)

> I like to be somewhere at least where you can see a few girls around once in a while, even if they're only scratching their arms or blowing their noses or even just giggling *or something*. (3)

... he hardly ever got up to recite or go to the blackboard *or anything*. (171)

Almost 50 years later, Angela Chase and her friends follow Holden's lead:

> It seems like some people have to die young. Like it fits them *or something*.

> Not that I'd attack him *or anything*, but I wouldn't leave me alone with him either.

> I know this is your house *and all*.

Plus, the *MSCL* teenagers have added the phrase "or whatever" to serve the same function:

> Today I tried to explain to her that I'm sorry—*or whatever*.

> I have to write a paragraph, *or whatever*, about that bug guy.

This teenage propensity to repeat favorite phrases and avoid elaborating on a topic also is seen on *MSCL* in the repetitive use of "thing" preceded by a variety of modifiers:

> a very guy thing to do

> this fashion thing
> the whole holiday basket thing
> that extra credit thing
> this hair flick thing
> this video thing

So when Rayanne mentions "this gun thing," she's actually referring to an in-school shooting incident that has scared students and angered parents. And when Brian mentions "this Delia thing," he's alluding to a new student who has a crush on him, and to the fact that he has no idea about how to handle the situation.

Costello discusses another typical tendency of 1950's teenage vernacular that can be found in *MSCL* as well: "constant repetition of a few favorite words . . . with little regard to specific meaning" (49). Take, for example, an adjective that is overused in both the novel and the series: "stupid." Although the characters occasionally may use this term to mean "ignorant," more often the literal meaning of the word has nothing to do with the noun it modifies. Instead, this word choice is usually indicative of the speaker's irritable mood:

I was sitting on his *stupid* towel. (Salinger 31)

. . . especially on top of that *stupid* hill. (4)

Here's her *stupid* backpack. (*MSCL*)

. . . one *stupid* gunshot. (*MSCL*)

. . . some *stupid* band. (*MSCL*)

. . . this *stupid* play. (*MSCL*)

Holden, Angela and company also violate a number of grammatical rules, a teenage tendency that seems to traverse the 50 year gap. For example, both are careless about correct pronoun use:

I think I probably woke *he* and his wife up. (Salinger 174)

My dad thinks every person in the world is having more fun than *him*. (*MSCL*)

Whereas Holden's "most common rule violation is the misuse of 'lie' and 'lay'" (Costello 51), the *MSCL* teens have regular adverb problems:

I can sing as *loud* and *obnoxious* as Tino.

Maybe if you'd dress more *normal*.

She took your hair *real calm*.

You have to wash the pants *separate*.

What's more interesting than these predictable grammatical gaffes, however, is how these teenagers creatively manipulate language to serve their linguistic needs. Specifically, they often adapt a word normally used as a particular part of speech to function as a different part. For example, Holden tends to turn nouns into adjectives by simply adding a -y: "perverty," "Christmassy," "pimpy," "show-offy," "vomity" (Costello 49-50). His 1990's counterparts take this process a bit further by turning a modified noun into an adjective:

. . . her *Popular Jock* phase.

. . . her *Awkward But Sensitive Guy* phase.

You can figure out some clever *Chess Club* way to get in.

Holden can even use nouns as adverbs—"She sings it very *Dixieland* and *whorehouse* . . ." (114-15)—while Angela can turn a noun into a verb ("It was the perfect moment for him to kiss me, to *anything* me"). And sometimes Angela and her friends simply invent their own words by adding a prefix to existing words: "unfunny," "non-shockable," and "non-unusual."

One of the most noticeable (and sometimes annoying) ways that *MSCL* accurately reflects the colloquial speech of the 1990's teenager is through the characters' nonstandard use of "like" (<u>not</u> meaning "similar to" or "approximately"):

What I, *like*, dread is when people who know you in completely different ways end up in the same area. You have to develop this, *like*, combination you on the spot.

Although this word seems to be peppered randomly and thoughtlessly throughout the characters' speech, Robert Underhill argues that the syntax and pragmatics of nonstandard *like* "is closely rule-governed" (243). Specifically, it "functions with great reliability as a marker of new information and focus" (234). In other words, the intrusive *like* focuses on the most important part of the sentence (238):

> Seeing a teacher's actual lunch is, *like*, so depressing.
>
> Sometimes I feel, *like*, numb or something.
>
> But when you're yearbook photographer, you're, *like*, never in the picture.

This is especially true when *like* is used in questions (239):

> So, you believe in, *like*, evil spirits?
>
> Did you ever try to protect someone so much that it, *like*, hurt?
>
> You know how sometimes the last sentence you said, *like*, echoes in your brain?

Additionally, *like* can be used to set off unusual and unbelievable notions (241):

> Maybe teachers have a hidden life, where they're actually, *like*, human.
>
> He was, *like*, making her beg for her shoe!

Mine are probably getting a citation for, *like*, best penmanship on a tax return or something.

Ironically, Underhill (in 1988) notes that he doesn't hear *like* as much as he used to, and he suggests that it may be becoming "archaic" (234). However, a cursory review of *MSCL* dialogue should indicate that he needn't worry!

Angela and her friends also use a nonstandard language construction to introduce dialogue—"be + like" (as opposed to "say" or "go"):

> I *was like*, "Hi," and he *was like*, "Hi."

Several linguistic studies of this feature (including one I co-authored with Kathleen Ferrara) demonstrate how widespread this variable is among teenage speakers. One reason we believe this variable is growing in popularity with teenagers is because of its flexibility—for example, it can introduce internal dialogue as well as actual speech. Here Jordan recalls a conversation he's had with Ricki:

> *He's like*, "I'm gonna light a candle for you," (speech) and *I'm like*, "Don't waste your match" (thought).

In both the series and the novel, the teenagers employ different figures of speech. For example, they make regular use of hyperbole to heighten the dramatic effect of a situation. In many cases, the exaggerated feature is a number. For example, Brian says he "thought about it for, like, 50 hours," Rayanne makes an offhand comment that "there's, like, 50 guns at school at any given moment," and a stressed Sharon complains that she has "two million presents to wrap" and "50,000 social events" she agreed to attend. Similarly, Holden claims that Pencey Prep advertises "in about a thousand magazines" (Salinger 2), an alumnus made a speech that started with "about 50 corny jokes" and lasted "about 10 hours" (16), and it takes Ackley "about five hours" (36) to get ready to go out.

Although this type of exaggeration is typical, it's hardly original. However, the characters' use of simile and metaphor is often witty, inspired and even funny. For example, Holden observes that Mr. Spencer handles his "exam paper like it was a turd or something" (11) and "[t]hat guy Morrow was about as sensitive as a goddam toilet seat" (55). When Rayanne tells Angela that her dad is attractive, Angela remarks, "When someone compliments your parents, there's, like, nothing to say. It's like a stun gun to your brain." In another scene, the camera surveys the school lunch room, eventually focusing on an unsuspecting Brian as his lunch tray is overturned by an 18-year-old thug. Angela's voice-over explains: "Cafeteria is the embarrassment capital of the world. It's like a prison movie." And when she and her classmates are taken on an obligatory field trip to a museum, Angela notes that "[f]ield trips are so intense. It's like everybody's been let out of their cages or something, and we're all roaming around."

These quotes also illustrate another similarity between the novel and the series: both make interesting use of a first-person narrator. Holden narrates *Catcher* from what seems to be a psychiatric hospital in California, after his adventures in New York and subsequent breakdown: "I'll just tell you about this madman stuff that happened to me around last Christmas just before I got pretty run-down and had to come out here and take it easy" (1). On *MSCL*, Angela's voice-overs narrate and provide commentary about what's happening on screen.

In many instances, both Holden and Angela make observations that are insightful and accurate. For instance, Holden comments on the character of a woman who cries during a sentimental movie:

> You'd have thought she did it because she was kindhearted as hell, but I was sitting right next to her, and she wasn't. She had this little kid with her that was bored as hell and had to go to the bathroom, but she wouldn't take him. She kept telling him to sit still and behave himself. She was about as kindhearted as a goddam wolf. (139-40)

Here Holden's insight "sharply exposes the contradiction in [the woman's] behavior" (Shaw 108). At the end of an episode in which Angela struggles with her appearance and stereotypical notions of beauty, she makes this observation:

> Sometimes it seems like we're all living in some kind of prison, and the crime is how much we all hate ourselves. It's good to get really dressed up once in a while and admit the truth—that when you really look closely, people are so strange and so complicated that they're actually beautiful. Possibly even me.

Thus Angela begins to understand the difference between internal and external standards of beauty, and her conclusion rings true.

More typical, however, are those instances in which the narrator's observations are inaccurate and completely unreliable. When Anne Goodman reviewed *Catcher* in 1951, she remarked that "this reader at least suffered from an irritated feeling that Holden was not quite so sensitive and perceptive as he . . . thought he was" (24). Since then many critics have called attention to Holden's "mutually inconsistent opinions, the gaps between his professed values and his behavior, and his uneven insight into his own behavior" (Cowan 43).

For example, throughout the novel Holden expresses contempt for the movies with comments like:

> If there's one thing I hate, it's the movies. Don't even mention them to me. (2)

> I hate the movies like poison . . . (29)

For someone who hates movies, however, Holden has seen his fair share. He's familiar enough with musicals to imitate them for Stradlater (29), plus he's able to describe in amazing detail the movie he saw at Radio City ("It was so putrid I couldn't take my eyes off it," he protests—perhaps too much). Holden also claims that "I never care too much when I lose something" (89), but this assertion falls flat as well. It's obvious to the reader that losing his brother, Allie, to leukemia has affected Holden deeply. He explains how he broke all the windows in the garage with his fist on the night Allie died (39). Since then, Allie has become the standard against which Holden evaluates those he comes in contact with: "'Just because somebody's dead,'" Holden tells Phoebe, "'you don't stop liking them . . . especially if they were about a thousand times nicer than the people you know that're *alive* and all . . .'" (171). And when Holden is lonely, depressed and near the breaking point, he talks to Allie, repeating, "'Allie, don't let me disappear'" (198).

Viewers must take many of Angela's observations with the same grain of salt. Matt Zoller Seitz asserts that *MSCL* "showcases the most sophisticated use of the unreliable narrator ever seen in network drama," and that "[t]he gap between appearance and reality . . . has rarely been detailed . . . so sharply" (34). He suggests that in order to discover the Truth, viewers must consider the opposites of Angela's thoughts (34).

Consider Angela's evaluation of Jordan, for whom she has a "thing." "He's always closing his eyes," she muses, watching him apply several drops of Visine, "like it hurts him to look at things." However, the viewer soon realizes that the elusive Jordan is not quite as deep as Angela would have us believe. As he struggles to grasp Kafka, Jordan asks: "So, getting back to that *Metamorphosis* story . . . It's made up, right?" In a later episode, Jordan and Angela finally hit the making-out stage. In a voice-over Angela explains, "We barely talked. So when we did, it came out sounding really meaningful." But in the next line of dialogue, Jordan asks, "Is that your stomach or my stomach?"

Their narration reveals that both Holden and Angela underestimate their parents' intelligence at times. When Holden thinks about calling Phoebe on the phone, he's afraid one of his parents will answer instead. Although he considers hanging up if that happens, he finally decides against the whole idea because, "They'd know it was me. My mother always knows it's me. She's psychic" (67). Angela makes a similar comment when her dad asks an obvious question about her love life: "Out of nowhere, they suddenly turn psychic."

Sometimes the narrators contradict themselves within the span of a single sentence. As Holden discusses his favorite authors (Thomas Hardy, Isak Dinesen), he remarks, "I'm quite illiterate, but I read a lot" (18). And when Angela visits Rayanne's retro-hippie home for the first time, she thinks, "Walking into someone's house for the first time is like entering another country. Not that I've been to another country." Although Goodman believes this type of inconsistency to be "irritating," I find it very refreshing. This kind of narration realistically illustrates the confusion, subjectivity and naivete of these adolescent protagonists who are struggling to make sense of their lives.

Throughout this struggle, a common theme runs through both the novel and the series: phoniness. In *Catcher*, Holden continually expresses hatred for all of the phony people (Mr. Spencer), conversations (about the Lunts' play), words ("grand"), and institutions (Pencey), he's encountered. He daydreams about moving out West and building himself a cabin where he'd live for the rest of his life: "I'd have this rule that nobody could do anything phony when they visited me. If anybody tried to do anything phony, they couldn't stay" (205).

Ironically, however, "Holden shares in the phoniness he loathes" (Edwards 149). For example, even though he criticizes phony conversations, Holden takes part in them himself. When he visits with Mr. Spencer, Holden "[shoots] the bull" (12), telling his teacher exactly what he wants to hear. And when he meets a classmate's mother on the train, he begins "chucking the old crap around" (56) by pretending to be someone else. Holden's lack of self-awareness isn't contemptible—rather, it's typical. Like any other teenager, Holden is trying to find a place for himself, trying to fit in. Duane Edwards observes that "Holden conforms to phoniness because he wants so badly to join the human race" (156).

Like Holden, Angela is very aware of the phoniness that surrounds her. For example, she recognizes the inherent hypocrisy in producing a yearbook: "It's like everybody's in this big hurry to make this book, to supposedly remember what happened. Because if you made a book of what really happened, it'd be a really upsetting book." But unlike Holden, Angela recognizes that she participates in the phoniness, too. When Brian accuses her of being an "act," she responds "Everyone's an act."

In the pilot, we first meet Angela as she hits a turning point in her life. "Things were getting to me," she says, "just how people are—how they always expect you to be a certain way, even your best friend." And so Angela's search for an identity begins as she distances herself from her safe childhood friend, Sharon, and takes up with the uninhibited Rayanne. In doing so, she identifies with Anne Frank:

> . . . so whatever she'd been like with her friends or her teachers, that was over. She was hiding. But in this other way, she wasn't. She, like, stopped hiding. She was free.

As the series progresses, Angela tries on a variety of personas, trying to find the one that fits. Much of this "acting" has to do with her infatuation with Jordan. For example, she tells him she could care less about going to the school dance, although she's hoping he'll ask. When Jordan then explains his noncommittal "philosophy" of "whatever happens, happens," Angela remarks, "I have to say, I really respect that." But when Brian feeds her the same line, she responds, "That's the stupidest thing I've ever heard in my life." Before long Angela is skipping geometry classes and doing Jordan's homework for him—a far cry from the Angela who used to panic when she heard the tardy bell.

Holden would call Angela a phony, but that label seems to assume the existence of a "real" Angela—how can she tell which is which? In the pilot, Angela observes:

It just seems like you agree to have a certain personality or something. For no reason. Just to make things easier for everyone. But when you think about it, I mean, how do you know it's even you?

The point is, she **doesn't** know, and neither does Holden.

Amid all of this confusion, however, we do gain brief glimpses of the "real" Holden and Angela. One night when Holden is cold, lonely and depressed, he sneaks home to talk to Phoebe. When she quizzes him about what he'd really like to be if he had his choice, Holden describes his fantasy of being "the catcher in the rye":

> Anyway, I keep picturing all these little kids playing some game in this big field of rye and all. Thousands of little kids, and nobody's around—nobody big, I mean—except me. And I'm standing on the edge of some crazy cliff. What I have to do, I have to catch everybody if they start to go over the cliff—I mean if they're running and they don't look where they're going I have to come out from somewhere and *catch* them. That's all I'd do all day. I'd just be the catcher in the rye and all. (173)

Holden's noble yet naive desire to protect the innocents of the world is reflected in Angela during the Christmas episode, "So-Called Angels." After being abused and finally kicked out of his home, Ricki seeks refuge in an abandoned warehouse that is inhabited by dozens of homeless kids. When Angela discovers Ricki's situation, she agonizes over how to help him and the others. But the ever practical Rayanne explains, "You can't, like, be responsible for the whole world." Yet the very fact that both Holden and Angela yearn to take on this responsibility of "catching" the helpless despite the overwhelming odds demonstrates more about their true character than the frequent contradictions between their words and actions.

Thus in Angela Chase is much of Holden Caulfield reincarnated. They speak similar languages and say whatever occurs to them whenever it occurs to them as they search for identity and acceptance. This search landed Holden in the hospital, but he's got a good shot at recovery. Angela and her friends, however, landed on ABC's cancellation list. Oh well. As Holden said, "Don't ever tell anybody anything. If you do, you start missing everybody" (214)—or whatever.

From *Studies in Popular Culture* 19.1 (October 1996): 47-57. Copyright © 1996 by *Studies in Popular Culture*. Reprinted with permission of *Studies in Popular Culture* and Barbara Bell.

Works Cited

Costello, Donald P. "The Language of *The Catcher in the Rye.*" *American Speech* 34 (1959): 172-81. Rpt. in *Critical Essays on Salinger's* The Catcher in the Rye. Ed. Joel Salzberg. Boston: G. K. Hall, 1990. 44-53.

Cowan, Michael. "Holden's Museum Pieces: Narrator and Nominal Audience in *The Catcher in the Rye.*" *New Essays on* The Catcher in the Rye. Ed. Jack Salzman. Cambridge: Cambridge UP, 1991. 35-55.

Edwards, Duane. "Holden Caulfield: 'Don't Ever Tell Anybody Anything.'" *English Literary History* 44 (1977): 556-67. Rpt. in *Critical Essays on Salinger's* The Catcher in the Rye. Ed. Joel Salzberg. Boston: G. K. Hall, 1990. 148-58.

Ferrara, Kathleen and Barbara Bell. "Sociolinguistic Variation and Discourse Function of Constructed Dialogue Introducers: The Case of be + like." *American Speech* 70 (1995): 265-90.

Goodman, Anne L. "Mad About Children." *New Republic* 125 (1951): 20-21. Rpt. in *Critical Essays on Salinger's* The Catcher in the Rye. Ed. Joel Salzberg. Boston: G. K. Hall, 1990. 23-24.

Martin, James. "Perfect Pitch." *America* 17 Sept. 1994: 24.

My So-Called Life. Created by Marshall Herskovitz and Edward Zwick. ABC Television Network. 1994-5. Personal video collection.

Salinger, J. D. *The Catcher in the Rye*. 1951. New York: Bantam, 1968.

Salzberg, Joel, ed. Introduction. *Critical Essays on Salinger's* The Catcher in the Rye. Boston: G. K. Hall, 1990.

Seitz, Matt Zoller. "Never Trust a Narrator Who's Under 16." *New York Times* 30 Oct. 1994, sec. 2: 34.

Shaw, Peter. "Love and Death in *The Catcher in the Rye.*" *New Essays on* The Catcher in the Rye. Ed. Jack Salzman. Cambridge: Cambridge UP, 1991. 97-114.

Smith, Harrison. "Manhattan Ulysses, Junior." *The Saturday Review* 34 (1951): 12-13. Rpt. in *Critical Essays on Salinger's* The Catcher in the Rye. Ed. Joel Salzberg. Boston: G. K. Hall, 1990. 28-30.

Underhill, Robert. "*Like* is, like, focus." *American Speech* 63 (1988): 234-46.

Waters, Harry F. "Review of *My So-Called Life.*" *Newsweek* 21 Feb. 1994: 66, 68.

Holden Caulfield's Legacy

David Castronovo

The Catcher in the Rye is, of course, more than a novel. A lightning rod for a new sensibility, a wisdom book for postwar students, a behavior manual for the age of impulse, it has had a life apart from the literary world and cultural significance and staying power beyond its literary value. Inferior in quality to the greatest consciousness-shaping works of American modernism—among them, *The Great Gatsby, The Sun Also Rises, Invisible Man*—it nevertheless has the power to distill states of mind, spark identification, and live beyond its covers. Like certain songs or movie characters, it has become a part of the shared experience of a vast number of people in the second half of the twentieth century. People know the book who haven't read it with any care; others—like nineteenth-century people who had heard about Mr. Pickwick or Anna Karenina—have heard the news of Holden Caulfield just by being alive. There are websites devoted to the novel; people live by it and, although we live in an un-Arnoldian age, it is probably one of our last remaining literary touchstones—youth and resentment and joy and angst, in book rather than CD, TV, or net form.

It came out in 1951, not exactly an *annus mirabilis* for American literature, but not such a bad year, either. *From Here to Eternity* was also published and became a bestseller. The gap between the two books is the gap between an older world of naturalism—with its careful chronicling of injustices and hard luck and hard living—and an entirely new rendering of the American situation: the distance between Jones's war in the Pacific and Salinger's peace and prosperity is hardly the crucial point; *Catcher* has a language, texture, and view of what counts that places it firmly in America's future; *From Here to Eternity* belongs with the classics of the past. 1951 was not a notable year for cultural change in America, either. Rock 'n roll, Brando's motorcycle in *The Wild One*, Dean's red jacket in *Rebel Without a Cause*—the spring blossoms of the coming age of antinomianism—were nowhere in sight. What was plentifully available? Endless anti-communist screeds, anxieties about conformity, books about Social Problems, music that was sentimental and kitschy or part of the wit and heart of old Tin Pan Alley (the obnoxious kid Stradlater in *Catcher* whistles themes from "Song of India" and "Slaughter on Tenth Avenue"), liberal arts students who wanted jobs and not ideologies. Salinger's book was the first embraceable book to appear after the war: the first book with an idiom and an attitude of its own, something that made young people newly aware of themselves. The novels that were still coming out about the war didn't quite do the job for these new readers. They needed their own book, one that spoke to the younger brothers who were just kids at the time of the war. They also needed a book that didn't employ the locutions of the Depression, the rhetoric of the left and right, or the language of the war years, whether the staunchly patriotic slogans of the majority or the disaffected idiom of the isolationists among the intellectuals.

At first blush, Salinger's novel, a younger brother's account of himself, seems like a reinvention of a familiar story in earlier twentieth-century literature: like *Winesburg, Ohio* or *Look Homeward, Angel* or even Hemingway's Nick Adams stories, it's about a lonely young boy who thinks there is something wrong with the world, something essentially dead and phony and disgusting about the arrangement of things. But once linked with these books, *Catcher* detaches itself, for the most part because it isn't a story about development. Holden Caulfield has no unfolding destiny, no mission, not even the dramatic moments of Nick or his avatars in battle or Eugene Gant overcoming his mother's influence. Holden is a drifter whose life story is a muddle, a series of pathetic, comic, poignant incidents that are altogether unlike the destiny-building moments of the earlier books. Salinger turns against the "*David Copperfield* crap" and most other patterns as well. The book is anti-literary in a new way: its pages are filled with babbling rather than talk that builds to a climax; impressions that are overtaken by afterthoughts, comic contradictions, half-recognitions, and canceled insights. While sharing the basic subject of Hemingway and Anderson—lonely youth—Salinger invents a mode of his own: a managed incoherence, an attractive breakdown of logic that appeals to the confused adolescent in all of us. Sweeping denunciations are followed by abject apologies—only to be followed by other ridiculous pronouncements. Holden the muttering self fires off Holdenism after Holdenism. Try one of these: "I'm quite illiterate, but I read a lot." Or, "I hate the movies like poison, but I get a bang imitating them." Or, "A horse is at least human, for God's sake." Or, "The show wasn't as bad as some I've seen. It was on the crappy side, though." Or, "Listen. What's the routine on joining a monastery?"

Holden's idiom is the novel's glory, the property that has appealed to audiences for fifty years. A blend of explosive denunciation and heart-on-sleeve sentiment, it maintains a high tension for a little over two hundred pages. Since Salinger employs only the thinnest of plots—a linking of loosely connected incidents in Holden's downward journey—the rambling, ranting, and rhapsodizing are the main events. The idiom takes over as Holden's speech becomes the central conflict. How will he react next? We lurch from *aperçu* to *aperçu*, epigram to epigram—all of them drawing on carefully chosen contrasts: the boy's rendering of his world employs popular culture and classic literature, upper-middle-class taste and a thorough knowledge of urban tackiness, refinement and grossness, tender solicitude and harsh condemnation. The book is charged and energetic to the end because it never quite settles into a consistent point of view: as exasperating as this may be for readers who want character logic and clear motivation, the scattered remarks and volatility of the prose have taken hold. Its unreasoned judgments have also dug deep into our consciousness and connected with the unexplainable part of our lives. Can we account for every aspect of our own irritation, repulsion, contempt? Are there clearly drawn correlatives for Holden's disgust, anger, and disillusionment? Do we have any evidence that the people he mocks are quite as pathetic as he would have it? Ackley with his pimples and bragging about sex, Stradlater with his dapper appearance and swagger, Sally Hayes with her hard-edged practicality and her little ice-skating skirt, the out-of-towners Marty and Laverne at the Lavender Lounge with their grammar errors and their gawking at celebrities? Are they enough to warrant what is magnified into what we see as Holden's *contemptu mundi*? If you have followed the crazy reasoning, listened to Holden's standards—sincerity, kindness, dignity—you will follow such judgments. These people are pathetic, either phonies or flops.

Holden's discontents and diatribes are infectious because we all have our irascibility and fastidiousness, and Salinger has managed to play on us by summoning up the perfect, grating details. Like Browning or Dickens, he has an extensive inventory of annoyances and human weaknesses, stupid locutions and exasperating habits. The book is a treasury of the ludicrous, and its absurdities remain fresh a half century later. Take Pencey's headmaster with his forced jokes and his toadying to rich parents; or the man at Radio City who says of the Rockettes, "that's precision"; or Sally Hayes conspicuously embracing a gray-flanneled acquaintance as if they were "old buddyroos." Recall some Dickens characters—despite Holden's self-conscious impatience with *David Copperfield*—and you will be in the same literary territory: Pecksniff with his "moral throat," Fagin's "my dear," Pumblechook with his hectoring. Like Dickens, Salinger has a masterful command of pretensions. At the Wicker Bar Holden observes the singer, "Old Janine": "And now we like to geeve you our impression of Vooly Voo Fransay. Eet ess the story of a leetle Fransh girl who comes to a beeg ceety, just like New York, and falls in love wees a leetle boy from Brookleen." He captures the manner of Carl Luce, a blasé intellectual, with dead-on accuracy: "He never said hello or anything when he met you. The first thing he said when he sat down was that he could only stay a couple of minutes." There's no place quite like *Catcher* for savoring the cant and swill of contemporary life: "Newsreels. Christ almighty. There's always a dumb horse race, and some dame breaking a bottle over a ship, and some chimpanzee with pants on riding a goddamn bicycle."

But once you have had your fill of Holden denouncing anything and everything, you naturally wonder what it all amounts to. Does Salinger deliver any real insight, any recognition? Is it all clever schtick or carefully managed nastiness? Are the mots a kind of superior talk radio? Pure spleen hasn't much staying power; negativism, as Cyril Connolly once remarked, dates quickly. But *Catcher* mixes its cynicism and irascibility with a rich brew of sentiment and idealism, a child-like faith that life contains more than pretensions and phoniness. In some ways it is more a wisdom book than a novel, a collection of pronouncements about living well and discovering useable truths. After thundering at the world, it offers compact packages of insight. Holden, the comic instructor incapable of running his own life, proposes exempla for his listeners: he's the half-cracked advisor who gets our attention by the strange slant of his doctrines. The most affecting doctrine of course is that of the Catcher in the Rye: this teaching—which twists Robert Burns's line from "meet" to "catch"—is a typical Holdenism; half-informed, but totally emphatic, it produces meaning in the midst of confusion. It takes a highly recognized poem, mixes childish naïveté with the poetry and mangles the original sense. The result is a curious restatement of the New Testament exhortation to be thy brother's keeper: your mission in life is to catch little children before they fall off the cliff. No sooner do you see the odd simplicity and innocence of the doctrine's packaging than you recognize its powerful connection with other such statements in world literature. Salinger, by redesigning a sentiment about love and mercy and the innocence of children, takes a modest but quite definite place in the romantic movement; his imagery—either in the figure of the individual child (Phoebe Caulfield or the little boy who sings a snatch from "Comin' Through the Rye") or the vision of crowds of children endangered—is strongly reminiscent of Blake's language in *Songs of Innocence and Experience*. His moment of pure joy at first reminds us of Blakean joy. Looked at from a Blakean point of view, it's the all-but-incoherent utterance of the innocent, for example the voice in "Infant Joy": "I happy am/ Joy is my

Holden Caulfield's Legacy 145

name.—/ Sweet joy befall thee!" But the more specific insight of *Catcher* is a lesson out of Wordsworth.

The doctrine of *Catcher* is presented in Salinger's characteristic spatterdash, free-associational way. In a scene with Phoebe, he enunciates his position, but does so by raking through the past and stumbling inadvertently on truth: the emotional truth of the Catcher "comes" to Holden—as it has to romantic poets, particularly to the Wordsworth of "Resolution and Independence"—after he has reviewed the spectacle of himself, rejected that self and the world that made it, and by chance discovered truth embodied in the quotidian, in the unproclaimed and unproclaiming world of everydayness; that truth is distilled in the actions of the nuns collecting for their order at the station, in the schoolteacher who mercifully covers the body of a young suicide, and in the sacred actions of Holden's dead brother, Allie. Like Wordsworth, Salinger favors the didactic colloquy as a prelude to emotional awakening. A teacher—without a schoolroom, of course—prepares the pupil for the recognition. Along the same lines, the leech gatherer in Wordsworth, an old man who endures despite poverty and the harshness of the environment, has a few direct, simple words—"apt admonishment" for a narrator who is depressed and caught in a web of self-absorption; he has his message, his example, his acceptance of life. Salinger's Phoebe Caulfield has her corresponding childish insights to offer an older brother caught in a similar emotional crisis.

Like Wordsworth, Salinger prefers a symbolic action or a dramatic scene to reasoning or mere words. Holden listening to Phoebe's childish jabbering and the narrator of "Resolution and Independence" listening to the old man's sparse advice: each character is more influenced by the personal situation than by the particular words. And each work is carried by spectacle and scene rather than by specific doctrine. Talk is important, but reasoned explanation will not yield insight. *Catcher*'s last dramatic scene shows Phoebe riding the carrousel in Central Park, reaching for the gold ring. The depiction includes Holden's reaction, a joyous response, something that cannot be accounted for logically or through an examination of motive: "I felt so happy all of a sudden, the way old Phoebe kept going around and around. I was damn near bawling, I felt so damn happy, if you want to know the truth." In its way this is our recent literature's most memorable equivalent of Wordsworth's great awakening scenes: the discovery of joy and heightened understanding and the capacity for close identification with others who are experiencing instinctual pleasure or fulfillment or satisfactory endurance. "By our spirits are we deified," Wordsworth put it. The awakening is like John Stuart Mill's famous recognition scene in his *Autobiography:* Mill's own depression lifted when he discovered the inner sense of Wordsworth's poetry. "What made Wordsworth's poems a medicine for my state of mind was that they expressed, not mere outward beauty, but states of feeling, and of thought colored by feeling, under the excitement of beauty." Hard as it is to think of human feeling as a news item at the turn of the millennium—after nearly two hundred years of writers, poets, singers, and attitudinizers prying out the meaning of emotions—it seems new to us when Salinger is the investigator. Holden watching his sister has given contemporary American literature a moment like that of "Resolution and Independence" and that of Mill emerging from his despondency: the melancholy observer awakens to the joy of life by observing another's deep involvement in some form of release or reclamation. Mill calls the process of his awakening through poetry "the culture of the feelings." In reading Wordsworth's poems, he recollects, "I seemed to draw from a source of inward joy, of sympathetic and imaginative pleasure, which could be shared in by all human beings." When Holden Caulfield was so happy he felt like "bawling," he wanted to pass on the elation—"God, I wish you could've been there." Be it said that the source of newfound joy—the culture of the feelings—is a child on a carrousel, not a series of poems. Renewal in the twentieth century is the raw experience of being in the midst of life, colliding with joy and not wanting to account for why or wherefore; Mill's highly analytic account of renewal through the cultivation of feelings assumes a world where the individual moves easily among books and abstract ideas and ordinary experiences.

The mystery of emotional awakening is Salinger's main obsession in the book; his fear is that the discovery he has made—the connection between the innocent wise child and joyous renewal—will in some way be mocked or cheapened or otherwise devalued. Or generalized about or analyzed. He also fears himself and his all-too-human inclination to traduce his own vision. Afraid to publish, afraid of the sentiment that he himself has dispersed, he has become an elderly Holden, AWOL from the responsibility to give an account of himself; in Salinger's case he has bitterly resisted the responsibilities of authorship as we generally recognize it, including the obligation to be heard periodically. *Catcher*—since its publication—has been its author's holy book, never to be defiled by stage, screen, or other profane translations. As any reader of Ian Hamilton's book on Salinger will easily recognize, the protectiveness of this author for his property is something that goes well beyond our ordinary understanding of author's rights. And the book itself provides its own self-absorbed defense against cheapness and meanness; hardly a sentence passes without the narrator's making sure that he is not falling into the ways of the world. Holden wants to immunize himself against corny rhetoric by employing every kind of hard-boiled phrase and cynical dismissal that the publishers of 1951 will permit. The scenes of pure joy and transcendence come in the main near the end of a book that has taken devastating aim at the cheap emotionalism, histrionics, sappy effects, warm and fuzzy recognition scenes in movies, books, and life. The author has his own defensive tactics—whatever it takes to keep the sacred texts from being defiled.

Salinger's idea of joy and renewal should be seen against the backdrop of Hollywood schlock; it's the awkward, hand-designed, and naive sentiment that stands out against the formulaic and corny. Askew and spontaneous, the story line is far from the calculated mass product that Holden remembers from the movies. Contrast it, for example, with his favorite love-to-hate movie, a travesty of renewal about an Englishman who suffers from amnesia after the war. Holden tells us that the character Alec staggers around on a cane until he meets a "homey babe" who wants to rejuvenate him, share her love of Dickens—as well as get help in her floundering publishing business, help badly needed since her cracked-up surgeon brother has been spending all the profits. The complications—involving Alec's ducal status and his other girlfriend—are hilariously related by Holden, whose own complications have none of the factitious neatness of this sort of plot. "Anyway it ends up with Alec and the homey babe getting married. . . . All I can say is don't see it if you don't want to puke all over yourself." Hollywood in this case is the culprit, but elsewhere human feeling is mangled by the cant of prep school teachers, New York sophisticates, phony intellectuals, doting upper-middle-class parents, even earlier writers. Dickens's *David Copperfield* crap is the best hint of all about Salinger's ambition to achieve his own breakthrough. True to the great project of romanticism, *Catcher* throws off the meretricious past, purifies its spirit with a new diction, tone, and objects of attention. The decorum of earlier literature disappears, along with the dignity and seriousness and measured speech of modernist heroes like Jake Barnes or Jay Gatsby. In the carrousel scene, the rain pours down and mixes with the strains of "Smoke Gets in Your Eyes" and "Oh Marie" and the spectacle of Holden in his hunting hat. No Frederic Henry here. The ludic, manic mode can't and won't account for a hero, refuses to unpack clear causes or offer careful delineations. The literary tradition is something to get a kick out of—the way Holden does from Hardy's Eustachia Vye—but not something to talk about much, or follow in much detail. When Salinger taught writing at Columbia, he was disdainful of the whole notion of classroom analysis of works. Just read them. We murder to dissect. We even murder to account for or scrutinize.

This contempt for disciplined analysis and careful tracing of literary filaments from the past does not mean the book doesn't champion other kinds of personal discipline. The central doctrine of the book—that each of us has a Catcher in the Rye lodged within—implies a strict code for living. In its ramshackle way, *Catcher* is a conduct book for the age of anxiety and conformity. No section of the book is without its precepts, prohibitions, and practical tips for cant-free living. It is, in this sense, one of the first manuals of cool, a how-to guide for those who would detach themselves from the all-American postwar pursuit of prosperity and bliss. Holden the drop-out and outsider speaks like some crazed, half-literate Castiglione as he discourses on everything from clothing and bearing to the appropriate responses of a cool person in any situation.

The following precepts are crucial:

—Ignore the messages of mass media. ("The goddamn movies. They can ruin you.")

—Be "casual as hell."

—Avoid any air of superiority or trace of competitiveness.

—Value digressions more highly than logical arguments.

—Never use the word "grand."

—Scorn routine sociability.

—Observe the margins of life: the remarks of children, the conduct of nuns; ignore the main acts. (The guy who plays the kettle drums at Radio City Music Hall is more important than the "Christmas thing" with "O Come All Ye Faithful.")

After fifty years these teachings remain a central element of our culture. Young people and their fearful elders know that coolness is the only way. Formal discourse, sequential thinking, reverence for the dignified and the heroic: these acts closed by the 1960s. The voice of Holden played a part in shutting them down. Its tone—directed against prestige and knowingness—is as cutting today as it was in 1951: "I could see them all sitting around in some bar with their goddamn checkered vests, criticizing shows and books and women in those tired, snobby voices." Cancel the checkered vests and you're right at home at the millennium.

But for all its durability, does *Catcher* continue to make sense to the mature mind? Is it infantile and simplistic, reductive and negative, expressing the attitude of a kid who is soon to get the therapy he needs? One can only say that the scorn for conventions and the search for joy are a part of the ongoing romantic project that started in the eighteenth century. Exasperating, irrational, and dangerous as these pursuits have sometimes proven, they show no signs of coming to an end. Salinger's ardor and disdain have a bracing quality of their own, inferior to that of the great romantic artists but nevertheless still important at a time when we need to resist our own age of reason, its monoliths and abstract ideas of human progress. With its horror of groupthink of all kinds—be it remembered that, like George Orwell, the Salinger of *Catcher* has nothing good to say about politics, power blocks, commercial modernity, or any orthodoxy—the book is free of the worst tendencies of the late 1940s. Like Orwell, too, Salinger has profound respect for the decencies, pleasures, and truths that can be found anywhere. But unlike Orwell, Salinger is an anti-enlightenment weaver of fantasies and denouncer of hard-headed thinking. If truth be told, his Blakean celebration of joy and wonder foreshadowed the wooliness of the beatniks and hippies and would become flabby and sententious even by the time of the Glass family stories of the late 1950s. While Franny and Zooey's complaints about civilization are preachy and humorlessly tiresome, though, Holden's negativity remains wonderfully fresh in its inconsistency. He remains a bearer of a permanent truth: that you can't fake an affectional life; that you must live through absurdity, indignity, and pain in order to get a small return of happiness.

From *New England Review* 22.2 (Spring 2001): 180-186. Copyright © 2001 by *New England Review*. Reprinted with permission of *New England Review*.

The Catcher in the Rye and All:
Is the Age of Formative Books Over?
Sanford Pinsker

> The best thing, though, in that museum was that everything always stayed right where it was. Nobody'd move. . . . Nobody'd be different. The only thing that would be different would be *you*.
>
> —Holden Caulfield[1]

I first read these lines about Holden's recollections in anxiety long before I could have identified the allusion to Wordsworth, long before I fell half in love with easeful death and Keats's "Ode on a Grecian Urn," long before I would scrawl "stasis" on the blackboard when lecturing about *The Catcher in the Rye*. And even though I hadn't the foggiest idea about which subway line takes one to the Museum of Natural History, I understood, at sixteen, what Holden was talking about.

In short, there was a time when books—or at least some books—used to matter. One wonders if the same excitements, the same confusions, the same affections persist. Or have formative books gone the way of penny candy and *un*organized baseball games? Perhaps our age is too restless, too sophisticated to suspend its disbelief, much less to sit still long enough to read a book. What follows, then, is an attempt, admittedly autobiographical, to talk about certain connections between reading and culture—not as a "reader-response" theorist, not as a statistics-and-graph sociologist, but rather as one who fell in love with *The Catcher in the Rye* early, and who has been trying to figure out what that has meant ever since.

About some underlying things I am fairly certain: the public indicators that presumably separate one generation in its youth from another (e.g., hairstyling, popular music) are finally less important than the conditions they share. "So much of adolescence," the poet Theodore Roethke once wrote, "is an ill-defined dying, . . . A longing for another time and place,/ another condition."[2] Roethke may have been wrong about the death wish that I, for one, didn't have, but he was dead right about my ill-defined longings. Like Holden, I yearned for a world more attractive, and less mutable, than the one in which we live and are forced to compete. As Holden puts it, with a sadness he does not fully comprehend:

> That's the whole trouble. You can't ever find a place that's nice and peaceful, because there isn't any. You may think there is, but once you get there, when you're not looking, somebody'll sneak up and write "Fuck you" right under your nose. Try it sometime. I think, even, if I ever die, and they stick me in a cemetery, and I have a tombstone and all, it'll say "Holden Caulfield" on it, and then what year I was born and what year I died, and then right under that it'll say "Fuck you." I'm positive, in fact. (p. 184)

That Holden renders a diffuse, universal condition in vivid particulars and that he gives eloquent expression to what I could not have articulated myself are both ways of saying that *The Catcher in the Rye* was, for me, a formative book. Others, no doubt, have candidates of their own: Mother Goose, *Treasure Island*, *The Adventures of Sherlock Holmes*—whatever books they remember as making the imagination's power immanent. But I would argue that our most important formative books are those which lead double lives as cultural statements, fastened as firmly to the here and now as they are to fiction's universals. One wrestles with genuinely formative books, often in ways that are as divided as they are paradoxical. Recalling his own experiences with such books, Lionel Trilling put the matter this way: "The great books taught me, they never made me dream. The bad books made me dream and hurt me; I was right when 4 years ago I said that the best rule-of-thumb for judgment of a good novel or play was—Do you want to be the hero? If you do, the work is bad."[3]

One could claim, and with some justification, that *The Catcher in the Rye* encourages precisely the sort of dreaming and heroic identification that Trilling stands four-square against. Indeed, if moral complexity were the sole issue, one would need look no further than Trilling's *The Middle of the Journey* (1949), an extraordinary novel published a scant two years before *The Catcher in the Rye*. But that said, who would be comfortable in claiming *The Middle of the Journey* as a formative book? To be sure, accessibility is part of the formula, but timing is equally important. A formative book catches its reader at a point when options loom larger than certainties, when an admonition to "change your life" can still have teeth.

For those who grew up in the 1950's, *The Catcher in the Rye* was *the* formative book. My own case, as I struggle to reconstruct it, was one of sharply divided loyalties, of as many repulsions as attractions. A part of me—the part that was reading a book called *On the Road* by an author whose name no one in my literary crowd could even pronounce—wanted, more than anything in the world, to be a beatnik. There were, clearly, *no* beatniks—at least none in the Kerouac mold—at a cushy joint like Holden's Pencey Prep. My dilemma, I hasten to add, was hardly unusual: formative books come in bunches and, more often than not, send contradictory messages about exactly how one goes about changing one's life. To make matters even more confusing, I kept testing what I read against the life I was actually living. When, for example, ol' Phoebe keeps repeating "Daddy'll *kill* you," I knew, even at sixteen, that this was so much Oedipal bluster. On the other hand, my father really would have leveled me—that is, if I had pissed away even *half* the money Holden did, or lugged home a single *C*, much less a fistful of *F*'s.

It was Holden's *voice*, rather than his circumstances, that hooked me. Long before the book appeared in its now-familiar bright red, plainly lettered, paperback cover—a dead giveaway that the novel has become a "classic" and can move off the shelf on its own power—I kept faith with a well-thumbed copy sporting a picture of an apple-cheeked, perplexed Holden (wearing his reversed hunting cap) gazing on the debauchery that was, presumably, New York City. Apparently, the cover designer sought to blend brows high and low, the lurid (soft porn à la 1955) with the literary (Daisy Buchanan eyeballing Manhattan on the dust jacket of *The Great Gatsby*). Anyway—as Holden might put it—it was the voice that got me each time I turned to the first page; to get the voice going—or, if you will, *talking*—all you had to do was sit back and read:

> If you really want to hear about it, the first thing you'll probably want to know is where I was born, and what my lousy childhood was like, and how my parents were occupied and all before they had me, and all that David Copperfield kind of crap, but I don't feel like going into it, if you want to know the truth. (p. 5)

To call a Dickens novel crap—and in the same sentence that heaves in a "lousy" no less!—was to yank literature away from those who pronounced it "lit-er-ah-tour." Huckleberry Finn warms up to his task by telling us that Mark Twain "told the truth, mainly," but Holden really *does* it, without an apology or so much as a "by your leave."

At least that was the way I read the book when I was sixteen and itching to pull down a few vanities myself. In those days Holden was my "secret sharer," the part of me that knew, down deep, that whatever Life was, it was decidedly *not* a game: "Game, my ass [Holden thinks as Spencer hectors him about yet another poor academic performance]. Some game. If you get on the side where all the hot-shots are, then it's a game all right—I'll admit that. But if you get on the *other* side, where there aren't any hot-shots, then what's a game about it? Nothing. No game" (p. 11). To be sure, what Holden said in bald print I dared only whisper *sotto voce*. That I could live with. It was having to share my secret sharer with others that gave me the gripes. Holden was fast becoming a doppelgänger-in-residence for an entire generation, including those who pointed to the obligatory fart-in-the-chapel scene and guffawed. *What right have any of you*, I wanted to shout, *to think of Holden as a fellow traveler?* Holden would expose *you* as a "secret slob," as a Joe Flit, as a phony.

It took some years before I realized the painful truth—namely, that Holden would probably say the same or worse about me. As Holden would have it, you can count the nonphonies on the fingers of one hand: Allie, his dead brother; Phoebe, his little sister, and of course Holden himself. Everybody else stands either suspect or convicted.

I took a measure of comfort from those passages in which even *Holden* wonders if he hasn't pulled the self-righteous trigger too quickly. Mr. Antolini, for example, might—or might not—have been a "pervert." What seemed clear enough when Holden was sleeping on Antolini's couch turns complicated when he hits the Manhattan street: ". . . What *did* worry me was the part about how I'd woke up and found him patting me on the head and all. I mean I wondered if just maybe I was wrong about thinking he was making a flitty pass at me. I wondered if maybe he just liked to pat guys on the head when they're asleep. I mean how can you tell about that stuff for sure?" (p. 175).

By this time I was in college: a place where I acquired for the first time that phenomenon known as a roommate, a place where novels like *The Catcher in the Rye* were dissected and placed under critical microscopes. It had taken the New Criticism two decades to trickle down to the small liberal-arts college I attended, but we soon learned to sniff out a paradox or an ambiguity with the best of them. If Salinger hadn't written *The Catcher in the Rye*, one of my professors certainly *would* have. At least that was the way it seemed, so unerring were they on those quirky Salinger touches we enjoyed without quite knowing how to talk, or write, about them: the kings Jane Gallagher kept in the back row; the question Holden keeps asking about the ducks of Central Park; the whole business of being a "catcher in the rye."

A few years later, while browsing through back issues of *Modern Fiction Studies*, I heard snippets of their dazzling lectures once again, but this time the insights were attached to names I kept bumping into in graduate school: Arthur Mizener, Leslie Fiedler, Alfred Kazin, James E. Miller, Jr., Frederick L. Gwynn, Joseph L. Blotner—none of whom, I hardly need add, taught at my college. No wonder my professors had wowed the pants off the undergraduates in the third row! Everything they said was safely tucked away in the MLA Bibliography—more critical articles on Salinger than on Hemingway or Fitzgerald or Faulkner. What had started out as an effort to give critical respectability (the Academy's Seal of Approval) to a wildly popular book had turned into a gusher of ink.

In short, the burgeoning Salinger industry did its best, but *The Catcher in the Rye* held up, and together, better than most similarly "saturated" books. After such knowledge, there was—in my case at least—forgiveness. So what if the intimations that would become Holden Caulfield could be unearthed in the wanderings of Odysseus, in the legends surrounding the Grail knights, in Huck Finn's adventures among con men and scalawags, in Quentin Compson's obsession with *his* sister? So what if my undergraduate professors took in the best that had been thought and printed about Holden's world and then modified it into their own lectures? Salinger's book was more or less the same book it had always been, and Salinger was, of course, still Salinger.

The truth is, however, that our formative books survive not only subsequent readings but also *ourselves*. In the case of *The Catcher in the Rye*, it even managed to survive what I would not then have believed possible—a time when I no longer counted myself among the Holden-lovers. The well-meaning but ineffectual Mr. Antolini came to strike me as a better model—despite his bows to Wilhelm Stekel and his penchant for stump speeches about the Great Tradition:

> ... you'll find [he tells a shaken Holden] that you're not the first person who was ever confused and frightened and even sickened by human behavior. You're by no means alone on that score, you'll be excited and *stimulated* to know. Many, many men have been just as troubled morally and spiritually as you are right now. Happily, some of them kept records of their troubles. You'll learn from them—if you want to. Just as someday, if you have something to offer, someone will learn something from you. It's a

Is the Age of Formative Books Over?

beautiful, reciprocal arrangement. And it isn't education. It's history. It's poetry. (pp. 170-71)

Indeed, there will probably come that dreaded day when a bathrobed, bumpy-chested avatar of Mr. Spencer will stare back at me from the mirror. And no doubt I will find him a good deal more sympathetically drawn than I did when I first encountered him reeking of Vicks Nose Drops and made to carry the symbolic role of Sickness Personified.

Teaching Holden's saga in Belgium (under the auspices of a Fulbright grant), I was struck by ironies better than I could have concocted myself, ironies that surely would have made even a Salinger smile. For example, in a university where *Fuck You*'s are scrawled on nearly every bathroom wall (graffiti, apparently, requires plain-talking, Anglo-Saxon words; in Belgium, neither French nor Flemish would suffice), my students—reading *The Catcher in the Rye* in the expurgated Penguin edition—had trouble figuring out what the dash in "——— You" stood for. Nonetheless, they fell in love with Holden at first sight. Our most *American* books—everything from *Adventures of Huckleberry Finn* to *Invisible Man*—are as portable as they are powerful. To be sure, my Belgian students had some difficulty understanding the easy arithmetic we make between the American West and the American Dream. When, for example, Holden imagines lighting out for the West, we read the passage with Huck Finn and Frederick Turner firmly in mind:

> Finally, what I decided I'd do, I decided I'd go away. I decided I'd never go home again and I'd never go away to another school again.... What I'd do, I figured, I'd go down to the Holland Tunnel and bum a ride, and then I'd bum another one, and another one, and another one, and in a few days I'd be somewhere out West where it was very pretty and sunny and where nobody'd know me and I'd get a job. (pp. 178-79)

My Belgian students knew about the American West by watching *Dallas* and *Dynasty*, but they also knew that riding westward—to, say,

Ghent—is at best only a two-hour drive from the German border. In short, they found it hard to make the translation, to feel—as well as to "know"—just how big, how sprawling, America is.

On the other hand, the things that made Holden "fed up"—the competitive and the materialistic, as well as, of course, the phony—struck an easy, sympathetic chord, even in those who found themselves attracted by his description of life among the corporate lawyers: "All you do is make a lot of dough and play golf and play bridge and buy cars and drink Martinis and look like a hot-shot." At this point the line between my Belgian students and the American students with whom I'm more familiar began to blur. In roughly the same way that the well-heeled students at my college in Pennsylvania cheer when the film series shows "Breaking Away," Belgian students have no trouble empathizing with Holden while simultaneously keeping their eyes on the main chance. Which is simply to say that *The Catcher in the Rye* has always had more appeal to rebels under the skin than to those who actually lugged their failing transcripts from one prep school to another.

What did *not* change in my development, however, was my abiding sense of a formative book's continuing power. Granted, I may have accounted for the power in language that changed with the decades, I may have shifted this allegiance, altered that loyalty, to its characters, but the plain truth is that Salinger's death-haunted tale of spiritual yearning, of youthful *angst*, of dream and nightmare, has much to do with the how-and-why I plug away at teaching literature to a generation willing to settle for a safe job and a three-piece suit. I say this not as Mr. Antolini, much less as Holden; not as Spencer, much less as Salinger. Each of them has become a part of me in the way that Hester and Huckleberry, together with Madame Bovary and Leopold Bloom—from other formative books—also share in the making of my sensibility.

Indeed, the very plurality of formative books is worth speculating about. There was a time, of course, when the *Zeitgeist* defined itself by a single book: the Bible. In our age, however, one might argue that the itch for *the* formative book has been replaced by a series of one-night stands: the *I Ching*, the *est Reader*, the *Beverly Hills Diet Book*. To update Thoreau, the mass of men, and women, now lead lives of noisy desperation—either screaming "I'm *ter-rrr-if-ic*" at an Amway sales rally or shelling out two-hundred bucks to learn the secrets of Greenspring. In this sense, formative books still abound. People stick them in your face with a missionary zeal not unlike those who waved copies of *The Sayings of Chairman Mao* during the Cultural Revolution. To be sure, the American equivalents are more diversified, more concerned with the pursuit of happiness (defined as everything from "inner harmony" to outer appearance) than with ideological purity, but they share the general belief that a single book can change things utterly.

Intellectuals, presumably, know better. In the late 1930's Bernard Smith proposed a series of essays in which specialists would choose a work of nonfiction and then show how it had helped to shape the contemporary American mind. After all, as far back as Franklin, we have been makers of lists and lovers of the opinion poll. *The New Republic* warmed to the idea instantly and conducted a lively symposium in its pages. The result is a curious volume entitled *Books That Changed Our Minds*, edited by Malcolm Cowley and Bernard Smith. I say *curious* not because the choices or the discussion about them is odd (e.g., Charles A. Beard on Turner's *The Frontier in American History* or David Daiches on I. A. Richards' *The Principles of Literary Criticism*), but, rather, because the book was published in 1939, even as the world tottered on the brink of a war that would call these academic assessments of culture into deep question. (E. L. Doctorow's recent novel *World's Fair* makes a similar point about the celebrated exposition held in New York during the same ominously foreshadowing and pivotal year.)

That the disillusionments of World War I gave birth to the roaring jazz-age twenties, that the stock market's crash ushered us into the Great Depression, that Hitler's invasion of Poland plunged us into the nightmare of World War II, that Eisenhower's benign, smiling face represented the fifties in bold relief—these become the convenient shorthand we use to mark the passing of one decade to another. And in large measure, literature seemed to cooperate—the jazz-age flappers of Fitzgerald giving way to the tight-lipped Hemingway heroes of the 1930's, the anxious, world-weary protagonists of World War II fiction giving way to the spiritually questing beatniks of the 1950's.

History, of course, does not always cooperate—as we discovered when, for example, President Kennedy had the doubly bad fortune to be assassinated in 1963, a year that teetered uneasily between whatever was left of the somnambulant fifties and what was yet to be born as the militant sixties. Shaped by the art and lives that mattered—in the twenties by *The Waste Land*, by *Ulysses*, by *In Our Time*, by *The Great Gatsby*; in the thirties by Faulkner, by Steinbeck, by Dos Passos; in the forties by a series of brilliant debuts (Bellow, Mailer, Ellison)—successive generations of critics held faith with the belief that *their* decade would also revolve around a handful of Great Books. That it has, alas, not been so—not in the counterculture's grip on the 1960's, not during the nondescript 1970's, not as we pass the midpoint of the 1980's—has come as something of a rude, perplexing shock. Indeed, some literary critics began to make much ado about the death of fiction: literature (or, as it came to be fashionably called, "print media in the linear mode") could no longer compete with film, with television, with the dizzying speed and sheer *power* of popular culture. As my students used to put it in the late sixties: "Literature just ain't where it's at." Now they tell me it's not "cost effective."

All of which brings me back to *The Catcher in the Rye* and the Holden Caulfield who roamed Manhattan's unsympathetic streets. When the novel first appeared in 1951, Holden was seventeen years old. To imagine him now in *his* early fifties is rather like playing one of those Victorian parlor games that encouraged speculation about Ophelia's childhood or about the life Pip and Estella might lead beyond the final page of *Great Expectations*. The difference, of course, is that American culture takes its blurrings of Art & Life quite seriously. Those who find some measure of solace in Jerry Rubin's turnabout from a Yippie member of the Chicago Seven to a Yuppie wheeler-dealer on the stock exchange are precisely those likely to be cheered by the thought of Holden getting his comeuppance in a *New Yorker* cartoon.

Mr. Antolini, we remember, had some thoughts about how a moral uncompromiser like Holden might end up:

> "I have a feeling that you're riding for some kind of a terrible, terrible fall. . . . It may be the kind where, at the age of thirty, you sit in some bar hating everybody who comes in looking as if he might have played football in college. Then again, you may pick up just enough education to hate people who say, 'It's a secret between he and I.' Or you may end up in some business office, throwing paper clips at the nearest stenographer. I just don't know. . . ." (p. 168)

To be sure, Mr. Antolini has difficulty imagining Holden *beyond* thirty, but in that regard he is in good American company. Long before the counterculture turned it into the stuff of slogan, Henry David Thoreau made it abundantly clear that he had "lived some thirty years on this planet, and [had] yet to hear the first syllable of valuable or even earnest advice from my seniors." Graybeards—that is, those over thirty—were simply not to be trusted. And in our century, it was F. Scott Fitzgerald, more than any other writer of stature, who equated life in one's thirties with the loss of all that was once held dear: youth, good looks, romance, infinite possibility. As Dexter Green, the protagonist of "Winter Dreams," puts it:

> The dream was gone. Something had been taken from him. . . . He wanted to care, and he could not care. For he had gone away and he could never go back any more. The gates were closed, the sun was gone down, and there was no beauty but the gray beauty of steel that withstands all time. Even the

grief he could have borne was left behind in the country of illusion, of youth, of the richness of life, where his winter dreams had flourished.

"Long ago," he said, "long ago there was something in me, but now that thing is gone. Now that thing is gone, that thing is gone. I cannot cry. I cannot care. That thing will come back no more."[4]

No other American writer gave himself so completely to our capacity for Dream, and no writer was better equipped than Fitzgerald to write its Romantic elegy. The wags in Hollywood insisted that he was a "failure at failure," but they were dead wrong. Failure was Fitzgerald's *subject*, just as it is Holden's, just as it is at the center of every sensitive adolescent's complaint. In Theodore Roethke's notebooks—where he did not mince words, where he did not have to curry favor or cover his flanks—he wrote Fitzgerald down in a single, telling sentence: "He was born, and died, a Princeton sophomore."[5]

Holden, of course, remains frozen in his adolescence—in a novel dominated by images of stasis, of freezing (the snowballs he lovingly packs but refuses to throw at cars or fire hydrants because they, too, look "nice and white"; the icy lake of Central Park; the unmoving, Keatsian figures at the museum). And despite our knowing better, we hope against hope that Salinger will also remain the same pipe-smoking, tweed sports-coated, "sensitive" young author who appears on the dust jacket of *The Catcher in the Rye*'s first edition. After all, didn't Salinger himself say, in a contributor's note he wrote for *Harper's* in 1946, "I almost always write about very young people"? And as the Glass family saga unfolded through the 1960's, Salinger kept faith with his manifesto. He wrote *of* the young and *for* the young, so it seemed only fair that the work should continue to be written *by* the young as well. No matter that the mind knows Salinger is now old enough to collect social security; the heart insists that he remain, like his characters, forever fixed, red hunting cap pulled over his ears, the broken pieces of "Little Shirley Beans" in his pockets.

This insistence takes a bizarre, fabulist turn, in W. P. Kinsella's recent *Shoeless Joe*, a novel in which a cast of improbable characters (e.g., Shoeless Joe Jackson, Moonlight Graham, and J. D. Salinger himself) are assembled at a baseball stadium the protagonist has built in, of all places, Iowa City. Baseball is the stuff that American Dreams are made of. When an announcer's "voice" tells Ray Kinsella "If you build it, he will come," Ray turns his bulldozer on the cornfield and—*voila!*—Shoeless Joe Jackson appears. And when the voice tells him to "Ease his pain," Kinsella sets off for Salinger's New Hampshire retreat, fully prepared to kidnap him, to drive him across country to Iowa, to "ease his pain."

The rub, of course, is that Salinger's major pain is being pestered by the adoring, the curious, and the downright crazy. As Salinger, the character, puts it:

> Serenity is a very elusive quality. I've been trying all my life to find it. I'm very ordinary. I've never been able to understand why people are so interested in me. Writers are very dull. It's people like you who keep me from achieving what I'm after. You feel that I must be unhappy. A neurotic, guilt-torn artist. I'm *not* unhappy. And I have no wisdom to impart to you. I have no pain for you, unless . . . you and your family were to be plagued with strangers lurking in your bushes, trampling your flower beds, looking in your windows. . . . Once someone stole the valve caps off my jeep. I suppose he sold them or displays them under glass in his library. I don't deserve that![6]

One could argue that he doesn't deserve a fate as "character" either. After all, a public writer like Norman Mailer leads with a cocked right fist; that he is dragged, kicking and screaming, into Alan Lelchuck's novel, *American Mischief*, has a measure of poetic justice about it. By contrast, Salinger has been eloquent about his "silence." Unfortunately, *any* public figure appears to be fair game in an age that takes a special delight in blurring the distinctions between what we used to know as *fiction* and what we have learned to call "the new journalism."

Part of Salinger's problem, of course, is that he represents a time when *literature* formed literature, when allusions to *Romeo and Juliet* and *Return of the Native*, to *The Great Gatsby* and *A Farewell to Arms*, could be incorporated into the fabric of a novel like *The Catcher in the Rye*. No doubt the deconstructionists would give Holden poor marks, but he is a critic of sorts, nonetheless:

> The book I was reading was this book I took out of the library by mistake. They gave me the wrong book, and I didn't notice it till I got back to my room. They gave me *Out of Africa*, by Isak Dinesen. I thought it was going to stink, but it didn't. It was a very good book. I'm quite illiterate, but I read a lot. . . . What I like best is a book that's at least funny once in a while. I read a lot of classical books, like *The Return of the Native* and all, and I like them, and I read a lot of war books and mysteries and all, but they don't knock me out too much. What really knocks me out is a book that, when you're all done reading it, you wish the author that wrote it was a terrific friend of yours and you could call him up on the phone whenever you felt like it. (pp. 19-20)

One has the sinking feeling these days that Holden's counterparts at, say, Yale or Johns Hopkins would prefer to shoot the theoretical breeze with imaginative critics rather than with imaginative writers.

Small wonder, then, that most discussions about Salinger's work begin and, all too often, end in nostalgia. As John Romano would have it:

> . . . those who were young and literate in the Eisenhower and Kennedy years can be said to have received such pictures [e.g., Zooey's blue eyes, which were "a day's work to look into"; Franny muttering the Jesus prayer under her breath; Phoebe, in her blue coat, going around and around on the carrousel] with utter credulity and in a state of mind resembling awe. Some of us founded not only our literary taste but also a portion of our identity on Holden Caulfield and Franny Glass: we were smart kids in a dumb world or sensitive kids in a "phony" one, and Salinger was playing our song.[7]

Now it is Ann Beattie who plays somebody else's song in the pages of *The New Yorker*, but the tunes that blare out of her characters' radios sound unfamiliar, and the characters themselves strike us as inarticulate. Allusions shrink to last season's TV schedule, a movie, a "hot" rock album. To be sure, people in *New Yorker* stories still suffer *angst*, but if technique is still style, theirs is a threadbare version.

In this sense, Jay McInerney's recent *Bright Lights, Big City* is also a book about the glitz, the fashion, the *tempora et mores* of Manhattan's faster lanes. As Holden's saga is simultaneously a satiric attack and a cautionary tale, so too is McInerney's. Moreover, behind *Bright Lights, Big City*'s smart talk about Bolivian Marching Powder (i.e., cocaine) and its quick studies in SoHo eccentricity lies a long history of American writers who equated the City with infinite possibilities, and who surrendered themselves to its Dream: the Hawthorne of "My Kinsman, Major Molineux," the Whitman of *Leaves of Grass*, the Dos Passos of *Manhattan Transfer*, and of course the Fitzgerald of *The Great Gatsby*.

Bright Lights, Big City has its Salingeresque connections—in the way, for example, that its protagonist describes one woman as having "cheek-bones to break your heart" or another as having a voice "like the New Jersey State Anthem played through an electric shaver"—and, more important, in the way it has apparently been adopted by many as an etiquette book for the eighties.[8] But the *real* connections, the shivery ones, are to F. Scott Fitzgerald. Jay McInerney is News—whether the "news" be about the $200,000 he received to turn *Bright Lights, Big City* into a Hollywood screenplay or his accounts of "partying" with Mick Jagger. He is sleek, handsome, barely past thirty, and an "established author" on the strength of one book. In short, McInerney is a secret sharer with the Fitzgerald who rocketed to stardom, literary and otherwise, by way of *This Side of Paradise*.

But this is also a case in which history repeats itself with a difference. If Fitzgerald's account of "parlor snakes" and "petting parties," of Princeton undergrads who got "boiled" at dances and vamps who had been kissed by "dozens of boys," was both a sensation and a Victorian shocker, McInerney's guided tour of Manhattan night life will, no doubt, strike even the most permissive parent as an updated, and upsetting, equivalent:

> You are not the kind of guy who would be at a place like this at this time of morning. But here you are, and you cannot say that the terrain is entirely unfamiliar, although the details are fuzzy. You are at a nightclub talking to a girl with a shaved head. The club is either Heartbreak or the Lizard Lounge. . . . Somewhere back there you could have cut your losses, but you rode past that moment on a comet trail of white powder and now you are trying to hang on to the rush.[9]

Shimmering surface details are, of course, only a small part of what make Fitzgerald and McInerney such fascinating *doppelgängers*. At a deeper, more significant level, what they share is a vision about failure, about breakdown, about crack up. With an *i* dotted here, a *t* crossed there, this passage from *Bright Lights, Big City* might have been lifted from the Old Master:

> You started on the Upper East Side with champagne and unlimited prospects, strictly observing the Allagash rule of perpetual motion: one drink per stop. Tad's mission in life is to have more fun than anyone else in New York City, and this involves a lot of moving around, since there is always the likelihood that where you aren't is more fun than where you are. You are awed by his strict refusal to acknowledge any goal higher than the pursuit of pleasure. You want to be like that. You also think he is spoiled and dangerous. His friends are all rich and spoiled. . . .[10]

This is the sort of world my students can "relate" to, the sort of world they hope to discover themselves after graduation. That most of them are not yet reading the book McInerney has written is a matter we

Is the Age of Formative Books Over?

will take up—with mixed results, I suspect—when *Bright Lights, Big City* elbows its way into the syllabus for English 263: Contemporary American Novel. Then I will tell them that, in Holden Caulfield's day, the Joe Flits wore tattersall vests and gray suiting; now they deck themselves out in designer jeans and Reeboks. What doesn't change, however, is the single word required to write both down: *phony*.

No doubt my students will shake off what I say about *their* current favorite, and perhaps they should. After all, when those in the know about postmodernist fiction wag their fingers at *The Catcher in the Rye* and call it "counterfeit," I continue to listen to the voices that mattered, and that still matter—namely those in Salinger's novel. Given the choice of being "suckered in" by fiction or by a critic of fiction, I know where to take my stand. And I hope that my students do too.

What worries me, however, is not so much that a hot book like *Bright Lights, Big City* may or may not weather the storms of time (few novels do), but that the notion of formative books *per se* may be sunk. Our culture moves with a speed as blinding as it is fickle. Mark Twain once quipped that few humorists last forever, and then went on to define "forever" as thirty years. "Forever," I would submit, has grown considerably shorter in our own time, and if we have not quite reached Andy Warhol's dream of everyone in America being famous for fifteen minutes, we are coming dangerously close. Even the most "with-it" of my students would squirm if they had to read yellowing copies of *People* magazine or sit through reruns on MTV. That, they would argue, is so much *history*, which Henry Ford, in another time and place, called so much bunk.

Rather than formative experiences, contemporary culture demands *new* ones—slicker, trendier, and (most important of all) disposable. *Bright Lights, Big City*—sandwiched uneasily between a film like *St. Elmo's Fire* and the current Land's End catalogue—is simply the latest, most interesting example of "This is how the world goes. . . ." I take some consolation in reminding myself that this, too, shall pass—and no doubt with deliberate speed—but I take a larger measure of satisfaction from my certain knowledge that, despite everything, and at 50+, Holden Caulfield still has an honored place in the minds of what might well be the last generation to have formed its imagination, its sense of who we were, from the pages of a formative book.

From *Georgia Review* 40.4 (Winter 1986): 953-967. Copyright © 1986 by Sanford Pinsker. Reprinted with permission of Sanford Pinsker.

Notes

1. J. D. Salinger, *The Catcher in the Rye* (New York: New American Library, 1953), p. 121. Subsequent references are to this edition.

2. From "I'm Here" in *The Collected Poems of Theodore Roethke* (Garden City, N.Y.: Doubleday & Co., 1966), p. 162.

3. "From the Notebooks of Lionel Trilling," ed. Christopher Zinn, in *Partisan Review: The 50th Anniversary Edition*, ed. William Phillips (New York: Stein & Day, 1985), p. 15.

4. *The Stories of F. Scott Fitzgerald*, ed. Malcolm Cowley (New York: Charles Scribner's Sons, 1951), p. 145.

5. *Straw for the Fire: From the Notebooks of Theodore Roethke, 1943-63*, ed. David Wagoner (Garden City, N.Y.: Anchor Press/Doubleday, 1974), p. 249.

6. W. P. Kinsella, *Shoeless Joe* (Boston: Houghton Mifflin, 1982), pp. 78-79.

7. John Romano, "Salinger Was Playing Our Song," *The New York Times Book Review* (3 June 1979), 11.

8. In roughly the same way that *The Catcher in the Rye* taught my generation "how to speak"—and often in ways my prudish parents did not approve—*Bright Lights, Big City* is a manual about where, and how, the action is. That they represent cases in which Life imitates Art was brought home to me with especial force when a student of mine wondered, half seriously, if Jay McInerney might like to do a line of coke after his public lecture. McInerney, I hasten to add, declined the invitation.

9. Jay McInerney, *Bright Lights, Big City* (New York: Vintage Books, 1984), p. 1.

10. McInerney, pp. 2-3. Bret Easton Ellis' *Less Than Zero* (New York: Penguin Books, 1985) raises the "rich and spoiled" ante considerably. If McInerney is out to spin a cautionary tale about Manhattan night life, Ellis seems content simply to chronicle the high-fashion clothing and pricey dinners, the drugs and fast cars that apparently come with the territory of being young and rich in Los Angeles.

Cherished and Cursed:
Toward a Social History of
*The Catcher in the Rye*_____
Stephen J. Whitfield

The plot is brief: in 1949 or perhaps 1950, over the course of three days during the Christmas season, a sixteen-year-old takes a picaresque journey to his New York City home from the third private school to expel him. The narrator recounts his experiences and opinions from a sanitarium in California. A heavy smoker, Holden Caulfield claims to be already six feet, two inches tall and to have wisps of grey hair; and he wonders what happens to the ducks when the ponds freeze in winter. The novel was published on 16 July 1951, sold for $3.00, and was a Book-of-the-Month Club selection. Within two weeks, it had been reprinted five times, the next month three more times—though by the third edition the jacket photograph of the author had quietly disappeared. His book stayed on the best-seller list for thirty weeks, though never above fourth place.[1]

Costing 75¢, the Bantam paperback edition appeared in 1964. By 1981, when the same edition went for $2.50, sales still held steady, between twenty and thirty thousand copies per month, about a quarter of a million copies annually. In paperback the novel sold over three million copies between 1953 and 1964, climbed even higher by the 1980s, and continues to attract about as many buyers as it did in 1951. The durability of its appeal is astonishing. *The Catcher in the Rye* has gone through over seventy printings and has spread into thirty languages. Three decades after it first appeared, a mint copy of the first edition was already fetching about $200.[2]

Critical and academic interest has been less consistent; and how J. D. Salinger's only novel achieved acclaim is still a bit mystifying. After its first impact came neglect: following the book reviews, only three critical pieces appeared in the first five years. In the next four years, at least seventy essays on *The Catcher in the Rye* were published in American and British magazines. Salinger's biographer explained why: "A feature of the youthquake was, of course, that students could now tell their teachers what to read." Ian Hamilton also notes that by the mid-1950s the novel had "become the book all brooding adolescents had to buy, [and on campuses] the indispensable manual from which cool styles of disaffection could be borrowed."[3] No American writer over the past half-century has entranced serious young readers more than Salinger, whose novel about the flight from Pencey Prep may lag behind only *Of Mice and Men* on public-school required reading lists.[4] And his fiction has inspired other writers as well; the late Harold Brodkey, for example, considered it "the most influential body of work in English prose by anyone since Hemingway."[5]

One explanation for why *The Catcher in the Rye* has enjoyed such a sustained readership came over two decades after the novel was first published—from a middle-aged Holden Caulfield himself, as imagined by journalist Stefan Kanfer: "The new audience is never very different from the old Holden. They may not know the words, but they can hum along with the malady. My distress is theirs. They, too, long for the role of adolescent savior. They, too, are aware of the imminent death in life. As far as the sexual explosion is concerned, I suspect a lot of what you've heard is just noise." Sex "still remains a mystery to the adolescent. I have no cure, only consolation: someone has passed this way before." Objections to schlock and vulgarity and physical decline, and preferences for the pastoral over the machine continue to resonate, "Holden" suspects;[6] and so long as the United States continues to operate very much this side of paradise, a reluctance to inherit what the grown-ups have bequeathed is bound to enlist sympathy. The fantasy of withdrawal and retreat to the countryside ("Massachusetts and Vermont, and all around there . . . [are] beautiful as hell up there. It really is.") is not only a commonplace yearning but also advice Holden's creator elected to take by moving to Cornish, New Hampshire.[7]

But it should be conceded that generally it's the grown-ups who are in charge, and many of them have wanted to ban the widely beloved novel. Why *The Catcher in the Rye* has been censored (and censured) as well as cherished is a curiosity worth examining for its own sake. But how so transparently charming a novel can also exercise a peculiar allure and even emit disturbing danger signals may serve as an entrée into postwar American culture as well.

Bad Boys, Bad Readers

One weird episode inspired by *The Catcher in the Rye* involves Jerry Lewis. He tried to buy the movie rights, which were not for sale, and to play the lead. One problem was that the director did not read the book until the 1960s, when he was already well into his thirties. Playing the protagonist would have been a stretch, but *le roi de crazy* felt some affinity for Salinger (whom Lewis never met): "He's nuts also." Curiously Holden himself mentions the word "crazy" and its cognates (like "mad," "madman," and "insane") over fifty times, more than the reverberant "phony."[8]

Indeed the history of this novel cannot be disentangled from the way the mentally unbalanced have read it. In one instance the reader is himself fictional: the protagonist of John Fowles's first book, which captures the unnerving character of Salinger's only novel as an index of taste, perhaps of moral taste. In the second section of *The Collector*, told from the viewpoint of the victim, the kidnapped Miranda Grey recounts in her diary that she asks her captor, lepidopterist Frederick Clegg, whether he reads "proper books—real books." When he admits that "light novels are more my line," she recommends *The Catcher in the Rye* instead: "I've almost finished it. Do you know I've read it twice and I'm five years younger than you are?" Sullenly he promises to read it. Later she notices him doing so, "several times . . . look[ing] to see how many pages more he had to read. He reads it only to show me how hard he is trying." After the duty has been discharged, over a week later, the collector admits: "I don't see much point in it." When Miranda counters, "You realize this is one of the most brilliant studies of adolescence ever written?" he responds that Holden "sounds a mess to me."

"Of course he's a mess. But he realizes he's a mess, he tries to express what he feels, he's a human being for all his faults. Don't you even feel sorry for him?"

"I don't like the way he talks."

"I don't like the way you talk," she replies. "But I don't treat you as below any serious notice or sympathy."

Clegg acknowledges: "I suppose it's very clever. To write like that and all."

"I gave you that book to read because I thought you would feel identified with him. You're a Holden Caulfield. He doesn't fit anywhere and you don't."

"I don't wonder, the way he goes on. He doesn't try to fit."

Miranda insists: "He tries to construct some sort of reality in his life, some sort of decency."

"It's not realistic. Going to a posh school and his parents having money. He wouldn't behave like that. In my opinion."

She has the final word (at least in her diary): "You get on the back of everything vital, everything trying to be honest and free, and you bear it down."

Modern art, she realizes, embarrasses and fascinates Clegg; it "shocks him" and stirs "guilty ideas in him" because he sees it as "*all* vaguely immoral." For the mass audience at which William Wyler's 1965 film adaptation was aimed, Clegg's aesthetic world is made less repellent and more conventional, and the conversation about *The Catcher in the Rye* is abbreviated.[9]

In a more class-conscious society than is the United States, Fowles's loner finds something repugnant about the recklessness of the privileged protagonist. In a more violent society than England, types like Frederick Clegg might identify with Holden Caulfield's alienation from "normal" people so thoroughly that they become assassins. To be sure, *The Catcher in the Rye* is bereft of violence; and no novel seems less likely to activate the impulse to "lock and load." But this book nevertheless has exercised an eerie allure for asocial young men who, glomming on to Holden's estrangement, yield to the terrifying temptations of murder. "Lacking a sense of who he is," such a person "shops among artifacts of our culture—books, movies, TV programs, song lyrics, newspaper clippings—to fashion a character." Instead of authentic individuality, Priscilla Johnson McMillan has written, "all that is left is a collection of cultural shards—the bits and pieces of popular culture, torn from their contexts."[10]

In December 1980, with a copy of Salinger's novel in his pocket, Mark David Chapman murdered John Lennon. Before the police arrived, the assassin began reading the novel to himself and, when he was sentenced, read aloud the passage that begins with "anyway, I keep picturing all these little kids" and ends with "I'd just be the catcher in the rye and all" (pp. 224-25). Daniel M. Stashower has speculated ingeniously that Chapman wanted the former Beatle's innocence to be preserved in the only way possible—by death (the fate of Holden's revered brother Allie). Of course it could be argued that the assassin was not a conscientious reader, since Holden realizes on the carrousel that children have to be left alone, that they cannot be saved from themselves: "The thing with kids is, if they want to grab for the gold ring, you have to let them do it, and not say anything. If they fall off, they fall off" (pp. 273-74). No older catcher should try to intervene.[11]

Nor was Chapman the only Beatles fan to reify happiness as a warm gun. John Hinckley, Jr., described himself in his high school days as "a rebel without a cause" and was shocked to hear that Lennon had been murdered. A year later Hinckley himself tried to kill President Reagan. In Hinckley's hotel room, police found, along with a 1981 John Lennon color calendar, Salinger's novel among a half-dozen paperbacks. Noting the "gruesome congruences between these loners,"

Richard Schickel wondered whether Chapman and Hinckley could "really believe their disaffections were similar to Holden Caulfield's."[12]

One stab at an answer would be provided in John Guare's play *Six Degrees of Separation*, which opened in New York in 1990 and which he adapted for Fred Schepsi's film three years later. An imposter calling himself Paul insinuates himself into a well-heeled family; he is a perfect stranger (or appears to be). Pretending to be a Harvard undergraduate who has just been mugged, posing as the son of actor Sidney Poitier, Paul claims that his thesis is devoted to Salinger's novel and its odd connections to criminal loners:

> A substitute teacher out on Long Island was dropped from his job for fighting with a student. A few weeks later, the teacher returned to the classroom, shot the student unsuccessfully, held the class hostage and then shot himself. Successfully. This fact caught my eye: last sentence. *Times*. A neighbor described him as a nice boy. Always reading *Catcher in the Rye*.

Paul then mentions "the nitwit—Chapman" and insists that "the reading of that book would be his defense" for having killed Lennon. Hinckley, too, had said "if you want my defense all you have to do is read *Catcher in the Rye*. It seemed to be time to read it again." Paul reads it as a "manifesto of hate" against phonies,

> a touching story, comic because the boy wants to do so much and can't do anything. Hates all phoniness and only lies to others. Wants everyone to like him, is only hateful, and is completely self-involved. In other words, a pretty accurate picture of a male adolescent. And what alarms me about the book—not the book so much as the aura about it—is this: The book is primarily about paralysis. The boy can't function. And at the end, before he can run away and start a new life, it starts to rain and he folds.... But the aura around this book of Salinger's—which perhaps should be read by everyone *but* young men—is this: It mirrors like a fun house mirror and am-

plifies like a distorted speaker one of the great tragedies of our times—the death of the imagination, [which] now stands as a synonym for something outside ourselves.

A smooth liar, Paul later admits (or claims) that a Groton commencement address delivered a couple of years earlier was the source of his insights.[13]

Beloved and Banned

Holden has thus been born to trouble—yet another reminder that, in the opinion of long queues of literary critics, you can't know about him without your having read a book by Mr. Mark Twain called *The Adventures of Huckleberry Finn*, which told the truth mainly about the intensity of the yearning for authenticity and innocence that marks the picaresque quest. Huck and Holden share the fate of being both beloved *and* banned; such reactions were not unrelated. When the Concord (Massachusetts) public library proscribed *The Adventures of Huckleberry Finn* soon after its publication, the author gloated that not even his *Innocents Abroad* had sold more copies more quickly; and "those idiots in Concord" "have given us a rattling tip-top puff which will go into every paper in the country. . . . That will sell 25,000 copies for us sure."[14]

Salinger's novel does not appear to have been kept off the shelves in Concord but did cause enough of a stir to make the short list of the most banned books in school libraries, curricula, and public libraries.[15] In 1973 the *American School Board Journal* called this monster best-seller "the most widely censored book in the United States."[16] It was noted nearly a decade later that *The Catcher in the Rye* "had the dubious distinction of being at once the most frequently censored book across the nation and the second-most frequently taught novel in public high schools."[17] Anne Levinson, the assistant director of the Office of Intellectual Freedom in Chicago, called *The Catcher in the Rye* probably "a perennial No. 1 on the censorship hit list," narrowly ahead of *Of Mice and Men* and *The Grapes of Wrath* and perhaps of Eldridge Cleaver's *Soul on Ice* as well.[18] No postwar American novel has been subjected to more—and more intense—efforts to prevent the young from reading it.

Some examples: The National Organization for Decent Literature declared it objectionable by 1956. Five years later a teacher in a San Jose, California, high school who had included the novel on the twelfth-grade supplementary reading list was transferred and the novel dropped. *The Catcher in the Rye* was excised from the list of approved books in Kershaw County, South Carolina, after the sheriff of Camden declared part of the novel obscene.[19] In 1978 the novel was banned in the high schools of Issaquah, Washington, in the wake of a campaign led by a diligent citizen who tabulated 785 "profanities" and charged that including Holden in the syllabus was "part of an overall Communist plot in which a lot of people are used and may not even be aware of it."[20] Three school board members in Issaquah not only voted in favor of banning *The Catcher in the Rye* but also against renewing the contract of the school superintendent who had explicitly sanctioned the right of English teachers to assign the book. The board members were recalled, however. A school board member also confiscated a copy of Salinger's novel from a high school library in Asheville, North Carolina, in 1973. Several high school teachers have been fired or forced to resign for having assigned *The Catcher in the Rye*.[21]

California was the site of two well-reported incidents. The first erupted in 1962 in Temple City, near Pasadena, at a Board of Education meeting. Salinger's book had been assigned as supplementary reading for the eleventh grade. A parent objected, in the main, to the "crude, profane and obscene" language. For good measure, though, the book was also condemned for its literary assault on patriotism, "home life, [the] teaching profession, religion and so forth." Another vigilant parent, imploring the President of the United States summarily to fire anyone writing such a book, had obviously confused the reclusive novelist with John F. Kennedy's amiable press secretary, Pierre Salinger.[22]

The Catcher in the Rye was also banned from the supplementary reading list of Boron High School, located on the edge of the Mojave Desert. The proscription had an interesting effect. Salinger "has gained a new readership among townspeople," the *New York Times* reported, "and Helen Nelson, the local librarian, has a waiting list of fifteen people for the book that she says has been sitting on the shelf all these years pretty much unnoticed." The campaign against the book had been fueled by its profanity, which aroused the most heated objections. Vickie Swindler, the parent of a fourteen-year-old girl, was startled to see three "goddamns" on page 32. She recalled phoning the school and demanding to know: "How the hell [*sic*] did this teacher [Shelley Keller-Gage] get this book?" Locals who sympathized with the censors offered a curious interpretation of their motives, which they compared to Holden's dream of becoming a catcher in the rye to keep innocence intact; the protagonist and the parents trying to muzzle him shared a desire to exempt children from the vulgarity and corruption of the adult world. Yet, as Mrs. Keller-Gage noted, "Things are not innocent any more, and I think we've got to help them [i.e., children] deal with that, to make responsible choices, to be responsible citizens." Parents were "wanting to preserve the innocence of the children" in vain. The *Times* reported that she offered an alternative assignment for pupils whose parents were opposed to *The Catcher in the Rye:* Ray Bradbury's *Dandelion Wine*.[23]

When the ban took effect in the new term, Mrs. Keller-Gage put her three dozen copies of Salinger's novel "on a top shelf of her classroom closet, inside a tightly taped cardboard box." Raise high the bookshelf, censors. In place of *The Catcher in the Rye*, she announced, she would assign another Bradbury novel, *Fahrenheit 451*,[24] the title referring to the presumed "temperature at which book-paper catches fire, and burns." This dystopian novel about book-burning was published in 1953, though a shorter version, entitled "The Fireman," had appeared in *Galaxy Science Fiction* in 1950. Both versions were too early to allude to Salinger's novel, which is neither shown nor recited in François Truffaut's 1966 film adaptation (though one item visibly consumed is an issue of *Cahiers du Cinéma*).

Efforts at suppression were not confined to secondary schools. A prominent Houston attorney, "whose daughter had been assigned the novel in an English class at the University of Texas, threatened to remove the girl from the University," *Harper's* reported. "The aggrieved father sent copies [of the novel] to the governor, the chancellor of the university, and a number of state officials. The state senator from Houston threatened to read passages from the book on the senate floor to show the sort of thing they teach in Austin. The lawyer-father said Salinger used language 'no sane person would use' and accused the university of 'corrupting the moral fibers [*sic*] of our youth.'" He conceded that the novel "is not a hard-core Communist-type book, but it encourages a lessening of spiritual values which in turn leads to communism."[25]

In making appointments to the department of English at the University of Montana, Leslie A. Fiedler recalled that "the only unforgivable thing in the university or the state was to be 'controversial.'" He nevertheless "began to make offers to young instructors who had quarreled with their administrators, or had asked their students to read *Catcher in the Rye*, or had themselves written poetry containing dirty words, or were flagrantly Jewish or simply Black." The narrator of a recent academic novel, *Mustang Sally*, recalls that "the chairman of the department has asked us all to use our best judgment in avoiding confrontation with the evangelicals . . . such as the group who staged a 'pray-in' at the Greensburg High School library because *The Catcher in the Rye* was on the shelves. It has since been removed, along with the principal." No wonder, then, that one columnist, though writing for the newspaper of record, whimsically claimed to "lose count of the number of times the book has been challenged or banned."[26]

Such animosity had become a predictable feature of the far right by the 1980s, when an outfit named Educational Research Analysts, financed by Richard Viguerie, a leading fundraiser for right-wing organizations, was formed to examine nearly every textbook considered for adoption anywhere in the nation. "The group has assembled a list of 67 categories under which a book may be banned. Category 43 ('Trash') included *The Catcher in the Rye*," the *New Republic* reported. Perhaps Salinger should have counted his blessings, since the eclectic Category 44 consisted of the "works of questionable writers" like Malcolm X, Langston Hughes, and Ogden Nash.[27]

It is more surprising that moral objections surfaced in the pages of *Ramparts*, the brashest of the magazines to give a radical tincture to the 1960s. The monthly had begun under Roman Catholic auspices, however; and though Simone de Beauvoir's *The Second Sex* was deemed a work of depravity on the *Index Librorum Prohibitorum*, Salinger was accorded the same treatment as Genet, Proust, Joyce, and D. H. Lawrence: omission.[28] But individual Catholics could still get incensed over *The Catcher in the Rye*, as the new editor of *Ramparts*, Warren Hinckle, discovered one evening. He was having a conversation with the new fiction editor, Helen Keating, who was married to the magazine's new publisher. Hinckle recalled:

> A great debate somehow began over the rather precious subject of J. D. Salinger. The setting was vaguely Inquisitional. . . . They all listened attentively as [Edward] Keating, suddenly a fiery prosecutor, denounced Salinger for moral turpitude. Keating expressed similar opinions about the degeneracy of writers such as Tennessee Williams and Henry Miller: corruption, moral decay, the erosion of the classic values of Western Civilization, et cetera, ad infinitum. His special contempt for Salinger seemed to have something to do with the fact that he had found his oldest son reading a paperback book by the man.

Keating became enraged enough to make "the hyperbolic assertion, which he later retracted, that if he were President, he would put J. D. Salinger in jail! I asked why. 'Because he's dirty,' Ed said. I barely recalled something in *The Catcher in the Rye* about Holden Caulfield in the back seat unhooking a girl's bra," Hinckle recalled. Despite the lyric, "If a body catch a body," in fact few popular novels are so fully exempt from the leer of the sensualist; and even though Holden claims to be "probably the biggest sex maniac you ever saw," he admits it's only "in my *mind*" (p. 81).

In any case, Hinckle was baffled by Keating's tirade and "unleashed a more impassioned defense of Salinger than I normally would have felt impelled to make of a voguish writer whose mortal sin was his Ivy League slickness." The chief consequence of the argument was Keating's discovery of a "bomb," by which he meant "a hot story. The 'bomb' which exploded in the first issue of *Ramparts* was the idea of a symposium on J. D. Salinger"—with Hinckle for the defense and Keating and a friend of his for the prosecution. That friend, Robert O. Bowen, complained in the inaugural issue in 1962 that Salinger was not only anti-Catholic but somehow also "pro-Jewish and pro-Negro." Bowen accused the novelist of being so subversive that he was "vehemently anti-Army" (though Salinger had landed on Utah Beach on D-Day), "even anti-America," a writer who subscribed to "the sick line transmitted by Mort Sahl" and other "cosmopolitan think people." Though Bowen was vague in identifying the sinister campaigns this impenetrably private novelist was managing to wage, alignments with the Anti-Defamation League and "other Jewish pressure groups" were duly noted, and Salinger's sympathy for "Negro chauvinism" was denounced. "Let those of us who are Christian and who love life lay this book aside as the weapon of an enemy," Bowen advised.[29] Such was the level of literary analysis at the birth of *Ramparts*.

The Catcher in the Rye has even taken on an iconic significance precisely because it is reviled as well as revered. What if the Third Reich had won the Second World War by defeating Britain? one novelist has wondered. Set in 1964, *Fatherland* imagines a past in which Salinger is among four foreign authors listed as objectionable to the Greater Reich. Those writers, banned by the authorities, are esteemed by younger Germans "rebelling against their parents. Questioning the state. Listening to American radio stations. Circulating their crudely printed copies of proscribed books. . . . Chiefly, they protested against the war—the seemingly endless struggle against the American-backed Soviet guerrillas." But forget about a history that never happened. One of the two regimes that *had* supplanted the defeated Reich was the German Democratic Republic, whose censors were wary of American cultural imports. In the 1960s, Kurt Hager served as the leading ideologist on the Central Committee of the East German regime. Resisting publication of a translation of Salinger's novel, Hager feared that its protagonist might captivate Communist youth. Though a translation did eventually appear and proved popular among young readers in the GDR, Hager refused to give up the fight. Appropriate role models were "winners," he insisted, like the regime's Olympic athletes, not "losers" like Holden Caulfield.[30]

Yet anti-anti-Communism could make use of the novel too. Its reputation for inciting censorious anxiety had become so great by 1990 that in the film *Guilty by Suspicion*, a terrified screenwriter is shown burning his books in his driveway a few hours after testifying before a rump session of the House Un-American Activities Committee. Shocked at this bonfire of the humanities, director David Merrill (Robert De Niro) categorizes what goes up in flames as "all good books"—though the only titles he cites are *The Adventures of Tom Sawyer* and *The Catcher in the Rye*. The decision of writer-director Irwin Winkler to include Salinger's novel, however, is historically (if not canonically) implausible. When the film opens in September 1951, Merrill is shown returning from two months in France; a hot-off-the-press copy of the best-seller must therefore have been rushed to him in Paris if he could pronounce on the merits of the book on his first evening back in Los Angeles.

The attacks on *The Catcher in the Rye* gathered a momentum of their own and "show no signs of tapering off," one student of book-banning concluded in 1979. The novel became so notorious for igniting controversy "that many censors freely admit they have never read it, but are relying on the reputation the book has garnered."[31] Anne Levinson added: "Usually the complaints have to do with blasphemy or what people feel is irreligious. Or they say they find the language generally offensive or vulgar, or there is a sort of general 'family values' kind of complaint, that the book undermines parental authority, that the portrayal of Holden Caulfield is not a good role model for teenagers." It was judged suitable for Chelsea Clinton, however. In 1993 the First Lady gave her daughter a copy to read while vacationing on Martha's Vineyard. The *Boston Globe* used the occasion to editorialize against persistent censorship, since "Salinger's novel of a 1950s coming of age still ranks among the works most frequently challenged by parents seeking to sanitize their children's school reading."[32]

Assigning Meaning to Growing Up Absurd

Few American novels of the postwar era have elicited as much scholarly and critical attention as *The Catcher in the Rye*, and therefore little that is fresh can still be proposed about so closely analyzed a text. But the social context within which the novel has generated such anxiety remains open to interpretation. If anything new can be said about this book, its status within the cross-hairs of censors offers the greatest promise. What needs further consideration is not why this novel is so endearing but why it has inspired campaigns to ban it. Literary critics have tended to expose the uncanny artistry by which Salinger made Holden Caulfield into the loved one but have been far less curious about the intensity of the desire to muffle him. It is nevertheless possible to isolate several explanations for the power of this novel to affect—and disturb—readers outside of departments of English.

The "culture wars" of the last third of the twentieth century are fundamentally debates about the 1960s. That decade marked the end of what historian Tom Engelhardt has labeled "victory culture," indeed the end of "the American Way of Life," phrased in the singular. The

1960s constituted a caesura in the formation of national self-definition, nor has confidence in *e pluribus unum* been entirely restored. At first glance it might seem surprising for *The Catcher in the Rye* to have contributed in some small fashion to fragmentation. Nevertheless such a case, however tentative, has been advanced. Since nothing in history is created *ex nihilo*, at least part of the 1960s, it has been argued, must have sprung from at least part of the 1950s.

Literary critics Carol and Richard Ohmann, for example, concede that the young narrator lacks the will to try to change society. They nevertheless contend that his creator recorded "a serious critical mimesis of bourgeois life in the Eastern United States, ca. 1950—of snobbery, privilege, class injury, culture as a badge of superiority, sexual exploitation, education subordinated to status, warped social feeling, competitiveness, stunted human possibility, the list could go on." They praise Salinger's acuity "in imagining these hurtful things, though not in explaining them"—or in hinting how they might be corrected. *The Catcher in the Rye* thus "mirrors a contradiction of bourgeois society" and of "advanced capitalism," which promises many good things but frustrates their acquisition and equitable distribution. In this manner readers are encouraged at least to conceive of the urgent *need* for change, even if they're not able to reconfigure Holden's musings into a manual for enacting it.[33]

That moment would have to await the crisis of the Vietnam War, which "converted Salinger's novel into a catalyst for revolt, converting anomie into objectified anger," John Seelye has argued. *The Catcher in the Rye* became "a threshold text to the decade of the sixties, ten years after it appeared at the start of the fifties, [when it was] a minority text stating a minor view." In the axial shift to the left that occurred in the 1960s, the sensibility of a prep school drop-out could be re-charged and politicized: "*Catcher* likewise supplied not only the rationale for the antiwar, anti-regimentation movements of the sixties and seventies but provided the anti-ideological basis for many of the actual novels about Vietnam."[34]

The 1960s mavericks ("the highly sensitive, the tormented") who would brand social injustice as itself obscene were, according to Charles Reich, real-life versions of what Holden had groped toward becoming. Salinger's protagonist may be too young, or too rich, to bestir himself outward. But he was "a fictional version of the first young precursors of Consciousness III. Perhaps there was always a bit of Consciousness III in every teenager, but normally it quickly vanished. Holden sees through the established world: they are phonies and he is merciless in his honesty. But what was someone like Holden to do? A subculture of 'beats' grew up, and a beatnik world flourished briefly, but for most people it represented only another dead end," Reich commented. "Other Holdens might reject the legal profession and try teaching literature or writing instead, letting their hair grow a little bit longer as well. But they remained separated individuals, usually ones from affluent but unhappy, tortured family backgrounds, and their differences with society were paid for by isolation." In making America more green, Holden was portrayed as an avatar of "subterranean awareness."[35]

Daniel Isaacson also reads the novel as seeding later revolt. The narrator of E. L. Doctorow's *The Book of Daniel*, published exactly two decades after *The Catcher in the Rye*, even echoes Holden in self-consciously repudiating Dickens's contribution to Con II: "Let's see, what other David Copperfield kind of crap" should he tell you? But the personal quickly becomes political, when Daniel insists that "the Trustees of Ohio State were right in 1956 when they canned the English instructor for assigning *Catcher in the Rye* to his freshman class. They knew there is no qualitative difference between the kid who thinks it's funny to fart in chapel, and Che Guevara. They knew then Holden Caulfield would found SDS."[36]

Of course Daniel thinks of himself as an outcast and is eager to re-establish and legitimate his radical lineage, and so his assumption that the trustees might have been shrewd enough to foresee guerrillas in the mist must be treated with skepticism. But consider Tom Hayden, a founder of Students for a Democratic Society (and in the 1950s a parishioner of Father Charles Coughlin in Royal Oak, Michigan). As a teenager Hayden had considered Salinger's protagonist (along with novelist Jack Kerouac and actor James Dean) an "alternative cultural model." "The life crises they personified spawned . . . political activism," which some who had been adolescents in the 1950s found liberating. Hayden remembers being touched not only by Holden's assault on the "phonies" and conformists but by his "caring side," his sympathy for "underdogs and innocents." The very "attempt to be gentle and humane . . . makes Holden a loser in the 'game' of life. Unable to be the kind of man required by prep schools and corporations," Salinger's protagonist could find no exit within American society. Undefiant and confused, Holden nevertheless served as "the first image of middle-class youth growing up absurd," which Hayden would situate at the psychological center of the Port Huron Statement.[37]

The dynamism inherent in youthful revolt, one historian has claimed, can best be defined as "a mystique . . . that fused elements of Marlon Brando's role in *The Wild One*, James Dean's portrayal in *Rebel without a Cause*, J. D. Salinger's Holden Caulfield in *Catcher in the Rye*, the rebels of *Blackboard Jungle*, and the driving energy and aggressive sexuality of the new heroes of rock 'n' roll into a single image. The mystique emphasized a hunger for authenticity and sensitivity." But something is askew here, for Holden is too young to have felt the Dionysian effects of rock 'n' roll, which erupted about three years after he left Pencey Prep. A "sex maniac" only in his head, he hardly represents "aggressive sexuality" either. *The Wild One*, *Rebel without a Cause*, and *Blackboard Jungle* are "goddam movies," which Holden professes to hate, because "they can ruin you. I'm not kidding" (p. 136). His own tastes are emphatically literary, ranging from *The Great Gatsby* and *Out of Africa* to Thomas Hardy and Ring Lardner. Even if the bland official ethos of the 1950s ultimately failed to repress the rambunctious energies the popular arts were about to unleash, Roland Marchand understands that the "mystique" he has identified would not be easily radicalized. Indeed, it could be tamed. Conservative consolidation was a more predictable outcome: "If the problems of a society are embedded in its social structure and are insulated from change by layers of ideological tradition, popular culture is an unlikely source of remedy. It is far more likely to serve needs for diversion and transitory compensation . . . [and] solace."[38] Such dynamism could not be politicized.

The deeper flaw with interpreting *The Catcher in the Rye* as a harbinger of revolt is the aura of passivity that pervades the novel. Alienation does not always lead to, and can remain the antonym of, action. Salinger's own sensibility was definitively pre- (or anti-) Sixties. His "conviction that our inner lives greatly matter," John Updike observed in 1961, "peculiarly qualifies him to sing of an America, where, for most of us, there seems little to do but to feel. Introversion, perhaps, has been forced upon history" rather than the other way around. Therefore "an age of nuance, of ambiguous gestures and psychological jockeying" could account for the popularity of Salinger's work.[39]

Describing Holden as "a misfit in society because he refuses to adjust" and because he lacks the self-discipline to cultivate privacy, one young literary critic of the fifties was struck by "the quixotic futility" of the protagonist's "outrage" at all the planet's obscenities, by his isolation. Holden seems to have sat for psychologist Kenneth Keniston's portrait of uncommitted youth: those who have the most to live for but find no one to look up to; those who are the most economically and socially advantaged but feel the deepest pangs of alienation.[40] Jack Newfield ('60) was a charter member of SDS but remembers Hunter College as mired in an apathy "no public question seemed to touch." His fellow students "were bereft of passions, of dreams, of gods. . . . And their *Zeitgeist*—J. D. Salinger—stood for a total withdrawal from reality into the womb of childhood, innocence, and mystical Zen." Holden's creator, evidently, had captured the spirit of the Silent Generation.[41]

It may not be accidental that David Riesman, whose most famous book was a veritable touchstone of social analysis in the era, assigned *The Catcher in the Rye* in his Harvard sociology course on Character and Social Structure in the United States. He did so "perhaps," a *Time* reporter speculated, "because every campus has its lonely crowd of imitation Holdens." Indeed, Holden demonstrates the characteristics of anomie, which is associated with "ruleless" and "ungoverned" conduct, that Riesman had described in *The Lonely Crowd*; the anomic are "virtually synonymous with [the] maladjusted." Though Salinger's narrator does not quite exhibit "the lack of emotion and emptiness of expression" by which "the ambulatory patients of modern culture" can be recognized, he does display a "vehement hatred of institutional confines" that was bound to make his peers (if not his psychoanalyst) uneasy.[42] One reviewer, in true Fifties fashion, even blamed Holden himself for his loneliness, "because he has shut himself away from the normal activities of boyhood, games, the outdoors, friendship."[43] It is true that Holden hates schools like Pencey Prep, where "you have to keep making believe you give a damn if the football team loses, and all you do is talk about girls and liquor and sex all day, and everybody sticks together in these dirty little goddam cliques" (p. 170). But Holden remains confined to his era, unable to connect the dots from those cliques to a larger society that might merit some rearrangement. Nor does the novel expand the reader's horizons beyond those of the narrator; it does not get from pathos to indignation.

For *The Catcher in the Rye* is utterly apolitical—unlike its only rival in arousing the ire of conservative parents. Steinbeck's fiction directs the attention of susceptible young readers to exploitation of the weak and the abuse of power. But a serious critique of capitalism would not be found in Salinger's text even if a full field investigation were ordered. Certainly Holden's fantasy of secluding himself in a cabin in the woods is scarcely a prescription for social activism: "I'd pretend I was one of those deaf-mutes. That way I wouldn't have to have any goddam stupid useless conversations with anybody. If anybody wanted to tell me something, they'd have to write it on a piece of paper and shove it over to me. They'd get bored as hell doing that after a while, and then I'd be through with having conversations for the rest of my life" (pp. 257-58). Such passages will hardly alarm those wishing to repudiate or erase the 1960s, which is why *The Catcher in the Rye* does not belong to the history of dissidence.

Growing Up Absurd (1960) sports a title and a perspective that Holden might have appreciated, but Paul Goodman does not mention the novel. Published at the end of the tumultuous, unpredictable decade, Theodore Roszak's *The Making of a Counter Culture* (which *Newsweek* dubbed "the best guide yet published to the meaning . . . of youthful dissent") likewise fails to mention Salinger, though Holden certainly personifies (or anticipates) "the ethos of disaffiliation that is fiercely obnoxious to the adult society." In 1962 the editor of a collection of critical essays on Salinger—the future editor-in-chief of *Time*—found American campuses innocent of activism: "'Student riots' are a familiar and significant factor in European politics. The phenomenon has no equivalent in the United States."[44] That generalization would soon be falsified. But it should be noted that authors who have fathomed how the 1950s became the 1960s (like Morris Dickstein, Fred Inglis, Maurice Isserman, James Miller) ignore the impact of Salinger's novel.

Because any reading of the novel as a prefiguration of the 1960s is ultimately so unpersuasive, an over-reaction has set in. Alan Nadel, for example, has fashioned Holden into a Cold Warrior, junior division. "Donning his red hunting hat, he attempts to become the good Red-hunter, ferreting out the phonies and the subversives, but in so doing he emulates the bad Red-hunters," Nadel has written. "Uncovering duplicity was the theme of the day," he adds, so that "in thinking constantly about who or what was phony, Caulfield was doing no more than following the instructions of J. Edgar Hoover, the California Board of Regents, *The Nation* [*sic*], the Smith Act, and the Hollywood Ten. . . . Each citizen was potentially both the threat and the threatened." After all, hadn't Gary Cooper, testifying before HUAC, defined

Communism as something that was not "on the level"? Nadel equates Caulfield's "disdain for Hollywood" with HUAC's, nor could the young prostitute's mention of Melvyn Douglas have been accidental—since Congressman Richard Nixon had run against Helen Gahagan Douglas, and her husband was himself "a prominent Hollywood liberal." Nadel concludes that "the solution to Caulfield's dilemma becomes renouncing speech itself." Having named names, he realizes: "I sort of *miss* everybody I told about.... It's funny. Don't ever tell anybody anything," he advises; that is, don't be an informer. "If you do, you start missing everybody" (pp. 276-77). The narrator "spoke for the cold war HUAC witness," Nadel argued, "expressing existential angst over the nature and meaning of his 'testimony.'"[45] Such an interpretation is far-fetched: Holden is no more interested in politics than his creator, and he's considerably less interested in sanctioning conformity than were the Red-hunters.

Citizens who abhor the 1960s commonly deplore one of its most prominent legacies: the fragmentation into "identity politics," the loss of civic cohesion. Those worrying over this sin also will not find it in Salinger's book, which promotes no class consciousness, racial consciousness, or ethnic consciousness of any sort. Sol Salinger had strayed so far from Judaism that he became an importer of hams and cheeses;[46] and his son left no recognizably Jewish imprint on his fiction. Nor does his novel evoke the special plight of young women and girls. That omission would be rectified about two generations later, when Eve Horowitz's first novel appeared. Her young narrator and protagonist is not only female but emphatically Jewish, and she longs to meet her own Holden Caulfield. Jane Singer recalls: "I hadn't known any males who were as depressed as I was in high school, except for maybe Holden Caulfield, and I didn't really know him." As she's packing to leave Cleveland for Oberlin College, she muses, "besides clothes and shampoo and *The Catcher in the Rye*, I couldn't think of anything else to bring."[47] In her account of growing up female, Horowitz may have wanted to correct the imbalance David Riesman identified in 1961, when, attempting to explain the United States to a Japanese audience, he had commented on the inscrutable popularity of Salinger's novel: "Boys are frustrated because they aren't cowboys, and girls are frustrated because they aren't boys." The sociologist noted that "women have been the audience for American fiction and for movies. There are no girls' stories comparable to *Catcher in the Rye*. Yet girls can adapt themselves and identify with such a book, while a boy can't so easily identify with a girl."[48] In the literary marketplace, Riesman speculated, readers aren't turned off or away if the central characters are male but only if they are female. How many Boy Scouts and Explorer Scouts have been moved by reading *The Bell Jar*?

The Curse of Culture

Another way to understand the power of Salinger's novel to generate controversy is to recognize its vulnerability to moralistic criticism. From wherever the source—call it Puritanism, or puritanism, or Victorianism—there persists a tradition of imposing religious standards upon art or of rejecting works of the imagination because they violate conventional ethical codes. According to this legacy, books are neither good nor bad without "for you" being added as a criterion of judgment. This entwining of the aesthetic and the moralistic was obvious as prize committees struggled with the terms of Joseph Pulitzer's instructions that the novels to be honored in his name "shall best present the whole atmosphere of American life." But until 1927, the novels selected more accurately conveyed "the wholesome atmosphere of American life."[49] That eliminated Dreiser. Had the subtle revision of Pulitzer's own intentions not been overturned, virtually all great writers would have been categorically excluded. Nabokov comes quickly to mind. His most famous novel was given to the good family man Adolf Eichmann, then imprisoned in Israel, but was returned after two days with an indignant rejection: *"Das ist aber ein sehr unerfreuliches Buch"*—quite an unwholesome book. *Lolita* is narrated from the viewpoint of an adult, a pervert whose ornate vocabulary made the novel unintelligible to young readers, and so censors passed it by to target *The Catcher in the Rye*. It is a measure of Salinger's stature among other writers that, though famously dismissive of many literary giants, Nabokov wrote privately of his fellow *New Yorker* contributor: "I do admire him very much."[50]

But the reviewer for *The Christian Science Monitor* did not: *The Catcher in the Rye* "is not fit for children to read"; its central character is "preposterous, profane, and pathetic beyond belief." Too many young readers might even want to emulate Holden, "as too easily happens when immorality and perversion are recounted by writers of talent whose work is countenanced in the name of art or good intention."[51] Here was an early sign of trouble. Nor was respectability enhanced by the novel's first appearance in paperback, for it was offered as pulp fiction, a genre that beckoned with promises of illicit pleasure. The common 1950s practice of issuing serious books in pulp meant that "dozens of classic novels appeared in packages that were cartoonish, sordid or merely absurd." The aim of such marketing, Julie Lasky has suggested, was to grab "the attention of impulse shoppers in drugstores and bus depots; slogans jammed across the four-inch width of paperbound covers compressed the nuances of prizewinning authors into exaggerated come-ons." The 1953 paperback edition of Salinger's novel, for example, assured buyers that "this unusual book may shock you . . . but you will never forget it." The illustration on the cover depicted a prostitute standing near Holden and may have served as the only means by which some citizens judged the book. The cover so offended the author that it contributed to his move to Bantam when his contract with Signet expired. By then, the pulping of classics had largely ended in the wake of hearings by the House of Representatives' Select Committee on Current Pornographic Materials. But the availability of such cheap editions of books ranging from the serious to the lurid drew the curiosity of censors as well as bargain-hunters. The vulnerability of Salinger's novel testified to the aptness of Walter

Lippmann's generalization that censorship "is actually applied in proportion to the vividness, the directness, and the intelligibility of the medium which circulates the subversive idea." Movie screens, he wrote in 1927, therefore tend to be more censored than the stage, which is more censored than newspapers and magazines. But "the novel is even freer than the press today because it is an even denser medium of expression."[52] At least that was the case until the paperback revolution facilitated the expansion of the syllabus.

Of course, the paperback revolution was not the only cultural shift affecting the reception of the novel. The career of *The Catcher in the Rye* is virtually synchronous with the Cold War, and Holden Caulfield takes a stand of sorts: he calls himself "a pacifist" (p. 59). For men slightly older than Holden in 1949-50, military conscription was more or less universal, yet he predicts that "it'd drive me crazy if I had to be in the Army. . . . I swear if there's ever another war, they better just take me out and stick me in front of a firing squad. I wouldn't object." Indeed he goes further: "I'm sort of glad they've got the atomic bomb invented. If there's ever another war, I'm going to sit right the hell on top of it. I'll volunteer for it, I swear to God I will" (pp. 182, 183). Barely a decade later, Stanley Kubrick's pitch-black comedy *Dr. Strangelove* (1964) would confront nuclear terror by showing Major "King" Kong (Slim Pickens) doing precisely what Holden vows he will step forward to do. With such images in mind, one interpreter has thus boldly claimed that "the fear of nuclear holocaust, not the fear of four-letter words[,]" sparked controversy about *The Catcher in the Rye*.[53]

Salinger's novel may thus also be about history veering out of control, about the abyss into which parents could no longer prevent their offspring from staring, about the impotence to which a can-do people was unaccustomed. "The lack of faith in the American character expressed in the *Catcher* controversies," Professor Pamela Steinle has argued, "is rooted not in doubts about the strength of adolescent Americans' character but in recognition of the powerlessness of American adults—as parents, professionals and community leaders—to provide a genuine sense of the future for the adolescents in their charge." According to Steinle, the novel indicts "adult apathy and complicity in the construction of a social reality in which the American character cannot develop in any meaningful sense beyond adolescence." Nor does the novel warrant any hope that the condition can be remedied. The story is, after all, told from a sanitarium in California—a grim terminus given the common belief that the West offers a second chance. No wonder, then, that John Seelye, who ended his own revised version of *The Adventures of Huckleberry Finn* with Huck's bleakest pessimism ("I didn't much care if the goddamn sun never come up again"), could read Salinger's book "as a lengthy suicide note with a blank space at the end to sign your name."[54]

The advantage of Steinle's argument is that she situates the controversy over *The Catcher in the Rye* where it actually took place, which is less in the pages of *Ramparts* than at school board meetings. In such settings, the novel was branded by parents as a threat to their control and heralded by teachers as a measure of their professional autonomy and authority. But the disadvantage of Steinle's view is the scarcity of direct evidence that nuclear fears fueled the debate. Neither those who condemned *The Catcher in the Rye* nor its defenders made the specter of atomic catastrophe pivotal. Neither the moral nor the literary disputes were ventilated in such terms. Compared to Holden's far more pronounced resistance to maturation, compared to more immediate targets of his scorn, the Bomb hardly registered as a concern among objections to the novel.

But if "the essence of censorship," according to Lippmann, is "not to suppress subversive ideas as such, but to withhold them from those who are young or unprivileged or otherwise undependable,"[55] then Steinle's emphasis upon parental assertion of authority is not misplaced. In a more class-conscious society, the Old Bailey prosecutor of the publisher of *Lady Chatterley's Lover* could ask in his opening address to the jury, in 1960: "Is it a book that you would even wish your wife or your servants to read?"[56] But in the United States, overt conflicts are more likely to take generational form; and the first of Lippmann's categories deserves to be highlighted. Some of the books that have aroused the greatest ire place children at the center, like Richard Wright's *Black Boy*, Anne Frank's *Diary of a Young Girl*, and of course *The Adventures of Huckleberry Finn*; and despite the aura of "cuteness" hovering over Salinger's work, it emitted danger by striking at the most vulnerable spot in the hearts of parents. Nor could it have escaped the attention of alert readers that Holden's emotional affiliations are horizontal rather than vertical. His father, a corporate lawyer, is absent from the scene; and his mother is present only as a voice speaking from a dark room. The only relative whom the reader meets is Phoebe, the younger sister (and a mini-Holden).[57]

The contributor's note Salinger submitted to *Harper's* in 1946 was his credo: "I almost always write about very young people";[58] and the directness with which he spoke *to* them had much to do with his appeal—and with the anxiety that his literary intervention provoked in the internecine battle between generations. The effectiveness of his empathy posed a challenge to parents who invoked their right to be custodians of the curriculum, and the "legions of decency" may have sensed "a unique seductive power" which Salinger's biographer claims *The Catcher in the Rye* exudes. Even if the less sensitive or eccentric of its young readers might not try to assume Holden's persona, at least teenagers could imitate his lingo. A book that elicits such proprietary interest—succeeding cohorts believing in a special access to Salinger's meaning—was bound to arouse some suspicion that conventional authority was being outflanked.[59] Salinger's adroit fidelity to the feelings and experiences of his protagonist was what made the novel so tempting a target. Perhaps *The Catcher in the Rye* has been banned precisely because it is so cherished; because it is so easily loved, some citizens love to hate it.

Steinle has closely examined the local controversies that erupted over the book in Alabama, Virginia, New Mexico, and California as well as the debates conducted in such publications as the *PTA Maga-*

zine and the *Newsletter on Intellectual Freedom* of the American Library Association. She discovered a "division . . . over whether to prepare adolescents for or to protect them from adult disillusionment. . . . In the postwar period . . . recognition of the increasing dissonance between American ideals and the realities of social experience has become unavoidable, and it is precisely this cultural dissonance that is highlighted by Salinger's novel."[60] Its literary value got lost in the assertion of family values, in a campaign that must be classified as reactionary. "They say it describes reality," a parent in Boron, California, announced. "I say let's back up from reality. Let's go backwards. Let's go back to when we didn't have an immoral society."[61] When so idyllic a state existed was not specified, but what is evident is the element of anti-intellectualism that the struggle against permissiveness entailed. Here some of the parents were joined by Leonard Hall, the school superintendent of Bay County, Florida, who warned in 1987 against assigning books that were not state-approved because, he sagely opined, reading "is where you get ideas from."[62]

Attempts at vindication were occasionally made on the same playing field that censors themselves chose. Though Holden labels himself "sort of an atheist" (p. 130), he could be praised as a saint, if admittedly a picaresque one. One educator discerned in the protagonist a diamond in the rough: "He befriends the friendless. He respects those who are humble, loyal, and kind. He demonstrates a strong love for his family" (or for Phoebe anyway). Besides enacting such New Testament teachings, "he abhors hypocrisy. He values sex that comes from caring for another person and rejects its sordidness. And, finally, he wants to be a responsible member of society, to guide and protect those younger than he."[63] But a character witness is not the same as a literary critic, and such conflation seems to have gained little traction when the right of English teachers to make up reading lists was contested. If Holden's defense rested on a sanitized version of his character, then the implication was that assigned books with less morally meritorious protagonists might be subject to parental veto. Such a defense also assumed that disgruntled parents were themselves exegetes who had simply misread a text, that community conflicts could be resolved by more subtle interpretations. There is no reason to believe, however, that the towns where the novel was banned or challenged overlapped with maps of misreading. But such communities *were* places where parents tried to gain control of the curriculum, which is why *The Catcher in the Rye* would still have been proscribed even had it been re-read as a book of virtues.

For the objections that were most frequently raised were directed at the novelist's apparent desire to capture profuse adolescent profanity in the worst way. In the *Catholic World*, reviewer Riley Hughes disliked the narrator's "excessive use of amateur swearing and coarse language," which made his character simply "monotonous."[64] According to one angry parent's tabulation, 237 instances of "goddamn," 58 uses of the synonym for a person of illegitimate birth, 31 "Chrissakes," and one incident of flatulence constituted what was wrong with Salinger's book. Though blasphemy is not a crime, *The Catcher in the Rye* "uses the Lord's name in vain two hundred times," an opponent in Boron asserted—"enough [times] to ban it right there."[65] The statistics are admittedly not consistent. But it is incontestable that the text contains six examples of "fuck" or "fuck you," though here Holden is actually allied with the censorious parents, since he does not swear with this four-letter word himself but instead tries to efface it from walls. He's indignant that children should be subjected to such graffiti. Upon seeing the word even in the Egyptian tomb room at the Metropolitan Museum of Art, however, Holden achieves a melancholy and mature insight that such offenses to dignity cannot really be expunged from the world: "You can't ever find a place that's nice and peaceful, because there isn't any" (p. 264).[66]

What happened to *The Catcher in the Rye* wasn't always nice and peaceful because it took a linguistic turn. Though historians are fond of defining virtually every era as one of transition, it does make sense to locate the publication of Salinger's novel on the cusp of change. The novel benefitted from the loosening of tongues that the Second World

War sanctioned, yet the profanity in which Holden indulges still looked conspicuous before the 1960s. Salinger thus helped to accelerate the trend toward greater freedom for writers but found himself the target of those offended by the adolescent vernacular still rarely enough recorded in print. During the Second World War, the Production Code had been slightly relaxed for *We Are the Marines*. This 1943 *March of Time* documentary was permitted to use mild expletives like "damn" "under stress of battle conditions." Professor Thomas Doherty adds that, "in the most ridiculed example of the Code's tender ears, Noel Coward's *In Which We Serve* (1942), a British import, was held up from American release for seventeen words: ten 'damns,' two 'hells,' two 'Gods,' two 'bastards,' and one 'lousy.'"

Only three years before publication of Salinger's novel, homophonic language was inserted into Norman Mailer's *The Naked and the Dead* at the suggestion of his cousin, Charles Rembar. A crackerjack First Amendment attorney who would later represent such clients as Fanny Hill and Constance Chatterley, Rembar proposed the substitution of *fug* (as in "Fug you. Fug the goddam gun") partly because the president of the house publishing the novel feared his own mother's reaction. The U.S. Information Agency was nevertheless unpersuaded and banned Mailer's book from its overseas libraries. As late as 1952, the revised edition of *Webster's Unabridged* offered a simple but opaque definition of masturbation as "onanism; self-pollution."[67] The next year President Eisenhower delivered a celebrated plea at Dartmouth College: "Don't join the book-burners. . . . Don't be afraid to go into your library and read every book." His amendment is less cited—"as long as that document does not offend our own ideas of decency." Though the war in which Mailer and Salinger fought allowed some indecorous terms to go public, the 1960 Presidential debates included the spectacle of Nixon seeking to trump another ex-sailor by promising the electorate—after Harry Truman's salty lapses—to continue Ike's restoration of "decency and, frankly, good language" in the White House.[68]

In this particular war of words, Salinger was conscripted into a cause for which he was no more suited than any other. If he was affiliated with any institution at all, it was the *New Yorker*, which initially published most of his *Nine Stories* as well as the substance of his two subsequent books. In that magazine even the mildest profanity was strictly forbidden, and editorial prudishness would have spiked publication of excerpts from the final version of what became his most admired work. It may be plausible, as one scholar circling the text has noted, that "the radical nature of Salinger's portrayal of disappointment with American society, so much like Twain's in *Huck Finn*, was probably as much of the reason that *Catcher* (like *Huck*) was banned from schools and colleges as were the few curse words around which the battle was publicly fought."[69] But such ideological objections to Salinger's novel were rarely raised, much less articulated with any cogency; and therefore no historian of the reception of this book should minimize the salience of those "few curse words."

Could *The Catcher in the Rye* have avoided the turbulent pool into which it was so often sucked? Could the novel have been rescued from primitive detractors and retained an even more secure status in the public school curriculum? One compromise was never considered. It is the solution that Noah Webster commonly applied to dictionaries and spelling books, that Emerson recommended to Whitman for *Leaves of Grass*, and that Lewis Carroll intended to enact with a volume entitled *The Girl's Own Shakespeare:* expurgation. Had Holden's lingo been sanitized in accordance with the legacy of Dr. Thomas Bowdler, the moral (or moralistic) resistance to Salinger's novel would have evaporated. Bowdlerization constitutes what its leading student has called "literary slum clearance," but it also cordons off the censors. Of course Holden would not have been Holden with expletives deleted. The guileless integrity of his language makes him so memorable and therefore the novel so distinctive. Richard Watson Gilder had inflicted the kindest cuts of all on Huck's talk,[70] but by the 1950s no expurgators survived to spare Holden from the animosity he incurred. Such an explanation may be too obvious and all, if you really want to know. It's so simple it kills me, for Chrissake. But I really believe it's the best explanation. I really do.

From *The New England Quarterly* 70.4 (December 1997): 567-600. Copyright © 1997 by The New England Quarterly, Inc. Reprinted with permission of MIT Press.

Notes

The author appreciates the invitation of Professors Marc Lee Raphael and Robert A. Gross to present an early version of this essay at the College of William & Mary, and also thanks Professors Paul Boyer and John D. Ibson for their assistance.

1. Adam Moss, "Catcher Comes of Age," *Esquire*, December 1981, p. 57; Jack Salzman, ed., intro. to *New Essays on "The Catcher in the Rye"* (New York: Cambridge University Press, 1991), pp. 6, 7.

2. Salzman, intro. to *New Essays*, pp. 6, 19 n. 16; Ian Hamilton, *In Search of J. D. Salinger* (New York: Random House, 1988), p. 136; Moss, "Catcher Comes of Age," pp. 56, 57; Jack Skow, "Invisible Man," in *Salinger: A Critical and Personal Portrait*, ed. Henry Anatole Grunwald (New York: Pocket Books, 1963), p. 4.

3. David J. Burrows, "Allie and Phoebe" (1969), reprinted in *Holden Caulfield*, ed. Harold Bloom (New York: Chelsea House, 1990), p. 80; Hamilton, *In Search of Salinger*, pp. 155-56.

4. Salzman, intro. to *New Essays*, p. 22 n. 46; Skow, "Invisible Man," p. 4; Moss, "Catcher Comes of Age," p. 57.

5. Quoted by Nadine Brozan, "J. D. Salinger Receives an Apology for an Award," *New York Times*, 27 April 1991, p. 26.

6. Stefan Kanfer, "Holden Today: Still in the Rye," *Time*, 7 February 1972, pp. 50-51.

7. J. D. Salinger, *The Catcher in the Rye* (Boston: Little, Brown, 1951), p. 171. Subsequent page references, enclosed in parentheses in text, are to this edition.

8. Shawn Levy, *King of Comedy: The Life and Art of Jerry Lewis* (New York: St. Martin's, 1996), p. 271; Peter Shaw, "Love and Death in *Catcher in the Rye*," in *New Essays*, p. 100.

9. John Fowles, *The Collector* (Boston: Little, Brown, 1963), pp. 156-57, 192, 219-20, 246; John Simon, *Private Screenings* (New York: Macmillan, 1967), p. 165.

10. Priscilla Johnson McMillan, "An Assassin's Portrait," *New Republic*, 12 July 1982, pp. 16-18.

11. Moss, "Catcher Comes of Age," p. 58; Daniel M. Stashower, "On First Looking into Chapman's Holden: Speculations on a Murder," *American Scholar* 52 (Summer 1983): 373-77; Jack Jones, *Let Me Take You Down: Inside the Mind of Mark David Chapman, the Man Who Killed John Lennon* (New York: Villard Books, 1992), pp. 7,

22, 174-79, 184; Warren French, *J. D. Salinger, Revisited* (Boston: Twayne, 1988), pp. 17, 48.

12. Richard Schickel, *Intimate Strangers: The Culture of Celebrity* (Garden City, N.Y.: Doubleday, 1985), p. 280; Lincoln Caplan, *The Insanity Defense and the Trial of John W. Hinckley, Jr.* (Boston: David R. Godine, 1984), pp. 42-43.

13. John Guare, *Six Degrees of Separation* (New York: Random House, 1990), pp. 31-35, 107.

14. Quoted by Justin Kaplan, in *Mr. Clemens and Mark Twain* (New York: Simon & Schuster, 1966), pp. 268-69.

15. Frank Trippett, "The Growing Battle of the Books," *Time*, 19 January 1981, p. 85; Mary Jordan, "Reports of Censorship in U.S. Schools Up 50%," *International Herald Tribune*, 4 September 1992, p. 5.

16. Quoted by Salzman, in intro. to *New Essays*, p. 15.

17. Quoted in Salzman, intro. to *New Essays*, p. 15; Pamela Steinle, "'If a Body Catch a Body': The *Catcher in the Rye* Censorship Debate as Expression of Nuclear Culture," in *Popular Culture and Political Change in Modern America*, ed. Ronald Edsforth and Larry Bennett (Albany: State University of New York Press, 1991), p. 127; L. B. Woods, *A Decade of Censorship in America: The Threat to Classrooms and Libraries, 1966-1975* (Metuchen, N.J.: Scarecrow Press, 1979), p. 82.

18. Quoted by Seth Mydans, in "In a Small Town, a Battle Over a Book," *New York Times*, 3 September 1989, p. 22; Woods, *Decade of Censorship*, p. 150.

19. "*Catcher* in the News," *Esquire*, December 1981, p. 58; Salzman, intro. to *New Essays*, p. 14.

20. Quoted by Edward B. Jenkinson, in *Censors in the Classroom: The Mind Benders* (Carbondale: Southern Illinois University Press, 1979), p. 35.

21. Jenkinson, *Censors in the Classroom*, pp. 35, 156; Jack R. Sublette, *J. D. Salinger: An Annotated Bibliography, 1938-1981* (New York: Garland, 1984), pp. 160, 162, 164-67.

22. Marvin Laser and Norman Fruman, "Not Suitable for Temple City," in *Studies in J. D. Salinger: Reviews, Essays, and Critiques*, ed. Laser and Fruman (New York: Odyssey Press, 1963), pp. 124-29.

23. Mydans, "Small Town," p. 3.

24. Mydans, "Small Town," p. 3.

25. Willie Morris, "Houston's Superpatriots," *Harper's*, October 1961, p. 50; Laser and Fruman, "Community Critics . . . and Censors," in *Studies in Salinger*, p. 123.

26. Leslie A. Fiedler, *Being Busted* (New York: Stein & Day, 1969), pp. 59, 60; Edward Allen, *Mustang Sally* (New York: W. W. Norton, 1992), pp. 20-21; Anna Quindlen, "Don't Read This," *New York Times*, 1 October 1994, sec. 4, p. 23.

27. Timothy Noah, "Censors Right and Left," *New Republic*, 28 February 1981, p. 12.

28. Robert J. Clements, "Forbidden Books and Christian Reunion," *Columbia University Forum* (Summer 1963): 28; conversation with Jonas Barciauskas, librarian for theology, Boston College, 28 October 1996.

29. Warren Hinckle, *If You Have a Lemon, Make Lemonade* (New York: Bantam Books, 1976), pp. 41-42, 44-45; Robert O. Bowen, "The Salinger Syndrome: Charity

Against Whom?" *Ramparts*, May 1962, pp. 52-60.

30. Robert Harris, *Fatherland* (London: Hutchinson, 1992), p. 17; Robert Darnton, *Berlin Journal, 1989-1990* (New York: W. W. Norton, 1991), p. 205.

31. Woods, *Decade of Censorship*, pp. 149-50.

32. Quoted by Mydans, in "Small Town," p. 22; "Censorship's Coming of Age," *Boston Globe*, 3 September 1993, p. 14.

33. Carol and Richard Ohmann, "Reviewers, Critics, and *The Catcher in the Rye*," *Critical Inquiry* 3 (Autumn 1976): 34-36.

34. John Seelye, "Holden in the Museum," in *New Essays*, pp. 24, 32.

35. Charles A. Reich, *The Greening of America* (New York: Random House, 1970), pp. 222-23.

36. E. L. Doctorow, *The Book of Daniel* (New York: Random House, 1971), p. 95.

37. Tom Hayden, *Reunion: A Memoir* (New York: Random House, 1988), pp. 8-9, 17-18.

38. Roland Marchand, "Visions of Classlessness, Quests for Dominion: American Popular Culture, 1945-1960," in *Reshaping America: Society and Institutions, 1945-1960*, ed. Robert H. Bremner and Gary W. Reichard (Columbus: Ohio State University Press, 1982), pp. 179, 181-82.

39. John Updike, "Franny and Zooey," in *Salinger: A Portrait*, pp. 58-59.

40. Paul Levine, "J. D. Salinger: The Development of a Misfit Hero," *Twentieth-Century Literature* 4 (October 1958): 97, reprinted in *If You Really Want to Know: A Catcher Casebook*, ed. Malcolm M. Marsden (Chicago: Scott, Foresman, 1963), p. 48; and "The Fiction of the Fifties: Alienation and Beyond," in *America in the Fifties*, ed. Anne R. Clauss (Copenhagen: University of Copenhagen, 1978), pp. 46-49; Kenneth Keniston, *The Uncommitted: Alienated Youth in American Society* (New York: Harcourt, Brace & World, 1965), pp. 7-8.

41. Jack Newfield, *A Prophetic Minority* (New York: Signet, 1967), pp. 28-29.

42. Skow, "Invisible Man," in *Salinger: A Portrait*, p. 5; David Riesman, with Nathan Glazer and Reuel Denney, *The Lonely Crowd: A Study of the Changing American Character*, abr. ed. (Garden City, N.Y.: Doubleday Anchor, 1953), pp. 278-82; French, *Salinger, Revisited*, pp. 57-58; James Lundquist, *J. D. Salinger* (New York: Ungar, 1979), pp. 65-67.

43. T. Morris Longstreth, "New Novels in the News," in *Christian Science Monitor*, 19 July 1951, p. 7, reprinted in *If You Really Want to Know*, p. 6.

44. Robert A. Gross, review of *Making of a Counter Culture*, in *Newsweek*, 15 September 1969, p. 98; Theodore Roszak, *The Making of a Counter Culture: Reflections on the Technocratic Society and Its Youthful Opposition* (Garden City, N.Y.: Doubleday Anchor, 1969), p. 174n; Grunwald, intro. to *Salinger: A Portrait*, p. xxx.

45. Alan Nadel, *Containment Culture: American Narratives, Postmodernism, and the Atomic Age* (Durham, N.C.: Duke University Press, 1995), pp. 71, 75, 79, 86, 181; "Communist Infiltration of the Motion Picture Industry," in *Thirty Years of Treason*, ed. Eric Bentley (New York: Viking, 1971), p. 149.

46. "The Complete J. D. Salinger," *Esquire*, December 1981, p. 58; Hamilton, *In Search of Salinger*, pp. 13-14.

47. Eve Horowitz, *Plain Jane* (New York: Random House, 1992), pp. 52, 200, 230.

48. David Riesman and Evelyn Thompson Riesman, *Conversations in Japan: Modernization, Politics, and Culture* (New York: Basic Books, 1967), p. 171.
49. John Hohenberg, *The Pulitzer Prizes* (New York: Columbia University Press, 1974), pp. 19, 55-56.
50. Hannah Arendt, *Eichmann in Jerusalem: A Report on the Banality of Evil*, rev. ed. (New York: Viking, 1964), p. 49; Vladimir Nabokov to John Leonard, 29 September 1971, in Nabokov's *Selected Letters, 1940-1977*, ed. Dmitri Nabokov and Matthew J. Bruccoli (San Diego: Harcourt Brace Jovanovich, 1989), p. 492.
51. Longstreth, "New Novels," pp. 5-6.
52. Julie Lasky, "Savage Puritans Ripped Her Bodice," *New York Times Book Review*, 12 November 1995, p. 67; Walter Lippmann, "The Nature of the Battle over Censorship" (1927), in *Men of Destiny* (Seattle: University of Washington Press, 1970), pp. 100-102.
53. Steinle, "If a Body," p. 136.
54. Steinle, "If a Body," p. 136; Seelye, "Holden in the Museum," p. 29, and *The True Adventures of Huckleberry Finn* (Evanston, Ill.: Northwestern University Press, 1970), p. 339.
55. Lippmann, "Nature of the Battle over Censorship," p. 99.
56. Quoted by Charles Rembar, in *The End of Obscenity* (New York: Random House, 1968), p. 156.
57. The absenteeism of Holden's parents is noted perceptively by Jonathan Baumbach, in *The Landscape of Nightmare* (New York: New York University Press, 1965), p. 65.
58. Quoted by Sanford Pinsker, in *Bearing the Bad News: Contemporary American Literature and Culture* (Iowa City: University of Iowa Press, 1990), p. 29.
59. Hamilton, *In Search of Salinger*, p. 4; Moss, "Catcher Comes of Age," p. 56.
60. Steinle, "If a Body," p. 131.
61. Quoted by Nat Hentoff, in *Free Speech for Me—But Not for Thee: How the American Left and Right Relentlessly Censor Each Other* (New York: HarperCollins, 1992), pp. 374-75.
62. Quoted by Joan DelFattore, in *What Johnny Shouldn't Read: Textbook Censorship in America* (New Haven: Yale University Press, 1992), p. 109.
63. June Edwards, "Censorship in the Schools: What's Moral about *The Catcher in the Rye*?" *English Journal* 72 (April 1983): 42.
64. Quoted by Salzman, in intro. to *New Essays*, pp. 5-6; Edward P. J. Corbett, "Raise High the Barriers, Censors," *America*, 7 January 1961, pp. 441-42, reprinted in *If You Really Want to Know*, pp. 68-70.
65. Riley Hughes, "New Novels," *Catholic World*, November 1951, p. 154, reprinted in *Holden Caulfield*, p. 8; Moss, "Catcher Comes of Age," p. 56; Steinle, "If a Body," p. 129; Quindlen, "Don't Read This," p. 23; Hentoff, *Free Speech for Me*, pp. 374-75.
66. French, *Salinger, Revisited*, p. 42.
67. Thomas Doherty, *Projections of War: Hollywood, American Culture, and World War II* (New York: Columbia University Press, 1993), pp. 54, 56; Hilary Mills, *Mailer: A Biography* (New York: Empire Books, 1982), pp. 90-93; Rembar, *End of*

Obscenity, p. 17n; Noel Perrin, *Dr. Bowdler's Legacy: A History of Expurgated Books in England and America* (New York: Atheneum, 1969), p. 251.

68. Quoted by Rembar, in *End of Obscenity*, p. 7; Walter L. Hixson, *Parting the Curtain: Propaganda, Culture, and the Cold War, 1945-1961* (New York: St. Martin's, 1997), p. 123; "The Third Debate," 13 October 1960, in *The Great Debates: Background, Perspective, Effects*, ed. Sidney Kraus (Bloomington: Indiana University Press, 1962), p. 397.

69. Gerald Rosen, "A Retrospective Look at *The Catcher in the Rye*," *American Quarterly* 29 (Winter 1977): 548, 557-58.

70. Perrin, *Dr. Bowdler's Legacy*, pp. 8, 105, 163, 167-72, 212, 220.

Reviewers, Critics, and
The Catcher in the Rye

Carol and Richard Ohmann

On the day *The Catcher in the Rye* was published, on Monday, July 16, 1951, the *New York Times* reviewed it; a review in the Sunday *Times* had appeared the day before, and a rush of other reviews followed. Through the later fifties and on into the sixties, *Catcher* engaged academic critics, and it still does, although the novel generates criticism at a slower rate today than it used to. By 1963 Warren French supposed that critics had written more on *Catcher* than on any other contemporary novel, and in 1965 James E. Miller, Jr., claimed, reasonably enough, that Salinger had stirred more interest among the public and critics alike than any writer since Fitzgerald and Hemingway.[1] By 1961, *Catcher* had sold 1,500,000 copies;[2] by 1965, 5,000,000;[3] last year the total of its sales stood at more than 9,000,000.[4]

The Catcher in the Rye arrived to stay and is older now than most of its audience when they read it for the first time. That quarter century is time enough to allow us to generalize not only about the book's reception in 1951 but about the consensus of critical opinion that developed afterwards. We are concerned, in brief, with how *Catcher* became a classic: this is a case study of capitalist criticism. And in it, we shall have in mind the distinction Raymond Williams makes in *Culture and Society* between the lives books lead in the minds of readers and the lives their readers (and writers) live in particular historical times.

I

To return to July 16, 1951: on that Monday, the front page of the *Times* carried eleven news stories. The largest headline, with the text beneath breaking into two parts, concerned the war in Korea, then a year old: one part told that peace talks between United Nations negotiators and Communists had resumed in Kaesong (they would, of course, be unsuccessful), and the other reported with extensive quotation a speech Secretary of State Dean Acheson made in New York to book and magazine publishers on the meaning of the Korean conflict; the State Department had released the speech "at the request of a number of those" who were present to hear it. An account of the fighting itself with maps and communiqués from the field and a list of casualties appeared on page two. The front-page news was not, in other words, of the combat and its immediate consequences but of verbal maneuvering in the conflict between Communism and the Western world and of the ideological interpretation our leading spokesman in foreign affairs wished to give to events in Korea. Apart from stories on a flood in Kansas City, the weather in New York (hot, dry, and hard on the water supply), and a request for funding for new schools in the City, all the other articles on the front page bore on the struggle between East and West, of which events in Korea were simply for the moment the most dramatic and costly example: in Teheran, 10,000 "Iranian Reds" rioted to protest the arrival of Averill Harriman, who had come as Truman's special assistant to talk with the Shah's government about the Iranian-British oil dispute; Admiral Forrest P. Sherman, Chief of Naval Operations, left for a week in Europe, which would include discussion in Spain about possibilities of "joint military cooperation"; the United States asked for the recall from Washington of two Hungarian diplomats in retaliation for the expulsion of two American officials from Budapest; a Republican congressman protested that his party's opposition to Truman's proposal for continued price, wage, and credit controls was not "sabotaging" those controls but aimed at stopping "socialistic power grabs" on the part of the Administration.

The front page of the *Times* on July 16, 1951, serves to outline, quickly enough, the situation of the world into which *The Catcher in the Rye* made such a successful and relatively well-publicized entrance. The main action of the world, the chief events of its days were occurring within a framework of struggle between two systems of life, two different ways of organizing human beings socially, politically, economically. The opposition between East and West, between socialist and capitalist, was determining what happened in Kaesong, Budapest, Madrid, Teheran, Washington, New York. Name-calling the Administration, Republicans threw out the term "socialist," and the bid for millions to build schools in the five boroughs of New York would finally have to dovetail with allocations of taxes for defense.

The review of *The Catcher in the Rye* in the back pages of the *Times* made no mention of any of this. The kind of reality reported on the front page belonged to one world; the new novel was about to be assimilated into another, into the world of culture, which was split from politics and society. And this separation repeated itself in other reviews: typically, they did not mention the framework of world history contemporary with the novel; they did not try to relate *Catcher* to that framework even to the extent of claiming that there was only a partial relationship or complaining, however simplistically, that there was none. Our concern from here on will be to try to sketch what reviewers and what academic critics after them did see in the novel and what they might have seen in it. We are interested in the conceptual frameworks, the alternatives to history, they used to respond to and interpret *Catcher* as they passed it on to its millions of lay readers.

Before turning to the world of culture, though, it seems useful to turn back one last time to the news of July 16, 1951, for even as it was being reported it was, of course, already being interpreted. The Secretary of State's speech in New York and the lead editorial were especially rich in interpretive intent. Acheson placed the Korean War in the perspective of an *ongoing* conflict between the United States and Russia, and urged us to prevail in that conflict: "Korea's significance is not the final crusade. It is not finally making valid the idea of collective security. It is important perhaps for the inverse reason that in Korea we prevented the invalidation of collective security." Even if peace was made in Korea, we should not relax, because further dangers resided in the awakening of the vast populations of Asia, populations which are beginning to feel that they should have and should exercise in the world an influence which is proportionate to their numbers and worthy of their cultures. We must manage our difficulties so prudently that we have strength and initiative and power left to help shape and guide these emerging forces so that they will not turn out to be forces which rend and destroy.

What Acheson implied to be the eventual happy ending of our present and future efforts is obvious and familiar: we would not only retain our present advantages economically and politically but augment them. Nations emerging in Asia would do so in ways compatible with rather than antagonistic to our hegemony, hence to our own well-being. The fundamental value to which Acheson appealed in his speech, the goal and the sanction of all that he urges, is comprehended in the phrase "national interests." Our nationalism was not, in the language of his argument, aggressive but defensive. "A blow has been struck at us in Korea." Another might be struck in a year elsewhere if we slackened in our defense effort; Asian nations would rend and destroy us if we did not guide them otherwise.

The lead editorial supported Acheson's policies and yet at the same time shifted the mode of justifying them:

> We would be less than humane if we did not urge and support any course of action that can spare the loss of life. No honest person wanted a war in Korea and all right-minded persons want to see it ended. Nevertheless, we are not willing to sacrifice honor and morality to our will to peace. The United Nations was right in the first place to resist aggression, and that rightness has not been changed. Obviously, the aggression that will have to be resisted now is political rather than military. Our defenses need to be as strong in one field as in the other.

The fundamental appeal here was to a timeless, extranational morality transcending particular interests. Sparing lives and living peacefully are good—everyone right-minded and honest and honorable believes that—but, regrettably and inexorably, the defense of freedom must come first. The United Nations was fighting for a self-determining, united Korea independent of foreign intrusion, and would go on fighting if that end was not achieved at the conference table in Kaesong.

In appealing to "national interests," Acheson did offer a justification, a definition of right, that is congruent with the historical moment; "national interests" fittingly named, though it certainly did not spell out, a clear-sighted interpretation of politico-economic realities in 1951: the United States, having determined the policy of the United Nations, was fighting in Korea to protect and eventually to extend America's post-World War II domination of the world's economic system. The editorial writer obscured the historical moment and mystified the Korean War: as an honorable nation, we were fighting north and south of the fortieth parallel to preserve morality. The transformation worked on historical fact between the front page and the editorial parallels, we think, the transformation reviewers and critics worked on *The Catcher in the Rye*. The novel does not, of course, mention the conflict between East and West. It does mirror a competitive, acquisitive society, where those who have, keep and press for more—the same society that put half a million troops on the field in Korea and sent Harriman to Teheran and Sherman to Madrid. *Catcher*, to anticipate our argument at this point, is precisely revealing of social relationships in midcentury America, and motives that sustained them, and rationalizations that masked them. In the hands of reviewers and critics, though, its precision and its protest were blurred and muted, masked not quite white but grayed by a steady application of interpretive terms that tended to abstract and merely universalize its characters and its action, dimming the pattern of their own historical time. As Acheson spoke of interests and the editorial writer of morality, Salinger wrote about power and wealth and reviewers and critics about good and evil and the problems of growing up.

From the *Times* directly or from other daily papers and from radio and television broadcasts purveying the same news, reviewers turned to *The Catcher in the Rye*. They were fairly consistent in their estimates of the novel; either they praised it or, finding some fault with it, they allowed that it was nonetheless brilliant or a tour de force or at the very least lively. What concerns us here, though, is not how the reviewers rated it but the categories under which they apprehended it. They viewed the novel as a novel, commenting especially on its most striking formal feature, Salinger's choice of a seventeen-year-old personal narrator and his matching of syntax and idiom to that choice. They were also concerned to label *Catcher* generically; they saw it as satire or comedy or tragicomedy, or at their most casual they called it funny or sad or both at once. And in a rudimentary way at least they positioned the novel in the history of fiction; it reminded them of Twain's work and Lardner's and Hemingway's. In other words, neither surprisingly nor inappropriately, the reviewers described *Catcher* as a literary work in itself and placed it vis-à-vis other works similar in genre and style. What they were concerned to do mostly, though, was to relate *Catcher* to life, and upon that relationship they hinged their estimates of its quality far more than they did on its stylistic or generic qualities. They assumed that a novel's most important function is mimetic and that insofar as it succeeds as representation, it succeeds as fiction. Theoretically, this standard might have integrated the two worlds which we have spoken of as separate. But in fact it did not because of the way the reviewers defined, and circumscribed, "life."

They were, first of all, concerned to describe Holden Caulfield as a person, and, doing that, they emphasized his youth; usually they went on to diagnose what ails him and, sometimes, to prescribe a cure and to guess what would happen to him next, beyond the point where the novel itself ends. In the *Times*, Nash K. Burger wrote: "Holden's mercurial changes of mood, his stubborn refusal to admit his own sensitiveness and emotions, his cheerful disregard of what is sometimes known as reality are typically and heartbreakingly adolescent."[5] Phrases similar to "typically and heartbreakingly adolescent" recur in other reviews: "[Salinger] charts the miseries and ecstasies of an adolescent rebel" (*Time*);[6] "[Holden is a] bright, terrible, and possibly normal sixteen-year-old" (Harvey Breit, *Atlantic*);[7] "Holden is not a normal boy. He is hypersensitive and hyper-imaginative" (S. N. Behrman, *New Yorker*);[8] "the reader wearies of this kind of explicitness, repetition and adolescence, exactly as one would weary of Holden himself" (Anne L. Goodman, *New Republic*).[9] The kind of typing implicit in these quotations is laid out plain in Ernest Jones' review: "[*Catcher*] is a mirror. It reflects something not at all rich and strange but what every sensitive sixteen-year-old since Rousseau has felt, and of course what each one of us is certain he has felt. . . . its insights . . . are not really insights; since they are so general, 'The Catcher in the Rye' becomes more and more a case history of all of us . . ." (*Nation*).[10] The reviewers differed on certain points: Holden is normal or he is not, but even those who say he is not or possibly not, have a norm in mind. They type Holden according to a timeless developmental standard. They do not fully agree on how to define adolescence, or on how far Holden fits the category (is he *hyper*sensitive? is he *especially* bright?), but they do agree that there is a norm or model and that Holden more or less matches it.

We would exaggerate if we said the reviewers had no awareness at all of Holden Caulfield's time and place. They did address themselves to Salinger's representation of his hero's society, although much less emphatically than they set about describing the hero himself, but here again, they showed a common disposition to typify or to categorize and to do so in remarkably similar ways. Harvey Breit called *Catcher* "a critique of the contemporary grown-up world" (*Atlantic*).[11] Harrison Smith referred to the "complexity of modern life" and "the spectacle of perversity and evil," which bewilder and shock Holden as they do so many youths (*Saturday Review*).[12] Both these reviewers alluded at least to the time of the novel's time. But Breit did not enlarge upon his point save to say that Holden is not a good observer, that we do not see the world through his eyes, only himself; the phrases Smith employed are very far from specific, and this disposition to abstraction is even more pronounced in some other reviews.

In S. N. Behrman's words, "[Holden] is driven crazy by 'phoniness,' a heading under which he loosely gathers not only insincerity but snobbery, injustice, callousness to the tears in things, and a lot more"; he is faced in the novel with "the tremendously complicated and often depraved facts of life" (*New Yorker*).[13] Burger, in the quotation above, attributed Holden's difficulties to "a world that is out of joint." In Virgilia Peterson's opinion, Holden "sees the mixtures, the inextricably mingled good and bad, as it is, but the very knowledge of reality is what almost breaks his heart" (*Herald Tribune Book Review*).[14] To say that modern life is complex is to say very little indeed about it, and to speak of "the tears in things" and "a world that is out of joint" and "reality" is to move *Catcher* altogether out of its contemporary setting, to see Holden's difficulties as everywhere and always the same. Even the reviews that make no explicit mention of modernity or of Holden's "world" imply by typing him as an adolescent that a sixteen-year-old's problems have been, are, and will remain the same.[15]

II

In the March 1957 issue of *The Nation*, David L. Stevenson remarked, "It is a curiosity of our age that J. D. Salinger . . . is rarely acknowledged by the official guardians of our literary virtue in the quarterlies."[16] That was accurate, though not perhaps so curious if, as we suppose to be the case, our official guardians then as now work primarily in our prestigious institutions of higher learning and work over a canonical list of English and American and other Western writers passed on down by those institutions. Although *The Catcher in the Rye* continued to be very much read through the fifties, there was a lag between its date of publication and the appearance of very much professional or academic criticism about the novel. Two years after Stevenson's comment, however, *The Nation* carried an article by George Steiner titled

"The Salinger Industry." "[Stevenson,]" Steiner wrote, "can now rest assured. The heavy guns are in action along the entire critical front."[17] What were they booming?

In Steiner's opinion, they were not only noisy but off target. He was concerned both to note the critical energy being expended on Salinger and to correct its aim. At the very time *Catcher* was being assumed into our literary canon, he was suggesting what bounds criticism should keep within and what conclusions it ought to be reaching. Salinger was a "gifted and entertaining writer with one excellent short novel and a number of memorable stories to his credit."

But criticism, Steiner complained, was busy comparing Salinger to *great* writers and speaking of his work in "complex" and "sublime" terms. Why so much activity, more than Salinger's merit (in Steiner's opinion) deserved, and why such exaggeration and pretension? Steiner gave two reasons, and to his mind they exposed what was wrong with criticism written in contemporary America: first, critics had grafted New Critical jargon onto Germanic scholarship and could no longer speak plainly; second, our academic institutions turned out too many critics, too many assistant and associate professors in need of promotions and fellowships and constrained to publish to get them. "Along comes a small though clearly interesting fish like Salinger and out go the whaling fleets. The academic critic can do his piece with few footnotes, it will be accepted by critical reviews or little magazines, and it is another tally on the sheet of his career."

Steiner's piece is in certain ways inaccurate. It tells what one might have expected to happen if one were predicting the nature of Salinger criticism in the later fifties from an exclusive and judgmental point of view of American academic institutions (too many critics on their way up the ladder, "too many critical journals, too many seminars, too many summer schools and fellowships for critics"); but it is skewed in its description of Salinger criticism as it actually did happen in the fifties. We have paused on Steiner because he did remark the arrival of the "Salinger industry" and because the prejudices he brings into the play are commonly leveled against academics. We want to distinguish our quarrel with the critics from Steiner's. As we see them, they were generously intentioned and more sincere, less dominated by New Criticism or any other "school" and more subtle, than they appeared to be in Steiner's account of a "vast machine in constant need of new raw material." If, as we go on to argue, they underestimated or overlooked or misread Salinger's rendering of contemporary American life, they do not appear to us to have done so because they were time-serving drudges fattening their bibliographies for promotion.

It is true that critics exercised their professional training in writing on Salinger, as they might be expected to do. They spoke of the novel's style; an article in *American Speech*, for example, scrutinized Holden's vocabulary and grammar, considering how far they conformed to teenage vernacular in the 1950s.[18] They clustered its images in significant patterns, interpreted its symbols, explained its literary allusions, brought to light principles of narrative repetition and variation that govern its structure, spoke of its time scheme, saw Holden in California as a novelist of sorts himself, looking back on his experience and shaping it to try to understand it. They paid, unsurprisingly, more precise and lengthier attention to the novel as a work of art than its reviewers had in 1951. And they cared much more than the reviewers about positioning *Catcher* with reference to other literary works, finding generic and literarily historical lodgings for it. In a particularly influential article in 1956, Arthur Heiserman and James E. Miller, Jr., identified *Catcher* as belonging to "an ancient and honorable narrative tradition" in Western literature, "the tradition of the Quest."[19] Other critics reiterated the idea of the quest, or they spoke of Holden's trip to New York as a journey to the underworld or through the waste land, or they called his series of adventures picaresque. And yet, academics though they were, the critics as a whole were less concerned, really, with typing the novel and less employed, even, with explication as an activity in itself than they were with elucidating the novel's rendering of human experience and evaluating its moral attitudes. In this they were close to the original concerns of the reviewers. And they give the impression less of elaborately trained professionals eager to display their learning and methodological expertise (while hungering after advancement) than they do of serious common readers approaching *Catcher* for what it reveals of life and offers in the way of wisdom.

We shall lower here a very plain but, we hope, serviceable grid on a number of critics and ask how they saw *Catcher* answering two questions: what went wrong with Holden, propelling him from Pencey Prep to New York to a psychiatrist's couch in California, and what, if anything, could have been, or could be, done about it?

One group of critics located the causes of Holden's predicament altogether or mainly in himself, in his soul or in his psyche. Flunking out of his third prep school, Holden is responding to inner rather than outer pressures; "he is a victim not so much of society as of his own spiritual illness" which forbids his discarding any of his experiences and condemns him to carry the burden of indiscriminate remembrance.[20] Or else he is saintly in his sensitivity, suffering and yet blessed in his inability to withhold either empathy or compassion.[21] Or else Holden is immature or spoiled, an adolescent who is too absolute in his judgments, too intolerant of human failings[22] or an "upper-class New York City boy" who is a "snob."[23] For his spiritual illness, there can be no cure unless he grows into spiritual perfection, finding God and living by His injunction to love. His immaturity calls for growth, for maturing into an acceptance of things as they are, and so does his snobbery.[24] These critics differed as to whether or not Holden is left arrested in his difficulties or moved toward or even through redemption or initiation or acceptance or adjustment. But in any case, these views of his predicament all imply that the answer to it, whether that answer is realized in the action of the novel or not, lies in some inward movement of the soul or psyche, a kind of resource that might be available to anyone any time and just as timelessly necessary to saints and sinners as bewildered young men.

More often than they held Holden responsible for his fate, for his breakdown and the events that led him to it, critics saw it derived more emphatically from external causes; they were disposed to blame the world instead of or along with the hero. For some, Holden collides with an unchanging set of antagonists which they speak of in religious or philosophical terms. Holden confronts "evil,"[25] an "immoral world,"[26] a "mutable and deceitful world";[27] his is, as everyman's always is, the existential condition. Like Hamlet, he "stand[s] aghast before a corrupt world."[28] He is "sickened by the material values and the inhumanity of the world."[29] In other readings, his antagonists are more particularly named American and modern. Holden is seen facing, and breaking on, forces characteristic of American life and, more particularly, twentieth-century American life. The people he meets are "innocently imperceptive and emotionally dead"; they impose standards of conformity, as they did on Thoreau and Henry Adams.[30] Or, Holden's society, worse than Thoreau's, and Adams' (and Huck Finn's), is complex, urbanized, dehumanized and dehumanizing; his is the condition of "contemporary alienation."[31] Holden is encircled by "phoniness, indifference and vulgarity"; "as a 'neo-picaresque,' [*Catcher*] shows itself to be concerned far less with the education or initiation of an adolescent than with a dramatic exposure of the manner in which ideals are denied access to our lives and the modes which mendacity assumes in our urban culture."[32] Contemporary America is afflicted with "neurosis and fatigue."[33] Society is "sick"; "our national experience hurtles us along routes more menacing than the Mississippi."[34] The critic who cast his net widest, aiming at both the enduring and the timely explanation, drew in the most reasons for Holden's fate, for the fact that his retrospective narration issues from a California institution for the mentally ill: "Holden could not face a world of age, death, sickness, ugliness, sex and perversion, poverty, custom, and cant."[35]

Most of these terms, we need hardly emphasize, conceptualize Holden's world in a general way. Many have a moral frame of reference (evil, deceit, corruption, inhumanity, mendacity); many have a psychological or emotional frame of reference (the individual feels the pressure to conform, or society is tired and disturbed). In either case, they tend away from precise description of the society Salinger renders in *Catcher*.

When *Catcher*'s society did draw pointed comments from critics, they were apt to be negative. Maxwell Geismar, for example, admired Salinger's creation of Pencey Prep, with "all the petty horrors, the banalities, the final mediocrity of the typical American prep school," but faulted his portrayal of Holden's family and class as vague and empty. Holden, he argued, comes to us from "both a social and a psychological void"; Salinger makes no reference to the "real nature and dynamics" of the hero's urban environment.[36] And Ihab Hassan conceded that *Catcher* is not a "sociological" novel: "No doubt social realities are repressed in the work of Salinger—note how gingerly he handles his Jews."[37] There is an assumption here that a novel that is satisfyingly realistic mirrors society sweepingly and fully, follows Mr. Caulfield into his corporate office and introduces the maid who lives in the room behind Phoebe's. And that assumption, we think, worked to obscure how much Salinger did represent of the contemporary world in *Catcher*, and how far he understood what he represented.

And when Holden's predicament *was* given external cause, at least in part, what could be done about it? What resolution if any did these critics see the novel reaching or at least implying? For certainly a difference in diagnosis would seem to entail a difference in prescription, especially when critics did invoke historical time and place to account for Holden's misadventures. They did not, however, differ very much from the critics above who addressed themselves primarily to the state of Holden's soul or psyche. Holden was searching, as they saw it, for truth or for wisdom or for personal integrity. And beyond reaching understanding and achieving his own identity, he needed to communicate and to love or to find an object for the love he was able to feel at least as the novel ended if not before. In *Catcher* Salinger showed that "the resources of the personality are sufficient for self-recovery and discovery."[38] Or they saw *Catcher* posing Holden's predicament without offering or even implying its solution. More rarely, they touched on the question of how society itself might change along with or apart from any change Holden might manage within his own psychic territory. America had lost its own innocence and, like Holden himself, needed to "face [the] problems of growing up."[39] Although facing them was more likely to lead to "despair" than to "hope."[40]

Of this common intellectual strategy, we can take James E. Miller's criticism as typical. In 1965, almost ten years after his article with Heiserman appeared, Miller wrote again about *Catcher*, this time in the Minnesota pamphlet series on American writers, where his responsibility was in part to voice the critical consensus that had developed. He did so in language that is by now familiar. Holden is on a threefold quest: for "the innocence of childhood," for "an ideal but un-human love," and for "identity." His is "the modern predicament." He is up against "the world as it is," and "the fundamental physicality of the human predicament," which is "a phenomenon of all human relationships, all human situations, by their very nature of being human." In spite of the word "modern," and some references to the atom bomb ("contemporary horrors"), Miller's epitomizing language takes the novel quite out of real history and makes it an eternal story of "death and rebirth."[41] This critical transformation, evidently, was what it took in the academic American fifties and sixties to claim for a literary work the status of a classic.

We fix on Miller, not because he was an inept critic, but because, on the contrary, he was one of the best. In 1965, had we written the Minnesota pamphlet, we surely would have written it in the same ideological key—and less well than Miller. But through another decade of history the book has come to lead a different kind of life in our minds, and it is to our present understanding that we now turn.

III

For us, as for almost all readers, Holden's sensitivity is the heart of the book, that which animates the story and makes it compelling.

Events are laden with affect for Holden. He cannot speak of an experience for long in a neutral way, apart from judgment and feeling. And of course those judgments and feelings are largely negative. Not so entirely negative as Phoebe says—"You don't like *any*thing that's happening"—but this novel is first the story of a young man so displeased with himself and with much of the world around him that his strongest impulse is to leave, break loose, move on. From his pain follows rejection and retreat.

But what exactly is it that puts Holden out of sorts with his life? What does he reject? The critics answer, as we have seen, phrases that universalize: an immoral world, the inhumanity of the world, the adult world, the predicament of modern life, the human condition, the facts of life, evil. As we see it, the leap is too quick and too long. Holden lives in a time and place, and these provide the material against which his particular adolescent sensibility reacts.

Holden has many ways of condemning, and an ample lexicon to render his judgments. Some people are bastards, others jerks. The way they act makes you want to puke. What they do and say can be—in Holden's favorite adjectives—depressing, corny, dopey, crumby, screwed-up, boring, phony. "Phony" is probably Holden's most frequent term of abuse, definitely his strongest and most ethically weighted. For that reason his application of the word is a good index to what he finds most intolerable in his life. And Holden is quite consistent in what he calls phony.

Holden says he left Elkton Hills, one of the schools he attended before Pencey, because he was "surrounded by phonies," in particular Mr. Haas the headmaster, "the phoniest bastard I ever met in my life." Haas earned this label in the following way:

> On Sundays [he] went around shaking hands with everybody's parents when they drove up to school. He'd be charming as hell and all. Except if some boy had little old funny-looking parents. You should've seen the way he did with my roommate's parents. I mean if a boy's mother was sort of fat

or corny-looking or something, and if somebody's father was one of those guys that wear those suits with very big shoulders and corny black-and-white shoes, then old Haas would just shake hands with them and give them a phony smile and then he'd go talk, for maybe half an *hour*, with somebody else's parents. I can't stand that stuff.[42]

In a word, snobbery. Haas toadies to those who comfortably wear the uniform of their class—some register of high bourgeois—and snubs those with padded shoulders and unfashionable shoes who have come lately to their money, or not at all. His gestures to the latter are inauthentic, and such contempt can wound. But only because class does exist: Haas is not just personally mean; his phoniness and his power to hurt depend on an established class system that institutionalizes slight and injury.

Just a bit later Holden tells of another phony, an old Pencey grad named Ossenburger who has "made a pot of dough" through a chain of "undertaking parlors all over the country that you could get members of your family buried for about five bucks apiece." Holden has little respect for Ossenburger's enterprise: "He probably just shoves them in a sack and dumps them in the river." Nonetheless, Ossenburger is an eminence at Pencey, to which he has given "a pile of dough," and where Holden's dormitory is named after him. On a football weekend Ossenburger comes to the school in "this big goddam Cadillac," receives an obligatory cheer at the game, and gives a speech in chapel "that lasted about ten hours." It is a pious affair, making obliquely the Calvinist connection between wealth and virtue. Ossenburger extols prayer:

> he started telling us how he was never ashamed, when he was in some kind of trouble or something, to get right down on his knees and pray to God. . . . He said *he* talked to Jesus all the time. Even when he was driving his car. That killed me. I can just see the big phony bastard shifting into first gear and asking Jesus to send him a few more stiffs. [pp. 16-17]

Holden demystifies in the telling, better than if he had said, "this man claims legitimacy for his money, his Cadillac, his business ethics, his eminence and class privilege, by enlisting religion on his side." Again, phoniness is rooted in the economic and social arrangements of capitalism, and in their concealment.

But a second motif in these scenes also deserves comment. The clues to phoniness lie in outward forms of conduct. Haas' phony smile follows an external convention, but accords poorly with emotional reality. His handshakes imply equality, but thinly hide the reverse of equality. Ossenburger talks within a framework of conventions: he is in chapel; he gives a sermon; he speaks of prayer. Holden's revulsion attends, in part, on ceremony itself: on prescribed forms that shape the flow of our words and movements. A smile, a handshake, a chapel assembly with boys seated in rows, a sermon, a prayer: none of these is a spontaneous expression of the self; all impose limits and bear conventional meaning. Holden resents these constraints, and delights in release from them. Hence:

> The only good part of [Ossenburger's] speech was right in the middle of it. He was telling us all about what a swell guy he was, what a hot-shot and all, then all of a sudden this guy sitting in the row in front of me, Edgar Marsalla, laid this terrific fart. It was a very crude thing to do, in chapel and all, but it was also quite amusing. Old Marsalla. p. 17]

We won't offer a disquisition on old Marsalla's fart, but these things may be noted: a fart is the antithesis of ceremony (in this society, anyhow). It asserts the body, assaults manners and convention. Here, it shatters Ossenburger's hypocrisy and boastfulness. But it also strikes at the social idea behind a *"speech"* itself. It mocks the meaning of "sitting in the *row.*" It is a "crude thing to do, in *chapel* and all." In brief, it is commendable ("quite amusing") because it challenges, not only Ossenburger's false ideology, but also the very existence of social forms.

These twin themes run through the book. When a situation or act seems phony to Holden, it evidences bad class relationships, or public ritual, or both. The first theme is foregrounded when Holden stigmatizes the word "grand," or the phrase "marvelous to see you"; the second when he notes the hollow formality of "glad to've met you." The first theme unites the Wicker Bar at the Seton Hotel, ambitious lawyers, the fashionable opinion that the Lunts are "angels," Spencer's deference to headmaster Thurmer, the night club set's public affection for pseudoculture (cute French songs), the "dirty little goddam cliques" at boys' schools (where "all you do is study so that you can learn enough to be smart enough to be able to buy a goddam Cadillac some day"), Andover, "Ivy League voices," men in "their goddam checkered vests, criticizing shows and books and women in those tired, snobby voices." The second theme is foregrounded in Sally Hayes' *letter*, inviting Holden to help trim the *Christmas tree*; in the black piano player, Ernie, and his "very phony, *humble*" *bow* to his philistine audience; in that audience's *applause*; in *actors'* conventional representation of people; in ministers' *sermons* ("they all have these Holy Joe voices. . . . I don't see why the hell they can't talk in their natural voice"); in Stradlater's *hello* to Ackley; in Holden's *handshake* with Ackley; in phony *parties* and smoking for show and *conversations* about art.

Holden rounds on mores and conventions that are a badge of class. He also revolts against convention itself. We would remark here that although these two feelings often blend, they have quite different origins. Society is imaginable without privilege, snobbery, unequal wealth. To banish *all* convention would be to end society itself. More of this later.

For now, we want to underline the first of the two conclusions we have reached by looking at what Holden calls phony. The novel's critique of class distinction may be found, not just between the lines of Holden's account, but in some of his most explicit comments on what's awry in his world. We must quote at some length from his digression on suitcases. When Holden meets the two nuns in the sandwich bar, their suitcases prompt him to say,

It isn't important, I know, but I hate it when somebody has cheap suitcases. It sounds terrible to say it, but I can even get to hate somebody, just *looking* at them, if they have cheap suitcases with them. Something happened once. For a while when I was at Elkton Hills, I roomed with this boy, Dick Slagle, that had these very inexpensive suitcases. He used to keep them under the bed, instead of on the rack, so that nobody'd see them standing next to mine. It depressed holy hell out of me, and I kept wanting to throw mine out or something, or even *trade* with him. Mine came from Mark Cross, and they were genuine cowhide and all that crap, and I guess they cost quite a pretty penny. But it was a funny thing. Here's what happened. What I did, I finally put *my* suitcases under *my* bed, instead of on the rack, so that old Slagle wouldn't get a goddam inferiority complex about it. But here's what he did. The day after I put mine under my bed, he took them out and put them back on the rack. The reason he did it, it took me a while to find out, was because he wanted people to think my bags were his. He really did. He was a very funny guy, that way. He was always saying snotty things about them, my suitcases, for instance. He kept saying they were too new and bourgeois. That was his favorite goddam word. He read it somewhere or heard it somewhere. Everything I had was bourgeois as hell. Even my fountain pen was bourgeois. He borrowed it off me all the time, but it was bourgeois anyway. We only roomed together about two months. Then we both asked to be moved. And the funny thing was, I sort of missed him after we moved, because he had a helluva good sense of humor and we had a lot of fun sometimes. I wouldn't be surprised if he missed me, too. At first he only used to be kidding when he called my stuff bourgeois, and I didn't give a damn—it *was* sort of funny, in fact. Then, after a while, you could tell he wasn't kidding any more. The thing is, it's really hard to be roommates with people if your suitcases are much better than theirs—if yours are really *good* ones and theirs aren't. You think if they're intelligent and all, the other person, and have a good sense of humor, that they don't give a damn whose suitcases are better, but they do. They really do. It's one of the reasons why I roomed with a stupid bastard like Stradlater. At least his suitcases were as good as mine. [pp. 108-9]

The source of Holden's feeling could hardly be clearer, or related with more social precision. He belongs by birthright at Elkton Hills; Dick Slagle presumably does not. Their situation—living together—calls for an equality of human beings. (School itself, the American institution that most supports our myth of equal opportunity, carries the same hope.) Likewise, Holden's desires point him toward a world in which human qualities like intelligence and a sense of humor would be the ground of relatedness, rather than Mark Cross luggage and the money that stands behind it.

Both boys are deformed by what they bring with them to their room from the social order outside. Holden is depressed, and wishes to find the right gesture (throw the suitcases away, trade with Slagle) to deny their socially imposed difference. He is hurt by Slagle's resentment, when it becomes more than kidding, and he finally gives up on the relationship. Slagle, naturally, suffers more. Shame over his suitcases is one thing. But worse are the contradictory feelings: he hates the class injustice, and strives through the word "bourgeois" ("He read it somewhere") for the ideas that would combat it; yet at the same time he longs to be on the *right* side of the barrier, to *benefit* from class antagonism by having others think he owns the Mark Cross suitcases. Clearly Holden understands all this; we can only suppose that Salinger does too.

It was the nuns' suitcases, and their straw baskets, that reminded Holden of Dick Slagle, and the nuns also stir in him reflections about money and the expression of social feeling. He tries to imagine women from his own class "collecting dough for poor people in a beat-up old straw basket," but it's "hard to picture." His aunt is "pretty charitable," but always dressed in a way that emphasizes her condescension. "I couldn't picture her doing anything for charity if she had to wear black clothes and no lipstick. . . ." As for Sally Hayes' mother: "Jesus Christ. The only way *she* could go around with a basket collecting dough would be if everybody kissed her ass for her when they made a contribution." If they didn't, she'd get bored and "go someplace swanky for lunch. That's what I liked about those nuns. You could tell, for one thing, that they never went anywhere swanky for lunch. It made me so damn sad . . ." (p. 114). At the root of Holden's sadness are lives confined by poverty, the loss of human connectedness, the power of feelings distorted by class to overcome natural bonds of affinity and friendship. In the end, one chooses to room with "a stupid bastard like Stradlater," whose suitcases are as good as one's own.

So we hold that the text of this novel, and the experience of it, warrant a formulation of what wounds Holden quite a lot more precise than the one given it by phrases like "the complexity of modern life," "the neurosis and fatigue of the world," or "our collective civilized fate." These epitomes are in fact strongly ideological. They displace the political emotion that is an important part of Salinger's novel, finding causes for it that are presumed to be universal.

Likewise, the majority opinion on what Holden yearns for—ideal love, innocence, truth, wisdom, personal integrity, etc. Let's examine one such idea in detail. James Miller writes, "Perhaps in its profoundest sense Holden's quest is a quest for identity, a search for the self. . . ." Holden tries various disguises, but "the self he is led to discover is Holden's and none other. And that self he discovers is a human self and an involved self that cannot, finally, break with what Hawthorne once called the 'magnetic chain of humanity.'"[43] Miller writes of the self as if it were innate, genetically coded, yet somehow repressed. When Holden does rediscover it, it is "human" and "involved."

These rather vague characterizations lack social content. Yet we doubt that Miller or anyone else believes the identity of a person to lie beyond social influence, not to say definition. Any society provides identities for its members to step into; Holden's is no exception. We can hardly consider his quest for identity apart, for instance, from the fact that his father is a corporation lawyer ("Those boys really haul it in") on the edge of the ruling class, who has tried, however fruitlessly, to open for Holden the way to a similar identity by apprenticing him in a series of private schools. For Holden, such an identity is imaginatively real, and coercive. He gives it a reasonably concrete description when Sally Hayes refuses his invitation to go live by a brook in Vermont. She says there will be time for such pleasures later, after college. Holden:

> No, there wouldn't be. There wouldn't be oodles of places to go at all. It'd be entirely different. . . . We'd have to go downstairs in elevators with suitcases and stuff. We'd have to phone up everybody and tell 'em good-by and send 'em postcards from hotels and all. And I'd be working in some office, making a lot of dough, and riding to work in cabs and Madison Avenue buses, and reading newspapers, and playing bridge all the time, and going to the movies and seeing a lot of stupid shorts and coming attractions and newsreels. [P. 133]

Holden understands well enough that such an identity is incompatible with the spontaneous feeling and relatedness he wishes for.

But what vision can he entertain of some alternate self? Here imagination darkens. Holden has no idea of changing society, and within the present one he can see forward only to the bourgeois identity that waits for him. So he fantasizes another identity which fulfills desire by escaping society almost entirely. He would hitchhike out West to "where it was pretty and sunny and where nobody'd know me," get a (working class) job at a filling station, and build a cabin at the edge of the woods. He would "pretend I was one of those deaf-mutes," thereby ending the necessity of having "goddam stupid useless conversations with anybody." If he married, it would be to a beautiful deaf-mute, and if they had children, "we'd hide them somewhere . . . and teach them how to read and write by ourselves" (pp. 198-99). No corporate structure and no Madison Avenue; but also no social production, no school, and no talk. In short, an identity for Holden that erases human history.

Here is the main equivocation of the book, and it seems to be both Holden's and Salinger's. We argued a while back that the force of Holden's severest judgment is divided. "Phony" stigmatizes both the manners and culture of a dominant bourgeoisie—class society—and ceremonies and institutions themselves—any society. As long as we listen to the critical themes of the novel, the equivocation doesn't matter much: after all, the only society around *is* bourgeois society. But when we listen to those hints in the novel of something better, of alternative futures, of reconstruction, it makes a great deal of difference. Given Salinger's perception of what's wrong, there are three possible responses: do the best you can with this society; work for a better one; flee society altogether. Only the second answers to the critical feeling that dominates the book, but Salinger omits precisely that response when he shows Holden turning from that which his heart rejects to that which has value, commands allegiance, and invites living into the future without despair. So, when Holden imagines an adult self he can think only of the Madison Avenue executive or the deaf-mute, this society or no society.

And what does he like in the present? Phoebe accuses him of not liking anything, but he likes much: his dead brother Allie, for inscribing poems on his baseball mitt; Jane Gallagher, for keeping her kings in the back row at checkers. Both violate convention, and show a disdain for winning. Richard Kinsella, who broke the rules of the Oral Expression class, and digressed upon his uncle's brace when he should have been telling about his father's farm. The nuns with their straw baskets, poor but outside competitive society. James Castle, who refused even the minimal compromise with society that would have saved his life. The Museum of Natural History, where the Eskimos remain as changeless as figures on a Grecian urn, and so defy historical process. For Holden, images of the valuable are generally images of people withdrawn from convention—people who are private, whimsical, losers, saints, dead. Holden's imagination cannot join the social and the desirable. At the beginning and again at the end of the novel he has the illusion of disappearing, losing his identity altogether—both times when he is crossing that most social of artifacts, a street.

So long as the choice is between this society and no society,

Holden's imagination has no place to go. He wants love and a relatedness among equals. These do not thrive in the institutions that surround him, but they cannot exist at all without institutions, which shape human feeling and give life social form. When Phoebe retrieves Holden from nothingness and despair she draws him, inevitably, toward institutions: the family, school, the Christmas play, the zoo in the park, the carrousel where "they always play the same songs." In short, toward the same society he has fled, and toward some of its innocent social forms, this time magically redeemed by love.

Holden returns to society, the only one available. It is unchanged; he has changed somewhat, in the direction of acceptance. To go the rest of the way back, he requires the help of another institution, and a psychoanalyst. Society has classified him as neurotic—a fitting response, apparently, to his having wanted from it a more hospitable human climate than it could offer. He will change more. Society will not. But that's all right, in the end: the very act of telling his story has overlaid it with nostalgia, and he misses everybody he has told about, "Even old Stradlater and Ackley, for instance. I think I even miss that goddam Maurice. It's funny. Don't ever tell anybody anything. If you do, you start missing everybody" (p. 214). In a word, *Art* forms the needed bridge between the desirable and the actual, provides the mediation by which social experience, rendered through much of the story as oppressive, can be embraced.

IV

The Catcher in the Rye is among other things a serious critical mimesis of bourgeois life in the Eastern United States, ca. 1950—of snobbery, privilege, class injury, culture as badge of superiority, sexual exploitation, education subordinated to status, warped social feeling, competitiveness, stunted human possibility, the list could go on. Salinger is astute in imaging these hurtful things, though not in explaining them. Connections exist between Holden's ordeal and the events reported on the front page of the *Times*, and we think that those connections are necessary to complete Salinger's understanding of social reality. Iran and Korea and the hard-pressed New York school system express the hegemony of Holden's class, as do Broadway and Pencey and Stradlater. Salinger's novel makes no reference to the economic and military scope of that class's power, but the manners and institutions he renders so meticulously are those of people who take their power for granted, and expect their young to step into it.

We say, further, that these themes are not just discernible to the eye of an obsessed political reader, as one might strain to give *Catcher* an ecological or existential or Seventh Day Adventist reading. They are central to the book's meaning and to the impact it has on us and other readers. Its power is located, all agree, in Holden's sensitivity, keen observation, and moral urgency, and in the language with which he conveys these in relating his story. For all his perceptiveness, though, he is an adolescent with limited understanding of what he perceives. Readers (adults, at least) understand more, and in this gap a poignancy grows. Most readers share or are won to Holden's values—equality, spontaneity, brotherhood—but sense that these values cannot be realized within extant social forms. The novel draws readers into a powerful longing for what-could-be, and at the same time interposes what-is, as an unchanging and immovable reality.

It does so in a way that mirrors a contradiction of bourgeois society: advanced capitalism has made it imaginable that there could be enough "suitcases" for everyone, as well as spontaneity and brotherhood, and it feeds these desires at the same time that it prevents their fulfillment. Only a few can hope for suitcases and spontaneity, at the expense of the many, and enjoyment of them depends on shutting out awareness of the many. Furthermore, even the few are somehow blocked from enjoyment by the antagonistic striving required to secure one's suitcases, by the snotty human relationships of the Wicker Bar and Madison Avenue, by what Philip Slater calls "our invidious dreams of personal glory." In short, the aesthetic force of the novel is quite precisely located in its rendering a contradiction of a particular society, as expressed through an adolescent sensibility that feels, though it cannot comprehend, this contradiction. Short of comprehension, both Holden and Salinger are driven to a false equation—to reject this society is to reject society itself—and a false choice—accept this society or defect from society altogether.

It is here that the novel most invites criticism, informed by history and politics. But the critics have instead, with few exceptions,[44] followed Salinger's own lead and deepened the confusion of the novel with the help of mystifications like "the adult world," "the human condition," and so on. Pressing for such formulations, they have left history and the novel behind. They have failed both to understand its very large achievement—for we consider it a marvelous book—and to identify the shortcomings of its awareness and its art. And in this way they have certified it as a timeless classic.

We have been speaking of "readers," "critics," and "criticism." This is itself, needless to say, a mystification. Most readers and almost all critics belong to the professional and managerial strata between the high bourgeoisie and the working class. Almost all the critics have been college teachers, and at a time when their (our) lives were affected dramatically by the course of American capitalism. Specifically, in the fifties and the sixties, these conditions wrought a significant change in the position of academic intellectuals: (1) America preserved, with great success at first, the world hegemony of capitalism through a policy of "containment" (Korea, etc.). (2) This achievement, along with rapid technical development and corporate expansion, allowed unprecedented use of the world's markets and resources (e.g., Iranian oil) for the enrichment of the American economy. (3) American higher education responds very directly to the needs of the economy: both the new imperialism and new technical development (television, computers, military hardware, etc.) resulted in a rapidly increasing demand for college trained people and for research. Hence the enormous expansion of the university system. (4) This happened just when new teachers had to be recruited from the small cohort of depression babies, while the *student* population began to swell as the much larger cohort born after the war reached school and college. In short, there was a sharp increase in demand for college teachers, and a corresponding improvement in our absolute and relative position in the society. Not great wealth, to be sure, but modest prosperity, quick advancement, more prestige, confidence and a new self-esteem.

Here we must leave the argument without perfect closure. It would be vulgar determinism to hold that from these economic conditions followed a "bourgeoisification" of the academic mind, and from that a capitalist misreading of *The Catcher in the Rye*. For one thing, this picture ignores McCarthyism, the pressure toward liberal conformity in the university, and the sweet, secret inducements proffered to intellectuals by the CIA through the Congress for Cultural Freedom, *Encounter*, *Partisan Review*, and all the instruments of cooptation.

But common sense and a belief in real connections between people's ideas and their material lives are enough, we think, to make it seem natural for a critical establishment so located in American capitalism to interpret and judge literary works in a way harmonious with the continuance of capitalism.

We need hardly say that the world is a different place in 1976 than it was in 1951 or 1971. Even from the American academy, capitalism now seems a less inevitable and friendly part of the landscape. Academic criticism, and indeed literary study, hold a less favored position than they did even five years ago, and all indications point to a further decline. As thousands of people in our field join the unemployed or ill-employed, it will be surprising if most teachers of English maintain a separation of culture from society, and keep on writing the kind of criticism that mediated *Catcher*'s acceptance as a classic.

From *Critical Inquiry* 3.1 (Autumn 1976): 15-37. Copyright © 1976 by The University of Chicago Press. Reprinted with permission of The University of Chicago Press.

Notes

1. Warren French, *J. D. Salinger* (New York, 1963), p. 102; James E. Miller, Jr., *J. D. Salinger* (Minneapolis, 1965), p. 5.
2. Robert Gutwillig, "Everybody's Caught 'The Catcher in the Rye,'" *The New York Times Book Review*, Paperback Book Section, 15 January 1961, p. 38.
3. Alice Payne Hackett, *70 Years of Best Sellers; 1895-1965* (New York, 1967), p. 13.
4. Our estimate, based on this information: Bantam has sold just over 5,000,000 copies since it became sole publisher of the novel in April, 1964 (thanks to Peter McCue of Bantam for this figure). Assuming that about 1,000,000 of these were sold before the end of 1965, we conclude that over 4,000,000 have been sold since Alice Payne Hackett's tally (see n. 3). *Catcher* was twelfth among all novels in American sales by 1965; our guess is that it is third or fourth now, and will soon be at the head of the list.
5. Nash K. Burger, *The New York Times*, 16 July 1951, p. 19.
6. "With Love & 20-20 Vision," *Time*, 16 July 1967, p. 96.
7. Harvey Breit, *The Atlantic* 188 (August 1951): 82.
8. S. N. Behrman, "The Vision of the Innocent," *The New Yorker*, 11 August 1951, p. 71.
9. Anne L. Goodman, "Mad About Children," *The New Republic*, 16 July 1951, p. 21.
10. Ernest Jones, "Case History of All of Us," *The Nation*, 1 September 1951, p. 176.
11. Breit, p. 82.
12. Harrison Smith, "Manhattan Ulysses, Junior," *Saturday Review*, 14 July 1951, p. 13.
13. Behrman, pp. 71, 75.
14. Virgilia Peterson, *Herald Tribune Book Review*, 15 July 1951, p. 3.
15. An exception is the review by William Poster, "Tomorrow's Child," *Commentary* 13 (January 1952): 90-92. He places Holden in the upper-middle or lower-upper class, estimates Mr. Caulfield's income at between $30,000 and $100,000 a year, and calls Holden "typical not so much of this adolescent class as a whole, but of a specific and extensive part of it, namely, those individuals who think of themselves as exceptions to their class by virtue of their superior taste," those who "have nothing further to strive for within their class and cannot accept its usual goals." We do not entirely agree with this account, as will become evident later; but at least Poster sees the book as socially precise. Other reviews appeared *in America*, 11 August 1951; *Catholic World*, November 1951; *Harper's*, August 1951; *New Statesman and Nation*, 18 August 1951; *Spectator*, 17 August 1951; *TLS*, 7 September 1971.
16. David L. Stevenson, "J. D. Salinger: The Mirror of Crisis," *The Nation*, 9 March 1957, p. 215.
17. George Steiner, "The Salinger Industry," *The Nation*, 14 November 1959, p. 360. Further quotations are from pp. 360-63, passim. The first entries under Salinger in the *MLA International Bibliography* appeared in 1956. Each succeeding year has car-

ried entries, whose number crested at 33 in 1963, when *Wisconsin Studies in Contemporary Literature* gave an entire issue to Salinger, as *Modern Fiction Studies* was to do in 1966. Both the *WSCL* and *MFS* issues included bibliographies of criticism on Salinger.

18. Donald P. Costello, "The Language of 'The Catcher in the Rye,'" *American Speech* 34 (October 1959): 172-81.

19. Arthur Heiserman and James E. Miller, Jr., "J. D. Salinger: Some Crazy Cliff," *Western Humanities Review* 10 (Spring 1956): 129.

20. William Wiegand, "J. D. Salinger: Seventy-Eight Bananas," *Chicago Review* 9 (Winter 1958): 4.

21. Donald Barr, "Saints, Pilgrims and Artists," *Commonweal*, 25 October 1957, pp. 88-90.

22. Peter J. Seng, "The Fallen Idol: The Immature World of Holden Caulfield," *College English* 23 (December 1961): 203-9.

23. Frederic I. Carpenter, "The Adolescent in American Fiction," *English Journal* 46 (September 1957): 314-15.

24. Unless of course Salinger himself was seen not only to have drawn an adolescent hero, but to have endorsed his attitudes in which case critics addressed themselves to the writer's shortcomings, e.g., Maxwell Geismar in "The Wise Child and the *New Yorker* School of Fiction," *American Moderns: From Rebellion to Conformity* (New York, 1958), pp. 195-209.

25. Jonathan Baumbach, "The Saint as a Young Man: A Reappraisal of *The Catcher in the Rye*," *Modern Language Quarterly* 25 (December 1964): 467.

26. Paul Levine, "J. D. Salinger: The Development of the Misfit Hero," *Twentieth-Century Literature* 4 (October 1958): 97.

27. Kermit Vanderbilt, "Symbolic Resolution in *The Catcher in the Rye:* The Cup, the Carrousel, and the American West," *Western Humanities Review* 17 (Summer 1963): 272.

28. George R. Creeger, *"Treacherous Desertion": Salinger's The Catcher in the Rye* (Middletown, Conn., 1961), p. 8.

29. Dan Wakefield, "Salinger and the Search for Love," *New World Writing* 14 (1958): 70.

30. Arthur Mizener, "The Love Song of J. D. Salinger, *Harper's*, February 1959, p. 90.

31. Stevenson, p. 216.

32. Ihab Hassan, "The Rare Quixotic Gesture," in *Salinger*, ed. Henry Anatole Grunwald (New York, 1962), pp. 148-49. Reprinted from Hassan's *Radical Innocence* (Princeton, 1961). First appeared in the *Western Humanities Review*, 1957.

33. Heiserman and Miller, p. 132.

34. Edgar M. Branch, "Mark Twain and J. D. Salinger: A Study in Literary Continuity," *American Quarterly* 9 (Summer 1957): 157.

35. Donald P. Costello, "Salinger and His Critics," *Commonweal*, 25 October 1963, p. 133.

36. Geismar, pp. 197-98.

37. Hassan, in Grunwald, p. 139.

38. Carl F. Strauch, "Kings in the Back Row: Meaning Through Structure—A Reading of Salinger's *The Catcher in the Rye*," *Wisconsin Studies in Contemporary Literature* 2 (Winter 1961): 27.
39. Carpenter, p. 316.
40. Branch, p. 154.
41. Miller, pp. 12-17.
42. *The Catcher in the Rye* (New York, 1964), pp. 14-15. Future page references to *Catcher* are in the text.
43. Miller, p. 13.
44. Notably these: (1) In "'Franny and Zooey' and J. D. Salinger" (*New Left Review* 15 [May-June 1962]: 72-82), Brian Way argued that *Catcher* is one of the few "contemporary American novels that have recreated in twentieth-century terms that simultaneous sense of character and society of the great nineteenth-century realists." School, he pointed out, "is the agency by which America more than most countries consciously socializes the immature for entry into the approved adult activities: and so a boy's relation to school becomes a microcosm of the individual's relation to his society. In this concentration upon a manageable network of representative relationships, we see at work the only method by which a novel can create with any living force the pressures of a society. . . ." Way went on to analyze both the successes and failures of the book in these terms, in an admirable essay. (2) Writing mainly about *Franny and Zooey*, but with reference to *Catcher* as well, Paul Phillips emphasized that "What Salinger's sensitive characters find so consistently repulsive is the vulgarity, the rampant selfishness, the fundamental hypocrisy and foulness of bourgeois conventions." We agree, though perhaps with milder epithets; and we think Phillips was nearly right in holding that "Salinger's major limitation as a satirist is that he is generally unconcerned with world issues" ("Salinger's *Franny and Zooey*," *Mainstream* 15 [January 1962: 32-39). (3) Three years earlier, also in *Mainstream*, Barbara Giles said of Holden, "In a vague sort of way he senses that the mannerisms and general make-believe he hates would not be worth hatred if they didn't proceed from a system in which the 'dirty movies' and the Broadway productions that his father, the corporation lawyer, helps to finance, play a directly debasing role. In the helplessness of his hatreds he may even be said to sense, still more vaguely, the extent of a power and corruption he cannot name." She went on to say that Salinger's young people reject this system, "but with it they reject any further study of motive itself, demanding only certificates of purity from themselves" ("The Lonely War of J. D. Salinger," *Mainstream* 12 [February 1959: 2-13). We would note that all three articles appeared in left wing journals, well out of the *academic* mainstream. Establishment critics did not take up their lead. We had not heard of the three articles before we set out to write this piece.

Catcher In and Out of History

James E. Miller, Jr.

Carol and Richard Ohmann, in "Reviewers, Critics, and *The Catcher in the Rye*" (*Critical Inquiry*, Autumn 1976), remind us that J. D. Salinger's youthful novel is a quarter century old. The reminder comes as a shock to me personally, inasmuch as I find myself given some prominence among those "Critics" of the title: as the co-author, with Arthur Heiserman, of one of the first critical essays on *Catcher* ("J. D. Salinger: Some Crazy Cliff," 1956) and as the author of the 1965 Minnesota pamphlet on Salinger. The Ohmanns treat both the article and the booklet with great tact and tenderness, while at the same time using them as focal points for their considerable disagreements. I do not want to come to the defense of these aging critical works, although I am tempted to identify in the early essay the flashes of genius in the passages written by the late Arthur Heiserman when he was young and energetic and we both were afire with ideas and plans. Both of us were bemused as we watched our essay become enshrined in a succession of Salinger casebooks: it had the distinction of being singled out as a target by George Steiner in a blast against the university critical enterprise in a piece entitled "The Salinger Industry." As the Salinger mania faded, Arthur and I sighed to ourselves that at least the anti-academic critics would not have our article to kick around anymore.

My Minnesota pamphlet on Salinger came after Salinger's lapse into silence, and soon after its appearance, Salinger seemed to fade from the public consciousness. But though he no longer appeared on the covers of *Time*, his novel was still and still is avidly read, especially by high school students the age of Holden Caulfield (16-17). I found this out when students coming into my contemporary American novel courses demonstrated such familiarity with *Catcher* that I dropped it from my reading list. I long ago assumed that *Catcher*, like *Billy Budd* and *Turn of the Screw*, had been so intensively examined by critics that little if anything was left to say. But I clearly reckoned without the Ohmanns and what might be termed a Marxist or neo-Marxist approach.

The Ohmann essay begins its argument by quoting headlines and editorials that appeared the day of *Catcher*'s publication (stories and commentaries revolving around the hot war in Korea and the cold war with Russia) and then goes on to show how the reviews of *Catcher* (and the critical essays on it) ignored the novel's relation to its moment in time and in effect "removed it from history" by concentrating on its universal elements. The essay can best speak for itself: *Catcher* is defined in essence as "a serious critical mimesis of bourgeois life in the Eastern United States, ca. 1950—of snobbery, privilege, class injury, culture as a badge of superiority, sexual exploitation, education subordinated to status, warped social feeling, competitiveness, stunted human possibility, the list could go on. Salinger is astute in imaging these hurtful things, though not in explaining them." These themes, we are told, are "central to the book's meaning and to the impact it has on us." The book's readers ("adults, at least") are "won to Holden's values—equality, spontaneity, brotherhood—but sense that these values cannot be realized within extant social forms. The novel draws readers into a powerful longing for what-could-be, and at the same time interposes what-is, as an unchanging and immovable reality."

Although the Ohmanns introduce some qualifiers in these summary generalizations, their reading of *Catcher* and their view of its limitations are in reality comprehensive and exclusive. If the reader grants their generalizations, he is likely to find that other views or approaches embodying his experience of the novel are no longer tenable. A close glance at the Ohmann reading reveals it as simplistic: Holden's warm, human values are pitted against a cold, selfish society; Holden's (and Salinger's) main failure (the "confusion of the novel") is in choosing only between rejoining or dropping out from this bourgeois, capitalistic society instead of opting for radical—that is, socialist—change.

Few would want to deny a political-economic dimension to

Catcher, and it is possibly true that this dimension has been slighted in past criticism. But to see Holden's malaise of spirit solely or even mainly caused by the evils of a capitalistic society is surely myopic; and to envision a utopian socialistic society (even were we to grant its possible creation) as miraculously erasing all the problems Holden faces is naive. The problems of a sensitive and perceptive adolescent moving painfully to maturity can never be solved by restructuring society politically and economically.

Early in the novel we hear Holden on his history teacher, "Old Spencer": ". . . you wondered what the heck he was still living for. I mean he was all stooped over, and he had very terrible posture, and in class, whenever he dropped a piece of chalk at the blackboard, some guy in the first row always had to get up and pick it up and hand it to him."[1] We learn that Holden's brother Allie died of leukemia some years before the novel opens, and that Holden has kept his memory alive through his baseball mitt on which Allie had copied out Emily Dickinson poems. In the dormitory room next to Holden's lives the unfortunate Robert Ackley, with "lousy teeth" that "always looked mossy and awful," who had "a lot of pimples" and a "terrible personality"—a "sort of nasty guy" (p. 19). When Holden's roommate Stradlater refuses to tell Holden whether he made it or not with Holden's friend Jane Gallagher, Holden strikes out and is struck down, bleeding. Over and over again Holden complains that nobody ever gives your message to anybody. Over and over again we hear Holden cry out: "I felt so lonesome, all of a sudden. I almost wished I was dead" (p. 48).

This catalogue of characters, incidents, expressions could be extended indefinitely, all of them suggesting that Holden's sickness of soul is something deeper than economic or political, that his revulsion at life is not limited to social and monetary inequities, but at something in the nature of life itself—the decrepitude of the aged, the physical repulsiveness of the pimpled, the disappearance and dissolution of the dead, the terrors (and enticements) of sex, the hauntedness of human aloneness, the panic of individual isolation. Headlines about Korea, Dean Acheson, and the cold war seem, if not irrelevant, essentially wide of the mark—if we define the mark as the heart and soul of *Catcher*.

The important comic scene in which Holden is victimized by the elevator operator Maurice and the prostitute Sunny surely must be read as something more than a revelation of "sexual exploitation" in a capitalistic society. The economic-political reading of the novel tends to pass over without mention Holden's groping about in desperation to come to terms with his sexuality, which both fascinates and threatens, lures and depresses him. His sexual feelings are central to the maturing process he is undergoing, and they lie obscurely behind his tender feelings for (and secret envy of) the various children he encounters: they remain in the pre-adult world of unsullied innocence. The title of the novel itself directs attention to Holden's dream, which he reveals to Phoebe, of standing on the edge of "some crazy cliff" near a playing field of rye, catching the kids before they fall over the cliff: the fall would surely be into sexuality, experience, adulthood.

It is difficult to see how the Marxist reading might come to terms with the crucial scene near the end of the novel, when Holden wakes up in fright to find his old and trusted teacher, Mr. Antolini, patting him on the head. Holden rushes away, to wonder later whether he had done the right thing, whether Antolini was really a "flit"—or a genuine friend in a generally hostile world. This self-questioning sets off a chain of events that brings Holden to a confrontation with his own death as he descends into the Egyptian tomb at the museum, sees again the ubiquitous obscene phrase he has rubbed off of Phoebe's school walls, and envisions his own tombstone with his name, the years of entry and exit, and the phrase pursing him into imagined death—"Fuck you" (p. 204). It is shortly after this that Holden, refusing to agree to Phoebe's running away to the west with him, announces that he has decided to stay—to rejoin the human race. As he watches Phoebe going around and around on the carrousel, grabbing for the gold ring, he realizes that he cannot shield her from experience: "If they [the kids] fall off, they fall off, but it's bad if you say anything to them" (p. 211). And the action of the novel closes as Holden feels so "damn happy" that he is "damn near bawling" watching Phoebe going around and around: he has fallen and survived, and he has discovered that he can be happy in the presence of an innocence he no longer has—without being a catcher in the rye.

The Ohmanns consider that the "shortcomings of [*Catcher*'s] awareness and its art" are manifest in its failure to show that Holden had an option of working for a better society. It is not at all clear, however, that Holden refuses this option. Mr. Antolini, in one of the novel's deepest moments, quotes Wilhelm Stekel to Holden: "The mark of the immature man is that he wants to die nobly for a cause, while the mark of the mature man is that he wants to live humbly for one" (p. 188). The comment comes at a critical turning-point for Holden, and is certainly lodged firmly in his psyche. But of course it is true that Holden does not turn his face into the sunrise at the end of the novel, expressing his determination to overthrow the bourgeois capitalistic society in favor of a socialist utopia. Indeed, the whole thrust of the novel seems to suggest that there is no social or political or economic structure that could insure sexual tranquility, banish pimples, outlaw old age, abolish death—or that would relieve Holden or any other human being of the tragic implications of his physical, sexual, emotional nature: to these he must reconcile himself, recognizing not only the "shortcomings" of man but also the "shortcomings" of himself.

But Holden is not so shortsighted, I think, as the Ohmanns suggest. In the closing lines of the novel, he confesses of the tale he has told: "I'm sorry I told so many people about it. About all I know is I sort of *miss* everybody I told about. Even old Stradlater and Ackley, for instance. I think I even miss that goddam Maurice. It's funny. Don't ever tell anybody anything. If you do, you start missing everybody" (p. 214). The Ohmanns consider this confession an overlay of "nostalgia." If it strikes them as naive or sentimental, it is hard to understand how they can believe so fiercely in a socialist utopia that must surely be based on some kind and measure of the human love—agape, not eros alone—Holden has attained at the end of *Catcher*. If a utopia is established without this kind of mutual love and understanding, is it not likely to turn into the kind of dictatorship with which the twentieth century is so familiar? In any event, the Ohmanns might have recognized that Holden has been awakened to a precondition of a better society—love of fellow human beings—before condemning Salinger for not instilling Holden with a vision of the kind of ideal state that has never existed before and seems not to exist now.

Would we really want Salinger to recycle the visions of *Looking Backward* or *A Traveler from Altruria*? The experience of the twentieth century has forced the literary imagination to portray the dark underside of such bright visions—as in *Brave New World* and *1984*. Holden joins a long succession of American "heroes" (Hawthorne's, Melville's, James', Twain's, and more) in discovering that experience is inevitably made up of good and bad, love and hate, light and dark. The Ohmanns have censured previous critics for removing *Catcher* from history. Do they not propose at the end to carry Holden out of baffling, muddled history into a tidy and clear-cut ideology?

From *Critical Inquiry* 3.3 (Spring 1977): 599-603. Copyright © 1977 by The University of Chicago Press. Reprinted with permission of The University of Chicago Press.

Note

1. *The Catcher in the Rye* (New York: Little, Brown, 1951; rpt. Bantam, 1964), pp. 6-7. All further page references appear after quotations in the text.

On First Looking into Chapman's Holden:
Speculations on a Murder
Daniel M. Stashower

Mark David Chapman, the young assassin, was carrying two things with him when he shot and killed John Lennon on the steps of the Dakota apartments in Manhattan: a pistol and a paperback copy of *The Catcher in the Rye*. The function of the pistol was obvious. Less obvious was the function of J. D. Salinger's novel. Yet the book, it seems fair to say, must have had some special significance to Mark Chapman. Any attempt to uncover its significance is, in the nature of the case, highly speculative. Yet some aspects of *The Catcher in the Rye*, set beside Mark Chapman's murder of John Lennon, seem so suggestive that not to speculate upon the connections between the two seems a temptation impossible to forgo.

J. D. Salinger's *Catcher in the Rye* was published in 1951. Like the Beatles, whose rise to fame came about roughly thirteen years later, the novel's adolescent hero, Holden Caulfield, became a spokesman for a generation of rebellious, supposedly much-misunderstood youth. An oversimplified yet functional reading of the Salinger novel might conclude that all that the book advocates would fall under the heading of "innocence" and all that it condemns falls under that of "phoniness." Holden Caulfield, during his somewhat aimless ramble through New York, feels overwhelmed by the phoniness he finds all around him. He struggles to preserve his own tenuous hold on youthful innocence—or, as he sometimes puts it, "niceness"—and despairs when he finds that innocence lost or threatened in the young people around him.

At his trial, Mark Chapman read what is perhaps *The Catcher in the Rye*'s most famous passage:

> I keep picturing all these little kids playing some game in this big field of rye and all. Thousands of little kids, and nobody's around—nobody big, I mean—except me. And I'm standing on the edge of some crazy cliff. What

> I have to do, I have to catch everybody if they start to go over the cliff—I mean if they're running and they don't look where they're going I have to come out from somewhere and *catch* them. That's all I'd do all day. I'd just be the catcher in the rye and all. I know it's crazy, but that's the only thing I'd really like to be. I know it's crazy.

While scarcely as succinct as John Wilkes Booth's "Sic semper tyrannus," or as compelling as Brutus's "Romans, countrymen, and lovers," the above passage was Chapman's sole attempt to justify the murder of John Lennon. It ought to be examined for anything in it that might have led Chapman from Salinger's rye fields to the Dakota apartments.

Probably no one will object too strenuously to the notion that Mark Chapman identified himself rather heavily with Holden Caulfield. Chapman would, after all, be only one of millions who felt that Salinger's book was written especially for him, that it addressed itself to his problems and, in the way that certain books do, eased his pain. If Chapman identified with Holden, what sort of view of the world would accompany the identification? *The Catcher in the Rye* is a book almost wholly concerned with the preservation of innocence. When Holden speaks of "coming out from somewhere" to catch the children, he hopes to save them from becoming the adult "phonies" of the kind he has been encountering in New York. He doesn't want the children to grow up into people who will "talk about how many miles their goddam cars get to the gallon." If Chapman also saw himself as a protector of innocence, why was he inspired to shoot Lennon? Here is a question of the kind Holden himself might have called "a real bastard."

Two possibilities come to mind: either Mark Chapman saw John Lennon as a corruptor of innocence, or he saw him as an innocent about to be corrupted. If Chapman imagined that Lennon was a threat to the innocence of youth, he certainly took his time in doing anything about it. After all, the man who in his music sang the joys of "Lucy in the Sky with Diamonds," and later posed nude on album covers while exhorting listeners to "open their thighs," was not exactly what one would call a Samaritan. But Lennon's last album, "Double Fantasy," was, by contrast, a Girl Scout manual. This album, which came after a silence of six years, dealt largely with the joys of home life and fatherhood. There was little in the album's songs that could he considered threatening; and the interviews that Lennon gave to promote it showed that he had settled into a comfortable, somewhat embourgeoisified life of baking bread and clipping coupons. Surely, this John Lennon was not the sort of person likely to threaten the innocence of children or of anyone else.

It is more likely, then, that Chapman saw Lennon as an innocent who was himself about to be corrupted. Some problems arise here, but the idea becomes at least plausible if considered in tandem with *The Catcher in the Rye*. Holden Caulfield provides some useful standards by which to judge innocence. His older brother, D. B., is the novel's clearest example of innocence gone bad. D. B., it will be recalled, was apparently a writer of great promise who "sold out" and began to "prostitute himself" in Hollywood by writing cheap movie scripts. Commercial success at the expense of artistic integrity is, in *The Catcher in the Rye*, the worst expression of phoniness. Throughout the novel Holden despairs that his once-noble brother has fallen.

This model of the fallen artist is easily applicable to the world of Mark Chapman. As a teenager, he idolized the Beatles, and a large part of the charm of the Beatles lay in their absolute unwillingness to compromise their integrity for the sake of commercial gain, as Holden's brother D. B. had. As it happens, the Beatles made fabulous sums of money anyway, but they often risked both their fortune and their popularity in unorthodox creative ventures. Sometimes, as with the album "Sgt. Pepper's Lonely Hearts Club Band," they succeeded in spite of their heterodoxy. Other times, as with their disastrous merchandising firm Apple Corps., they failed. But they always preserved their dedication to their fans and their art, which made them easily the world's most exciting rock band, while other bands clung to tested, profitable, and secondhand formulas. When the Beatles disbanded in 1970, their fans—including, one imagines, Mark Chapman—watched with interest to see what the individual members would do. Could any of the four men who had formed the Beatles achieve anything like a similar success on his own? Ringo Starr and George Harrison pursued fairly steady and largely uninteresting solo careers. Paul McCartney and John Lennon, divided by the stresses that had disrupted the Beatles, took off in two wildly divergent directions. Salinger himself couldn't have wished for two characters whose careers more clearly defined the two sides of *The Catcher in the Rye* dilemma.

James Paul McCartney, as almost everyone who once cared for the Beatles is aware, became the most successful male pop artist the world has ever known, but in the process he completely alienated his former fans. The man who had written such songs as "Hey Jude," "Let It Be," and "Yesterday" now churned out material that was designed, almost scientifically, to sell. From a purely commercial standpoint, McCartney was several times more successful than the Beatles ever were, but he had, like Holden's older brother, clearly sold out in producing obviously commercial music. If Chapman held to the definitions of "phoney" and "nice" as outlined by J. D. Salinger, Paul McCartney had become a phoney.

Turn now to John Lennon. Lennon's solo career was easily the most erratic of the four former Beatles. He released a series of albums that were alternately brilliant and peculiar, sometimes both, and then he dropped out of sight. "Dropped out of sight" actually means that he stopped recording and dedicated six years to raising his son, Sean, while his wife, Yoko, managed their business affairs and sold holstein cows for enormous sums. While McCartney was so much in the news that even his toes were once photographed for *Time*, John Lennon—and all his various parts—were hidden from sight. No one has ever made much sense out of Lennon's post-Beatle years, but one thing is certain: in the code of rock music, he preserved his Beatle integrity. He was not a phoney. Even his artistic failures were dignified, and his self-imposed exile did nothing to damage but rather strengthened the claim of some music critics that Lennon was, after Elvis Presley, the "king of rock."

Lennon's exile suggests an interesting and possibly illuminating parallel to *The Catcher in the Rye* as it might have been interpreted by Mark Chapman. Possibly America's most famous recluse is J. D. Salinger. For more than twenty years Salinger has isolated himself in his bunker-like retreat in New Hampshire. Like Lennon, Salinger has preserved the mystique that surrounds his early work, and he has accomplished this simply by removing himself from society. This isolation has done nothing to damage but rather has strengthened the claim of some literary critics that Salinger is one of the more important American writers in the postwar era.

Salinger's retreat from society is anticipated in *The Catcher in the Rye*. On a date with the pretty but vapid Sally Hayes, Holden suddenly asks:

> How would you like to get the hell out of here? Here's my idea. I know this guy ... we can borrow his car for a couple of weeks. What we could do is, tomorrow morning we could drive up to Massachusetts and Vermont, and all around there, see. It's beautiful as hell up there. . . . I have about a hundred and eighty bucks ... we'll stay in these cabin camps and stuff ...

Holden's plan is, obviously, unrealistic, a fact that, in the novel, Sally Hayes belabors at somewhat tedious length. But the desire to "get the hell out of here," which Holden expresses several times, is entirely consistent with the uncompromising line Holden draws between "nice" and "phoney," and his fantastical if winning desire to become a "catcher in the rye." "There were goddam phonies coming in the windows," Holden complains at one point. Thus overwhelmed, the logical recourse is escape. Salinger's own decision "to get the hell out of here" must mark one of the rare cases in literature in which an author has taken his character's advice.

Though one can hardly call holing up in the Dakota "getting the hell out of here," John Lennon did follow a course roughly like the one outlined by Holden. He, too, "got the hell out." If Chapman shared the views of Holden Caulfield, then the chances are fairly good that he very much admired Lennon's withdrawal from public life. When Lennon resurfaced in 1980, suddenly granting interviews and appearing in public, Chapman may have perceived a threat to the Salinger credo and a crack in the wall that protected Lennon's splendid innocence.

The self-promotion accompanying Lennon's re-entry into the world of high publicity was unlike anything he had ever done before, and it seems likely that Chapman found him listing dangerously toward commercialism. After six years of seclusion, news of John Lennon's doings was everywhere. The hermit of rock had become all too accessible, in a *People* magazine, vulgar way. In many respects he resembled Paul McCartney promoting his albums, which led John Lennon's fans to wonder, with some trepidation, what Lennon's long-awaited album would sound like.

Since his death, Lennon's last album, "Double Fantasy," has been hailed as a rock classic. At the time of its release, however, when Lennon was still alive, the album received a very lukewarm reception. In England, his home country, *The National Music Express* suggested that "the old man" ought to have stayed in retirement and pointed out striking similarities between this album and the work of Paul McCartney, which Lennon was known to have found distasteful. Fans who hoped for, or expected, another album of the quality of "Imagine" were disappointed.

We can only speculate, of course, upon what effect Lennon's re-emergence might have had on Mark Chapman. Perhaps Chapman had been perfectly content as long as Lennon remained in Salinger-like isolation. Now, however, Lennon thrust himself into the open with a McCartney-like publicity blitz and released what was generally acknowledged to be a mediocre piece of work. Lennon was in trouble; he was in danger of falling off the cliff, à la D. B. Caulfield and Paul McCartney. What could Mark Chapman do about it? If we examine the question with *The Catcher in the Rye* in mind, a most distressing, twisted solution arises. Simply put, it appears Chapman misread *The Catcher in the Rye*. He took the "catcher" passage to be the novel's solution, when in fact it is the crisis.

No one who has read *The Catcher in the Rye* will argue that Holden Caulfield was a seriously disturbed sixteen-year old. He wanders through New York with a genuine desire, to quote an old Beatles tune, to "take a sad song and make it better," but he doesn't know how to begin. As a result he develops an all-purpose, self-protective cynicism. When challenged by his younger sister Phoebe to justify this cynicism, he offers the famous "catcher" speech. But the book doesn't end there. What Holden has outlined in his "some crazy cliff" plan, and in his earlier "get the hell out" plan, is impossible. Holden Caulfield wants to stop reality. He wants to keep the children in the rye field from growing up. But growing up is the natural order of things. It cannot be stopped. Yet Holden longs to do the impossible. This is what brings about his crisis in *The Catcher in the Rye*.

Can it be that Mark Chapman, devoted J. D. Salinger reader, had his own difficulty in dealing with reality and responsibility in a world of grown-ups? In addition to *The Catcher in the Rye*, Chapman was known to favor a song of Lennon's called "Strawberry Fields Forever." Like Salinger's rye fields, Lennon's strawberry fields offered a frozen, unrealistic approach to life; it promised an eternity in a land where, to quote from the song, "nothing is real." If Chapman was madly drawn to both Holden Caulfield's "catcher" and John Lennon's "Strawberry Fields," it is not inconceivable that he would have wanted Lennon himself to remain "caught" in his protective retreat, where "nothing is real." Especially now, with the release of the mediocre album "Double Fantasy," Mark Chapman could have viewed John Lennon poised on the edge of the crazy cliff, and it was up to him, Chapman, to play catcher in the rye.

So Chapman flew to New York and began a sojourn very much like the one that takes place in *The Catcher in the Rye*. Although it is difficult to know for certain how Chapman filled the time, he was in the city for two full days before the shooting. He is said to have switched hotels (as Holden did); walked out of a movie theater ("I hate the movies," Holden says, "don't even mention them to me"); and regaled a cab driver with tales of a forthcoming Lennon/McCartney album, which he claimed to be producing ("I'm a terrific liar," Holden admits, "I have to watch myself sometimes").

* * *

Now comes the large question: Why did Chapman shoot Lennon? Given his Holden Caulfield state of mind, wouldn't it have made more sense to invite Lennon out for a nightcap somewhere or to go skating at Radio City, there to caution him against selling out? But Chapman was a confused, disturbed man. There are no easy explanations for why he did what he did. One answer is suggested in the pages of *The Catcher in the Rye*. Chapman may have believed that the highest possible attainment, at least as viewed through Salinger's novel, would be to achieve that permanent state of innocence suggested in the "catcher" passage. Only one character in *The Catcher in the Rye* manages that unimpeachable innocence—Holden's younger brother Allie. Allie is the only character in the novel, including Holden, who never shows any hint of phoniness, and who never will. How is this possible? It is possible only because Allie is dead.

Immediately preceding Caulfield's "catcher" speech, which Chapman found so significant and which he recited at his trial, there is a section in the novel in which Holden's sister Phoebe asks if her depressed brother can "name one thing" that he likes. Holden has a lot of trouble responding. He recalls a boy at school, James Castle, who, rather than taking back something he had said about a bully, jumped out of a fifth-floor window. Then he reveals what at first seems to be an unrelated piece of information: that he likes his brother Allie. "Allie's *dead*!" Phoebe cries, "You always say that! If somebody's dead and everything, and in *Heaven*, then it isn't really . . ."

"I know he's dead!" Holden returns. "Don't you think I know that? I can still like him though, can't I? Just because someone's dead, you don't just stop liking them, for God's sake—especially if they were about a thousand times nicer than the people you know that're *alive* and all."

In the traditional interpretation of the novel, Holden's reference to his brother is simply another indication of his unrealistic desire to freeze innocence and thwart phoniness. But Chapman, who wrote "This is my statement" in the flyleaf of his copy of the Salinger novel, was not a typical reader. To him, the "catcher" speech was the book's final and transcendent message, which would make Allie the real hero of *The Catcher in the Rye*. Allie, in this reading, is the only character to come out unscathed. Death, then, would have presented itself to Chapman as the only safeguard against loss of innocence.

Holden Caulfield and Mark Chapman were faced with the same crisis: an assault on innocence. Holden Caulfield could not find a way to preserve innocence forever and was forced to entertain the notion of growing up. If I am correct in my speculation, Chapman found a way. Taking as a model the only character in *The Catcher in the Rye* who achieved perpetual innocence, Chapman found his course clear. For John Lennon's innocence—which was essential to Chapman's own spiritual well-being—to remain intact, Lennon himself would have to die. Only then could his innocence, like Allie's, be preserved forever.

Unfortunately, this idea, as I have set it out here, is not as absurd or outrageous as it sounds. If Chapman's intention was to secure, and even to improve, the legend of John Lennon, the artist of perfect integrity, he succeeded. Gone now is the John Lennon who once smeared excrement on the walls of his dressing room; who claimed that the Beatles were a bigger item than Christ; and who appeared in a Los Angeles nightclub with a Kotex on his head. In his place is a sort of rock-and-roll Gandhi. Because of his violent death, anything about him that is base or even unkind has been erased. In the most extraordinary way, John Lennon today is viewed as a man of pristine innocence—"a genius of the spirit," Norman Mailer has called him. And all because Mark Chapman, standing outside the Dakota apartments, caught him in the rye.

Reprinted from *The American Scholar* 52.3 (Summer 1983): 373-377. Copyright © 1983 by the author. Reprinted by permission of the publisher.

The Language of *The Catcher in the Rye*
Donald P. Costello

A study of the language of J. D. Salinger's *The Catcher in the Rye* can be justified not only on the basis of literary interest, but also on the basis of linguistic significance. Today we study *The Adventures of Huckleberry Finn* (with which many critics have compared *The Catcher in the Rye*) not only as a great work of literary art, but as a valuable study in 1884 dialect. In coming decades, *The Catcher in the Rye* will be studied, I feel, not only as a literary work, but also as an example of teenage vernacular in the 1950s. As such, the book will be a significant historical linguistic record of a type of speech rarely made available in permanent form. Its linguistic importance will increase as the American speech it records becomes less current.

Most critics who looked at *The Catcher in the Rye* at the time of its publication thought that its language was a true and authentic rendering of teenage colloquial speech. Reviewers in the Chicago *Sunday Tribune*, the London *Times Literary Supplement*, the *New Republic*, the New York *Herald Tribune Book Review*, the New York *Times*, the *New Yorker*, and the *Saturday Review of Literature* all specifically mentioned the authenticity of the book's language. Various aspects of its language were also discussed in the reviews published in *America*, the *Atlantic*, the *Catholic World*, the *Christian Science Monitor*, the *Library Journal*, the Manchester *Guardian*, the *Nation*, the *New Statesman and Nation*, the New York *Times Book Review*, *Newsweek*, the *Spectator*, and *Time*.[1] Of these many reviews, only the writers for the *Catholic World* and the *Christian Science Monitor* denied the authenticity of the book's language, but both of these are religious journals which refused to believe that the 'obscenity' was realistic. An examination of the reviews of *The Catcher in the Rye* proves that the language of Holden Caulfield, the book's sixteen-year-old narrator, struck the ear of the contemporary reader as an accurate rendering of the informal speech of an intelligent, educated, Northeastern American adolescent.[2]

In addition to commenting on its authenticity, critics have often remarked—uneasily—the 'daring,' 'obscene,' 'blasphemous' features of Holden's language. Another commonly noted feature of the book's language has been its comic effect. And yet there has never been an extensive investigation of the language itself. That is what this paper proposes to do.

Even though Holden's language is authentic teenage speech, recording it was certainly not the major intention of Salinger. He was faced with the artistic task of creating an individual character, not with the linguistic task of reproducing the exact speech of teenagers in general. Yet Holden had to speak a recognizable teenage language, and at the same time had to be identifiable as an individual. This difficult task Salinger achieved by giving Holden an extremely trite and typical teenage speech, overlaid with strong personal idiosyncrasies. There are two major speech habits which are Holden's own, which are endlessly repeated throughout the book, and which are, nevertheless, typical enough of teenage speech so that Holden can be both typical and individual in his use of them. It is certainly common for teenagers to end thoughts with a loosely dangling 'and all,' just as it is common for them to add an insistent 'I really did,' 'It really was.' But Holden uses these phrases to such an overpowering degree that they become a clear part of the flavor of the book; they become, more, a part of Holden himself, and actually help to characterize him.

Holden's 'and all' and its twins, 'or something,' 'or anything,' serve no real, consistent linguistic function. They simply give a sense of looseness of expression and looseness of thought. Often they signify that Holden knows there is more that could be said about the issue at hand, but he is not going to bother going into it:

... how my parents were occupied and all before they had me (5)[3]

... they're *nice* and all (5)

I'm not going to tell you my whole goddam autobiography or anything (5)

... splendid and clear-thinking and all (6)

But just as often the use of such expressions is purely arbitrary, with no discernible meaning:

... he's my *brother* and all (5)

... was in the Revolutionary War and all (6)

It was December and all (7)

... no gloves or anything (7)

... right in the pocket and all (7)

Donald Barr, writing in the *Commonweal*, finds this habit indicative of Holden's tendency to generalize, to find the all in the one:

> Salinger has an ear not only for idiosyncrasies of diction and syntax, but for mental processes. Holden Caulfield's phrase is 'and all'—'She looked so damn *nice*, the way she kept going around and around in her blue coat and all'—as if each experience wore a halo. His fallacy is *ab uno disce omnes*; he abstracts and generalizes wildly.[4]

Heiserman and Miller, in the *Western Humanities Review*, comment specifically upon Holden's second most obvious idiosyncrasy: 'In a phony world Holden feels compelled to reenforce his sincerity and truthfulness constantly with, "It really is" or "It really did."'[5] S. N. Behrman, in the *New Yorker*, finds a double function of these 'perpetual insistences of Holden's.' Behrman thinks they 'reveal his age, even when he is thinking much older,' and, more important, 'he is so aware of the danger of slipping into phoniness himself that he has to repeat over and over "I really mean it," "It really does."'[6] Holden uses this idiosyncrasy of insistence almost every time that he makes an affirmation.

Allied to Holden's habit of insistence is his 'if you want to know the truth.' Heiserman and Miller are able to find characterization in this habit too:

> The skepticism inherent in that casual phrase, 'if you want to know the truth,' suggesting that as a matter of fact in the world of Holden Caulfield very few people do, characterizes this sixteen-year-old 'crazy mixed up kid' more sharply and vividly than pages of character 'analysis' possibly could.[7]

Holden uses this phrase only after affirmations, just as he uses 'It really does,' but usually after the personal ones, where he is consciously being frank:

> I have no wind, if you want to know the truth. (8)

> I don't even think the bastard had a handkerchief, if you want to know the truth. (34)

> I'm a pacifist, if you want to know the truth. (44)

> She had quite a lot of sex appeal, too, if you really want to know. (53)

> I was damn near bawling, I felt so damn happy, if you want to know the truth. (191)

These personal idiosyncrasies of Holden's speech are in keeping with general teenage language. Yet they are so much a part of Holden and of the flavor of the book that they are much of what makes Holden to be Holden. They are the most memorable feature of the book's language. Although always in character, the rest of Holden's speech is more typical than individual. The special quality of this language comes from its triteness, its lack of distinctive qualities.

Holden's informal, schoolboy vernacular is particularly typical in its 'vulgarity' and 'obscenity.' No one familiar with prep-school speech could seriously contend that Salinger overplayed his hand in this respect. On the contrary, Holden's restraints help to characterize him as a sensitive youth who avoids the most strongly forbidden terms, and who never uses vulgarity in a self-conscious or phony way to help him be 'one of the boys.' *Fuck*, for example, is never used as a part of Holden's speech. The word appears in the novel four times, but only when Holden disapprovingly discusses its wide appearance on walls. The Divine name is used habitually by Holden only in the comparatively weak *for God's sake*, *God*, and *goddam*. The stronger and usually more offensive *for Chrissake* or *Jesus* or *Jesus Christ* are used habitually by Ackley and Stradlater; but Holden uses them only when he feels the need for a strong expression. He almost never uses *for Chrissake* in an unemotional situation. *Goddam* is Holden's favorite adjective. This word is used with no relationship to its original meaning, or to Holden's attitude toward the word to which it is attached. It simply expresses an emotional feeling toward the object: either favorable, as in 'goddam hunting cap'; or unfavorable, as in 'ya goddam moron'; or indifferent, as in 'coming in the *goddam* windows.' *Damn* is used interchangeably with goddam; no differentiation in its meaning is detectable.

Other crude words are also often used in Holden's vocabulary. *Ass* keeps a fairly restricted meaning as a part of the human anatomy, but it is used in a variety of ways. It can refer simply to that specific part of the body ('I moved my ass a little'), or be a part of a trite expression ('freezing my ass off'; 'in a half-assed way'), or be an expletive ('Game, my ass.'). *Hell* is perhaps the most versatile word in Holden's entire vocabulary; it serves most of the meanings and constructions which Mencken lists in his *American Speech* article on 'American Profanity.'[8] So far is Holden's use of *hell* from its original meaning that he can use the sentence 'We had a helluva time' to mean that he and Phoebe had a decidedly pleasant time downtown shopping for shoes. The most common function of *hell* is as the second part of a simile, in which a thing can be either 'hot as hell' or, strangely, 'cold as hell'; 'sad as hell' or 'playful as hell'; 'old as hell' or 'pretty as hell.' Like all of these words, *hell* has no close relationship to its original meaning.

Both *bastard* and *sonuvabitch* have also drastically changed in meaning. They no longer, of course, in Holden's vocabulary, have any connection with the accidents of birth. Unless used in a trite simile, *bastard* is a strong word, reserved for things and people Holden particularly dislikes, especially 'phonies.' *Sonuvabitch* has an even stronger meaning to Holden; he uses it only in the deepest anger. When, for example, Holden is furious with Stradlater over his treatment of Jane Gallagher, Holden repeats again and again that he 'kept calling him a moron sonuvabitch' (43).

The use of crude language in *The Catcher in the Rye* increases, as we should expect, when Holden is reporting schoolboy dialogue. When he is directly addressing the reader, Holden's use of such language drops off almost entirely. There is also an increase in this language when any of the characters are excited or angry. Thus, when Holden is apprehensive over Stradlater's treatment of Jane, his *goddams* increase suddenly to seven on a single page (p. 39).

Holden's speech is also typical in his use of slang. I have catalogued over a hundred slang terms used by Holden, and every one of these is in widespread use. Although Holden's slang is rich and colorful, it, of course, being slang, often fails at precise communication. Thus, Holden's *crap* is used in seven different ways. It can mean foolishness, as 'all that David Copperfield kind of crap,' or messy matter, as 'I spilled some crap all over my gray flannel,' or merely miscellaneous matter, as 'I was putting on my galoshes and crap.' It can also carry its basic meaning, animal excreta, as 'there didn't look like there was anything in the park except dog crap,' and it can be used as an adjective meaning anything generally unfavorable, as 'The show was on the crappy side.' Holden uses the phrases *to be a lot of crap* and *to shoot the crap* and *to chuck the crap* all to mean 'to be untrue,' but he can also use *to shoot the crap* to mean simply 'to chat,' with no connotation of untruth, as in 'I certainly wouldn't have minded shooting the crap with old Phoebe for a while.'

Similarly Holden's slang use of *crazy* is both trite and imprecise. 'That drives me crazy' means that he violently dislikes something; yet 'to be crazy about' something means just the opposite. In the same way, to be 'killed' by something can mean that he was emotionally affected either favorably ('That story just about killed me.') or unfavorably ('Then she turned her back on me again. It nearly killed me.'). This use of *killed* is one of Holden's favorite slang expressions. Heiserman and Miller are, incidentally, certainly incorrect when they conclude: 'Holden always lets us know when he has insight into the absurdity of the endlessly absurd situations which make up the life of a sixteen-year-old by exclaiming, "It killed me."'[9] Holden often uses this expression with no connection to the absurd; he even uses it for his beloved Phoebe. The expression simply indicates a high degree of emotion—any kind. It is hazardous to conclude that any of Holden's slang has a precise and consistent meaning or function. These same critics fall into the same error when they conclude that Holden's use of the adjective *old* serves as 'a term of endearment.'[10] Holden appends this word to almost every character, real or fictional, mentioned in the novel, from the hated 'old Maurice' to 'old Peter Lorre,' to 'old Phoebe,' and even 'old Jesus.' The only pattern that can be discovered in Holden's use of this term is that he usually uses it only after he has previously mentioned the character; he then feels free to append the familiar *old*. All we can conclude from Holden's slang is that it is typical teenage slang: versatile yet narrow, expressive yet unimaginative, imprecise, often crude, and always trite.

Holden has many favorite slang expressions which he overuses. In one place, he admits:

> 'Boy!' I said. I also say 'Boy!' quite a lot. Partly because I have a lousy vocabulary and partly because I act quite young for my age sometimes. (12)

But if Holden's slang shows the typically 'lousy vocabulary' of even the educated American teenager, this failing becomes even more obvious when we narrow our view to Holden's choice of adjectives and adverbs. The choice is indeed narrow, with a constant repetition of a few favorite words: *lousy, pretty, crumby, terrific, quite, old, stupid*—all used, as is the habit of teenage vernacular, with little regard to specific meaning. Thus, most of the nouns which are called 'stupid' could not in any logical framework be called 'ignorant,' and, as we have seen, *old* before a proper noun has nothing to do with age.

Another respect in which Holden was correct in accusing himself of having a 'lousy vocabulary' is discovered in the ease with which he falls into trite figures of speech. We have already seen that Holden's most common simile is the worn and meaningless 'as hell'; but his often-repeated 'like a madman' and 'like a bastard' are just about as unrelated to a literal meaning and are easily as unimaginative. Even Holden's nonhabitual figures of speech are usually trite: 'sharp as a tack'; 'hot as a firecracker'; 'laughed like a hyena'; 'I know old Jane like a book'; 'drove off like a bat out of hell'; 'I began to feel like a horse's ass'; 'blind as a bat'; 'I know Central Park like the back of my hand.'

Repetitious and trite as Holden's vocabulary may be, it can, nevertheless, become highly effective. For example, when Holden piles one trite adjective upon another, a strong power of invective is often the result:

He was a goddam stupid moron. (42)

Get your dirty stinking moron knees off my chest. (43)

You're a dirty stupid sonuvabitch of a moron. (43)

And his limited vocabulary can also be used for good comic effect. Holden's constant repetition of identical expressions in countless widely different situations is often hilariously funny.

But all of the humor in Holden's vocabulary does not come from its unimaginative quality. Quite the contrary, some of his figures of speech are entirely original; and these are inspired, dramatically effective, and terribly funny. As always, Salinger's Holden is basically typical, with a strong overlay of the individual:

He started handling my exam paper like it was a turd or something. (13)

He put my goddam paper down then and looked at me like he'd just beaten hell out of me in ping-pong or something. (14)

That guy Morrow was about as sensitive as a goddam toilet seat. (52)

Old Marty was like dragging the Statue of Liberty around the floor. (69)

Another aspect in which Holden's language is typical is that it shows the general American characteristic of adaptability—apparently strengthened by his teenage lack of restraint. It is very easy for Holden to turn nouns into adjectives, with the simple addition of a *-y:* 'perverty,' 'Christmasy,' 'vomity-looking,' 'whory-looking,' 'hoodlumy-looking,' 'show-offy,' 'flitty-looking,' 'dumpy-looking,' 'pimpy,' 'snobby,' 'fisty.' Like all of English, Holden's language shows a versatile combining ability: 'They gave Sally this little blue butt-twitcher of a dress to wear' (117) and 'That magazine was some little cheerer upper' (176). Perhaps the most interesting aspect of the adaptability of Holden's language is his ability to use nouns as adverbs: 'She sings it very Dixieland and whorehouse, and it doesn't sound at all mushy' (105).

As we have seen, Holden shares, in general, the trite repetitive vocabulary which is the typical lot of his age group. But as there are exceptions in his figures of speech, so are there exceptions in his vocabulary itself, in his word stock. An intelligent, well-read ('I'm quite illiterate, but I read a lot'), and educated boy, Holden possesses, and can use when he wants to, many words which are many a cut above Basic English, including 'ostracized,' 'exhibitionist,' 'unscrupulous,' 'conversationalist,' 'psychic,' 'bourgeois.' Often Holden seems to choose his words consciously, in an effort to communicate to his adult reader clearly and properly, as in such terms as 'lose my virginity,' 'relieve himself,' 'an alcoholic'; for upon occasion, he also uses the more vulgar terms 'to give someone the time,' 'to take a leak,' 'booze hound.' Much of the humor arises, in fact, from Holden's habit of writing on more than one level at the same time. Thus, we have such phrases as 'They give guys the ax quite frequently at Pencey' and 'It has a very good academic rating, Pencey' (7). Both sentences show a colloquial idiom with an overlay of consciously selected words.

Such a conscious choice of words seems to indicate that Salinger, in his attempt to create a realistic character in Holden, wanted to make him aware of his speech, as, indeed, a real teenager would be when communicating to the outside world. Another piece of evidence that Holden is conscious of his speech and, more, realizes a difficulty in communication, is found in his habit of direct repetition: 'She likes me a lot. I mean she's quite fond of me' (141), and 'She can be very snotty sometimes. She can be quite snotty' (150). Sometimes the repetition is exact: 'He was a very nervous guy—I mean he was a very nervous guy' (165), and 'I sort of missed them. I mean I sort of missed them' (169). Sometimes Holden stops specifically to interpret slang terms, as when he wants to communicate the fact that Allie liked Phoebe: 'She killed Allie, too. I mean he liked her, too' (64).

There is still more direct evidence that Holden was conscious of his speech. Many of his comments to the reader are concerned with language. He was aware, for example, of the 'phony' quality of many words and phrases, such as 'grand,' 'prince,' 'traveling incognito,' 'little girls' room,' 'licorice stick,' and 'angels.' Holden is also conscious, of course, of the existence of 'taboo words.' He makes a point of mentioning that the girl from Seattle repeatedly asked him to 'watch your language, if you don't mind' (67), and that his mother told Phoebe not to say 'lousy' (160). When the prostitute says 'Like fun you are,' Holden comments:

> It was a funny thing to say. It sounded like a real kid. You'd think a prostitute and all would say 'Like hell you are' or 'Cut the crap' instead of 'Like fun you are.' (87)

In grammar, too, as in vocabulary, Holden possesses a certain self-consciousness. (It is, of course, impossible to imagine a student getting through today's schools without a self-consciousness with regard to grammar rules.) Holden is, in fact, not only aware of the existence of 'grammatical errors,' but knows the social taboos that accompany them. He is disturbed by a schoolmate who is ashamed of his parents' grammar, and he reports that his former teacher, Mr. Antolini, warned him about picking up 'just enough education to hate people who say, "It's a secret between he and I"' (168).

Holden is a typical enough teenager to violate the grammar rules, even though he knows of their social importance. His most common rule violation is the misuse of *lie* and *lay*, but he also is careless about relative pronouns ('about a traffic cop that falls in love'), the double negative ('I hardly didn't even know I was doing it'), the perfect tenses ('I'd woke him up'), extra words ('like as if all you ever did at Pencey was play polo all the time'), pronoun number ('it's pretty disgusting to watch somebody picking their nose'), and pronoun position ('I and this friend of mine, Mal Brossard'). More remarkable, however, than the instances of grammar rule violations is Holden's relative 'correctness.' Holden is always intelligible, and is even 'correct' in many usually difficult constructions. Grammatically speaking, Holden's language seems to point up the fact that English was the only subject in which he was not failing. It is interesting to note how much more 'correct' Holden's speech is than that of Huck Finn. But then Holden is educated, and since the time of Huck there had been sixty-seven years of authoritarian schoolmarms working on the likes of Holden. He has, in fact, been overtaught, so that he uses many 'hyper' forms:

I used to play tennis with he and Mrs. Antolini quite frequently. (163)

She'd give Allie or I a push. (64)

I and Allie used to take her to the park with us. (64)

I think I probably woke he and his wife up. (157)

Now that we have examined several aspects of Holden's vocabulary and grammar, it would be well to look at a few examples of how he puts these elements together into sentences. The structure of Holden's sentences indicates that Salinger thinks of the book more in terms of spoken speech than written speech. Holden's faulty structure is quite common and typical in vocal expression; I doubt if a student who is 'good in English' would ever create such sentence structure in writing. A student who showed the self-consciousness of Holden would not *write* so many fragments, such afterthoughts (e.g., 'It has a very good academic rating, Pencey' [7]), or such repetitions (e.g., 'Where I lived at Pencey, I lived in the Ossenburger Memorial Wing of the new dorms' [18])

There are other indications that Holden's speech is vocal. In many places Salinger mildly imitates spoken speech. Sentences such as 'You could tell old Spencer'd got a big bang out of buying it' (10) and 'I'd've killed him' (42) are repeated throughout the book. Yet it is impossible to imagine Holden taking pen in hand and actually writing 'Spencer'd' or 'I'd've.' Sometimes, too, emphasized words, or even parts of words, are italicized, as in 'Now *shut up*, Holden. God damn it—I'm *warn*ing ya' (42). This is often done with good effect, imitating quite perfectly the rhythms of speech, as in the typical:

> I practically sat down in her *lap*, as a matter of fact. Then she *really* started to cry, and the next thing I knew, I was kissing her all over–*any*where—her eyes, her *nose*, her forehead, her eyebrows and all, her *ears*—her whole face except her mouth and all. (73)

The language of *The Catcher in the Rye* is, as we have seen, an authentic artistic rendering of a type of informal, colloquial, teenage American spoken speech. It is strongly typical and trite, yet often somewhat individual; it is crude and slangy and imprecise, imitative yet occasionally imaginative, and affected toward standardization by the strong efforts of schools. But authentic and interesting as this language may be, it must be remembered that it exists, in *The Catcher in the Rye*, as only one part of an artistic achievement. The language was not written for itself, but as a part of a greater whole. Like the great Twain work with which it is often compared, a study of *The Catcher in the Rye* repays both the linguist and the literary critic; for as one critic has said, 'In them, 1884 and 1951 speak to us in the idiom and accent of two youthful travelers who have earned their passports to literary immortality.'[11]

From *American Speech: A Quarterly of Linguistic Usage* 34.3 (October 1959): 172-181. Copyright © 1959 by Duke University Press. All rights reserved. Reprinted with permission of Duke University Press.

Notes

1. See reviews in *America*, LXXV (August 11, 1951) 463, 464; *Atlantic*, CLXXXVIII (1951), 82; *Catholic World*, CLXXIV (1951), 154; Chicago *Sunday Tribune*, July 15, 1951, Part 4, p. 3; *Christian Science Monitor*, July 19, 1951, p. 9; *Library Journal*, LXXVI (1951), 1125; *Times* [London] *Literary Supplement*, September 7, 1951, p. 561; Manchester *Guardian*, August 10, 1951, p. 4; *Nation*, CLXXIII (September 1, 1951), 176; *New Republic*, CXXV (July 16, 1951), 20, 21; *New Statesman and Nation*, XLII (August 18, 1951), 185; New York *Herald Tribune Book Review*, July 15, 1951, p. 3; New York *Times Book Review*, July 15, 1951, p. 5; New York *Times*, July 16, 1951, p. 19; *New Yorker*, XXVII (August 11, 1951), 71-76; *Newsweek*, XXXVIII (July 16, 1951), 89, 90; *Saturday Review of Literature*, XXXIV (July 14, 1951), 12, 13; *Spectator*, CLXXXVII (August 17, 1951), 224; *Time*, LVIII (July 16, 1951), 96, 97.

2. If additional evidence of the authenticity of the book's language is required, one need only look at the phenomenal regard with which *The Catcher in the Rye* is held by today's college students, who were about Holden's age at the time the book was written. In its March 9, 1957, issue, the *Nation* published a symposium which at-

tempted to discover the major influences upon the college students of today. Many teachers pointed out the impact of Salinger. Carlos Baker, of Princeton, stated: 'There is still, as there has been for years, a cult of Thomas Wolfe. They have all read J. D. Salinger, Wolfe's closest competitor.' Stanley Kunitz, of Queens College, wrote: 'The only novelist I have heard praised vociferously is J. D. Salinger.' Harvey Curtis Webster, of the University of Louisville, listed Salinger as one of the 'stimulators.' R. J. Kaufman, of the University of Rochester, called *The Catcher in the Rye* 'a book which has complexly aroused nearly all of them.' See 'The Careful Young Men,' *Nation*, CLXXXIV (March 9, 1957), 199-214. I have never heard any Salinger partisan among college students doubt the authenticity of the language of their compatriot, Holden.

3. Whenever *The Catcher in the Rye* is substantially quoted in this paper, a page number will be included in the text immediately after the quotation. The edition to which the page numbers refer is the Signet paperback reprint.

4. Donald Barr, 'Saints, Pilgrims, and Artists,' *Commonweal*, LXVII (October 25, 1957), 90.

5. Arthur Heiserman and James E. Miller, Jr., 'J. D. Salinger: Some Crazy Cliff,' *Western Humanities Review*, X (1956), 136.

6. S. N. Behrman, 'The Vision of the Innocent,' *New Yorker*, XXVII (August 11, 1951), 72.

7. Heiserman and Miller, *op. cit.*, p. 135.

8. See H. L. Mencken, 'American Profanity.' *American Speech*, XIX (1944), 242.

9. Heiserman and Miller, *op. cit.*, p. 136.

10. *Ibid.*

11. Charles Kaplan, 'Holden and Huck: The Odysseys of Youth,' *College English*, XVIII (1956), 80.

The Saint as a Young Man:
A Reappraisal of *The Catcher in the Rye*
Jonathan Baumbach

J. D. Salinger's first and only novel, *The Catcher in the Rye* (1951), has undergone in recent years a steady if overinsistent devaluation. The more it becomes academically respectable, the more it becomes fair game for those critics who are self-sworn to expose every manifestation of what seems to them a chronic disparity between appearance and reality. It is critical child's play to find fault with Salinger's novel. Anyone can see that the prose is mannered (the pejorative word for stylized); no one actually talks like its first-person hero Holden Caulfield. Moreover, we are told that Holden, as poor little rich boy, is too precocious and specialized an adolescent for his plight to have larger-than-prep-school significance. The novel is sentimental; it loads the deck for Holden and against the adult world; the small but corrupt group that Holden encounters is not representative enough to permit Salinger his inclusive judgments about the species. Holden's relationship to his family is not explored: we meet his sister Phoebe, who is a younger version of himself, but his father never appears, and his mother exists in the novel only as another voice from a dark room. Finally, what is Holden (or Salinger) protesting against but the ineluctability of growing up, of having to assume the prerogatives and responsibilities of manhood? Despite these objections to the novel, *Catcher in the Rye* will endure both because it has life and because it is a significantly original work, full of insights into at least the particular truth of Holden's existence. Within the limited terms of its vision, Salinger's small book is an extraordinary achievement; it is, if such a distinction is meaningful, an important minor novel.

Like all of Salinger's fiction, *Catcher in the Rye* is not only about innocence, it is actively for innocence—as if retaining one's childness were an existential possibility. The metaphor of the title—Holden's fantasy-vision of standing in front of a cliff and protecting playing children from falling (Falling)—is, despite the impossibility of its realization, the only positive action affirmed in the novel. It is, in Salinger's Manichean universe of child angels and adult "phonies," the only moral alternative—otherwise all is corruption. Since it is spiritually as well as physically impossible to prevent the Fall, Salinger's idealistic heroes are doomed either to suicide (Seymour) or insanity (Holden, Sergeant X) or mysticism (Franny), the ways of sainthood, or to moral dissolution (Eloise, D. B., Mr. Antolini), the way of the world. In Salinger's finely honed prose, at once idiomatically real and poetically stylized, we get the terms of Holden's ideal adult occupation:

> Anyway, I keep picturing all these little kids playing some game in this big field of rye and all. Thousands of little kids, and nobody's around— nobody big, I mean—except me. And I'm standing on the edge of some crazy cliff. What I have to do, I have to catch everybody if they start to go over the cliff—I mean if they're running and they don't look where they're going I have to come out from somewhere and *catch* them. That's all I'd do all day. I'd just be the catcher in the rye and all. I know it's crazy, but that's the only thing I'd really like to be. I know it's crazy.[1]

Apparently Holden's wish is purely selfless. What he wants, in effect, is to be a saint—the protector and savior of innocence. But what he also wants, for he is still one of the running children himself, is that someone prevent *his* fall. This is his paradox: he must leave innocence to protect innocence. At sixteen, he is ready to shed his innocence and move like Adam into the fallen adult world, but he resists because those no longer innocent seem to him foolish as well as corrupt. In a sense, then, he is looking for an exemplar, a wise-good father whose example will justify his own initiation into manhood. Before Holden can become a catcher in the rye, he must find another catcher in the rye to show him how it is done.

Immediately after Holden announces his "crazy" ambition to Phoebe, he calls up one of his former teachers, Mr. Antolini, who is both intelligent and kind—a potential catcher in the rye.

He was the one that finally picked up that boy that jumped out of the window I told you about, James Castle. Old Mr. Antolini felt his pulse and all, and then he took off his coat and put it over James Castle and carried him all the way over to the infirmary. (p. 226)

Though Mr. Antolini is sympathetic because "he didn't even give a damn if his coat got all bloody," the incident is symbolic of the teacher's failure as a catcher in the rye. For all his good intentions, he was unable to catch James Castle or prevent his fall; he could only pick him up after he had died. The episode of the suicide is one of the looming shadows darkening Holden's world; Holden seeks out Antolini because he hopes that the gentle teacher—the substitute father—will "pick him up" before he is irrevocably fallen. Holden's real quest throughout the novel is for a spiritual father (an innocent adult). He calls Antolini after all the other fathers of his world have failed him, including his real father, whose existence in the novel is represented solely by Phoebe's childish reiteration of "Daddy's going to kill you." The fathers in Salinger's child's-eye world do not catch falling boys—who have been thrown out of prep school—but "kill" them. Antolini represents Holden's last chance to find a catcher-father. But his inability to save Holden has been prophesied in his failure to save James Castle; the episode of Castle's death provides an anticipatory parallel to Antolini's unwitting destruction of Holden.

That Antolini's kindness to Holden is motivated in part by a homosexual interest, though it comes as a shock to Holden, does not wholly surprise the reader. Many of the biographical details that Salinger has revealed about him through Holden imply this possibility. For example; that he has an older and unattractive wife whom he makes a great show of kissing in public is highly suggestive; yet the discovery itself—Holden wakes to find Antolini sitting beside him and caressing his head—has considerable impact. We experience a kind of shock of recognition, the more intense for its having been anticipated. The scene has added power because Antolini is, for the most part, a good man, whose interest in Holden is genuine as well as perverted. His advice to Holden is apparently well-intentioned. Though many of his recommendations are cleverly articulated platitudes, Antolini evinces a prophetic insight when he tells Holden, "I have a feeling that you're riding for some kind of a terrible, terrible fall"; one suspects, however, that to some extent he is talking about himself. Ironically, Antolini becomes the agent of his "terrible, terrible fall" by violating Holden's image of him, by becoming a false father. Having lost his respect for Antolini as a man, Holden rejects him as an authority; as far as Holden is concerned, Antolini's example denies the import of his words. His disillusionment with Antolini, who had seemed to be the sought-for, wise-good father, comes as the most intense of a long line of disenchantments; it is the final straw that breaks Holden. It is the equivalent of the loss of God. The world, devoid of good fathers (authorities), becomes a soul-destroying chaos in which his survival is possible only through withdrawal into childhood, into fantasy, into psychosis.

The action of the novel is compressed into two days in which Holden discovers through a series of disillusioning experiences that the adult world is unreclaimably corrupt. At the start of the novel, we learn from Holden that he has flunked out of Pencey Prep for not applying himself; he has resisted what he considers foolish or "phony" authority. Like almost all of Salinger's protagonists, Holden is clearly superior to his surroundings; he functions by dint of his pure sight, his innocence and sensibility, as initiate in and conscience of the world of the novel. Allowing for the exaggerations of innocence, we can generally accept Holden's value judgments of people and places as the judgments of the novel. For example, when Holden observes about his seventy-year-old, grippe-ridden history teacher that

> Old Spencer started nodding again. He also started picking his nose. He made out like he was only pinching it, but he was really getting the old thumb right in there. I guess he thought it was all right to do because it was

> only me that was in the room. I didn't *care*, except that it's pretty disgusting to watch somebody pick their nose. (pp. 13-14)

he is not being gratuitously malicious; he is passing what amounts to a moral judgment, although he is consciously doing no more than describing his reactions. Whereas the adult observer, no matter how scrupulous, censors his irreverent or unpleasant responses because he is ashamed of them, the child (Holden is sixteen) tells all.

Like Jane Austen, Salinger treats fools, especially pretentious ones, mercilessly. Though Spencer is seventy years old and for that reason alone may be worthy of respect, he is nevertheless platitudinous and self-indulgent, interested less in Holden than in pontificating before a captive audience. In a world in which the child is the spiritual father of the man, old age represents not wisdom but spiritual blindness and physical corruption. Spencer is not only foolish and "phony" ("Life is a game, boy"), but in his self-righteous way also actively malicious. Though Holden's is ostensibly a social visit, the old man badgers the boy about having failed history ("I flunked you in history because you knew absolutely nothing") and then insists on reading aloud Holden's inadequate exam.

> He put my goddam paper down then and looked at me like he'd just beaten hell out of me in ping-pong or something. I don't think I'll ever forgive him for reading me that crap out loud. I wouldn't've read it out loud to *him* if *he'd* written it—I really wouldn't. (p. 17)

In this confrontation between Holden and Spencer, there is an ironic inversion of the traditional student-teacher, son-father relationship which extends throughout the novel and throughout Salinger's fictional world. While Spencer, out of a childish need for personal justification, insensitively embarrasses Holden (already wounded by his expulsion from Pencey), the boy is mature enough to be kind to his conspicuously vulnerable antagonist. Holden accepts the full burden of responsibility for his scholastic failure so as to relieve Spencer of his sense of guilt.

> Well, you could see he really felt pretty lousy about flunking me. . . . I told him I was a real moron, and all that stuff. I told him I would've done exactly the same thing if I'd been in his place, and how most people didn't appreciate how tough it is being a teacher. That kind of stuff. The old bull. (p. 17)

In protecting his teacher's feelings, Holden performs the role of wise father; he is here a kind of catcher in the rye for a clumsy old child. His compassion is extensive enough to include even those he dislikes, even those who have hurt him. As he tells Antolini later in the novel:

> But you're wrong about that hating business. . . . What I may do, I may hate them for a *little* while, like this guy Stradlater I knew at Pencey, and this other boy, Robert Ackley. I hated *them* once in a while—I admit it—but it doesn't last too long, is what I mean. After a while, if I didn't see them, if they didn't come in the room . . . I sort of missed them. (p. 243)

Both Antolini and Spencer are too corrupt to notice that Holden is unable to cope with the world not because he hates, but because he loves and the world hates.

Spencer symbolizes all the stupid and destructive teacher-fathers at Pencey Prep, which is in microcosm all schools—the world. In the short scene between Holden and Spencer, Salinger evokes a sense of Holden's entire "student" experience in which flunking out is an act of moral will rather than a failure of application. Here, as throughout the novel, the wise son resists the initiatory knowledge of the false ("phony") father and, at the price of dispossession, retains his innocence. Holden is not so much rebelling against all authority, or even false authority, as he is searching for a just one. That there are no good fathers in the world is its and Holden's tragedy. It is the tragedy of Salinger's cosmos that the loss of innocence is irremediable. Ejected from the fallow womb of the prep school, Holden goes out alone into the world of New York City in search of some kind of sustenance. His comic misadventures in the city, which lead to his ultimate disillusion and despair, make up the central action of the novel.

Holden not only suffers as a victim from the effects of the evil in this world, but for it as its conscience—so that his experiences are exemplary. In this sense, *Catcher in the Rye* is a religious or, to be more exact, spiritual novel. Holden is Prince Mishkin as a sophisticated New York adolescent; and like Mishkin, he experiences the guilt, unhappiness, and spiritual deformities of others more intensely than he does his own misfortunes. This is not to say that Holden is without faults; he is, on occasion, silly, irritating, thoughtless, irresponsible—he has the excesses of innocence. Yet he is, as nearly as possible, without sin.

The most memorable love affair Holden has experienced had its fruition in daily checker games with Jane Gallagher, an unhappy, sensitive girl who was his neighbor one summer. She has become the symbol to him of romantic love, that is, innocent love. When Holden discovers that his "sexy" roommate Stradlater has a date with her, he is concerned not only about the possible loss of Jane's innocence, but about the loss of his dream of her—the loss of their combined checker-playing, love-innocence. Holden has had one previous emotional breakdown at thirteen when his saint-brother, Allie,[2] died of leukemia. In Allie's death, Holden first recognized the fact of evil—of what appears to be the gratuitous malevolence of the universe. Allie, who was, Holden tells us, more intelligent and nicer than anyone else, has become for Holden a kind of saint-ideal. By rejecting an English theme on Allie's baseball glove that Holden has written for him, and by implying that he has "given Jane Gallagher the time," Stradlater spiritually maims Holden. Holden's sole defense, a belief in the possibility of good in the world, collapses: "I felt so lonesome, all of a sudden. I almost wished I was dead" (p. 62).

It is in this state of near-suicidal despair that Holden leaves for New York. That Stradlater may have had sexual relations with Jane—the destruction of innocence is an act of irremediable evil in Holden's world—impels Holden to leave Pencey immediately (but not before he quixotically challenges the muscular Stradlater, who in turn bloodies his nose). At various times in New York, Holden is on the verge of phoning Jane, and actually dials her number twice—that he is unable to reach her is symbolic of his loss of her innocence. The sexually experienced Stradlater, who is one of Holden's destructive fathers in the novel, has destroyed not Jane's innocence so much as Holden's idealized notion of her.[3]

Obliquely searching for good in the adult world, or at least something to mitigate his despair, Holden is continually confronted with the absence of good. On his arrival in the city, he is disturbed because his cabdriver is corrupt and unsociable and, worst of all, unable to answer Holden's obsessional question: where do the Central Park ducks go when the lake freezes over? What Holden really wants to know is whether there is a benevolent authority that takes care of ducks. If there is one for ducks, it follows that there may be one for people as well. Holden's quest for a wise and benevolent authority, then, is essentially a search for a God-principle. However, none of the adults in Holden's world has any true answers for him. When he checks into a hotel room, he is depressed by the fact that the bellboy is an old man ("What a gorgeous job for a guy around sixty-five years old"). As sensitized recorder of the moral vibrations of his world, Holden suffers the indignity of the aged bellhop's situation for him, as he had suffered for Spencer's guilt and Ackley's self-loathing. Yet, and this is part of his tragedy, he is an impotent saint, unable either to redeem the fallen or to prevent their fall.

If the world of Holden's school was a muted purgatory, the world of his New York hotel is an insistent Hell. The window of his room provides him with a view of the other rooms in the hotel. In one, he sees a man dress himself in women's clothes, and in another, a man and woman who delight (sexually) in squirting water at each other from their mouths. This is the "real" world, with its respectable shade lifted, which fascinates and seduces Holden by its prurience. Having lost the sense of his innocence, he seeks sexual initiation as a means of redemption. His attraction to older women suggests that his quest for a woman is really a search for a mother whose love will protect him against the corrupt world as well as initiate him into it. Where the father-quest is a search for wisdom and spirit (God), the mother-quest is a search not for sex but ultimately for Love. They are different manifestations, one intellectual, the other physical, of the same spiritual quest. His search for sexual experience, Salinger indicates, is the only love alternative left Holden after he loses Jane. Once the possibility of innocent love ceases to exist, sexual love seems the next best thing, a necessary compensation for the loss of the first. However, Holden is only mildly disappointed when he is unable to arrange a date with a reputedly promiscuous girl whose telephone number he has inherited from a Princeton acquaintance. For all his avowed "sexiness," he is an innocent, and his innocence-impelled fear dampens his desire. Though the women he meets are by and large less disappointing than the men, they too fail Holden and intensify his despair. That they are not as good as he would like them to be seems to him *his* fault, *his* responsibility, *his* failure.

If Jane represents sacred love profaned, the prostitute who comes to Holden's room represents profane love unprofaned. After he has agreed to have her come to his room (the elevator operator, Maurice, is go-between), he refuses to make love to her once she is there. The scene is a crucial one in defining Holden's nontraditional sainthood. Holden refuses the prostitute not because of moral principle, but because the condition of her existence (she is about Holden's age and a kind of lost-innocent) depresses him.

> I took her dress over to the closet and hung it up for her. It was funny. It made me feel sort of sad when I hung it up. I thought of her going in a store and buying it, and nobody in the store knowing she was a prostitute and all. The salesman probably just thought she was a regular girl when she bought it. It made me feel sad as hell—I don't know why exactly. (p. 125)

He would save her if he could, but she is far too fallen for any catcher in the rye. But as child-saint, Holden is quixotic. In not sleeping with her, he means to protect her innocence, not his own; he is spiritually, hence physically, unable to be a party to her further degradation. The consequences are ironic. Holden as saint refuses to victimize the prostitute, but he is victimized by the girl and her accomplice, Maurice. Though Holden has paid the girl without using her, Maurice beats Holden and extorts an additional five dollars from him. This episode is a more intense recapitulation of the Stradlater experience. In both cases Holden is punished for his innocence. If the hotel is a symbolic Hell, Maurice, as far as Holden is concerned, is its chief devil. In offering Holden the girl and then humiliating him for not accepting his expensive gift, Maurice is another of Holden's evil fathers.

After his disillusionment with Antolini, who is the most destructive of Holden's fathers because he is seemingly the most benevolent, Holden suffers an emotional breakdown. His flight from Antolini's house, like his previous flights from school and from the hotel, is an attempt to escape evil. The three are parallel experiences, except that Holden is less sure of the justness of his third flight and wonders if he has not misjudged his otherwise sympathetic teacher.

> And the more I thought about it, the more depressed I got. I mean I started thinking maybe I *should've* gone back to his house. Maybe he *was* only patting my head just for the hell of it. The more I thought about it, though, the more depressed and screwed up about it I got. (p. 253)

The ambivalence of his response racks him. If he has misjudged Antolini, he has wronged not only his teacher, but he has wronged himself as well; he, not Antolini, has been guilty of corruption. Consequently, he suffers both for Antolini and for himself. Holden's guilt-ridden despair manifests itself in nausea and in an intense sense of physical ill-being, as if he carries the whole awful corruption of the city inside him. Walking aimlessly through the Christmas-decorated city, Holden experiences "the terrible, terrible fall" that Antolini had prophesied for him.

> Every time I came to the end of a block and stepped off the goddam curb, I had this feeling that I'd never get to the other side of the street. I thought I'd go down, down, down, and nobody'd ever see me again. Boy, did it scare me. You can't imagine. I started sweating like a bastard—my whole shirt and underwear and everything. . . . Every time I'd get to the end of a block I'd make believe I was talking to my brother Allie. I'd say to him, "Allie, don't let me disappear. Allie, don't let me disappear. Allie, don't let me disappear. Please, Allie." And then when I'd reach the other side of the street without disappearing, I'd *thank* him. (pp. 256-57)

Like Franny's prayer to Jesus in one of Salinger's later stories, Holden's prayer to Allie is not so much an act of anguish as an act of love, though it is in part both. Trapped in an interior hell, Holden seeks redemption, not by formal appeal to God or Jesus, who have in the Christmas season been falsified and commercialized, but by praying to his saint-brother who in his goodness had God in him.

Like so many heroes of contemporary fiction—Morris' Boyd, Ellison's Invisible Man, Malamud's Frank, Salinger's Seymour—Holden is an impotent savior. Because he can neither save his evil world nor live in it as it is, he retreats into fantasy—into childhood. He decides to become a deaf-mute, to live alone in an isolated cabin, to commit a kind of symbolic suicide. It is an unrealizable fantasy, but a death wish nevertheless. However, Holden's social conscience forces him out of spiritual retirement. When he discovers an obscenity scrawled on one of the walls of Phoebe's school, he rubs it out with his hand to protect the innocence of the children. For the moment he is a successful catcher in the rye. But then he discovers another such notice, "*scratched* on, with a knife or something," and then another. He realizes that he cannot possibly erase all the scribbled obscenities in the world, that he cannot catch all the children, that evil is ineradicable.

This is the final disillusionment. Dizzy with his terrible awareness, Holden insults Phoebe when she insists on running away with him. In his vision of despair, he sees Phoebe's irrevocable doom as well as his own, and for a moment he hates her as he hates himself—as he hates the world. Once he has hurt her, however, he realizes the commitment that his love for her imposes on him; if he is to assuage her pain, he must continue to live in the world. When she kisses him as a token of forgiveness and love and, as if in consequence, it begins to rain, Holden, bathed by the rain, is purified—in a sense, redeemed.

A too literal reading of Holden's divulgence that he is telling the story from some kind of rest home has led to a misinterpretation of the end of the novel. Holden is always less insane than his world. The last scene, in which Holden, suffused with happiness, sits in the rain and watches Phoebe ride on the merry-go-round, is indicative not of his crack-up, as has been assumed, but of his redemption. Whereas all the adults in his world have failed him (and he, a butter-fingered catcher in the rye, has failed them), a ten-year-old girl saves him—becomes his catcher. Love is the redemptive grace. Phoebe replaces Jane, the loss of whom had initiated Holden's despair, flight, and quest for experience as salvation. Holden's pure communion with Phoebe may be construed as a reversion to childlike innocence, but this is the only way to redemption in Salinger's world—there is no other good. Innocence is all. Love is innocence.[4]

The last scene, with Holden drenched in Scott Fitzgerald's all-absolving rain,[5] seems unashamedly sentimental. Certainly Salinger overstates the spiritually curative powers of children; innocence can be destructive as well as redemptive. Yet Salinger's view of the universe, in which all adults (even the most apparently decent) are corrupt and consequently destructive, is bleak and somewhat terrifying. Since growing up in the real world is tragic, in Salinger's ideal world time must be stopped to prevent the loss of childhood, to salvage the remnants of innocence. At one point in the novel, Holden wishes that life were as changeless and pure as the exhibitions under glass cases in the

Museum of Natural History. This explains, in part, Holden's ecstasy in the rain at the close of the novel. In watching Phoebe go round and round on the carrousel, in effect going nowhere, he sees her in the timeless continuum of art on the verge of changing, yet unchanging, forever safe, forever loving, forever innocent.

Salinger's view of the world has limited both his productivity and his range of concerns. In the last nine years, he has published only four increasingly long and increasingly repetitive short stories, all of which treat some aspect of the mythic life and times of the Glass family, whose most talented member, Seymour, committed suicide in an early story, "A Perfect Day for Bananafish." But though Salinger may go on, as Hemingway did, mimicking himself, trying desperately to relocate his old youthful image in some narcissistic internal mirror, his achievement as a writer cannot be easily discounted. All his stories, even the least successful, evince a stunning and original verbal talent, despite some stylistic debt to Fitzgerald and Lardner. Like *The Great Gatsby*, which both Holden and Salinger admire, *Catcher in the Rye* is, as far as the human eye can see, a perfect novel; it is self-defining, that is, there seems to be an inevitability about its form. Although the craft of the author is unobtrusive, everything of consequence that happens in the novel has been in some way anticipated by an earlier episode or reference. The rain that baptizes Holden at the end is, in symbol, the same rain that had fallen on Allie's gravestone and had depressed Holden; the scurrying of the visitors as they left the cemetery to seek shelter in their cars had emphasized Allie's immobility, his deadness. In praying to Allie, Holden implicitly accepts the fact of his brother's immortality which his earlier response had denied. Through association, Salinger suggests that the purifying rain is a manifestation of Allie's blessed and blessing spirit. Like Phoebe's kiss, Allie's rain is an act of love.

From *Modern Language Quarterly* 25.4 (1964): 461-472. Copyright © 1964 by Duke University Press. All rights reserved. Reprinted with permission of Duke University Press.

Notes

1. J. D. Salinger, *The Catcher in the Rye* (Boston, 1951), pp. 224-25; all page references are to this edition.

2. Holden's relationship to Allie, though less intense, is the equivalent of Buddy's to Seymour in the several Glass family stories.

3. Another destructive father is Ackley, who refuses Holden solace after Holden has been morally and physically beaten by Stradlater. (The father concern is intentional on Salinger's part.) Both Ackley and Stradlater are two years older than Holden, and at one point Ackley reproves Holden's lack of respect, telling him, "I am old enough to be your father."

4. Like the narrator in "For Esmé—With Love and Squalor," Holden is redeemed by the love of an innocent girl. In both cases the protagonist is saved because he realizes that if there is any love at all in the world—even the love of one child—Love exists.

5. At the graveside service for Gatsby, as rain falls on his coffin, Nick hears someone say, "Blessed are the dead that the rain falls on." I suspect that Salinger had the Fitzgerald passage in mind.

In Memoriam:
Allie Caulfield in *The Catcher in the Rye*

Edwin Haviland Miller

Although J. D. Salinger's *Catcher in the Rye* deserves the affection and accolades it has received since its publication in 1951, whether it has been praised for the right reasons is debatable. Most critics have tended to accept Holden's evaluation of the world as phony, when in fact his attitudes are symptomatic of a serious psychological problem. Thus instead of treating the novel as a commentary by an innocent young man rebelling against an insensitive world or as a study of a youth's moral growth,[1] I propose to read *Catcher in the Rye* as the chronicle of a four-year period in the life of an adolescent whose rebelliousness is his only means of dealing with his inability to come to terms with the death of his brother. Holden Caulfield has to wrestle not only with the usual difficult adjustments of the adolescent years, in sexual, familial and peer relationships; he has also to bury Allie before he can make the transition into adulthood.[2]

Life stopped for Holden on July 18, 1946, the day his brother died of leukemia. Holden was then thirteen, and four years later—the time of the narrative—he is emotionally still at the same age, although he has matured into a gangly six-foot adolescent. "I was sixteen then," he observes concerning his expulsion from Pencey Prep at Christmas time in 1949, "and I'm seventeen now, and sometimes I act like I'm about thirteen."[3]

On several occasions Holden comments that his mother has never gotten over Allie's death, which may or may not be an accurate appraisal of Mrs. Caulfield, since the first-person narrative makes it difficult to judge. What we can deduce, though, is that it is an accurate appraisal of Holden's inability to accept loss, and that in his eyes his mother is so preoccupied with Allie that she continues to neglect Holden, as presumably she did when Allie was dying.

The night after Allie's death Holden slept in the garage and broke "all the goddam windows with my fist, just for the hell of it. I even tried to break all the windows on the station wagon we had that summer, but my hand was already broken and everything by that time, and I couldn't do it. It was a very stupid thing to do, I'll admit, but I hardly didn't even know I was doing it, and you didn't know Allie" (p. 39). The act may have been "stupid"—which is one of his pet words to denigrate himself as well as others—but it also reflects his uncontrollable anger, at himself for wishing Allie dead and at his brother for leaving him alone and burdened with feelings of guilt. Similarly, the attack on the station wagon may be seen as his way of getting even with a father who was powerless either to save Allie or to understand Holden. Because he was hospitalized, he was unable to attend the funeral, to witness the completion of the life process, but by injuring himself he received the attention and sympathy which were denied him during Allie's illness. His actions here as elsewhere are inconsistent and ambivalent, but always comprehensible in terms of his reaction to the loss of Allie.

So too is Holden's vocabulary an index to his disturbed emotional state—for all that it might seem to reflect the influence of the movies or his attempts to imitate the diction of his older brother, D. B. At least fifty times, something or somebody *depresses* him—an emotion which he frequently equates with a sense of isolation: "It makes you feel so lonesome and depressed" (p. 81). Although the reiteration of the word reveals the true nature of his state, no one in the novel recognizes the signal, perceiving the boy as a kind of adolescent clown rather than as a seriously troubled youth. As his depression deepens to the point of nervous breakdown, furthermore, Holden—who at some level of awareness realizes that he is falling apart—seeks to obscure the recognition by referring to everything as "crazy" and by facetiously likening himself to a "madman."

"Crap," another word he uses repeatedly, is similarly self-reflexive. Although it is his ultimate term of reductionism for describing the world, like "crazy" it serves to identify another of his projections. He feels dirty and worthless, and so makes the world a reflection of his self-image. Similarly, if he continually asserts, almost screams, that the phony world makes him want to "puke," it is because Holden's world itself has turned to vomit. In his troubled, almost suicidal state he can incorporate nothing, and, worse, he believes there is nothing for him to incorporate. In turn, the significance of his repeated use of variations on the phrase "that killed me" becomes almost self-evident: reflecting his obsession with death, it tells the unsuspecting world that he wishes himself dead, punished and then reunited with Allie.

Although his consistently negative and hostile language thus reflects Holden's despair and is his way of informing the world of his plight, if no one listens it is primarily his own fault. For with the usual fumbling of the hurt he has chosen a means which serves his purposes poorly. While his language may serve to satisfy his need to act out his anger, at the same time it serves to isolate and to punish him further. If in his hostile phrases he is calling for help, he makes certain that he does not receive it. Ashamed of his need—a sixteen-year old crying for emotional support—and unable to accept kindness since in his guilt he feels he does not deserve it, Holden is locked into his grief and locked out of family and society.

In this respect, the first paragraph of *Catcher in the Rye* is one of the most deceptively revealing possible. Although Holden, the would-be sophisticate, relegates his familial background to "David Copperfield kind of crap," he talks about little else except his "lousy childhood." Arguing that he will not divulge family secrets so as not to cause pain, and pretending to respect the feelings of his parents, he verbally mutilates them, and in an ugly way; but if he is to suffer, so must they. He retaliates in kind, not in kindness. Yet the aggressive, assertive tone masks a pitiful, agonized call for emotional support and love.

Equally revealing of Holden's problem is his observation, as he stands alone on a hill that cold December, his last day at Pencey Prep, looking down at the football field where his classmates are participating collectively in one of the rites of adolescence: "it was cold as a witch's teat, especially on top of that stupid hill" (p. 4). What he wants is the good mother's breast. And why he needs this maternal comfort so much is implicitly suggested when he descends the hill to say good-by to his history teacher, who cannot understand why in answering a question about Egyptian history on an examination Holden should have begun and ended with a description of the preservation of mummies. The teacher cannot know that Holden has no interest in the Egyptians, only in what happened to Allie, and that he cannot focus on ancient history until he has come to terms with his own past. Nor can he know that Holden has misinterpreted as rejection his father's concern for his future, that the boy wants to be at home, and that to accomplish his goal he has failed in four different schools.

But lest one think that this insensitivity is a fault of the older generation, Salinger next portrays the response of one of Holden's peers to the first of a number of roles he will play in his desperate attempt to disguise his obsession with Allie's death, on the one hand, and his need for parental comfort, on the other. Thus when Holden pulls his red hunting cap over his eyes and says histrionically, "I think I'm going blind. . . . Mother darling, everything's getting so *dark* in here. . . . Mother darling, give me your hand," the response of his classmate is: "You're nuts. . . . For Chrisake, grow up" (pp. 21-22). Ackley cannot know that Holden assumes Allie's red hair when he puts on the red cap, that the simulated blindness is descriptive of Holden's state, or that he uses the script as a (futile) means of asking for the maternal hand that he believes has been denied to him.

If Ackley does not appreciate the extent to which the death of Holden's red-haired brother informs his posturing, even less is his room-mate Stradlater aware of the chain of associations that he sets off when he asks Holden to write a composition for him. Unable to write about a "room or a house" Holden writes about Allie's baseball mitt—an object which is a complex version of a child's security blanket, a sacred relic of the living dead, at the same time that it reminds Holden of betrayal. And thus as he writes about the mitt, we learn directly for the first time of Allie's death and of Holden's self-punishing rage.

By coincidence, Stradlater has a date that evening with Jane Gallagher, the girl to whom Holden had shown the glove in a combined attempt to sympathize with her for her unhappy childhood and to solicit her sympathy for himself. Worried that Stradlater will make "time" with an attractive girl with whom Holden plays checkers—the only kind of play of which the self-styled sex maniac is capable—Holden presses to know what has happened on the date. And when Stradlater implies that he got what he wanted, Holden lashes out with the hand he injured on the day of Allie's death. Subsequently pinned to the floor until he promises to stop his ridiculing insults, as soon as he is released, Holden shouts, "You're a dirty stupid sonuvabitch of a moron," and then he receives the blow that subconsciously he wants. "You asked for it, God damn it," Stradlater says, and he is right for reasons he does not understand (pp. 44-45).

And so on his last day at Pencey Prep Holden makes a clean sweep of it: he writes off the school, his chums, and even Jane. There is no Tom Sawyer to rescue him when he eventually quotes Huck Finn: "I felt so lonesome, all of a sudden. I almost wished I was dead" (p. 48). Suddenly Holden decides to leave late that evening even though his family is not expecting him until the following Wednesday. His Mark Cross luggage packed, he is "sort of crying. I don't know why. I put my red hunting hat on, and turned the peak around to the back, the way I liked it, and then I yelled at the top of my goddam voice, '*Sleep tight, ya morons!*'" Thus, in his usual hostile fashion, Holden makes sure that he will be rejected. Protected only by the red hat, which he now wears like a baseball catcher as he evokes Allie's favorite sport, he stumbles down the stairs and "damn near broke my crazy neck" (p. 52).

On the train to New York he strikes up a conversation with a Mrs. Morrow, who turns out to be the mother of one of his former classmates. He lies through his teeth praising her son who is "about as sensitive as a goddam toilet seat" (p. 55). But "Mothers are all slightly insane. The thing is, though, I liked old Morrow's mother," who happens to be proud of her moronic son. When she wonders whether Holden is leaving school before the beginning of vacation "because of illness in the family," he casually informs her, "I have this tiny little tumor on the brain" (p. 58). The fib achieves the expected result, Mrs. Morrow's genuine sympathy for an ill "son."

Though Holden plans to spend the next few days in a hotel, he is "so damn absent-minded" that he gives the cab driver his home address. After he realizes his "mistake," they drive through Central Park, and Holden asks the driver whether he knows what happens to the ducks in the pond during the winter. The "madman" replies angrily, "What're ya tryna do, bud? . . . Kid me?" (p. 60). Worried that he has antagonized the man, Holden invites him for a drink. When the driver refuses, Holden, "depressed," retaliates against "father": "He was one of those bald guys that comb all their hair over from the side to cover up the baldness" (p. 61).

In the hotel he is bored but "feeling pretty horny" (p. 63), as a sixteen-year-old is supposed to feel, and he calls up a whore but lets her put him off. ("I *really* fouled that up.") Then he thinks of telephoning his sister Phoebe, who "has this sort of red hair, a little bit like Allie's was" (p. 67), but he is afraid his mother will answer. He goes to the bar in the hotel and dances with some older women from Seattle who are in New York to see the celebrities, not to provide Holden with entertainment or solace. He punishes them for neglecting him when he fibs that Gary Cooper has just left the room. On the way to a bar frequented by his older brother D. B., who is now, according to Holden, prostituting himself in Hollywood, he asks a cabby named Horwitz about the ducks in the lagoon in Central Park. Horwitz gets "sore" and counters in a typical New York taxi discussion that "The *fish* don't go no place" (p. 82). Desperate for companionship, Holden invites Horwitz for a drink. The driver refuses and has the last word: "If you was a fish, Mother Nature'd take care of *you*, wouldn't she? Right? You don't think them fish just *die* when it gets to be winter, do ya?" (p. 83). Holden does not comment, but Horwitz unwittingly summarizes the boy's dilemma.

Later, in D. B.'s nightclub Holden glosses over his loneliness by observing the behavior of the phonies in the club, and then rejects the invitation of one of D. B.'s girlfriends as others have rejected him. When Holden returns to his hotel, an elevator operator named Maurice sets him up with a call girl, but when "Sunny" arrives, he is "more depressed than sexy" (p. 95), and asks her to stay and talk. He pays her $5.00 and then "depressed" begins "talking, sort of out loud, to Allie" (p. 98).

Maurice returns with Sunny and demands another $5.00 for services not rendered. Holden tries to defend his rights but begins to cry. Sunny wants to leave quietly after she takes money from Holden's wallet, but Maurice "snapped his finger very hard on my pajamas. I won't tell you *where* he snapped it, but it hurt like hell." (The sudden self-protective chastity is an amusing and effective detail.) When Holden calls Maurice "a stupid chiseling moron," for the second time that evening he is smacked, with a "terrific punch" in his stomach (p. 103). Hardly able to breathe, fearing he is drowning, he stumbles toward the bathroom. "Crazy," he acts out a scenario: with a bullet in his gut, he goes down the stairs and puts six shots into Maurice's "fat hairy belly," and then throws the gun down the elevator shaft. He calls up Jane, who comes over and bandages his wound: "I pictured her holding a cigarette for me to smoke while I was bleeding and all." Finally he goes to sleep: "What I really felt like, though, was committing suicide. I felt like jumping out the window. I probably would've done it too"—except for the "stupid rubbernecks" (p. 104).

Holden's protestations to the contrary, the associations in this scene are only superficially from the "goddam movies." Maurice threatens Holden with castration, even though he has not had sex with Sunny, and then pummels him in the stomach. In retaliation Holden commits parricide. In his fantasy he summons Jane, who is associated with Allie through her knowledge of the baseball mitt, and has her play the role of mother.

When Holden thinks of jumping out the window, he is recalling an event which the reader does not learn about until later. A few years earlier Jimmy Castle, a classmate, was so tortured and brutalized, presumably genitally, by a bunch of students that he leaped from a window, wearing Holden's turtleneck sweater. As though Holden is not sufficiently burdened with his unresolved grief for Allie, he has had to cope with this tie to an unfortunate classmate. Sunny, the prostitute, anticipates the appearance of Phoebe, who is both the kid sister and by mythic association the sun goddess. Sunny offers Holden sex, Phoebe will offer him love. Unable to handle sex, Holden wants Sunny to be a confidante, a role which she is unable to handle. Yet she tries unsuccessfully to protect him from Maurice's aggression, which may be Holden's construction of his mother's ineffectual role in the Caulfield household.

At breakfast on the following morning he meets two nun school teachers, and begins a conversation which shortly turns to *Romeo and Juliet*. If the scene with Sunny reveals that Holden is not ready for sexual relationships—he is a "sex maniac" only in his head—his comments on the tragedy solely in terms of Romeo's culpability in Mercutio's death confirm the arrestment. He is attracted to the nuns, or mothers, who remind him of "old Ernest Morrow's mother" (p. 112), but they also remind him that his father was a Catholic until he "married my mother." This leads him to recall some unpleasant associations with Catholics, and when he says good-by to the nuns, "by mistake I blew some smoke in their faces. I didn't mean to, but I did it" (p. 113). In atonement for his unkindness Holden makes a symbolic apology to the nuns when he imagines them standing in front of a department store raising money for charity. He tries "to picture my mother or somebody, or my aunt, or Sally Hayes's crazy mother, standing outside some department store and collecting dough for poor people in a beat-up old straw hat. It was hard to picture." Since his "picture" of his mother is too harsh, and anxiety-producing, he guiltily corrects it: "Not so much my mother, but those other two" (p. 114).

Walking along the street, he sees a family coming from church—"a father, a mother, and a little kid about six years old." Holden "sees" the family, but only in terms of his own situation. Without evidence he initially assumes that the parents are neglecting the boy who walks along the curb singing to himself, "If a body catch a body coming through the rye"—or so Holden imagines. For it is doubtful that the six-year old, if he knows the poem in the first place, duplicates Holden's misreading of the famous lines. What Holden "hears" anticipates the grandiose fantasy he will later relate to Phoebe in which he catches and saves children. For a moment he is charmed with his fantasy of a self-contained kid whose parents are at hand to protect him: "It made me feel not so depressed any more" (p. 115).

In the afternoon Holden escorts Sally Hayes to a Broadway show and goes ice skating at Rockefeller Center. Then they sit down for a chat—about Holden. He pours out his anger at the phony world, and when Sally tries to be sensible, he almost screams at her, "I don't get hardly anything out of anything. I'm in bad shape. I'm in *lousy* shape" (p. 131). Sally can hardly be expected to understand how empty he feels, or know how to respond to his cry for sympathy. Then he proposes what he knows she cannot agree to, that they run off together to New England. When she objects to the scheme, he verbally assaults her but not without self-pity: "she was depressing the hell out of me" (p. 133).

After this rejection, which in his usual fashion he makes inevitable, he tries to lift the depression by evoking earlier, happier days when the Caulfield family was intact. He goes to Radio City Music Hall, where, with the parents in another part of the theater, Allie and he had sat by themselves watching a favorite drummer. But pleasant memories of Allie cannot rescue him, and he goes to a bar to meet a former classmate named Luce. Although Holden wants Luce's companionship and assistance, he subjects him to an offensive, crude interrogation about his sex life. Twice Luce asks, repeating the question put earlier by Ackley, "When are you going to grow up?" (p. 144). After Holden confesses that his sex life "stinks," Luce reminds him that once before he had advised him to see an analyst. At once Holden asks for more information and comes as close as his pride permits to begging for the kind of aid which Luce of course cannot provide. When Luce gets ready to leave for his date, Holden implores, "Have just one more drink. Please. I'm lonesome as hell" (p. 149).

Now "*really* drunk" and wounded, because Luce like the others betrays him, he replays the scenario of "that stupid business with the bullet in my guts again. I was the only guy at the bar with a bullet in their guts. I kept putting my hand under my jacket, on my stomach and all, to keep the blood from dripping all over the place. I didn't want anybody to know I was even wounded. I was con*ceal*ing the fact that I was a wounded sonuvabitch" (p. 150). Even in fantasy his self-pity turns into self-disparagement: he hates himself as he screams for attention.

He decides to call up Jane Gallagher, but by "mistake"—it is almost a comedy of errors—he dials Sally Hayes and makes up for his insults. Then he goes to the men's room, dunks his head in a washbowl, and sits on a radiator to dry himself. When the pianist, a "flitty-looking guy," enters, Holden asks him to arrange a date with the singer at the club. The pianist tells him to go home.

> "You oughta go on the radio," I said. "Handsome chap like you. All those goddam golden locks. Ya need a manager?"
> "Go home, Mac, like a good guy. Go home and hit the sack."
> "No home to go to. No kidding—you need a manager?" (p. 152)

Holden, who needs "a manager," is crying as he goes for his coat. When the middle-aged attendant gives him his coat even though he has lost his check, he returns the kindness by asking her for a date. She laughs, but not derisively, and, intuiting the role he wants her to play, makes him put on his red hunting hat. His teeth chattering, Holden goes to Central Park to "see what the hell the ducks were doing" (p. 153). On the way, one "accident" following another, he drops the phonograph record he has bought for Phoebe. If, as he believes, nothing has been given to him, he cannot give even to his favorite sister and must punish her as he has been punished. When he finds the pond he nearly falls in. "Still shivering like a bastard," he imagines that he has pneumonia and dies.

In this fantasy he acts out his anger against his parents and inflicts upon them the ultimate punishment, his death. His funeral is mobbed and everybody cries: "They all came when Allie died, the whole goddam stupid bunch of them." He feels "sorry as hell for my mother and father. Especially my mother, because she still isn't over my brother Allie yet" (p. 155). In this reenactment of Allie's funeral he displaces his brother and enjoys exclusively the love of his mother. But not for long, since his "picture" cannot lift his guilt, dissolve his rage, or make over reality. People will not mourn him long, no longer than they mourned Allie, and life in the phony world will go on without him. Like Allie he will lie in the cemetery exposed to the elements.

To take his "mind off getting pneumonia and all," he skips "the quarters and the nickel" across the lagoon. "I don't know why I did it, but I did it." Perhaps he imitates a game Allie and he played together, but when he throws away his money, there is only one place he can go—home. Which he does, although he disguises the desire by preserving his fantasy: he goes there to see Phoebe "in case I died and all" (p. 156). In the foyer of the Caulfield apartment he recognizes "a funny smell that doesn't smell like any place else" (p.158), and he finds Phoebe asleep in D. B.'s bed: "I felt swell for a change" (p. 159). Safe and protected, he begins to relax and no longer worries "whether they'd catch me home or not" (p. 163). What he does not say is that he would like to be caught. At first Phoebe is "very affectionate" until she guesses that he has been kicked out of Pencey Prep. Then, hurt and angry, a reaction which he cannot understand, she beats him with her fists and says over and over, "Daddy'll *kill* you!" At last Holden tellingly replies, "No, he won't. The worst he'll do, he'll give me hell again, and then he'll send me to that goddam military school. That's all he'll do" (p. 166).

In this climactic scene Phoebe plays a double role. About Allie's age when he died, she is the sister disappointed in the failures of her idealized brother, but she is also an underaged, undersized mother figure. Firmly but affectionately Phoebe presses Holden to explain why he has been expelled. He pours forth all his phony rationalizations, most of which begin and end with something or somebody "depressing" him. When Phoebe suggests that the fault may be his—"You don't like anything that's happening"—he is "even more depressed" (p. 169). She insists, now perhaps not unlike the lawyer father, that he name some things he likes. Unable to "concentrate" on her disturbing questions, Holden thinks of the two nuns and of Jimmy Castle's suicide—kind mothers and a dead son. Relentlessly but not without a concession, Phoebe asks him to tell her "one thing" he likes.

> "I like Allie," I said. "And I like doing what I'm doing right now. Sitting here with you, and talking, and thinking about stuff, and—"
> "Allie's *dead*—You always say that! If somebody's dead and everything, and in *Heaven*, then it isn't really—"
> "I know he's dead! Don't you think I know that? I can still like him, though, can't I? Just because somebody's dead, you don't just stop liking them, for God's sake—especially if they were about a thousand times nicer than the people you know that're *alive* and all." (p. 171)

Phoebe is silent. Holden believes that "she can't think of anything to say." More perceptive than her older brother, she gives him time to recognize the significance of what he has said: that Allie is dead. Then, like the parents and the teachers, but with an affection that dilutes his anger, she tries to direct Holden to a consideration of a future which—as she tactfully does not say—must be lived without Allie. When she suggests that he may want to be a lawyer, Holden is unable to reply precisely, not merely because he is trapped in his negations, but also because, in spite of his anger, he can only attack the father by indirection. "Lawyers are all right, I guess," he replies, with wayward antecedents, "but it does not appeal to me." He draws a picture of lawyers "saving innocent guys' lives"—which is another rescue fantasy and a disguised self-reference. When he discusses, from his hurt viewpoint, the role of the corporation lawyer, he deflects the indictment of his father through use of the second-person pronoun: "All you do is make a lot of dough and play golf and play bridge and buy cars and drink Martinis and look like a hot-shot" (p. 172). Ironically, Holden emulates his father's behavior, from his Mark Cross luggage to his drinking and "hot-shot" attacks on phonies.

Soon Holden confides his most heroic fantasy, undeterred when Phoebe corrects the misquotation of Burns's poem on which it is based.

> "I thought it was 'If a body catch a body,'" I said. "Anyway, I keep picturing all these little kids playing some game in this big field of rye and all. Thousands of little kids, and nobody's around—nobody big, I mean—except me. And I'm standing on the edge of some crazy cliff. What I have to do, I have to catch everybody if they start to go over the cliff—I mean if they're running and they don't look where they're going I have to come out from somewhere and *catch* them. That's all I'd do all day. I'd just be the catcher in the rye and all. I know it's crazy, but that's the only thing I'd really like to be. I know it's crazy." (p. 173)

This is the most complex of all the rescue fantasies. Holden has the "crazy" idea that he should have saved Allie, and that in the future he will save children abused by adults. If he is savior, he is also victim. For he himself is at "the edge of some crazy cliff" and feels himself, as he puts it later, going "down, down, down" (p. 197). He acts out the role he wants the adult world, particularly his father, to play: that of rescuer.

When a moment later Phoebe and Holden horse around and dance about the bedroom, the youth's delight illuminates his desire for a childhood where there are no fears, only joy and protection. The idyll ends abruptly when the parents come home, and Holden, fearing rejection, hides in a closet. Before he leaves, he borrows Phoebe's Christmas money. For the fourth time he begins to cry: "I couldn't help it. I did it so nobody could hear me, but I did it." For the first time he achieves what he has cried for from the beginning: Phoebe, now the mother, not the little sister, "put her old arm around my neck, and I put my arm around her, too, but I still couldn't stop for a long time" (p. 179). Before he goes, he almost tells the truth about himself as well as about the catcher-in-the-rye fantasy. "I didn't give much of a damn any more if they caught me. I really didn't. I figured if they caught me, they caught me. I almost wished they did, in a way" (p. 180).

Holden leaves to spend the night with a former teacher at a preparatory school, now an English professor at New York University. Antolini has been a role model, a good father, for Holden: he carried the body of Jimmy Castle to the infirmary after his suicide, and he banters in the witty style of D. B. Holden is disappointed when Antolini informs him that he has had lunch with Mr. Caulfield and shares the father's concern that "you're riding for some kind of a terrible, terrible fall" (p. 186). The professor tries intellectually to check the boy's self-destructive tendencies, as Phoebe does in her quite different way. Antolini puts the boy to bed on a couch in the living room, and says "Good night, handsome." Later Holden wakens to find "something on my head, some guy's hand" (p. 191). "Shaking like a madman," he concocts an excuse to leave and spends the rest of the night sleeping on a bench in Grand Central Station. "I think," he writes, "I was more depressed than I ever was in my whole life" (p. 194).

Although initially Holden interprets Antolini's caress as a sexual advance, in the morning he has doubts, "I mean I wondered if just maybe I was wrong about thinking he was making a flitty pass at me" (pp. 194-95). Whatever his intentions, sexual or paternal, Antolini sets off the not unusual homosexual panic of adolescents. But Holden's problem is not primarily sexual. He cannot connect with anyone in any way until the burden of Allie's death is lifted.

Alone, depressed, he walks up Fifth Avenue in the morning looking for the two nuns—looking for mother—when something "very spooky" happens. "Every time I came to the end of a block and stepped off the goddam curb, I had this feeling that I'd never get to the other side of the street. I thought I'd just go down, down, down, and nobody'd ever see me again." Once more he is at the cliff, and there is no one to catch him, to keep him from going "down, down, down"—except Allie. He cries out, "Allie, don't let me disappear" (pp. 197-98).

Holden has at last touched bottom, although he is not to be spared further indignities, some of his own making. Never again will he summon Allie, which means that he begins to turn from the past and death and to move into the present and toward the living. The inevitable fantasy that he creates in moments of crisis subtly changes. He plans to go "out West, where it was very pretty and sunny and where nobody'd know me" (p. 198). When Holden proposes to Sally that they run off to Vermont or Massachusetts, the flight is in the direction of Maine, where Allie died. In going west he moves toward the living, for D. B. is in Hollywood. Still damaged and still hungering for security, he pictures himself as a deaf mute working at a filling station and—most important—married to another deaf mute. "If we had any children," he declares, with obvious reference to his own lot, "we'd hide them somewhere. We could buy them a lot of books and teach them how to read and write by ourselves" (p. 199). At last Holden's locked world is opening up.

He goes to Phoebe's school to say good-by and to return her Christmas money. He is upset to find "Fuck you" scrawled on a wall, no doubt more upset than the kids who share neither his naive ideas of purity, despite his verbal profanities, nor his fears of sexuality. While he waits for Phoebe at the museum, two boys ask the way to the mummies. As Holden leads them to the Egyptian room, he begins to repeat the information given in his history examination at Pencey Prep about the process of preservation, and frightens the lads who do not share his obsession with death. Instead of a savior or a catcher, Holden turns out to be a bogey man—as unfeeling as the unfeeling adults who have never understood him. Alone in the tomb, he is mocked again by the ugly epithet of sexual assault which he finds on the walls. Typically he overreacts and at the same time punishes himself as he pictures his tombstone: Holden Caulfield—"Fuck you" (p. 204).

If this debasement is not enough, he suddenly has diarrhea, and passes out on the floor of a toilet. It is as though he must experience an elemental purging—get all the "crap" out of his distorted picture of life and of himself. Compulsively he creates still another fantasy of flight. This time he is a thirty-five-year-old man living by himself: "I even started picturing how it would be when I came back. I knew my mother'd get nervous as hell and start to cry and beg me to stay home and not go back to my cabin, but I'd go anyway" (p. 205). If he is still punishing his mother—and himself—at least he pictures himself alive and at the middle of the journey.

When Phoebe comes to the museum with her luggage because she plans to go west too, once again she reaches out to her brother. The act of love is almost too much for Holden. "I got sort of dizzy and I thought I was going to pass out or something again" (p. 206). But he does not fall nor pass out. Instead like the loved-hated parents or like a protective older brother—in short like all the other adults—he automatically advances all the sensible reasons why Phoebe's plans are "crazy." When he begins genuinely to think of someone else's lot, he assumes responsibility. He is no longer the kid who needs and demands everybody's attention.

When Phoebe proves stubborn, he returns her gift of love with another gift. He escorts her to Central Park, not to the duck pond—with its associations with death—but to the carrousel. "When she was a tiny little kid, and Allie and D. B. and I used to go to the park with her, she was mad about the carrousel" (p. 210). In the bedroom Holden and Phoebe had danced together like two kids, but at the carrousel Holden refuses to ride with her and watches her reach for the gold ring. In turn, when he promises to go home with Phoebe, he delights her and at the same time achieves the goal hinted at on the first page of his narrative: "I felt so damn happy all of a sudden, the way old Phoebe kept going around and around. I was damn near bawling, I felt so damn happy" (p. 213).

In the epilogue, Chapter 26, Holden writes of himself at age seventeen in an institution near Hollywood, not far from D. B. After a period of rest and therapy there has been no fabulous transformation, although there has been change. His language is no longer negative, nor is his attitude. He is not sure that he is going to apply himself when he returns to school in September: "I *think* I am, but how do I know? I swear it's a stupid question" (p. 213). Although he has to put up token resistance—after all, he is Holden Caulfield—he is ready to go "around and around" in the game of life and no longer needs Allie's mitt or hat to protect him. Nor must he picture himself as the victim of insensitive adults; the psychoanalyst's advice is not "bull."

When D. B. asks him about "all the stuff I just finished telling you about," he replies truthfully, without a defensive wisecrack. "About all I know is, I sort of *miss* everybody I told about." At last he cuts through his "crap," his evasions and hostile defenses. He wants, as he has always wanted, to establish connections, and he is well on his way to doing just that, for in his narrative he has at least established connections with readers.

"Don't ever tell anybody anything," he writes at the conclusion; "if you do, you start missing everybody" (p. 214). But telling is precisely what he has been doing and in the process Holden has finished mourning. Allie now rests in peace.

This essay originally appeared in *Mosaic*, a journal for the interdisciplinary study of literature, vol. 15, no. 1, pp. 129-140. Copyright © 1982 by *Mosaic*. Reprinted with permission of *Mosaic*.

Notes

1. Holden Caulfield has been called "a lout," a saint, a "sad little screwed-up" neurotic, and a "beatnik Peter Pan," but he deserves none of these epithets, positive or negative. The novel has been read as a critique of "the academic and social conformity of its period" (Maxwell Geismar), as a modern version of the Orestes-Iphigeneia story (Leslie Fiedler), as a commentary on the modern world in which ideals "are denied access to our lives" (Ihab Hassan), or as a celebration of life (Martin Green). These essays appear in *Salinger—A Critical and Personal Portrait*, ed. Henry Anatole Grunwald (New York, 1962).

2. James Bryan recognizes that "the trauma" behind Holden's problems is the death of his brother Allie, but he proceeds to examine the work in terms of Holden's psychosexual growth when clearly the youth's development is emotionally arrested. See "The Psychological Structure of *The Catcher in the Rye*," *PMLA*, 89 (1974), 1065-74.

3. J. D. Salinger, *The Catcher in the Rye* (New York, 1964), p. 9.

Symbolic Resolution in *The Catcher in the Rye*:
The Cap, the Carrousel, and the American West
Kermit Vanderbilt

The ending of J. D. Salinger's *The Catcher in the Rye* has, I believe, been consistently slighted or misinterpreted. The result has been a number of misreadings of the ultimate meaning of the novel. The final pages, as heavily laden with symbols as a Salinger short story, not only illuminate the previous chapters, but also suggest a hopeful resolution of Holden's crippling search for himself and his America.

The climactic final action centers on Holden Caulfield and his ten-year-old sister Phoebe. They meet to say goodbye at the museum in New York City. She has brought her suitcase and wants to join Holden in his flight to the West. He refuses to let her come along. They go to the zoo and then to the carrousel. Phoebe rides on the carrousel, and Holden, standing in the rain, suddenly feels happy. We next discover, in the postscript final chapter, that Holden afterwards had gone home, and that he is now recovering in the West.

For economy, we shall view this action as it focuses on the pervading symbol of the novel, Holden's cap, and with it two accompanying symbols, the carrousel and the American West. Holden's cap may well be the happiest symbolic device in recent American fiction. It works unobtrusively to suggest every aspect of Holden's thwarted search for external reality and private identity. Before interpreting the ending, we must briefly examine the ways in which Salinger has employed this symbolic device earlier in the novel. First are the obvious uses of the cap early in the novel. Holden wears his cap backwards, 180 degrees out of phase, as a badge of his nonconformity and his rebellion against the rest of society. He buys it originally, it will be remembered, to wear as a gesture of defiance after losing the fencing foils of his teammates on the New York subway. It represents his need for individual identity, for a sense of his private self. And his wearing it backwards suggests not only his defiant withdrawal from his teammates, but more generally, his basically recessive tendencies. He wants to retreat backward into the world he is leaving—that of childhood innocence—rather than advance into adolescence, maturity, and the world of adult American society. Again, the cap suggests his yearning for innocence because, as a reversed cap, it becomes also a baseball cap—specifically the catcher's. Hence Holden's misquoting the Burns poem and fancying himself the *catcher* in the rye, a companion and protector of children in their everlastingly innocent field of rye. As a catcher's cap it carries us even more intimately into Holden's rather disturbed psyche. The red cap ties him closely with his idealized younger brother, the red-haired Allie, who played baseball and wrote poems in green ink on his baseball glove. The possibility here is that Holden is doing more than merely trying to evade the reality of his own adolescence, or even to regain his lost brother (recall his guilty conversations with Allie when he becomes very depressed). Through the reversed baseball cap, he presumably is *identifying* himself with his dead brother Allie. Salinger drops hints which the amateur psychologist can hardly miss. He describes the traumatic shock which Holden experienced when Allie died of leukemia. Obviously despairing at the cosmic injustice of such an early death, the highly sensitive Holden punched his fist through all the windows of the Caulfield garage and broke his hand. In his continuing identification with Allie (as well as his strong preoccupation with the equally idealistic James Castle, who committed suicide at Elkton Hills school), Holden can be interpreted as seeking, in an ultimate regression, the comfort of death itself. This will be the only successful release from the agonizing complexities of a mutable and deceitful world.

    The circumstances surrounding and issuing from Allie's death then, rather than the phoniness of the prep school and American society at large, are quite clearly set forth as the important, underlying cause of Holden's present maladjustment.[1] Had Salinger intended Holden to be the young social critic *par excellence* he would scarcely have supplied Holden with this private childhood trauma and overly charged emotional equipment for his entry into the world of adolescence. By the time of the present action in the novel, the schizophrenia, or "phoniness," of American society, which Holden does rightly sense, has become the correlative and secondary cause of his own exaggerated schizoid tendencies. And so, with a dim awareness of his sickness, but not its primary sources, Holden frequently refers to himself as a "madman," while all occasions in American life inform against him and conspire to drive him "crazy," as he says. In what enlarges to a world-destruction fantasy, he broods over the insecurity of the ducks in winter, and clings to symbols of security and changelessness: the monastic life, the serene nuns amid the circus atmosphere of Grand Central Station, and more clearly fusing with his concern with death, the Egyptian mummies and the Indian figures in the museum. Phoebe's intuition about Holden's paranoid symptoms (he even suspects courageous lawyers of disguising base motives of self-aggrandizement) expresses itself in her simple statement to Holden, "You don't like *any*thing that's happening. . . . Name one thing." After long musing, Holden replies, "I like Allie." Phoebe, with unwitting accuracy, points next to Holden's private obsession with death by simply reminding him, "Allie's *dead*."[2]

Partly through the concentration of symbolic meanings in the cap, then, Salinger has created a complex adolescent whose ambition to be a catcher in the rye has to be understood from a wider frame of reference than that of a muck-raking "problem" novel about social conformity in midcentury America. By first relating Holden's sickness to Allie's death, Salinger dissociates Holden from the immediate social environment. Then rather than his being psychoanalyzed after Allie's death, as his parents had briefly considered, this young Raskolnikov is forced to discover his unlikely redemption in the world, first in the morally dishonest associations of the American prep school at Elkton Hills, Whooton, and Pencey Prep; and then in his odyssey through New York City. In short, Holden's private salvation, his return to wholeness, must come, if it does come, through a deepened moral vision which can reconcile him to his world. He can then stop trying on caps—the desperate and futile gestures of adolescent self-discovery.

It is through the innocent Phoebe, at the end, that Holden initially moves toward this redemption. As she is running to meet him at the museum, he sees her because she is wearing his red duck-hunting cap—his "people-shooting" rather than duck-shooting cap. He had given her the cap after he had decided to leave New York, vaguely to hitchhike to the West. Phoebe, he discovers, has packed her suitcase and now asks if she can flee with him. Salinger describes Holden's sudden reaction: "I almost fell over when she said that. I swear to God I did. I got sort of dizzy and I thought I was going to pass out or something again" (185). For the first time in the novel, he has begun to realize that the idea of wholesale retreat from human associations must be re-examined. He discovers that he does not want to save this young innocent from the phoniness and obscenity of New York City. Disappointed and angry, Phoebe hurls the cap at Holden. He puts the cap not on his head but into his pocket. Phoebe then walks ahead of him to the zoo, where Holden is able briefly to observe the animals all safe and well-fed in winter. Next they arrive at the carrousel. Holden's mind now fixes on the significance of the carrousel.

First, the carrousel comforts Holden because he discovers here a permanent and secure spot in New York, specifically because in the fixed center comes the same old song year after year. His earlier preoccupation with change and death is still active. And it becomes more highly charged as Phoebe climbs up onto the carrousel and it begins to whirl. He sees the innocent children in danger of falling from the circling carrousel as they reach for the stationary gold ring. But the moment suddenly becomes also, for Holden, the instant of revelation. He reflects,

> The thing with kids is, if they want to grab for the gold ring, you have to let them do it, and not say anything. If they fall off, they fall off, but it's bad if you say anything to them. (190)

Then between rides, Phoebe comes over to Holden, gives him a kiss, it starts to rain, she puts his cap back on his head and then returns to take her chances on the turning carrousel again. As Holden watches, standing in the downpour with his cap on, he is suddenly overwhelmed with happiness:

> My hunting hat really gave me quite a lot of protection, in a way, but I got soaked anyway. I didn't care, though. I felt so damn happy all of a sudden, the way old Phoebe kept going around and around. (191)

The novel proper closes on this scene. The carrousel has suggested to Holden the dangers and insecurities in life which children must risk as they grow up and reach for their fixed star. The ride has its perils, but all children must risk them. One cannot make life stand still in an eternal moment of childhood innocence. The carrousel, with all of its dangers, however, still has a fixed center—an unchanging music in the midst of external movement, a still point in the turning world.[3] In this confronting of reality, Holden has begun to lose his delusional obsession to be a catcher in the rye. There can be no protector to break the fall from innocence into adolescence and maturity. Holden also declines the gesture of wearing his red hunting cap backwards while forestalling his own progress into maturity. When Phoebe has placed the cap on Holden's head, he does not swing it around to the back. Nor does he retreat for cover from the rain which falls here almost as a baptismal downpour at Holden's moment of illumination. And he realizes that the cap, his pseudo-identity and gesture of escape from life, provides, at best, only a partial protection from the unexpected drenching.

But the ending is not quite so pat. Holden's ordeal is not yet over. Earlier, the reader has seen the merging of manic and depressive states in the unstable young hero. Without knowing why, during a moment of depression, Holden will suddenly begin "horsing around." After the brutal physical assault by Maurice, the pimp elevator-operator at the Edmont Hotel, Holden's spirit is momentarily shattered; then suddenly, he goes into a manic Hollywood act, identifying himself with a wounded gunman in a gangster movie. Shortly thereafter, acute depression returns and he contemplates suicide. Again, after calling Sally Hayes a foul name, Holden admits that he felt bad; but then "all of a sudden, I did something I shouldn't have. I laughed" (122). And at the end, while describing Phoebe on the whirling carrousel, Holden remarks, "I was damn near bawling, I felt so damn happy, if you want to know the truth. I don't know why" (191). His discovery of who he is remains imperfect, just as his reunion with society yet remains to be achieved.

II

And so Holden does go to the American West, there to recover both his physical and mental well-being. Several critics, by passing over the previous scene, have read this last chapter as an ironic commentary on Holden's final helplessness in the face of modernism, phoniness, and psychotherapy. Three of these critics, all having used Huck Finn as touchstone, arrive at a remarkably happy agreement about Holden's imminent surrender to the forces of evil in American society:

> Ironically, he is revealed as telling us his narrative from an institution of some kind—psychiatric, we are led to suspect—having also been trapped by the people who want to "sivilize" him.[4]

> Supremely ironical, then, is our last glimpse of Holden making recovery and adjustment in the sanitarium—a prelude to compromise in the outside world. . . . Modern therapy takes over, Holden will return. For Holden's sake we wouldn't have it otherwise, even though it's a return to the big money and dopey newsreels.[5]

> And we can see, on the final note of irony in the book, that that frontier West which represented escape from "sivilization" for Huckleberry Finn has ended by becoming the symbol for depravity and phoniness in our national shrine at Hollywood.[6]

Perhaps if we look at what Salinger has actually written in this final chapter, we may find that the outlook for Holden is not quite this bleak. Certain signs can be taken as encouraging. The first is Holden's response to the psychoanalyst, who has asked Holden if he is going to change and apply himself in school during the coming autumn. Holden answers like the common-sense American frontiersman of old:

> It's such a stupid question, in my opinion. I mean how do you know what you're going to do till you *do* it? The answer is, you don't. I *think* I am, but how do I know? I swear it's a stupid question. (192)

Despite Hollywood, modern psychoanalysis, and power of positive thinking around him, Holden in the West is beginning to face reality in the pragmatic frontier spirit and intends to discover his private, workable solutions to life in America. As the children on the carrousel must do, he will live through his experience as it comes. What he *thinks* he should do—his private idealism—will be put to the test of American pragmatism, what he *does* and must do.

The second encouraging sign appears in Holden's reaction to his Hollywood brother D. B.'s question: what does Holden *think* about his recent crisis? Again, Holden does not intellectualize his problem. But he makes a confession that points to an advance over his previous gestures of rebellion and retreat, as well as his unsuccessful attempts to break through the wall of phoniness in American society to achieve love and community. He recognizes the need for a balance between the size of the head (Professor Antolini's earlier emphasis) and the size of the heart. What Holden says at the close is, "About all I know is, I sort of *miss* everybody I told about. Even old Stradlater and Ackley, for instance. I think I even miss that goddam Maurice" (192). The prospect for Holden is that he may now be able to give people a "buzz" on the phone and achieve communication.[7]

If Holden's comments at the end point the way out of sickness and into wholeness, one can only assume that Salinger has placed his hero in the vaguely defined West for the same reason that Mark Twain, with similar vagueness, in *Huckleberry Finn*, held out the promise of a revitalizing West for an even younger American individualist. Both writers at the end are working not on the level of realism but on the lower stratum of American myth. What Salinger suggests in his final page is that, while the America represented for Holden by Pencey Prep, New York City, and even the new West, is a far cry from the pastoral America which Holden periodically has cherished in fantasy, still that earlier *spirit* of self-knowledge through private action and self-reliance endures unchanged to serve as a source of emotional strength to young Americans. Holden's reaction to the psychiatrist's question tells us that he, at least, will not be poured forthwith into the modern mould of Ivy-League conformity and Madison Avenue commercialism. And second, Holden, like that earlier New York transcendentalist, Walt Whitman, has recognized too the "hollowness at heart" of an urban society shot through with every form of "deceit in the spirit"; and yet Holden at the end, also like Whitman, is able to affirm a social brotherhood with the complex humanity of men. Why should we invite ourselves to lament this passing of a naïve idealism and, in effect, to have Holden remain little more than a modern, uncompromising Young Goodman Brown?[8]

Through the symbols of the cap, the carrousel, and the American West, Salinger traces on the final pages Holden's first steps on the way to his discovery of a new life. Whether this symbolic ending tries to imply too much while rendering too little is not the issue here. What is important is that the symbols need to be adequately accounted for if we are to know what the novel has finally tried to say. I have suggested that they reinforce each other and point the way to Holden's redemption into life rather than alienation and withdrawal from it. His too-innocent idealism has begun to give way to the hopeful beginnings of maturity and a saner view both of himself and of the America in which he must live.

From *Western Humanities Review* 17.3 (Summer 1963): 271-277. Copyright © 1963 by *Western Humanities Review*. Reprinted with permission of *Western Humanities Review*.

Notes

1. The sociologically oriented reader is doubtless tempted to relate Holden's instability to another cause, the Caulfield's rather improvised homelife—the mother being a chain-smoking insomniac and the father an ex-Catholic and peripatetic lawyer. But Salinger neither suggests that this home environment is abnormal in our time nor that it has played a decisive part in moulding Holden's acutely sensitive reactions to the world. In virtually all of Salinger's fiction, for that matter, the parents are relegated to a humiliating role of insignificance in the lives of their precocious children.

2. *The Catcher in the Rye* (New York, 1953), pp. 153, 154. All subsequent quotations are taken from this edition.

3. Two interpretations of the carrousel present a less optimistic view of Holden's progress. Edgar Branch writes that the carrousel "goes round and round, going nowhere—a dynamic moment of happy, static immaturity eternalized in his mind." ("Mark Twain and J. D. Salinger: A Study in Literary Continuity," *American Quarterly*, IX, Summer, 1957, 149.) Arthur Heiserman and James E. Miller, Jr., hold out even less hope for Holden: "So at the end, like the hero of *Antic Hay*, Holden delights in circles—a comforting, bounded figure which yet connotes hopelessness.... From that lunatic delight in a circle, he is shipped off to the psychiatrist. For Holden loves the world more than the world can bear." ("J. D. Salinger: Some Crazy Cliff," *Western Humanities Review*, X, Spring, 1956, 131.)

4. Charles Kaplan, "Holden and Huck: The Odysseys of Youth," *College English*, XVIII (November, 1956), 78.

5. Branch, *op. cit.*, p. 156.

6. Heiserman and Miller, *op. cit.*, p. 134.

7. Critical opinion here again has insisted that Holden remains a confirmed isolate at the end of the book. Alfred Kazin includes Holden in the sweeping pronouncement that "in Salinger's work the two estates—the world and the cutely sensitive young—never really touch at all." ("J. D. Salinger: 'Everybody's Favorite,'" reprinted in *Contemporaries*, Boston, 1962, p. 238.) For Maxwell Geismar, Holden's statements represent the smugly removed "peak of well-to-do and neurotic anarchism." ("J. D. Salinger: The Wise Child and the *New Yorker* School of Fiction," in *American Moderns: From Rebellion to Conformity*, New York, 1958.) Peter J. Seng, otherwise perceptive in noting Holden's obvious incapacity to act as an arbiter of moral values in an adult society, insists that Holden at the end is the tragic author of his own undoing. Holden's "flaw" resides in "a naïve refusal to come to terms with the world in which he lives." ("The Fallen Idol: The Immature World of Holden Caulfield," *College English*, XXIII, December, 1961, 209.)

8. Authors Heiserman and Miller, *op. cit.*, p. 137, come rather close to such a conclusion: "As we leave Holden alone in his room in the psychiatric ward, we are aware of the book's last ironic incongruity. It is not Holden who should be examined for a sickness of the mind, but the world in which he has sojourned and found himself an alien. To 'cure' Holden, he must be given the contagious, almost universal disease of phony adultism; he must be pushed over that 'crazy cliff.'"

The Burning Carousel and the Carnivalesque:
Subversion and Transcendence at the Close of *The Catcher in the Rye*

Yasuhiro Takeuchi

Beyond the controversy that has surrounded *The Catcher in the Rye* since it first appeared, and beyond contemporary assessments of the novel's political/cultural relevance, J. D. Salinger's *Catcher* [*The Catcher in the Rye*] merits ongoing consideration because of the subversion it conducts, a revolt against all fixed values. Ironically, the comment of one editor who rejected *Catcher* for publication is suggestive of the nature of this revolt: "Is Holden Caulfield supposed to be crazy?" (Hamilton 114). It is the sense of madness, often expressed in the novel through Holden's characteristic humor, that—as Mikhail Bakhtin observes in regard to carnival—"makes men look at the world with different eyes, not dimmed by 'normal,' that is by commonplace ideas and judgments" (*Rabelais* 39). This carnivalesque aspect of *Catcher* has yet to be explored fully, but it is fundamental to the novel's import and value.

In addition to madness and laughter, Bakhtin identifies other principles of the carnivalesque that offer liberation from conventional values, principles that illuminate the essential concerns of *Catcher*. These include a "peculiar festive character without any piousness, [and] complete liberation from seriousness" (*Rabelais* 254); "free and familiar contact among people"; "behavior, gesture, and discourse . . . freed from the authority of all hierarchical positions (social estate, rank, age, property)" (*Dostoevsky's Poetics* 123); and "disguise—that is, carnivalistic shifts of clothing and of positions and destinies in life" (125). In the spirit of the carnivalesque, Holden's story is set in the festive Christmas season, yet it is far from pious.[1] Holden himself delights in and encourages the "liberation" of a classmate who farts under his headmaster's watchful eye during the speech of a respected alumnus. During Holden's two day stay in New York, he enjoys "free and familiar contact" with diverse people, regardless of "social estate, rank, age, [and] property"; these people range from a nine-year-old girl (his sister Phoebe's friend) to a married society woman in her forties (his classmate's mother), and from a prostitute to a pair of nuns. Finally, "shifts of clothing" are a recurring motif for Holden and those around him, with lendings and borrowings of his hound's-tooth jacket, his turtleneck sweater, and his famous hunting hat. How these exchanges of clothing signify shifts of "positions and destinies" shall be considered at greater length below. It is worth noting first, however, that the received values that the novel aims to subvert encompass not merely prevailing social conventions but also fundamental binary oppositions, including self/other, body/mind, father/mother, heaven/hell, life/ death, writer/reader, and notably, savior/saved.

This subversion of binary oppositions takes center stage at the novel's ending, the ambiguity of which has long divided *Catcher*'s critics. During the final carousel scene, Holden has the following thought in reference to the children on the carousel: "If they fall off, they fall off, but it's bad if you say anything to them" (274). Holden's willingness to let his beloved sister fall has perplexed many readers because it seems to contradict his dream of becoming a "catcher in the rye"—one who saves children from falling (224). Some critics have failed even to appreciate the ambiguity resulting from this contradiction. Warren French, for instance, maintains that "Holden no longer sees himself as a catcher in the rye" (121) at the novel's conclusion. Sanford Pinsker argues that "one thing is clear—Holden, the narrator, no longer clings to the same desperate scenarios that defined him as a participant in his story" (96). Underpinning such views of the novel's ending is the notion that to catch and not to catch are opposing, irreconcilable actions that cannot be taken (or aspired to) simultaneously.

Other critics have regarded the final carousel scene as less clear-cut, but have viewed its ambiguity as cause for complaint. Carl Strauch calls the novel's conclusion a "blunted, ambiguous ending" (29), and Maxwell Geismar derides it as belonging to "the *New Yorker* school of ambiguous finality" (198). Gerald Rosen likewise concludes that "ultimately, the problems faced by Holden . . . have no 'answer' that we can hold on to" (561).

Such readings fail to appreciate that the ambiguity of the novel's ending itself provides a kind of "answer" in its blurring of the binary oppositions through which we come to understand Holden. Critics sensitive to this quality of blurring have found insight into *Catcher* in the perspective of Zen Buddhism, which according to Zen master Daisetz Suzuki, "takes us to an absolute realm wherein there are no antitheses of any sort" (68). In their pioneering study "Zen and Salinger," Bernice and Sanford Goldstein observe Holden's Zen-like identification with the very people he criticizes, as well as the underlying unity ("wherein there are no antitheses") reflected in the catcher Holden's being caught by both Phoebe and his deceased younger brother Allie (322).[2] Dennis McCort extends this perspective by considering the specific influence of Suzuki on Salinger, maintaining that in the carousel scene, Holden transcends the "contradiction between permanence and change" (266). In the readings of these critics, Zen Buddhism affords substantial insight into the ambivalence of *Catcher*'s conclusion. Yet the Zen approach to *Catcher* is less successful in explaining the novel's blasphemous, carnivalesque aspect. In concluding that Holden "is caught by love" (322), for instance, the Goldsteins privilege a static principle (love/hate) that, in a larger sense, *Catcher* overturns[3]—a typical reversal of binary oppositions upon which Bakhtin, perhaps, casts a clearer light than Zen.

However, both Eastern and Western thought inform the novel's ultimate ambiguity, and a third perspective—that of Carl Jung—offers an initial vantage from which Zen and Bakhtinian readings resolve to be complementary.[4] Through Jung, a Zen-informed Bakhtinian perspective[5] affords a reassessment of Holden's ideal of becoming a catcher in the rye. More specifically, Jung and Bakhtin—neither of whom have figured prominently in previous studies of Salinger—afford a deepening of the Zen understanding of why Holden, in the end, accepts falling (death). Finally, these critical perspectives expose seemingly negative values, such as phoniness, as essential to the process of "catching," or salvation, leading us (as *Catcher*'s readers) toward the goal of "all legitimate religious study," as Seymour Glass put it in Salinger's "Zooey": "unlearning the differences, the illusory differences, between boys and girls, animals and stones, day and night, heat and cold" (67).

The Identity Between the Hunter and His Prey

Salinger's catcher-related imagery is paradoxical: Holden is both savior and saved; Holden's younger siblings Phoebe and Allie, as shall be shown, represent the caught even as they act to catch Holden. The image of Jesus Christ that Jung develops in *Aion* embodies a similar paradox, and will prove helpful to a discussion of the identity between the savior and the saved in *Catcher*.[6]

Jung considers Christ as being both fisherman and fish, remarking that "the Christian Ichthys is a fisher of men par excellence" (*Aion* 112). Jung observes that as "Christ wants to make Peter and Andrew 'fishers of men,'" and as a "miraculous draught of fishes (Luke 5:10) is used by Christ . . . as a paradigm for Peter's missionary activity" (89), Jesus is himself a fisher of men. Yet as Jung notes, the fish has become a universal symbol of Jesus Christ because "*Ichthys*" or "*Ichthus*," an abbreviation of "Iesous CHristos THeou Uios Soter" (Greek for "Jesus Christ Son of God Savior"), means "fish" ("Fish"). Jung's conception of the "identity between the hunter and his prey" (112) thus poses a challenge to conventional notions of the hunter (savior) and the prey (saved) as existing in an overdetermined hierarchical relationship.

Salinger explores a similar conception of the hunter (savior)/prey (saved) relationship through similar imagery. In his later story, "Seymour: An Introduction," narrator Buddy Glass refers to the unity of fisherman and fish directly:

The hazards of fishing in general were themselves a favorite subject of Seymour's. Our younger brother Walt was a great bent-pin fisherman as a small boy, and for his ninth or tenth birthday he received a poem from Seymour—one of the major delights of his life, I believe—about a little rich boy who catches a lafayette in the Hudson River, experiences a fierce pain in his own lower lip on reeling him in, then dismisses the matter from his mind, only to discover when he is home and the still-alive fish has been given the run of the bathtub that he, the fish, is wearing a blue serge cap with the same school insignia over the peak as the boy's own; the boy finds his own name-tape sewn inside the tiny wet cap. (143-44)

Clearly, the fisher boy has caught himself as prey. Considering the fish as a symbol of Jesus Christ, the two identical caps in Seymour's poem not only suggest the identity of savior and saved, but also bring to mind the case of Holden Caulfield in particular, who as savior/catcher, wears a hat—the red hunting cap that he both gives to and has returned by Phoebe (exchanges to be considered in detail below).

In light of the cap in Seymour's poem, the significance of Holden's calling his cap "a people shooting hat" is clear. If the hat were "a deer shooting hat," as Holden's dormitory neighbor Ackley suggests, it would represent the conventional binary opposition of hunter and prey. However, Holden firmly states that "[t]his is a people shooting hat . . . I shoot people in this hat" (30), an assertion that resonates with the Jungian identity of hunter (savior)/prey (saved). Furthermore, although Holden's cap confers a hunter identity, Holden often imagines himself as a wounded, suffering gunshot victim (135, 195). Holden is thus at once the shooter and the shot, an ambivalent hunter akin to Jung's fisherman, Jesus.

The nature of "catching" in the novel lends nuance to its representation of "the identity between the hunter and his prey." Imagining a catcher in the rye, Holden dreams of preventing children from falling off a cliff, a notion of catching that presupposes the conventional binary opposition of life and death, in which life is preferable to death.

But Holden's dream (like this conventional notion of the life/death opposition) is informed by the many acts of picking up the fallen—as opposed to catching the falling—that occur throughout the novel.[7]

A particularly resonant instance of picking up concerns a phonograph record that Holden buys as a present for Phoebe but drops and breaks before giving to her. The fictional song on this record, "Little Shirley Beans," concerns a girl who has lost two of her front teeth. Considered in light of *Catcher*'s Christmas setting, this song is surely patterned on the 1949 hit "All I Want for Christmas (Is My Two Front Teeth)," sung by Spike Jones and His City Slickers. This real song tells us how the little girl lost her teeth: she "slid down the banister just as fast as . . . [she] could" (Jones), and was injured. Like the fictional fallen record, the girl in the real song falls and is not caught. Given this parallel, it follows that the broken pieces of the record can be understood to represent the fallen. Significantly, Holden picks up these broken pieces and gives them to Phoebe despite their condition. Phoebe responds, "I'm *saving* them" (212, emphasis added); the fallen girl can be understood to merit the same treatment: to be picked up and saved.

Another fallen figure, James Castle, is also picked up after having hit the ground.[8] James falls to his death after an incident of bullying, and as Holden recalls, his body is picked up by Holden's former teacher Mr. Antolini:

> He was the one that finally *picked up* that boy that jumped out the window I told you about, James Castle. Old Mr. Antolini felt his pulse and all, and then he took off his coat and put it over James Castle and carried him all the way over to the infirmary. He didn't even give a damn if his coat got all bloody. (226-27, emphasis added)

In Holden's eyes, Mr. Antolini's heroism in this scene qualifies him as "the best teacher . . . [he] ever had" (226), and even after Antolini attempts to seduce him, Holden retains his respect for his teacher because of Antolini's treatment of James: "I mean I started thinking that even if he [Antolini] was a flit he certainly'd been very nice to me. I thought . . . how he was the only guy that'd even gone *near* that boy James Castle I told you about when he was dead" (253). Given Holden's reaction to Antolini's advances—and his casual use of the epithet "flit"—Holden clearly ascribes conventional notions of corruption to Antolini, yet nonetheless Holden views him as a savior. Finally, it bears mentioning that another James, the oldest half-brother of Jesus Christ, was martyred (and thus saved) by being thrown down "from the pinnacle of the temple" (Eusebius 125). James Castle's suicide (221-22) thus deeply informs the development of the theme of falling in *Catcher*, and indeed, Holden conceives of his ideal of the catcher in the rye almost immediately after relating this episode (224-25).

Considering how falling (death, corruption, and betrayal) thus fuse into the process of salvation, it is significant that at the time of his fall, James is wearing Holden's sweater as if he were disguised, in a sense, as Holden. Because of this sweater, many readers have identified James with Holden, seeking psychological and other similarities between the two characters,[9] but the greater significance of the sweater lies in the differences between the characters' positions. That is, the fallen (James) and the catcher (Holden) are unified through the sweater, which thus represents a Bakhtinian disguise in that it transposes the characters' "positions and destinies in life." Bakhtin's view that "[b]irth is fraught with death, and death with new birth" (*Dostoevsky's Poetics* 125) provides further insight into the fusion of James's death and Holden's salvation: death gives rise to its opposite, life or birth, and indeed the two principles interpenetrate.[10]

Aspects of salvation or new being can also be discerned in falls that Holden himself experiences later in the novel. During his visit to Mr. Antolini, whom Holden has presumably sought out in the hope of being caught, Antolini tells Holden that he may soon experience a fall: "This fall I think you're riding for—it's a special kind of fall, a horrible kind. The man falling isn't permitted to feel or hear himself hit bottom.

He just keeps falling and falling" (243). As Holden wanders about town the following day, he feels like he is "just go[ing] down, down, down" (256). At this point, a fall is indeed something horrible for Holden, as Antolini foresaw. Soon after, however, falling takes on a positive aspect when Holden faints and falls to the floor in the museum lavatory. Although Holden narrates, "I could've killed myself when I hit the floor," he is physically restored by the fall, thinking, "I felt better after I passed out. I really did" (265).

Bakhtin offers further insight into this particular fall, insofar as Holden has diarrhea immediately before collapsing. Bakhtin regards images of feces as "presenting at the same time the death of the old and the birth of the new world" (*Rabelais* 149), and that "feces and urine are ambivalent. . . . [T]hey debase, destroy, regenerate, and renew simultaneously. They are blessing and humiliating at the same time" (151).[11] From this perspective, the proximity of feces to this moment of falling allows us to view the episode as prefiguring the subversion of positions in the subsequent scene, in which a debased Holden moves from being a catcher of children (savior) to one of the fallen in need of being saved.

In this, the novel's climactic scene, Holden's savior (catcher) is herself a child—Holden's sister Phoebe—a reversal that reflects a subversion of values best appreciated in view of the scene's setting: the carousel in Central Park. This fictional carousel offered Salinger a fitting locale for consummating his exploration of the ambivalence of life and death because it is based upon a real carousel that itself fell—in a fire on November 8, 1950, eight months before *Catcher*'s publication ("Carrousel Burns"). In a manner of speaking, the carousel experienced death, or in the novel's chronology (the novel is set in 1948 or 1949), faced imminent death. Salinger, born in 1919 and brought up in New York, surely rode on the Central Park carousel, which went into service in 1922. News of its destruction saddened many New Yorkers ("A Day of Disappointment"), no doubt including Salinger. However, by rendering the carousel within his novel as the site of the great joy that Holden finds while watching his sister (275), Salinger locates renewal and rebirth within destruction, changing the news from sad to happy.[12]

Significantly, Salinger represents the fusion of binary opposites in this scene, as in others, through a pairing of elements of the novel with elements that have foundations in the real world. As the fallen phonograph record in the novel is paired with the fallen girl of the real song on which it is based, and as the fallen James Castle of the novel is paired with the fallen martyr of the Bible, this scene pairs Phoebe's imminent potential fall from the fictional carousel with the actual fall of the real burnt carousel. Coming at the ending of a novel in which falling figures so prominently, the happiness that befalls Holden in this scene must be seen to suggest that to fall—in general, and contrary to conventional notions—is indeed a blessing.

The Caulfield Quaternity

In accord with Bakhtin, Jung too recognizes the coincidence of such binary opposites as death and life, maintaining that "the corruption of one is the generation of the other, an indication that this death is an interim stage to be followed by a new life" (*Psychology* 95). Let us now consider how death and rebirth mediate between catcher and caught (and/or fallen) in the relationships of Holden and his siblings, the central characters in both Holden and the novel's figurative pantheons. By overturning the static relationship of savior and saved, these relationships reveal the birth of a new savior to be a process that subverts and transcends conventional oppositions.

The family member with the greatest need of being caught, arguably, is Allie Caulfield (because of his fatal leukemia), and Allie must be seen as the primary inspiration for Holden's dream of becoming a catcher in the rye. However, Holden takes on so many of Allie's characteristics that he emerges as possessing a desire to become Allie (the fallen) which infuses and redefines his desire to be a catcher in the rye.

For instance, we learn that on the night that Allie died, Holden broke all the windows of his family's garage with his fist, permanently injuring his right hand (50). This act of grief and anger is associated with Allie's left-handedness; Holden may have ruined his chances of becoming "a goddam surgeon or a violinist" (51), but the impairment of his right hand[13] has entitled him to Allie's "left-handed fielder's mitt" (49), the baseball glove that equipped Allie as a catcher.[14]

Baseball and other games played on fields also link Allie and Holden through Holden's red hunting hat, which Holden often wears in the style of a baseball catcher (with the peak at the back). In explaining "what kind of red hair he [Allie] had" (50), Holden invokes a childhood memory of seeing Allie sitting outside the fence surrounding a golf course on which Holden was playing. Later, when Holden elaborates to Phoebe his ideal of becoming a catcher in the rye, the catcher he describes stands watch over children playing "some game in this big field of rye" (224), much as Allie watches Holden playing golf. The catcher, moreover, is "standing on the edge of some crazy cliff" (224), an image that intensifies the sense of boundary produced by the "fence that went all around the course" (50) that separated Allie from Holden in Holden's childhood memory. In view of these connections, Holden's prized red hunting hat suggests the identity of the catcher Holden and the red-haired Allie, serving much like the fish's cap in Seymour's poem to embody the oneness of catcher and caught.

There are, furthermore, strong suggestions that Holden desires to reenact Allie's fall (death) himself. As described above, Holden is identified with James Castle, the classmate who leapt from a window to his death. Holden earlier toys with the idea of jumping out of a window (136), and another suicide fantasy of Holden's resonates specifically with Allie's cause of death: "Anyway, I'm sort of glad they've got the atomic bomb invented. If there's ever another war, I'm going to sit right the hell on top of it. I'll volunteer for it, I swear to God I will" (183). Leukemia, the cause of Allie's death, is widely understood to be a common fatal consequence of atomic bomb fallout.[15]

Holden eventually succeeds in joining his brother, not in death, but through the rain at the close of the novel's climactic carousel scene. As Holden watches Phoebe riding the carousel from a nearby bench, a drenching rain suddenly pours down. Everyone standing nearby dashes for shelter, but Holden stays out in the rain and gets completely soaked (275). With this sudden downpour, the carousel scene becomes paired with the scene that Holden described earlier in which he makes a visit with his family to Allie's grave (201-02). As in the carousel scene, rain falls suddenly during this family visit, and in both scenes everyone flees except for one person who gets soaked: Holden in the carousel scene, and Allie in the gravesite visit. Given this parallel structure, the rain of the carousel scene can be understood as identifying Holden with his deceased brother Allie—they are both dead men in the rain.[16]

Jonathan Baumbach characterizes the "purifying rain" of the carousel scene as "a manifestation of Allie's blessed and blessing spirit" (472), a description that points to the salvation inherent in transcending binary oppositions. When Holden takes the place of the deceased Allie in the rain, he realizes his dream of becoming the catcher even as he becomes one with the fallen/caught (i.e., Allie), and this is the reason for his great joy. To put it another way, the catcher (savior) is saved (blessed) by identifying himself with the caught/fallen (saved). Death brings about birth through the rain; as Jung put it in a similar context, "the water is that which kills and vivifies" (*Psychology* 80).

The saved must experience a fall (death) in the process of salvation, and thus Holden in this scene bears witness to Phoebe's imminent potential fall from the carousel, even as we bear witness to the fall of the real Central Park carousel immanent in the fictional carousel upon which Phoebe rides. Phoebe, like Allie, is instrumental to these reversals of life and death (and of catcher and caught) in the carousel scene, as closer consideration of her relationship to Holden will illustrate.

First, it is suggestive that Phoebe—a child like the children in the rye field over whom Holden's catcher watches—bears the name of the

Greek goddess of the hunt ("Artemis"); Holden, with his hunting hat, views himself as a hunter of people ("I shoot people in this hat"), yet it is Phoebe who catches Holden at key junctures of the novel. Exchanges of the hunter/prey roles between the two are signaled, appropriately enough, by exchanges of Holden's red hunting hat. After telling Phoebe his dream of being a catcher, Holden narrates, "I took my hunting hat out of my coat pocket and gave it to her" (233). This moment marks their exchange of roles: Holden, the catcher, becomes the caught/fallen, while Phoebe, in possession of the hat, soon comes to catch, or rather pick up, Holden. As shown earlier, Holden's fall gains momentum during his visit to Mr. Antolini in the subsequent scene, and hits bottom with his literal collapse on the lavatory floor at the museum.[17] It is Phoebe, in the role of catcher—indeed, transformed by the hat into the former Holden—who comes to Holden's rescue:

> Finally, I saw her. I saw her through the glass part of the door. The reason I saw her, *she had my crazy hunting hat on*—you could see that hat about ten miles away.
> I went out the doors and started down these stone stairs to meet her. The thing I couldn't understand, she had this big suitcase with her. She was just coming across Fifth Avenue, and she was dragging this goddam big suitcase with her. She could hardly drag it. When I got up closer, I saw *it was my old suitcase*, the one I used to use when I was at Whooton. I couldn't figure out what the hell she was doing with it. "Hi," she said when she got up close. *She was all out of breath* from that crazy suitcase. (266, emphases added)

Phoebe wears Holden's hat, drags Holden's suitcase, is out of breath as Holden often is, and during the ensuing scene refuses to return to school (269) as Holden himself has decided to refuse.[18]

Yet their reversed relationship is again reversed when Phoebe returns the hat to Holden: "All she did was, she took off my red hunting hat—the one I gave her—and practically chucked it right in my face"

(269). Salinger here again uses clothing as a formal device signaling an exchange of position: once more in possession of the hat, Holden again assumes the catcher/hunter role and pursues Phoebe as prey. However, although this time Holden tries to catch Phoebe literally, his prey eludes him.

Playing the role of prey but still acting in accord with her identity as goddess of the hunt, Phoebe teaches Holden a new technique for catching people; this paradoxical way of catching—catching by way of not catching—is dramatized by the dynamic of their hunter/prey relationship in this scene. Holden narrates, "I sort of tried to get hold of her old hand, but she wouldn't let me" (268), and goes on to make numerous similar attempts to reconnect with her physically (268-71). However, Phoebe rebuffs Holden definitively when he becomes too forceful: "I *took a hold of* the belt at the back of her coat, just for the hell of it, but *she wouldn't let me.* She said, '*Keep your hands to yourself,* if you don't mind'" (271-72, emphases added). If one tries to hunt the prey by catching it, one fails in hunting. Not only do the roles of hunter and prey resolve to be interchangeable, but the very act of catching resolves to be its opposite: not catching. This ambivalent way of catching, akin to Zen archery,[19] dissolves the binary opposition of catching/not catching, and only by adopting it does Holden become a real people hunter embodying the identity between his prey and himself.

Having mastered this lesson, Holden narrates, "Then what she did—it damn near killed me—she reached in my coat pocket and took out my red hunting hat and put it on my head" (274). Beyond signifying the exchange of roles in the Holden-Phoebe relationship, the red hunting hat has been performing what Bakhtin calls "[c]rowning/ decrowning . . . a dualistic ambivalent ritual, expressing the inevitability and at the same time the creative power of the shift-and-renewal" (*Dostoevsky's Poetics* 124). The shifts of the hunting hat signal not merely exchanges of fixed hunter/catcher-prey/ caught roles, but also rebirth through these role changes, as well as the underlying identity of the roles themselves. This "dualistic ambivalent ritual" recognizes no difference between the catcher and the caught, between catching and not catching, or even between life and death. Watching Phoebe and other children as they face an imminent fall (from a carousel informed by an immanent fall), Holden thinks, "If they fall off, they fall off" (274). It is indeed through a fall (death) that new life is born—in this case, a new catcher who embodies the oneness of Phoebe, Allie, and Holden, joined by the carousel and the rain.

Only D. B., eldest of the four Caulfield children, remains to be saved after the carousel ride and the rain. We first encounter D. B. in the novel's opening paragraph, in which Holden introduces him as having once been "a regular writer" but having since become a "prostitute" Hollywood scriptwriter, and thus fallen (4). Holden furthermore reveals that his favorite book is D. B.'s *The Secret Goldfish*; from the outset, his relationship with D. B. is defined as that of reader and writer.

D. B.'s salvation is set in motion at the novel's beginning when he and Holden—like Holden and Allie, and Holden and Phoebe—exchange roles. That is, although D. B. is a writer, it is Holden who tells his story to D. B., the story of *The Catcher in the Rye:* "I'll just tell you about this madman stuff that happened to me. . . . I mean that's all I told D. B. about, and he's my *brother* and all" (3). Holden thus assumes the role of writer and D. B. that of reader, even as Holden identifies himself as a reader of D. B.'s story.[20]

Recalling that the story by D. B. that Holden admires is "The Secret Goldfish," it is reasonable therefore to consider how Holden, in his authorial role as narrator of *Catcher*, undertakes to tell his own fish story. From this perspective, the novel can be viewed simply as the story of Holden as *Ichthys*. However, like the ambivalent fish symbolism that Salinger employs in "Seymour: An Introduction," fish in *Catcher* portray a far from orthodox vision of Christian salvation, as Holden's encounter with the taxi driver Horwitz reveals.

Horwitz explains how fish survive the winter to Holden as follows:

"Their *bodies*, for Chrissake.... They got their *pores* open the whole time. That's their *nature*, for Chrissake.... Listen," he said, "If you was a fish, Mother Nature'd take care of *you*, wouldn't she? Right? You don't think them fish just *die* when it gets to be winter, do ya?" (108-09)

In this explanation of fish—the only one that Holden is to receive—"bodies" rather than the spirit are emphasized, as is "Mother Nature" rather than the Holy Father, and "hell" rather than heaven (Holden observes that Horwitz drives "off like a bat out of hell" [109]). These emphases undermine the primacy assigned to spirit, Father, and heaven in Christian orthodoxy, rendering equivocal their values *vis-à-vis* body, Mother, and hell, much as death and the caught are to fuse into birth and the catcher as the novel progresses. Thus, *Ichthys* in Holden's Christmas story represents not a traditional Christ but rather a Jungian version of an ambivalent Christ.

That D. B. visits Holden in the hospital suggests his desire to help—to save, in a sense—his younger brother, but in receiving Holden's *Ichthys* story, it is D. B. who is saved. Since it was his own fish story, "The Secret Goldfish," that conferred D. B.'s status as a "regular" writer initially, Holden's gift of a fish story may be seen as restoring that status. Once again in possession of a fish story, D. B. is no longer a "prostitute" (4) at the novel's close. Thus D. B. experiences a rebirth like that of Mary Magdalene, the penitent prostitute who bore first witness to the resurrected Savior.

D. B.'s birthday present to Holden of a book by Ring Lardner lends further significance to the brothers' exchange of roles. As noted above, the Lardner book contains the story "There Are Smiles," which culminates with a death in the rain. The story that Holden offers to revive D. B.—the narrative of *Catcher*—also depicts a death (i.e., rebirth) in the rain, and thus comprises a fitting gift for D. B.'s (re)birthday at the end of the novel. By becoming both giver and receiver of stories, D. B. is restored to the status from which he fell.

Finally, by appearing in both the first and final chapters of *Catcher*,

D. B. provides the novel with a circular structure through which its own birth (beginning) and death (end) are connected. In this regard, it seems likely that the initials D. B. are an abbreviation of *D*eath and *B*irth. It is noteworthy that these initials reverse the conventional order of these words; death precedes birth as falling precedes salvation. The character of D. B. may be understood to embody the flux between and ultimate oneness of these binary opposites.

Despite the contrasts between Holden and his three siblings, they have merged by the end of the novel in such perfect harmony through their exchanges (and fusions) of roles that we come to recognize the fundamental unity of this quaternity of siblings. Their identity—the identity of savior and saved, life and death, and other binary oppositions—finds clear expression in the novel's final rain, the circular movement of the carousel, and Holden's closure of his story to his brother. Furthermore, in the devices by which Salinger connects the novel to the real world—the phonograph record, James Castle, and the carousel itself[21]—we recognize the creative principle implicit in the underlying unity of opposites. Thus as we witness the carousel in the novel, we are conscious of its Phoenix-like rebirth from the burnt carousel that was its precursor in reality. We may also find fire, the agent of its rebirth, to be informed by the "deeply ambivalent" image of fire in carnival, the fire that—as Bakhtin remarks—"simultaneously destroys and renews the world" (*Dostoevsky's Poetics* 126).

The Identity Between the Novel and Its Reader

Beyond the binary oppositions considered above, *Catcher* explores the dynamics and underlying unity of a range of oppositions worthy of further study: mind/body, father/mother, man/woman, nun/prostitute, sun/moon, fiction/fact, and of course real/phony. On the topic of sexuality alone, for instance, the novel repeatedly undermines conventional fixed values. Although Holden seemingly accepts his society's conventional prejudices against homosexuality, the only two people that

Holden respects other than family members are Antolini and Carl Luce, the novel's gay or bisexual characters.[22] As if to reflect the blurred relationship of sexual innocence and guilt, to take another example, Holden ends his meetings with the prostitute (134) and the nuns (143) by giving the same amount of money, ten dollars, to each. *Catcher* offers fertile ground for further readings that look to such subversions of conventional oppositions.

Studies of Salinger would benefit, too, from a broadened theoretical perspective. Although Salinger has long been considered in terms of the influence of Zen Buddhism, the perspective of Western mysticism has been largely neglected, despite its relevance to Salinger's struggle against the hierarchical binary oppositions that constitute central principles of Western thought.[23] As yet largely unconsidered *vis-à-vis* Salinger, Jung, in particular, promises further insight in this regard, not only into the problem of sexuality, but also the relations of heaven and hell, mind and body, and other binary oppositions beyond the scope of this essay. Finally, this essay's concern with Bakhtin represents an initial approach to the postmodern point of view on Salinger, yet this perspective, too, remains to be fully developed.

But it must be noted that, regardless of theoretical perspective, any analytic reading that focuses upon the dissolution of binary oppositions cannot evade the risk of self-betrayal. Analysis necessarily divides the analyst and the analyzed, introducing a binary opposition of the very sort it aims to interrogate. To conclude, therefore, let us apply our reading of the identity between catcher and caught to ourselves, the analysts, in our experience of reading the novel.

First, the notion of the underlying identity of binary opposites developed thus far suggests that as readers of *Catcher*, we cannot "catch" the novel unless we are "caught" by the novel. That is, to stand outside of the novel scrutinizing it is to miss the point; rather, the novel must be experienced, because only experience affords the possibility of self-evidential knowledge beyond analysis. In exploring such a possibility, John T. Irwin quotes Wittgenstein's remark that "[t]here are, indeed, things that cannot be put into words" (97). Words—doubts, questions, even explanations—are predicated upon the separation of subject from experience. What is anterior to this separation literally cannot be said. It can only be shown.

A more analytical Holden might share this view, for Holden's experience at the end of *Catcher* is to witness the self-evident: that which lies beyond language or analysis. Thus Holden, bearing witness to Phoebe on the carousel, narrates, "I don't know why. It was just that she looked so damn *nice*, the way she kept going around and around, in her blue coat and all" (275); Holden shares with us his own deed not by explaining it, but by showing us what he witnesses even as we read (witness) the novel.

It furthermore bears mention that as a reader (of D. B.'s stories, *The Great Gatsby*, and other literary works), Holden himself does not analyze literary experience so much as he lives it—as a Gatsby-like, blessed dead man in the rain, for example, and as a mystical *Ichthys* like D. B.'s secret goldfish; Holden's reading experience is manifested thus in his own life rather than in his thoughts or beliefs. As readers of Holden's story, we, in turn, must live and experience Holden's story, for its essential fusions of binary oppositions lie in the realm, not of analysis, but rather of "what cannot be said." Holden, verging on tears, reveals this to us directly as he shares his happiness at watching his sister on the carousel: "God, I wish you could've been there" (275). Holden simply cannot explain the truth he witnesses in words, but his longing to share it with us is its own fulfillment. Addressed directly by Holden's words, we step inside the novel to experience it by his side. With the collapse of this final boundary—the boundary between novel and reader—the *Catcher*'s subversion of binary oppositions is completed; the boundaries dividing Holden-Allie, savior-saved, life-death, Gatsby's fictional world-Holden's real world (book-reader), and finally writer-reader dissolve in the rain.

This moment is one deeply informed by the sensibility of carnival, a chief value of which is the elision of the boundary between performer and spectator. As Bakhtin remarks, "Carnival is a pageant . . . without a division into performers and spectators. . . . [E]veryone is an active participant" (*Dostoevsky's Poetics* 122). In keeping with this sensibility, Salinger has orchestrated this conclusive moment around a structure much akin to a central feature of carnival, what Bakhtin describes as "a special structure (usually a vehicle adorned with all possible sorts of gaudy carnival trash) called 'hell.' . . . [A]t the close of carnival this 'hell' . . . [is] triumphantly set on fire" (*Dostoevsky's Poetics* 126). Joining Holden by the carousel in the rain, we as readers share Holden's triumphal realization, witnessing it in the nimbus of fire surrounding the original carousel that links it to reality.[24]

From *Studies in the Novel* 34.3 (Fall 2002): 320-336. Copyright © 2002 by the University of North Texas Press. Reprinted with permission of the University of North Texas Press.

Notes

I would like to thank John T. Irwin and Larzer Ziff for their generosity and guidance during a period of research at the Johns Hopkins University. I am also grateful to Michael Keezing for his helpful suggestions.

1. For example, Holden finds it amusing to hear a Christmas tree called "sonuvabitch" (255) and finds absurd "this Christmas thing [performance] they have at Radio City," of which he observes, "[O]ld Jesus probably would've puked if He could see it" (178).

2. Though less concerned with Zen Buddhism, Clinton Trowbridge argues along similar lines in observing that Holden himself is a phony because he often recognizes images of himself in those of phony people. See Trowbridge, "Character and Detail" 74-79, and "Symbolic Structure" 691-92.

3. For a view similar to Goldsteins', see also Trowbridge 78. Without specific reference to Zen, critics including John M. Howell and Jonathan Baumbach have also suggested that Holden is saved by the love of his younger siblings. See Howell 375, and Baumbach 472.

4. Like Salinger, Jung held a deep interest in Zen; indeed, Jung wrote the foreword to Suzuki's *An Introduction to Zen Buddhism*, of which Salinger was a likely reader. Given this connection, it is probably no coincidence that Luce, the son of a psychoanalyst in *Catcher*, shares Jung's first name. Carl Luce's Chinese girlfriend furthermore brings to mind what Jung refers to as a "(Chinese) alchemical tract" ("Foreword" xiv) that deeply influenced his alchemical study. The tract is *The Secret of the Golden*

Flower, the title of which bears an intriguing resemblance to *The Secret Goldfish*, a fiction by Holden's brother D. B. (discussed in detail below).

5. David Danow points out "at least a tentative correlation between the thought of Bakhtin and that of Jung" (148) on the grounds that the carnivalesque represents an archetypal pattern inherent in the human psyche.

6. *Aion* was originally published in Germany in 1947. An English version was published in 1951, the year of *Catcher*'s publication.

7. To offer several examples, Holden's teacher, Mr. Spencer, drops a piece of chalk that a student picks up (10), and drops a magazine and an exam paper that Holden picks up (14, 17). Holden later picks up the straw basket of one of the nuns he meets (142).

8. Interestingly, Castle's teeth are scattered "all over the place" (221) after his fall; he loses his teeth like the girl in the Spike Jones song upon which "Little Shirley Beans" is based.

9. Pinsker regards James as "a doppelgänger, a psychological double" (75). See also Trowbridge 74; Mellard 201.

10. A parallel incidence of disguise in the novel involves Stradlater, Holden's roommate and an embodiment of phoniness and sexual license. Stradlater borrows Holden's jacket, appropriately enough, for a date with Jane, Holden's ex-girlfriend (33-40). This exchange of roles suggests a provocative identity between the violator and defender of innocence.

11. See also Jung, *Memories* 39-40. As a schoolboy, Jung had a vision in which he perceived the destruction of a cathedral by an enormous piece of feces falling from God as an incidence of grace.

12. Biographers Ian Hamilton and Paul Alexander contend that Salinger completed the manuscript of *Catcher* by the summer or early fall of 1950—that is, before the fire. See Hamilton 113; Alexander 146. However, Salinger's daughter Margaret maintains that during the 1950-51 school year, when the fire occurred, Salinger wrote to his future wife Claire that "he was hard at work finishing a novel" (11). Margaret furthermore maintains that during this period, Salinger may have made changes to his text to please Claire. McCort also raises the possibility of revisions during the winter of 1950 and the spring of 1951. See McCort 267.

13. We learn that Holden is right-handed when he strikes Stradlater: "It probably would've hurt him a lot, but I did it with my *right* hand, and I can't make a good fist with that hand. On account of that injury I told you about" (56, emphasis added).

14. In a different sense than that presented here, Mellard suggests that Holden and Allie are identical in relation to their parents, viewing Holden's broken right hand as a "reminder" of the loss of his brother (203-05).

15. It is furthermore intriguing that Allie died of leukemia on July 18, only two days after the anniversary of the invention of the atomic bomb on July 16, 1945 ("Atomic Bomb"). This near-miss creates an ambiguous connection akin to that which Salinger introduces in his short story, "For Esmé—with Love and Squalor." In this story, the protagonist, Sergeant X, meets Esmé on April 30, 1944, a date that Ian Hamilton maintains is "a subtle reference to Exercise Tiger, a tragic U.S. Army exercise that took place on April 28-29" (82). Pursuing this line of thought further, it is also in-

triguing that *Catcher* was published on July 16, 1951, and thus that the novel conveying Holden's ideal of the catcher in the rye came to life on the same date as the atom bomb associated with Allie's death.

16. Salinger reinforces Holden's association with death in the rain through references to three stories that conclude with rainy death scenes: *A Farewell to Arms*, a story by Ring Lardner, and *The Great Gatsby*—all favorites of Holden's brother D. B. (182-83). The Lardner story referred to here can only be "There Are Smiles," which Holden mentions earlier (25), though without reference to the fatal rain at the story's close.

17. Referring to Holden's own image of the catcher in the rye, French views Holden's collapse as a sign that he "has fallen over the 'crazy cliff'" (121).

18. See also Trowbridge, "Symbolic Structure" 691.

19. A similar catching technique is described in Seymour Glass's advice to his younger brother in "Seymour: An Introduction." Seymour instructs his younger brother not to target his friend's marbles directly with his own, thereby—as Buddy describes it—"instinctively getting at something very close in spirit to the sort of instructions a master archer in Japan will give when he forbids a willful new student to aim his arrows at the target" (241).

20. Holden's twofold identity as both reader and writer is informed by the extent to which his narrative is shaped by his own reading experience. A reader of Charles Dickens's story about the boy Copperfield (3), Holden, in turn, narrates the story of the boy Caulfield (himself). Holden furthermore attempts to erase the words "fuck you" from the walls of his sister's school (261), behaving like the narrator of *The Great Gatsby*, his favorite book, who removes "an obscene word, scrawled by some boy with a piece of brick" (Fitzgerald 188) on the front steps at Gatsby's house. For further discussion of similarities between *Catcher* and *The Great Gatsby*, see McSweeney 67. As described in n. 16, moreover, the death in the rain in Holden's story is informed by three stories that Holden has read. Finally, the novel's title itself is a windfall of Holden's creative rephrasing of a Robert Burns poem. Holden's experience of reading his own precursors thus makes possible the generation of his life and narrative.

21. It is worth noting with regard to these images how Salinger constructs links between the real world and fiction as if the two are different sides of the same coin. Two of these images (set in 1948 or 1949) concern fictional events that precede their real world models (the phonograph record/the 1949 hit song and the carousel/the 1950 fire) evoking a sense of the real world following the fictional in a literal reversal of fiction and fact.

22. Holden "used to think he [Luce] was sort of flitty himself, in a way" (186).

23. For a discussion of binary oppositions and Western thought, see Montrose 396.

24. If we were readers specifically of *Catcher*'s first edition, designed by Michael Mitchell, we would find upon closing the book an image directly suggestive of the burning carousel. Mitchell designed the book jacket around a carousel image colored an infernal red from its base all the way to the upper edge of the cover.

Works Cited

"A Day of Disappointment." *New York Times* 9 Nov. 1950, late ed.: A1.

Alexander, Paul. *Salinger, A Biography*. Los Angeles: Renaissance Books, 1999.

"Artemis." *World Encyclopaedia*. 2nd ed. Tokyo: Heibonsha, 1998.

"Atomic Bomb." *Encyclopedia Americana*. 1996 ed.

Bakhtin, Mikhail. *Problems of Dostoevsky's Poetics*. Ed. and trans. Caryl Emerson. Minneapolis: U of Minnesota P, 1984.

──────. *Rabelais and His World*. Trans. Helene Iswolsky. Bloomington: Indiana UP, 1984.

Baumbach, Jonathan "The Saint as a Young Man: A Reappraisal of *The Catcher in the Rye*." *Modern Language Quarterly* 25.4 (1964): 461-72.

"Carrousel Burns in Central Park." *New York Times* 9 Nov. 1950, late ed.: A1.

Danow, David. *The Spirit of Carnival*. Lexington: UP of Kentucky, 1995.

Eucebius. *Church History, Life of Constantine the Great, and Oration in Praise of Constantine*. Trans. Arthur Cushman McGiffert. Grand Rapids: Wm. N. Eerdmans, 1890.

"Fish." *An Encyclopedic Supplement to the Dictionary for the General Reader*. Tokyo: Kenkyusha, 1994.

Fitzgerald, F. Scott. *The Great Gatsby*. New York: Scribner's Sons, 1925.

French, Warren. *J. D. Salinger*. Revised ed. Boston: Twayne, 1976.

Geismar, Maxwell. *American Moderns from Rebellion to Conformity*. New York: Hill and Wang, 1958.

Goldstein, Bernice, and Sanford Goldstein. "Zen and Salinger." *Modern Fiction Studies* 12.3 (1966): 313-24.

Hamilton, Ian. *In Search of J. D. Salinger*. London: Heinemann, 1988.

Howell, John M. "Salinger in the Waste Land." *Modern Fiction Studies* 12.3 (1966): 367-75.

Irwin, John T. *American Hieroglyph*. Baltimore: Johns Hopkins UP, 1980.

Jones, Spike. "All I Want for Christmas (Is My Two Front Teeth)." By Don Gardner. Warner Brothers Music, 1947.

Jung, C. G. *Aion*. 1951. Trans. R. F. C. Hull. 2nd ed. Princeton: Princeton UP, 1969.

──────. Foreword to the Second German Edition. *The Secret of the Golden Flower*. 1931. Trans. Richard Wilhelm. San Diego: Harcourt Brace & Company, 1962.

──────. *Memories, Dreams, Reflections*. Trans. Richard and Clara Winston. New York: Vintage Books, 1989.

──────. *The Psychology of the Transference*. 1954. Trans. R. F. C. Hull. 2nd ed. Princeton: Princeton UP, 1969.

McCort, Dennis. "Hyakujo's Geese, Amban's Doughnuts and Rilke's Carrousel: Sources East and West for Salinger's *Catcher*." *Comparative Literature Studies* 34.3 (1997): 260-78.

McSweeney, Kerry. "Salinger Revisited." *Critical Quarterly* 20.1 (1978): 61-68.

Mellard, James M. "The Disappearing Subject: A Lacanian Reading of *The*

Catcher in the Rye." *Critical Essays on Salinger's The Catcher in the Rye.* Ed. Joel Salzberg. Boston: G. K. Hall, 1990. 197-214.

Montrose, Louis. "New Historicisms." *Redrawing the Boundaries.* Ed. Stephen Greenblatt and Giles B. Gunn. New York: The Modern Language Association of America, 1992. 392-418.

Pinsker, Sanford. *The Catcher in the Rye: Innocence Under Pressure.* New York: Twayne, 1993.

Rosen, Gerald. "A Retrospective Look at *The Catcher in the Rye.*" *American Quarterly* 29.5 (1977): 547-62.

Salinger, J. D. *The Catcher in the Rye.* Boston: Little, Brown, 1951.

_____. "Seymour: An Introduction." *Raise High the Roof Beam, Carpenters, and Seymour: An Introduction.* Boston: Little, Brown, 1963.

_____. "Zooey." *Franny and Zooey.* Boston: Little, Brown, 1961.

Salinger, Margaret A. *Dream Catcher.* New York: Washington Square Press, 2000.

Strauch, Carl F. "Kings in the Back Row: Meaning through Structure—A Reading of Salinger's *The Catcher in the Rye.*" *Wisconsin Studies in Contemporary Literature* 2.1 (1961): 5-30.

Suzuki, Daisetz. *Essays in Zen Buddhism.* New York: Grove Press, 1964.

Trowbridge, Clinton W. "Character and Detail in *The Catcher in the Rye.*" *Holden Caulfield.* Ed. Harold Bloom. New York: Chelsea House, 1990. 74-79.

_____. "The Symbolic Structure of *The Catcher in the Rye.*" *The Sewanee Review* 74.3 (1966): 681-93.

RESOURCES

Chronology of J. D. Salinger's Life

1919	Jerome David Salinger, the second child of Sol and Miriam (née Grace) Salinger, is born on January 1 in New York City. His sister, Doris, is eight years older.
1937	After struggling in a number of prep schools, "Sonny" Salinger matriculates at New York University but stays less than a year. His father sends him to Vienna, Austria, to study the family business, meat and cheese importing.
1938	Salinger returns to the United States and enrolls at Ursinus College in Pennsylvania. He stays one semester and returns to New York to live with his parents. He starts to write short stories.
1939	Salinger, determined to be a writer, enrolls in a creative-writing class at Columbia University. His first published story appears the following year.
1942	Salinger is drafted into the Army and serves two difficult years during World War II in the European theater.
1946-51	Salinger establishes his reputation among the foremost short-story writers of the era, publishing more than a dozen stories in prestigious major-market magazines. In the story "Slight Rebellion off Madison" (1946), the character Holden Caulfield appears for the first time.
1951	On July 16, Salinger's first, and only, novel, *The Catcher in the Rye*, is published. It becomes a national best seller and a cultural phenomenon.
1953	Seeking privacy, Salinger moves to a remote 90-acre farm in rural Cornish, New Hampshire.
1953-65	Salinger publishes three collections of short stories centered on the Glass family; each is a best seller. He appears on the cover of the September 15, 1961, issue of *Time* magazine, although he refuses to be interviewed for the story.

1965	On July 19, Salinger's story "Hapworth 16, 1924" appears in *The New Yorker*—it will be his last work published in his lifetime.
1974	Bothered by the fact that a pirated edition of his short stories is circulating on the West Coast, Salinger gives his first—and last—full-dress public interview, with the *New York Times*.
1986	Salinger again emerges from seclusion to file a lawsuit against an unauthorized biography by British writer Ian Hamilton that quotes unpublished letters from Salinger. After more than a year of legal arguments, the U.S. Supreme Court denies Salinger's petition and the biography is published.
1988	*New York Post* photographer Paul Adao takes the only photo of Salinger in more than thirty years—a shot of an agitated Salinger attempting to stop the photographer from taking a picture. The photo becomes world famous.
1992	In October, fire sweeps through Salinger's Cornish farmhouse. The property suffers significant damage, including to a reported cache of unpublished manuscripts, although that is never confirmed.
2010	On January 27, Salinger dies quietly in his sleep in his Cornish home at the age of ninety-one.

Works by J. D. Salinger

Long Fiction
The Catcher in the Rye, 1951

Short Fiction
Nine Stories, 1953
Franny and Zooey, 1961
"Raise High the Roof Beam, Carpenters" and *"Seymour: An Introduction,"* 1963

Bibliography

Bloom, Harold, ed. *Holden Caulfield*. New York: Chelsea House, 1990.

_____, ed. *J. D. Salinger's "The Catcher in the Rye."* New ed. New York: Chelsea House, 2009.

Branch, Edgar. "Mark Twain and J. D. Salinger: A Study in Literary Continuity." *American Quarterly* 9 (Summer 1957): 144-58.

Bryan, James. "The Psychological Structure of *The Catcher in the Rye*." *PMLA* 89.5 (1974): 1065-74.

Bryfonski, Dedria, ed. *Depression in J. D. Salinger's "The Catcher in the Rye."* Detroit: Greenhaven Press, 2008.

Crawford, Catherine, ed. *"If You Really Want to Hear About It": Writers on J. D. Salinger and His Work*. New York: Thunder's Mouth Press, 2006.

French, Warren. *J. D. Salinger, Revisited*. Boston: Twayne, 1988.

Grunwald, Henry Anatole, ed. *Salinger: A Critical and Personal Portrait*. New York: Harper, 1962.

Gwynn, Frederick L., and Joseph L. Blotner. *The Fiction of J. D. Salinger*. Pittsburgh: University of Pittsburgh Press, 1958.

Hamilton, Ian. *In Search of J. D. Salinger*. New York: Random House, 1988.

Hassan, Ihab H. "Rare Quixotic Gesture: The Fiction of J. D. Salinger." *Western Review* 21.4 (Summer 1957): 261-80.

Heiserman, Arthur, and James E. Miller, Jr. "J. D. Salinger: Some Crazy Cliff." *Western Humanities Review* 10 (Spring 1956): 129-37.

Laser, Marvin, and Norman Fruman, eds. *Studies in J. D. Salinger: Reviews, Essays, and Critiques of "The Catcher in the Rye" and Other Fiction*. New York: Odyssey Press, 1963.

Lundquist, James. *J. D. Salinger*. New York: Frederick Ungar, 1979.

Marsden, Malcolm M., ed. *If You Really Want to Know: A "Catcher" Casebook*. Chicago: Scott, Foresman, 1963.

Modern Fiction Studies. Special issue on Salinger. 12.3 (1966).

Nadel, Alan. "Rhetoric, Sanity, and the Cold War: The Significance of Holden Caulfield's Testimony." *Centennial Review* 32.4 (Fall 1988): 351-71.

Notes on Contemporary American Literature. Special issue on Salinger. 32.4 (2002).

Pinsker, Sanford. *"The Catcher in the Rye": Innocence Under Pressure*. New York: Twayne, 1993.

Reiff, Raychel Haugrud. *J. D. Salinger: "The Catcher in the Rye" and Other Works*. Tarrytown, NY: Benchmark Books, 2008.

Rosen, Gerald. "A Retrospective Look at *The Catcher in the Rye*." *American Quarterly* 29.5 (Winter 1977): 547-62.

Salzberg, Joel, ed. *Critical Essays on Salinger's "The Catcher in the Rye."* Boston: G. K. Hall, 1990.

Salzman, Jack, ed. *New Essays on "The Catcher in the Rye."* New York: Cambridge University Press, 1991.

Seng, Peter J. "The Fallen Idol: The Immature World of Holden Caulfield." *College English* 23.3 (December 1961): 203-9.

Slawenski, Kenneth. *J. D. Salinger: A Life*. New York: Random House, 2011.

Steed, J. P., ed. *"The Catcher in the Rye": New Essays*. New York: Peter Lang, 2002.

Steinle, Pamela Hunt. *In Cold Fear: The "Catcher in the Rye" Censorship Controversies and Postwar American Character*. Columbus: Ohio State University Press, 2000.

Strauch, Carl F. "Kings in the Back Row: Meaning through Structure—A Reading of Salinger's *The Catcher in the Rye*." *Wisconsin Studies in Contemporary Literature* 2.1 (1961): 5-30.

Wakefield, Dan. "Salinger and the Search for Love." *New World Writing*. Vol. 14. New York: New American Library, 1958.

CRITICAL
INSIGHTS

About the Editor

Joseph Dewey is Associate Professor of Modern and Contemporary American Literature for the University of Pittsburgh. He has taught American literature at the university level since 1979. He is the author of four studies of contemporary American literature that have looked at the relationship between literature and religion: *In a Dark Time: The Apocalyptic Temper of the American Novel in the Nuclear Age* (1990), *Novels from Reagan's America: A New Realism* (1997), *Understanding Richard Powers* (2001), and *Beyond Grief and Nothing: A Reading of Don DeLillo* (2006). In addition, Dr. Dewey has coedited two casebooks, *"The Finer Thread, The Tighter Weave": The Short Fiction of Henry James* (1995) and *Under/Words: A Casebook on "Underworld"* (2003). His essays, more than one hundred, have appeared in a variety of literary journals over the past thirty years. His subjects of interests have included Edward P. Jones, Rick Moody, Marilynne Robinson, Harry Crews, Michael Chabon, and Frederick Buechner, among many others. In addition, Dr. Dewey has published a variety of articles in casebooks that have treated, among other subjects, Sherwood Anderson's *Winesburg, Ohio*, the Beats, British novelist Graham Swift, and the Southern writer Reynolds Price.

In his writings, Dr. Dewey has sought to introduce the work of major contemporary writers to audiences coming to these landmark figures for the first time. He is a regular reviewer for *Aethlon: The Journal of Sport Literature*, *Nuclear Texts and Contexts*, *Review of Contemporary Fiction*, and *Modern Fiction Studies*. He has presented papers at national and international conferences over the past three decades, with especial interest in examining the evolution of spirituality in modern and contemporary American and British literature. Dr. Dewey holds a B.A. in literature from Villanova University and an M.A. and Ph.D. in modern American literature from Purdue University. He joined the Department of English for the University of Pittsburgh in 1987. Since that time, he has been recognized as both the University Teacher of the Year (1992) and his division's Outstanding Teacher (2009).

About *The Paris Review*

The Paris Review is America's preeminent literary quarterly, dedicated to discovering and publishing the best new voices in fiction, nonfiction, and poetry. The magazine was founded in Paris in 1953 by the young American writers Peter Matthiessen and Doc Humes, and edited there and in New York for its first fifty years by George Plimpton. Over the decades, the *Review* has introduced readers to the earliest writings of Jack Kerouac, Philip Roth, T. C. Boyle, V. S. Naipaul, Ha Jin, Ann Patchett, Jay McInerney, Mona Simpson, and Edward P. Jones, and published numerous now-classic works, including Roth's *Goodbye, Columbus*, Donald Barthelme's *Alice*, Jim

Carroll's *Basketball Diaries*, and selections from Samuel Beckett's *Molloy* (his first publication in English). The first chapter of Jeffrey Eugenides's *The Virgin Suicides* appeared in the *Review*'s pages, as have stories by Rick Moody, David Foster Wallace, Denis Johnson, Jim Crace, Lorrie Moore, and Jeanette Winterson.

The *Paris Review*'s renowned Writers at Work series of interviews, whose early installments include legendary conversations with E. M. Forster, William Faulkner, and Ernest Hemingway, is one of the landmarks of world literature. The interviews received a George Polk Award and were nominated for a Pulitzer Prize. Among the more than three hundred interviewees are Robert Frost, Marianne Moore, W. H. Auden, Elizabeth Bishop, Susan Sontag, and Toni Morrison. Recent issues feature conversations with Jonathan Franzen, Norman Rush, Louise Erdrich, Joan Didion, Norman Mailer, R. Crumb, Michel Houellebecq, Marilynne Robinson, David Mitchell, Annie Proulx, and Gay Talese. In November 2009, Picador published the final volume of a four-volume series of anthologies of *Paris Review* interviews. The *New York Times* called the Writers at Work series "the most remarkable and extensive interviewing project we possess."

The *Paris Review* is edited by Lorin Stein, who was named to the post in 2010. The editorial team has published fiction by Lydia Davis, André Aciman, Sam Lipsyte, Damon Galgut, Mohsin Hamid, Uzodinma Iweala, James Lasdun, Padgett Powell, Richard Price, and Sam Shepard. Recent poetry selections include work by Frederick Seidel, Carol Muske-Dukes, John Ashbery, Kay Ryan, Mary Jo Bang, Sharon Olds, Charles Wright, and Mary Karr. Writing published in the magazine has been anthologized in *Best American Short Stories* (2006, 2007, and 2008), *Best American Poetry*, *Best Creative Non-Fiction*, the Pushcart Prize anthology, and *O. Henry Prize Stories*.

The magazine presents three annual awards. The Hadada Award for lifelong contribution to literature has recently been given to Joan Didion, Norman Mailer, Peter Matthiessen, John Ashbery, and, in 2010, Philip Roth. The Plimpton Prize for Fiction, awarded to a debut or emerging writer brought to national attention in the pages of *The Paris Review*, was presented in 2007 to Benjamin Percy, to Jesse Ball in 2008, and to Alistair Morgan in 2009. In 2011, the magazine inaugurated the Terry Southern Prize for Humor.

The *Paris Review* was a finalist for the 2008 and 2009 National Magazine Awards in fiction and won the 2007 National Magazine Award in photojournalism. The *Los Angeles Times* recently called *The Paris Review* "an American treasure with true international reach," and the *New York Times* designated it "a thing of sober beauty."

Since 1999 *The Paris Review* has been published by The Paris Review Foundation, Inc., a not-for-profit 501(c)(3) organization.

The Paris Review is available in digital form to libraries worldwide in selected academic databases exclusively from EBSCO Publishing. Libraries can contact EBSCO at 1-800-653-2726 for details. For more information on *The Paris Review* or to subscribe, please visit: www.theparisreview.org.

Contributors

Joseph Dewey is Associate Professor of Modern American Literature for the University of Pittsburgh. His books include *In a Dark Time: The Apocalyptic Temper of the American Novel in the Nuclear Age* (1990), *Novels from Reagan's America: A New Realism* (1997), *Understanding Richard Powers* (2001), and *Beyond Grief and Nothing: A Reading of Don DeLillo* (2006). He has coedited casebooks on the fiction of Henry James and on Don DeLillo's *Underworld*. In addition, he has published essays and book chapters on a variety of post-World War II American writers, most recently Rick Moody, Edward P. Jones, and Marilynne Robinson.

David Klingenberger received his B.A in English from St. Joseph's College in Rensselaer, Indiana, and his M.A. in English from the University of Illinois-Chicago. For the past twenty years, he has taught the AP English Language class at Niles West in Skokie, Illinois. He has devoted his career to high school teaching and developing curricula in both American literature and film studies. For the past twelve years, he has served as one of the national readers for the AP Language Examination and in that capacity has worked extensively to develop curricula programs to empower high school students in the study of language and literature. He is a certified College Board consultant who has facilitated teacher workshops around the county on analysis, argumentation, and composition.

David Matthews is the author of the memoir *Ace of Spades* and the biography *Kicking Ass and Saving Souls*. His writing has appeared in the *New York Times*, the *Washington Post*, *Salon*, and the *Huffington Post*, and in the essay collection *The Autobiographer's Handbook*. He lives in New York City, not coincidentally, Holden Caulfield's hometown.

Robert Miltner is Associate Professor of English at Kent State University-Stark and teaches poetry in the Northeast Ohio MFA in Creative Writing program. Coeditor of *New Paths to Raymond Carver: Essays on His Life, Fiction, and Poetry* and *Not Far from Here: The Paris Symposium on Raymond Carver*, he also edits *The Raymond Carver Review*. He has published articles and book chapters on Carver, J. D. Salinger, John Steinbeck, Haniel Long, Virginia Woolf, Albert Goldbarth, Richard Adams, Terry Tempest Williams, and James Joyce. His *Hotel Utopia*, winner of the New Rivers Press Poetry Prize, appeared in 2011.

Jeff Pruchnic is Assistant Professor of New Media Rhetoric and Writing in the Department of English at Wayne State University in Detroit, Michigan. He received his doctorate from Penn State University. His writings and research are focused primarily on the impacts of technology and new media on contemporary reading, writing, culture, and, politics. His essays have appeared in such journals as *Rhetoric Review*, *Configurations*, and *JAC*.

Matthew Evertson is Associate Professor in the Department of English and Humanities at Chadron State College in Chadron, Nebraska, where he teaches American literature, Native American literature, the literature of the American West, and writing. He is currently working on a book-length comparative study of Stephen Crane and Theodore Roosevelt, tentatively titled *Strenuous Lives: Stephen Crane, Theodore Roosevelt, and the American 1890s*. He also teaches, researches, and writes about the regional influences on the literature of the Great Plains.

Jill Rollins received her Honors English B.A. from McGill University (Montreal), her teaching diploma from Bishop's University (Lennoxville, Canada), and her M.A. from the University of New Brunswick. She pursued Ph.D. studies in English at the Université de Montréal. For more than forty years, she was Department Head in English at the high school level. She also taught college-level (in Montreal) and A-level English at Raffles Junior College in Singapore. Retired since 2008, she continues to write and teach part-time.

Carl Freedman is Professor of English at Louisiana State University. He is the author of many articles and books, including *The Incomplete Projects: Marxism, Modernity, and the Politics of Culture* (2002) and *Critical Theory and Science Fiction* (2000).

Tom Teicholz is a successful film producer in Los Angeles as well as a ubiquitous commentator on American pop culture via his online award-winning column "Tommywood." Most known as a consummate interviewer of celebrities (he has published two highly successful collections of his conversations with writers S. J. Perelman and Jerzy Kozinski), he maintains a special interest in exploring the expressions of the Jewish sensibility in contemporary American literature and film.

Adam Gopnik is a prolific commentator on American postmodern culture, both on radio and in print. He is largely known through his long association (since 1986) with *The New Yorker*. He has written fiction (a children's fantasy titled *King in the Window*), but he is most known for his nonfiction, notably the critically praised *Paris to the Moon* (2001), a collection of essays from five years he and his wife and son lived in Paris.

Barbara Bell is Associate Professor of English at Santa Barbara City College. Her research interests are varied, and she has published and presented in the areas of composition and rhetoric, linguistics, writing centers, eighteenth-century literature, and popular culture.

David Castronovo, the C. Richard Pace Professor of English at Pace University in New York City, is a widely published critic and cultural and literary historian as well as a respected academic. He is the author of *Edmund Wilson* (a *New York Times* Notable Book in 1984), *Beyond the Gray Flannel Suit: Books from the 1950s That Made American Culture, Critic in Love: A Romantic Biography of Edmund Wilson* (with Janet Groth), and two companion cultural studies, *The English Gentleman: Images and Ideals in Literature and Society* (1987) and *The American Gentleman: Social Prestige and the Modern Literary Mind* (1991).

Sanford Pinsker, for more than thirty-five years Professor of English at Franklin and Marshall College (Lancaster, Pennsylvania), is the author or editor of more than a dozen books on mid-twentieth-century American literature, with a special interest in Jewish American fiction, including groundbreaking studies of Philip Roth, Cynthia Ozick, Joseph Heller, and J. D. Salinger. In a prolific career in which he has distinguished himself as a proponent of postwar literature, he has published more than eight hundred articles, essays, chapter studies, editorials, and book reviews on literature and culture.

Stephen J. Whitfield holds the Max Richter Chair in American Civilization at Brandeis University. A distinguished teacher, trained as a historian, he has held residency appointments at universities around the world. He has focused his teaching and research on politics, culture, and ideas in the twentieth century. He is the author of eight books, most notably *Into the Dark: Hannah Arendt and Totalitarianism* (1980), *American Space, Jewish Time* (1988), and *The Culture of the Cold War* (1991, second edition 1996).

Carol Ohmann is Associate Professor of English at Wesleyan University in Middlebury, Connecticut. She is the author of *Ford Madox Ford: From Apprenticeship to Craftsman* (1964). In addition to her work in British literature, most notably the novels of Charlotte Brontë and Virginia Woolf, she is a pioneer in women's studies and gender studies.

Richard Ohmann is Benjamin Waite Professor of English, Emeritus, at Wesleyan University in Middlebury, Connecticut. A prolific scholar in both British and American literatures and cultural histories, he is the author of *Politics of Letters* (1987) and *Shaw: The Style and the Man* (1962). As a career academic, he has also published provocative works on the challenges facing contemporary American education generally and the university system specifically.

James E. Miller, Jr., was a distinguished scholar of American literature and the Helen A. Regenstein Professor Emeritus of English Language and Literature at the University of Chicago. He published more than twenty studies during a career spanning close to four decades, particularly seminal works on the poetry of Walt Whitman and T. S. Eliot and the experimental fiction of the 1920s. He is particularly known for his work on the textual evolution of Eliot's masterwork *The Waste Land*, and his 1967 *Quests Surd and Absurd: Essays in American Literature* is considered a foundational work on postwar American fiction. He also served as editor of the journal *College English* and as editorial adviser to the journals *Modern Philology*, *Critical Inquiry*, *Studies in American Fiction*, and *American Poetry*.

Daniel M. Stashower is known primarily for his edgy postmodern novels. He is the author of *The Boy Genius and the Mogul: The Untold Story of Television* (2002), a biography of inventor Philo T. Farnsworth, as well as the Edgar Award-winning *Teller of Tales: The Life of Arthur Conan Doyle* (2001). He has also written five highly experimental mystery novels, including *The Houdini Specter* (2001). In addition to his novels, he has been a freelance journalist for more than twenty years, with articles on culture and the arts appearing in the *New York Times*, the *Washington Post, Smithsonian Magazine*, and *Connoisseur*, among many others.

Donald P. Costello, Professor Emeritus of English at the University of Notre Dame, where he taught for more than half a century, is a much-published critic on the spiritual and religious aspects of British and American literature of the twentieth century as well as on European film. He is the author of seminal works on playwright George Bernard Shaw and Italian filmmaker Federico Fellini.

Jonathan Baumbach, longtime Professor of English at Brooklyn College of the City University of New York, has published ten works of experimental fiction (most recently *B: A Novel* in 2002) and a significant body of film criticism. In addition, he was among the earliest and most eloquent and prolific critics to address post-World War II American fiction, most notably in his groundbreaking 1965 study *The Landscape of Nightmare: Studies in the Contemporary American Novel*.

Edwin Haviland Miller, who died in September 2001 at the age of eighty-three, was widely regarded as among the preeminent postwar scholars on American literature and culture. He was known particularly for numerous biographies and critical studies on the American Renaissance, specifically the towering figures of Herman Melville, Walt Whitman, and Nathaniel Hawthorne. A career academic, he was Professor Emeritus of English at New York University. His eloquent writings inspired a generation of Americanists and helped defined the direction of the evolution of the field of American studies.

Kermit Vanderbilt is respected as one of the foremost explicators of nineteenth- and twentieth-century American literature. Distinguished Professor of English and Comparative Literature at San Diego State University, where he taught from 1962 to 1988, he published seminal studies on Edgar Allan Poe, William Dean Howells, Herman Melville, and F. Scott Fitzgerald, among many other figures. In addition, he was a major proponent of traditional literary study, most notably his controversial 1987 polemic *American Literature and the Academy: The Roots, Growth, and Maturity of a Profession*.

Yasuhiro Takeuchi is Associate Professor of Humanities and Comparative Cultures at the Graduate School of Nara Women's University in Japan. One of the most respected scholars of American literature in Japan, he is known to American readers primarily for his extensive work explicating the Buddhist influence on Salinger.

Acknowledgments

"The *Paris Review* Perspective" by David Matthews. Copyright © 2012 by David Matthews. Special appreciation goes to Christopher Cox, Nathaniel Rich, and David Wallace-Wells, editors at *The Paris Review*.

"Memories of Holden Caulfield—and of Miss Greenwood" by Carl Freedman. From *The Southern Review* 39.2 (2003): 401-417. Copyright © 2003 by Carl Freedman. Reprinted with permission of Carl Freedman.

"J. D. Salinger, Novelist of Modern Anomie, Dead at 91" by Tom Teicholz. From *Jewish Journal* 28 January 2010. Copyright © 2010 by Tom Teicholz. Reprinted with permission of Tom Teicholz.

"J. D. Salinger" by Adam Gopnik. From *The New Yorker* 8 February 2010, pp. 20-21. Copyright © 2010 by Condé Nast Publications. Reprinted with permission of Condé Nast Publications.

"'Holden Caulfield in Doc Martens': *The Catcher in the Rye* and *My So-Called Life*" by Barbara Bell. From *Studies in Popular Culture* 19.1 (October 1996): 47-57. Copyright © 1996 by *Studies in Popular Culture*. Reprinted with permission of *Studies in Popular Culture* and Barbara Bell.

"Holden Caulfield's Legacy" by David Castronovo. From *New England Review* 22.2 (Spring 2001): 180-186. Copyright © 2001 by *New England Review*. Reprinted with permission of *New England Review*.

"*The Catcher in the Rye* and All: Is the Age of Formative Books Over?" by Sanford Pinsker. From *Georgia Review* 40.4 (Winter 1986): 953-967. Copyright © 1986 by Sanford Pinsker. Reprinted with permission of Sanford Pinsker.

"Cherished and Cursed: Toward a Social History of *The Catcher in the Rye*" by Stephen J. Whitfield. From *The New England Quarterly* 70.4 (December 1997): 567-600. Copyright © 1997 by The New England Quarterly, Inc. Reprinted with permission of MIT Press.

"Reviewers, Critics, and *The Catcher in the Rye*" by Carol and Richard Ohmann. From *Critical Inquiry* 3.1 (Autumn 1976): 15-37. Copyright © 1976 by The University of Chicago Press. Reprinted with permission of The University of Chicago Press.

"*Catcher* In and Out of History" by James E. Miller, Jr. From *Critical Inquiry* 3.3 (Spring 1977): 599-603. Copyright © 1977 by The University of Chicago Press. Reprinted with permission of The University of Chicago Press.

"On First Looking into Chapman's Holden: Speculations on a Murder" by Daniel M. Stashower. Reprinted from *The American Scholar* 52.3 (Summer 1983): 373-377. Copyright © 1983 by the author. Reprinted by permission of the publisher.

"The Language of *The Catcher in the Rye*" by Donald P. Costello. From *American Speech: A Quarterly of Linguistic Usage* 34.3 (October 1959): 172-181. Copyright ©

1959 by Duke University Press. All rights reserved. Reprinted with permission of Duke University Press.

"The Saint as a Young Man: A Reappraisal of *The Catcher in the Rye*" by Jonathan Baumbach. From *Modern Language Quarterly* 25.4 (1964): 461-472. Copyright © 1964 by Duke University Press. All rights reserved. Reprinted with permission of Duke University Press.

"In Memoriam: Allie Caulfield in *The Catcher in the Rye*" by Edwin Haviland Miller. From *Mosaic* 15.1 (1982): 129-140. Copyright © 1982 by *Mosaic*. Reprinted with permission of *Mosaic*.

"Symbolic Resolution in *The Catcher in the Rye*: The Cap, the Carrousel, and the American West" by Kermit Vanderbilt. From *Western Humanities Review* 17.3 (Summer 1963): 271-277. Copyright © 1963 by *Western Humanities Review*. Reprinted with permission of *Western Humanities Review*.

"The Burning Carousel and the Carnivalesque: Subversion and Transcendence at the Close of *The Catcher in the Rye*" by Yasuhiro Takeuchi. From *Studies in the Novel* 34.3 (Fall 2002): 320-336. Copyright © 2002 by the University of North Texas Press. Reprinted with permission of the University of North Texas Press.

CRITICAL
INSIGHTS

Index

Adventures of Huckleberry Finn (Twain), 27, 50, 85, 107, 158, 176, 304
Antolini, Mr. (*The Catcher in the Rye*), 11, 26, 38, 40, 72, 156, 162, 238, 266, 292, 311; sexual orientation, 267

Bright Lights, Big City (McInerney), 166-168
Buddhism. *See* Zen Buddhism

Carousel, 73, 146, 149, 174, 238, 277, 294, 297, 300-301, 305, 307
Castle, James (*The Catcher in the Rye*), 24, 39, 41, 79, 227, 248, 267, 286, 298, 311-312, 315
Catcher in the Rye, The (Salinger); best-seller status, 5, 84, 170, 205; comparison with *My So-Called Life*, 126-139; comparison with "Paul's Case" (Cather), 67-76; controversies surrounding, vii, 5, 82, 171, 176-182, 191-195, 197; critical responses, 49, 81-92, 170, 189, 193, 207, 210-218, 230, 235-236, 251, 265; cultural influence of, 27, 91, 141, 184-185; discussion of in other fiction works, vii, 172, 175, 179, 182, 185, 190; first sentence, 22, 52, 126, 155, 281; language, 28, 128, 214, 251, 253-254, 256-263, 280-281; narrative voice, 4, 101, 127, 143, 154, 252; profanity in, 82, 178, 197, 252, 255-256
Caulfield, Allie (*The Catcher in the Rye*), 248, 314; and poetry, 110
Caulfield, D. B. (*The Catcher in the Rye*), 37, 43, 105, 110, 243, 319-321
Caulfield, Holden (*The Catcher in the Rye*); and Allie's death, 40, 52, 76, 136, 237, 248, 271, 279, 298-299, 314; comparisons with Hamlet, 50, 108, 216; comparisons with Huckleberry Finn, 28, 85, 107, 158, 261, 302; father, 37, 195, 225, 267, 290, 292; and Jane Gallagher, 46, 105, 237, 271, 283, 285; mental breakdown, 23, 72, 274, 293; and Mr. Antolini, 11, 26, 40, 72, 156, 238, 266, 274, 292, 311; sexuality, 7, 23, 29, 38, 181, 186, 238, 272, 286
Caulfield, Phoebe (*The Catcher in the Rye*), 10, 45, 105, 139, 146, 286, 289, 294; rescue of Holden, 72, 228, 276, 300, 317
Censorship, 83, 87, 172, 176, 182-183, 192, 194
Children, protection of, 33, 40, 74, 139, 145, 178, 192, 197, 238, 242, 265-266, 275, 291, 293
Christmastime setting, 12, 72, 275, 306, 311
Class issues. *See* Social class issues
Collector, The (Fowles), 172
Cultural studies, 34, 112

David Copperfield (Dickens), 8, 22, 53
Death and dying, 5, 39, 41, 74, 76, 136, 237-238, 248, 271, 279, 281-282, 289-290, 298-300, 315, 326. *See also* Suicide
Dickens, Charles, 8, 22, 53, 144
Disappearing, 22, 72, 227, 275, 293

Falling, 39-40, 72, 162, 174, 238-239, 243, 265, 268, 275, 300, 306, 310, 312, 316
Finn, Huckleberry (*Adventures of*

Huckleberry Finn), comparisons with Holden Caulfield, 28, 85, 107, 158, 261, 302
"For Esmé—with Love and Squalor" (Salinger), 122, 325

Gallagher, Jane (*The Catcher in the Rye*), 46, 105, 237, 271, 283, 285
Gender studies, 35, 78
Great Gatsby, The (Fitzgerald), 277-278, 323, 326

"Hapworth 16, 1924" (Salinger), 87
Hat. *See* Hunting hat
Hollywood. *See* Movies and Hollywood
Holocaust, influence on Salinger, 19, 110-111
Homosexuality, 78, 267, 292, 321
Huckleberry Finn. *See Adventures of Huckleberry Finn*
Hunting hat, 25, 282-283, 297-298, 300-301, 307, 310, 315, 317-318

In Search of J. D. Salinger (Hamilton), 21, 90, 148
Innocence, loss of, 40, 55, 102, 238, 241, 243, 265, 270-271, 274, 276, 298, 300

Language and vocabulary, 28, 128, 214, 251, 253-254, 256-263, 280-281. *See also* Narrative voice, Profanity
Loneliness, 237, 271, 280, 283, 288
Luce, Carl (*The Catcher in the Rye*), 38, 103, 144, 287, 322, 324

Marxist literary criticism, 61, 89, 116, 236, 238
Motifs. *See* Themes and motifs
Movies and Hollywood, 37, 43-46, 135, 148, 186, 243, 302

Museum of Natural History, 29, 61, 67, 152, 227, 277
My Ántonia (Cather), 65
My So-Called Life (television series), 126-139

Narrative voice, 4, 101, 127, 143, 154, 252-253. *See also* Language and vocabulary, Profanity
New Criticism, 83, 89, 156, 213
New Yorker, The; criticism of fiction in, 86-87; and Salinger short stories, 19-20, 81, 83, 119, 199

O Pioneers! (Cather), 65
Ossenburger (*The Catcher in the Rye*), 102, 113, 220

"Paul's Case" (Cather), 67, 69-71, 73-75; sexual orientation of protagonist, 79; viewpoint, 67
"Perfect Day for Bananafish, A" (Salinger), 119, 124, 277
Phoniness, 51, 54, 56, 103, 106, 113, 137, 189, 212, 219-222, 226, 241, 299
Plain Jane (Horowitz), 190
Profanity, 82, 178, 197, 252, 255-256. *See also* Language and vocabulary, Narrative voice

Rain, 76, 149, 175, 276, 301, 315, 320-321, 326
Red hat. *See* Hunting hat
"Resolution and Independence" (Wordsworth), 146

Sexuality, 186, 238, 272, 286, 321
"Seymour: An Introduction" (Salinger), 124, 309, 319, 326
Shoeless Joe (Kinsella), 163

Six Degrees of Separation (Guare), 91, 175
Sixty Years Later (California), 910
Slang. *See* Language and vocabulary
"Slight Rebellion off Madison" (Salinger), 19, 81, 119
Social class issues, 60, 112-116, 184, 190, 220, 222, 224-225, 229
Stradlater, Ward (*The Catcher in the Rye*), 102, 271-272, 282, 325
Suicide, 24, 39, 41, 75, 79, 122, 227, 248, 267, 285-286, 298, 302, 311-312, 315

Themes and motifs; carousel, 73, 146, 149, 174, 238, 277, 294, 297, 300-301, 305, 307; children's need of protection, 33, 40, 74, 139, 145, 197, 238, 242, 265-266, 275, 291, 293; death and dying, 5, 39, 41, 74, 76, 136, 237-238, 248, 271, 279, 281-282, 289-290, 298-300, 315, 326; disappearing, 22, 72, 227, 275, 293; falling, 39-40, 72, 162, 174, 238-239, 243, 265, 268, 275, 300, 307, 310, 311, 316; hunting hat, 25, 282-283, 297-298, 300-301, 307, 310, 315 317-318; loneliness, 237, 271, 280, 283, 288; loss of innocence, 40, 55, 102, 238, 241, 243, 265, 270-271, 274, 276, 298, 300; movies, 37, 43-46, 135, 148, 186, 243, 302; phoniness, 51, 54, 56, 103, 106, 113, 137, 189, 212, 219-222, 226, 241, 299; rain, 76, 149, 175, 276, 301, 316, 320-321, 326; suicide, 24, 39, 41, 75, 79, 122, 227, 248, 267, 285, 298, 302, 311-312, 315; violence, 24, 45, 285; writers and writing, 26, 37, 43, 53, 110, 243, 319, 326
"There Are Smiles" (Lardner), 320, 326

Violence, 24, 285; fantasies of, 24, 45

World War II, influence on Salinger, 25, 122
Writers and writing, 26, 37, 43, 53, 110, 243, 319, 326

Zen Buddhism, 12-14, 16, 20, 119, 307, 322, 324